Communicate as a Professional

T0314237

Communicate as a Professional

Edited by

Carel Jansen
Leon de Stadler
Aline Douma

Amsterdam University Press

Communicate as a Professional is largely based on a Dutch communication textbook: Steehouder, M., Jansen, C., Van Gulik, L., Mulder, J., Van der Pool, E., & Zeijl, W. (2016). *Leren communiceren* [Learning how to communicate] (7th, rev. ed.). First published in the Netherlands by © Noordhoff Uitgevers B.V., Groningen/Utrecht, The Netherlands

Illustrations interior pp. 6, 8, 44, 104, 144, 180, 216, 250, 296, 354, 388, 416: Rijksmuseum Amsterdam.
Cover illustration: *A writer trimming his pen*, Jan Ekels (II), 1784. Rijksmuseum Amsterdam.

Cover design: Coördesign, Leiden
Lay-out: Crius Group, Hulshout

ISBN   978 94 6298 810 1
DOI   10.5117/9789462988101
NUR   810

Foreword

Students across a wide range of programs in international higher education are all preparing themselves for a career in a particular professional field. Learning how to communicate as a professional is an essential part of that preparation. No matter how diverse the professional situations in which graduates are employed, they are always expected to behave professionally in their communication—both within their own organization and beyond.

In order to be able to carry out their communication tasks adequately, professionals must not only possess a large repertoire of knowledge and skills, they also need to be able to deploy that repertoire effectively and appropriately in their communication. They must make the right choices on what best suits the situation in which they are communicating with others and the goals they want to achieve.

During their training, students already come across a variety of tasks that are largely new to them. For these tasks, too, they need a broad knowledge and skills repertoire from which they can make the right choices. *Communicate as a Professional* offers a solid foundation for students to develop the communication knowledge and skills they need, both when working as a professional after they have graduated and when following an educational program that prepares them for this future.

In the first chapters of this textbook, the emphasis is on tools that can be used for the analysis of communication processes and products. In later chapters, the attention shifts to advice on how to apply this knowledge when performing more specialized communication tasks. These tasks can be complicated and demanding. This is the case, for example, when having to carefully and critically read diverse forms of professional literature, or when asked to write a research report. Carrying out such communication tasks is a bit like juggling: It may look quite easy when you see a professional do it, but if you try it yourself you will notice how difficult it is and how much experience you need to keep all the balls in the air.

This book does not offer customized recipes for performing communication tasks. The tasks are too difficult for this, and too much depends on the circumstances in which the tasks have to be carried out. What this volume does offer to the professional (or prospective professional) are tried and tested strategies to bring various communication tasks to a successful conclusion.

Each chapter opens with an image of a work of art that is directly or indirectly related to that chapter. We are grateful to the Rijksmuseum in Amsterdam for granting us the permission to use these images. More information about the works of art can be found on the website of *Communicate as a Professional*: www.communicate.amsterdam. This website also includes answers to and

The wardens of the Amsterdam drapers' guild, known as 'The syndics', Rembrandt van Rijn, 1662. The master drapers assess the quality of a number of cloth samples that were submitted to them as masterpieces by weavers who wanted to join the guild of the cloth makers.

Nowadays, students also have the ambition to gain entrance into an (informal) guild, when they are preparing for their careers. At the end of their training they, too, will have to deliver one or more masterpieces to show that they possess the knowledge, insights and skills needed to start a professional career.

explanations of the assignments in the book. Furthermore, it contains test questions and additional practice material.

As the editors of this book, we are grateful to the authors and the publisher of *Leren Communiceren*,[1] the Dutch textbook on which *Communicate as a Professional* is largely based. We also thank the many generations of Dutch students who have provided useful feedback on the seven editions of *Leren Communiceren* that have been published since 1979, and who have thus contributed to a textbook that we believe can be of value to students and other communicators not only in the Netherlands, but also in the rest of the world.

Aduard / Stellenbosch / Groningen, December 2018
Carel Jansen, Leon de Stadler, Aline Douma

1   Steehouder, M., Jansen, C., Van Gulik, L., Mulder, J., Van der Pool, E., & Zeijl, W. (2016). *Leren communiceren* [Learning how to communicate] (7th, rev. ed.). Groningen, The Netherlands: Noordhoff.

Contents

RHETORICÆ GRATOS SERMONI ASTVTA COLORES,
QVO DVLCIVS FLVAT IS AD AVREIS ADYCIT.

1 Communication

◀ *Rhetorica*, Cornelis Cort, after Frans Floris (I), 1565. Rhetorica sits on a chair and listens to the speech of a young man sitting behind her. An older man looking over the young man's shoulder inspects his concept. Through the window you can see the square in front of the building where a stage is being built. Rhetorica holds a messenger staff in her hand. The caption reads: 'She cleverly adds the pleasing hues of rhetoric to speech, by which it flows more sweetly to the ears.'

This chapter explains the basics of communication, so that you, through practice, guidance, and training, may embark on your career as a professional—just like the young man in this picture who is about to deliver a speech, and receives feedback from experienced communicators.

An impressive speech

Source: ANP/Andrew Gombert

On 17 July 2014, a plane crashed in the eastern part of Ukraine. Malaysia Airlines flight MH17 was on its way from Amsterdam to Kuala Lumpur when an attack from an officially still unknown party took the lives of 298 people, among them 196 passengers from the Netherlands.

Four days later, Frans Timmermans—then Foreign Minister of the Netherlands—gave an impressive speech to the UN Security Council. Among other things, he requested that the Netherlands and the other countries involved be enabled to safely bring home the victims' remains, and that an official international crime investigation be conducted. Below, parts of his speech are reprinted.

Mr. President,

We are here to discuss a tragedy: the downing of a commercial airliner and the death of 298 innocent people. Men, women and a staggering number of children lost their lives, on their way to their holiday destinations, their homes, loved ones, their jobs or international obligations. How horrible must have been the final moments of their lives, when they knew the plane was going down. Did they lock hands with their loved ones, did they hold their children close to their hearts, did they look each other in the eyes, one final time, in an unarticulated goodbye? We will never know.

[…]

For the Netherlands, one priority clearly stands out above all others: Bring the victims' remains home. It is a matter of human decency that remains should be treated with respect and that recovering victim's remains should be done without any delay.

The last couple of days we have received very disturbing reports of bodies being moved about and looted for their possessions. It must be unbearable first to lose your husband and then to have to fear that some thug might steal his wedding ring from his remains.

To my dying day, I will not understand that it took so much time for the rescue workers to be allowed to do their difficult jobs and that human remains should be used in a political game. I hope the world will not have to witness this again, any time in the future.

Images of children's toys being tossed around, luggage being opened or passports being shown are turning our grief and mourning into anger. We demand unimpeded access to the terrain. We demand respectful treatment of the crash site. We demand dignity for the victims and the multitudes who mourn their loss.

I call on the international community, on the Security Council, on anyone with influence on the situation on the ground: Allow us to bring the victims' remains home to their loved ones without any further delay. They deserve to be home.

[…]

I also welcome the setting up of a proper investigation into the cause of the tragedy of MH17, as envisaged in today's resolution. […]

Once the investigation ascertains who was responsible for the downing of the flight MH17, accountability and justice must be pursued and delivered. We owe that to the victims, to justice, to humanity. I call on all relevant countries to provide full cooperation.

My country will not rest until all facts are known and justice is served.

I thank you, Mr. President.

Source: Timmermans (2014).[2]

Timmermans' speech was a great success. The UN Security Council unanimously passed a resolution condemning the attack that had caused the downing of the aircraft, ordered the United Nations Civil Aviation Agency to perform an international investigation, and urged armed forces in the area to give access to the crash site. The speech also received a very favorable response from the general public, both in the Netherlands and around the world—although later there was also some criticism of Timmermans' striking depiction of what must have taken place in the plane in the final moments before the crash.

---

2   Timmermans, F. (2014, July 21). *Speech at the UN Security Council*. Retrieved from https://www.facebook.com/frans.timmermans/posts/765080793514782

The immediate effectiveness of this speech can, of course, partly be explained by the tragic event it referred to. But there is more to it than that. Frans Timmermans succeeded in reaching not only the minds but also the hearts of the people he addressed. He clarified what he wanted and why he wanted it. More importantly, he supported his demands by showing his emotions and by sketching a detailed and moving picture of what in his view had happened to the innocent people on the aircraft. It is hardly possible to listen to or read the speech without imagining the picture that is sketched and without being touched by it. Frans Timmermans proved to be a very proficient communicator by not only conveying factual information but also evoking emotions in his audience that contributed to the acceptance of his request.

Not every professional communication situation involves including such heavy emotional components in the messages exchanged by the communication parties. But as the *four-sides communication model* discussed in this chapter will show, messages that only convey factual information simply do not exist. Communication messages always reveal other information too—information that is often less explicit but that nevertheless can be decisive for their effect.

Analyzing communication

In order to see the strengths and weaknesses of a communication message clearly and to find possibilities for improvement, it is useful to have an analysis model. A model can also be useful when you develop effective messages yourself or when you discuss a particular message with someone else. In the analysis model that will be introduced in section 1.1, communication is understood as a goal-driven exchange of information between two parties. One party acts as a sender (writer, speaker, developer of a website, and so on); the other party acts as a receiver (reader, listener, user of a website, and so on).

When person A sends a message to somebody else, that person is called the sender *at that moment*, and person B who receives this message is called the receiver *at that moment*. We explicitly say 'at that moment' because the roles of sender and receiver can change very quickly. In fact, especially in oral communication, people are often both sender and receiver at the same time. Person A says something, and at the same time he or she notices how person B responds, with or without words—for instance by showing a facial expression. And vice versa: Person B hears or sees the message from person A and person B reacts immediately, often even before person A's message comes to an end.

The model presented in section 1.1 is called the *four-sides model of communication*. It was introduced by the German psychologist Friedemann Schulz von Thun. The model is based on the principle that a communication message always has four sides. Apart from the factual content, messages also always include information about the image created by the sender of him- or herself, the relationship between the sender and the receiver, and the goals that the sender and the receiver are trying to achieve.

Chapters 2 and 3 deal with the factual content of the information that is exchanged. In this chapter we discuss the other three sides of a communication message. The final section of this chapter will discuss how communication parties can let each other know how they are experiencing each other's messages.

1.1 The four-sides model of communication

What do we mean by the word *communication*? Studies in this field have proposed all kinds of descriptions and definitions. In this book, we stick to the basics. We regard communication as a goal-driven process in which messages are exchanged between two parties: senders and receivers. Communication messages include not only written or printed texts but also oral presentations, photos, videos, website pages, e-mails, messages on social media, and so on. In a conversation, we consider each individual contribution ('turn') of a participant as one short message.

A verbal message (an oral or written message in *words*) may consist of a single sentence, but it may also contain a number of sentences. If the sender uses signals other than words (posture, gestures, signs, images), we speak of non-verbal communication. Most forms of communication include both verbal and non-verbal elements.

Communication is more than simply exchanging messages. Communication always takes place with certain *goals* in mind. People who communicate always want to achieve something—even if that is only creating, establishing, or ending a relationship. Not only *senders* but also *receivers* have certain goals that lead them to pay attention to the messages they receive. One goal that cooperative senders and receivers always have in common is *mutual understanding*. Communication parties need each other in order to make progress on what they want to achieve. The content and form of a message are primarily determined by the goals of the sender, but sensible senders will also take the goals of their receivers into account.

When we consider the *content* of a message, we tend to primarily think of the factual information that is provided. To give some examples: A policy document sets out plans and proposals, a technical document describes an apparatus or a system, and a quotation presents the nature and costs of services offered to the potential customer. There is more to communication messages, however, than just factual information. Messages always present a certain image of the sender to the receiver, whether the sender wants to or not. Consciously or unconsciously, senders always provide information about themselves and about the organization they may represent. Communication messages also always show how the sender perceives the relationship with the receiver. When problems arise with a particular message, the causes often lie in these non-factual aspects of the communication at hand. In order to do justice to the complexity of communication, we distinguish four different sides of a communication message.

– The *matter side* concerns the actual subject of the message and the factual information provided about this subject.
– The *appeal side* concerns the purpose of the message: the goal or goals that the sender wants to achieve with the receiver.
– The *self-expression side* of the message concerns the image it reveals of the sender—his or her person, norms, and values.
– The *relationship side* concerns the way in which the sender views the receiver and also the relationship between the sender and the receiver, as attested by the message.

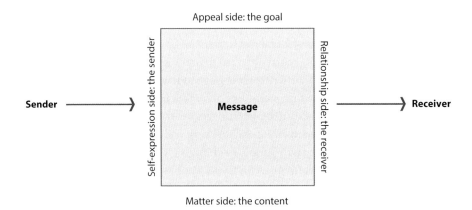

The four sides of a message.

Successful communication requires that the communication parties—both senders and receivers—consider the interplay of the four sides of their messages. Senders try to choose the content and form of their messages in such a way that their intentions in each respect are well understood by their receivers. And receivers try to interpret the sender's messages in each respect properly so that they can respond adequately.

Each message contains all four sides. The emphasis placed on the different sides may differ, however. The sender is always faced with the choice of whether to place the emphasis on the matter side, the appeal side, the self-expression side, or the relationship side. This choice is decisive for both the content and form of the message.

In the next three sections of this chapter, the focus will be on the appeal side (1.2), the self-expression side (1.3), and the relationship side of the message (1.4). The matter side will be further explored in chapters 2 and 3.

In the educational program *Advertising Psychology* at an Irish university, there have been multiple cases of plagiarism. Many students seem to habitually copy long parts of articles they found on the internet without proper references to the sources of their information. The program board has now decided that a clear warning is appropriate. They have asked George Wilbury, the program coordinator, not only to write an article for the university's digital newsletter, but also to design some posters that may draw the students' attention. The posters will be displayed in places where students often come. George is now faced with the question of what the emphasis in those posters should be on.

The first option is to provide a brief explanation of the concept of *plagiarism*, including the sanctions for students who get caught. In this option, the emphasis will be on the *matter side* of the message: What is plagiarism and which rules apply in our educational program?

George could also choose to let the students know that they have to keep away from everything that smells of plagiarism, and to refer them to a manual where they can find concrete advice on how to use sources carefully and prevent plagiarism. In this option, the emphasis will be on the *appeal side* of the message: the behavior that the staff wants to achieve among the students.

A third possibility is to make it clear that the staff members in this program despise every form of plagiarism and regard it as a form of deception. Now the emphasis will be on the *self-expression side* of the message: the image that the poster creates of the norms and values of the program staff.

Finally, George could use the posters to make it clear that the staff does not regard students as potential fraudsters but as prospective professionals who may not yet know how to prevent plagiarism. In this case, George puts the emphasis on the *relationship side* of the message: What view does the staff have of the students who participate in the program?

Differences in emphasis in a message about plagiarism.

It is important to distinguish between different communicative goals. Often, the first aim of a message is to change the knowledge of the receivers. Sometimes the communicative goal is limited to this knowledge aspect, for example in the case of news items that are only meant to provide information. However, most messages also aim to achieve other goals: in the case of the CDC (see the next page), influencing the beliefs, attitudes, and behavior of the receiver (safe sex) and ultimately improving the public health situation. Whether or not these goals are achieved often depends on more than just the quality of the communication.

1.2   The appeal side: communicative goals

The Centers for Disease Control and Prevention (CDC) aims to protect the USA from health, safety, and security threats, both foreign and at home. Part of its website (*cdc.gov/std/prevention/*) is devoted to the prevention of sexually transmitted diseases (STDs) such as chlamydia, HPV, and HIV/AIDS. Site visitors are informed about STDs and about the use of condoms and other means of preventing infections. From the website it is clear that the communicative goals are threefold: providing site visitors with sufficient knowledge about the subject of STDs, convincing them of the need to have safe sex, and informing them of what to do. The underlying goal is, of course, that more people have safe sex. If this goal is achieved, the next underlying goal is reached: The CDC has contributed to the improvement of the public health situation. Whether people have safe sex evidently does not depend solely on the CDC's website. There are also other factors that influence the behavior of the visitors, such as their social environment, possible psychological barriers, their partner's willingness to have safe sex, and also the availability of a condom.

Communicative goals and underlying goals.

In this section, we will first discuss the sender's communicative goals. Subsequently, underlying goals and the receiver's goals are discussed.

1.2.1   Communicative goals of senders

Through communication, senders want to influence the knowledge, skills, opinions, behavioral intentions, or emotions of the receivers of their messages. The following table shows a breakdown of communicative goals according to the type of influence senders may want to exert.

Communicative goal	The sender wants to	In order to exert influence on the receiver's
informative	inform	factual knowledge
instructive	instruct	skills
persuasive	persuade	beliefs, attitudes
motivational	motivate	behavioral intentions
affective	emotionally affect	feelings

Breakdown of possible communicative goals of senders.

- *Informative*. The sender wants to transfer knowledge, for example by reporting on an event, clarifying what products and services a company provides, or explaining the causes of a certain problem.
- *Instructive*. The sender wants to help the receiver in performing a specific task, such as setting up an *Apple Watch*, preparing an Ossobuco, or applying for a student grant.
- *Persuasive*. The sender wants to influence the receiver's view or position. By means of an advertising message, a company wants to convince the public of the quality of its products. By means of a policy paper, the government wants to convince the parliament that its position on a certain issue is justified or that a certain policy must be pursued.
- *Motivational*. The sender not only wants to convince the receiver of a point of view but also wants to ensure that the receiver is willing to do something, such as buying a product, attending a meeting, transferring money to a bank account, or quitting smoking.
- *Affective*. The sender wants to evoke certain emotions in the receiver, such as surprise, pleasure, anger, or fear.

In practice, different communicative goals are often combined; sometimes that is the only possibility. For example, a sender who wants to *convince* receivers of the quality of a certain product can hardly avoid providing *information* about that product as well. Most receivers will only be convinced if they are informed about the characteristics of the product. Moreover, most advertisers not only want to convince, they also want to *motivate* the public to actually buy the product.

The combination of communicative goals in a message is not arbitrary; there is almost always a certain hierarchy. Usually, there is one main goal that the other goals serve to support.

The Belgian city of Ghent publishes a brochure with information on the most important tourist sights, such as the Gravensteen castle, the Saint Bavo Cathedral, the belfry, and the Museum of Fine Arts. The goal of this brochure is first and foremost informative: The city wants to pass on factual knowledge. But that is not all, of course. The brochure also aims to convince the reader that Ghent is an attractive place to visit, and it wants to convey a positive feeling about the city. And even those goals are not what the text is ultimately all about. The brochure intends to persuade the reader to visit this city: The main goal of the brochure is therefore motivational. Once readers want to visit Ghent, they must also be informed on how to get there, how to book a room in a hotel, and so on. The brochure should therefore also include instructions.

Different communicative goals in a tourist brochure.

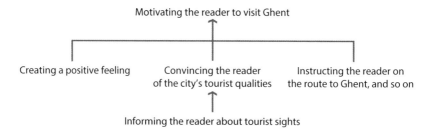

Coherence between communicative goals in a tourist brochure. The main goal is to motivate the reader (to visit Ghent); the other goals support this main goal.

Instruction manuals primarily serve an instructive goal. The reader has to learn, for example, how to operate a newly purchased orbital sander. The sender assumes that this is what the reader wants. The instructions, therefore, do not have to serve any motivational goal—with the exception of the warnings in the instruction manual, for instance that you should unplug the machine when you want to change the grinding belt. In order to motivate users to take this action, it is necessary to convince them of the risks they will run if they fail to do so. For this purpose, information must be provided: If you do not unplug the device, the machine may accidentally turn on while changing the grinding belt and you may get injured.

Various goals in an instruction manual.

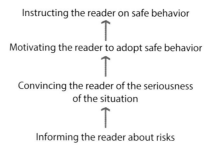

Different goals of warnings in instruction manuals. The main goal is to give instructions (on safe behavior); the other goals support this main goal.

1.2.2   Underlying goals

In section 1.2.1, the main focus was on the *communicative goals* of the sender. What does the sender want to achieve 'in the mind of the receivers': changing their knowledge, skills, beliefs, attitudes, behavioral intentions, or emotions? But communication in a professional context also always serves *the underlying goals* of a sender: an organization or an individual. These underlying goals determine to a large extent the content and the form the message needs to have.

The underlying goals of an organization can be arranged hierarchically. For instance, a Ministry of Education must, among other things, ensure good and affordable education (general goal). In that context, it must also provide facilities for children with learning difficulties (more specific goal). Various means are used for these more specific goals: money, labor, legislation, and in a number of cases also communication, for instance through the internet.

Just like organizations, individuals who communicate have underlying goals. If you apply for a job, you not only want to inform the selection committee about your education and experience. Above all, you want to convince the committee that you are the best candidate. In this case, your underlying goals will be to get a nice job, to develop your skills, and to earn an attractive income.

When we look at the messages of others, or when we communicate ourselves, we must always do so against the background of the underlying goals. After all, these goals determine to a large extent what the communicative goals will be, and what the content and form of the message will be.

The *Oblex Communication Consultancy* company receives an assignment from the Ministry of Education. They are asked to develop a new part of the ministry's website about the new rules for admitting children to special schools. The information is intended for parents who, possibly on the advice of the teacher, are considering a special school for their child. The new section on the website should serve two purposes. It should be informative (offering information on special schools) and it should be instructive (explaining what parents must do to have their child placed at a special school). *Oblex Communication Consultancy* gets access to the official texts of the new rules and the brochures that schools have already received.

Staff member Karen McDevor reads the information she has received and decides to visit a school for special education in order to experience the atmosphere. While she is there, she is informed that many parents find it difficult to send their child to a special school, but that almost all parents are very enthusiastic once they have done so. It therefore seems clear to Karen that the new pages on the website should not only be informative and instructive, but also persuasive and motivating. The website should convince parents of a child with learning difficulties of the advantages of sending their child to a special school, and encourage them to actually do so.

After two weeks, Karen is able to present a draft of the new pages to the client, a manager at the ministry. To her surprise, however, the client is not satisfied. He finds the information far too positive: He thinks it should be presented in a more neutral tone.

Karen explains why she presented the information in the way she did, but that does not convince the client.

What is the problem here? For a number of years now, the ministry has been following a 'joint schooling' policy. This policy implies that children with learning difficulties are cared for as much as possible within the mainstream primary education system by means of extra guidance, and that access to special education will be limited. Considering this policy, there is definitely no need for a highly persuasive and motivating text on the ministry's website.

Underlying goals of an organization play a decisive role in its communication messages.

1.2.3   Goals of receivers

As with the sender's goals, we can distinguish five types of goals that the receiver may have.
- *Acquiring knowledge.* One of the main reasons for receivers to pay attention to a message is that they want to know more about its subject, understand how it works, learn what is going on, and so on. The motives can vary: pure curiosity (people reading the newspaper), practical usefulness (potential customers collecting information about a smartphone because they want to buy one), but sometimes also external pressure (students studying a textbook for an examination). The acquisition of knowledge is also a prominent goal when, for example, the receiver listens to the radio news, watches a documentary on TV, or conducts an interview for a newspaper.
- *Acquiring skills.* Many texts that people have to read in their professional career are intended to enable them to perform certain tasks. The type of tasks can vary from operating a device to registering a new customer in the administration or dealing with a customer's complaint. More often than not, the receiver will want at least two questions answered: 'What should I do?' and 'How should I do it?'.
- *Defining your position.* An important motive for reading texts, participating in conversations, or listening to a presentation can be to find the answer to questions such as 'What do I think of [...]?' and 'How do I evaluate [...]?'. Sometimes the motivation is purely personal: People want to form their own opinion about something. There can also be a social motive: The people around you expect you to have an opinion on a certain subject. Are you for or against euthanasia? Do you think that the current immigration policy is humane or too strict? Should the regulations for receiving a study grant be changed or not?

- *Making a decision.* One step further than forming an opinion is making a decision: What am I going to do, or what is our organization going to do? What type of computer am I going to buy? Where am I going on holiday? What policy should be pursued? In which areas should we invest? Are we going to work with company X?
- *Being touched.* Messages can also touch the receiver. This effect is generally associated with reading a novel, watching a film, or attending a theatre performance. It is often thought that such affective goals do not play a role in professional communication, but this is an incorrect assumption. Even if it is not on the foreground, professional communication can (and should) also be pleasant, nice, and perhaps even exciting. Such an effect may even be decisive for the ultimate success of the communication.

When the goals of the receiver seamlessly fit those of the sender, we speak of *symmetrical* goals. The following table shows when this symmetry exists.

Type of goal	The sender wants to	The receiver wants to
informative	inform	know something
instructive	instruct	acquire skills, be able to do something
persuasive	persuade	take a position, form an opinion
motivational	motivate	make a decision, do something
affective	emotionally affect	be touched, have a good time

Symmetry between sender goals and receiver goals.

However, reality is often less clear-cut. Even if goals are symmetrical, that does not necessarily mean that both parties will achieve their goals. If a sender informs the receiver about a subject in which the receiver is not interested, or if the information is very unclear, then neither the sender nor the receiver will achieve their informative goal. And a politician who tries to arouse feelings of indignation at the government's scandalous proposal may find that many voters remain indifferent, even if they were willing to be moved.

Especially when it comes to convincing and motivating, the goal of the receiver is not always in line with the goal of the sender. If receivers want to form an opinion or make a decision, it does not always have to be the opinion that the sender wants to convince them of or the decision that the sender wants them to make.

Elisabeth Schulze is a member of a German political party. She is active as a volunteer in the reception of asylum seekers. The German media are discussing the question of whether the reception of asylum seekers should take place in a European context, or whether all European countries should define and pursue their own policies. An article in the party paper, written by a foreign policy specialist, argues in favor of the European approach. The article is intended as a persuasive text, and Elisabeth is interested in form-ing an opinion. The communicative goals are therefore symmetrical. But that does not mean that Elisabeth will be convinced by the arguments provided in the article. On the contrary, when Elisabeth reads that European policy will lead to a higher percentage of rejections of asylum applications, she is actually inclined to oppose that policy.

Sender and receiver goals are symmetrical, but the receiver does not accept what the sender wants to achieve.

Asymmetric goals do not necessarily create unsolvable problems. But sometimes things can go really wrong. The goals of the sender and the receiver may be so far apart that neither party can successfully attain their goals.

After studying electrical engineering, Sarah Ericsson joins ITF, a Swedish manufacturer of state-of-the-art telecommunications equipment. Her first task as a junior research assistant is to conduct a laboratory study into the reliability of three types of advanced interference suppression systems. At a certain point, she is asked to present her findings in a meeting of the management team. As a new employee, Sarah naturally tries to do her best. She prepares a presentation to explain in detail which measurement methods she has used. She makes digital slides of the measuring setups and she takes copies of a handout with her, with an overview of all the data analyses she has performed.

However, the reactions of the management team to the well-prepared presentation are disappointing. Most of the attendees clearly show a lack of interest: They are continu-ously looking at their smartphones and their paperwork. After only ten minutes, Sarah receives a friendly but urgent request to conclude her presentation quickly.

What went wrong? Sarah had assumed that the attendees would mainly be interested in detailed technical information. That turned out to be an incorrect assumption. The task of the management team was to define a position on the soundness of the various systems and to decide whether one of those should be put into production. The receiver goals were therefore quite different from the sender goals.

The goals of the sender do not match those of the receivers.

1.2.4 Unclear goals

We often communicate without being fully aware of our goals. That may be a good thing. If we had to think about our goals all the time, even the most ordinary conversations would be difficult. It is only when something goes wrong that we may find ourselves giving more thought to our goals and asking ourselves questions like 'What did I want from my audience?' or 'Why did I say that?'.

In more complex communicative situations, it is important to think in advance about what we want to achieve. Senders who have to write a report, take part in a meeting, or address a committee, should start by asking themselves what they want to achieve and also what the goals of the readers of the report, the other participants in the meeting, or the presentation's audience might be. From the perspective of the receiver, it is not always possible to deduce from the message what the sender exactly wants to achieve. It may be particularly difficult if the sender wants to influence the beliefs or the attitudes of the receiver without being explicit.

– Sometimes *senders think their communicative goal is clear enough* but in fact this is not the case at all. For example, the sender gives a hint ('It is quite cold in here!'), expecting that a receiver sitting next to a heater will understand the appeal included in the message and turn the heater on. Sometimes, however, such a hint is not clear enough: The receiver does not notice the appeal side of the message and takes no action.

– Sometimes *senders do not feel they are in a position to influence the receivers' behavior in a direct way*. Especially in organizations where hierarchy is important, junior employees may find it difficult to explicitly advise their superiors on the decisions to be made, even if they are convinced they have a better understanding of the issue than their superiors.

– Sometimes *senders consciously choose not to be too clear* because clarity also entails responsibility. Someone who unreservedly recommends making a certain purchase to the management may run into problems if the decision later turns out to be wrong. If senders want to avoid such problems, they may opt for a message with an appeal side that is not quite clear.

– Often, *politeness* is an important motive for lack of clarity about the communicative goals of senders. Senders want to give receivers the freedom to decide for themselves what to think or do and therefore do not explicitly say what they want to achieve. These messages are *indirect*. Fortunately, indirect messages do not necessarily lead to misunderstandings and communication failures. Indirectness is often more or less conventional. When someone asks you: 'Do you know where Jenny lives?' and you do know Jenny's address, you understand that probably a simple 'yes' will not do: The question was intended as a request for Jenny's address. Senders often count on the goodwill of the receivers to understand the meaning behind their literal message, and this confidence is usually justified.

A report from a company's internal audit department states: 'It was found that there is no overview of persons who are entitled to make payments of more than €5,000.' The writers do not explicitly say what they want to achieve with this message because they deem it self-evident: Such an overview is needed.

   The company's CEO, however, does not consider the appeal side of this message and does not notice its motivational goal, and therefore takes no action.

The sender wrongly thinks that the motivational goal is clear.

CEO Mathieu is a regular visitor of the meetings of her company's Sales Promotion Department. Today the colleagues have little to discuss with Mathieu, and the rest of the meeting's agenda is quite long. Unfortunately, Mathieu is very talkative: She elaborates extensively on all kinds of incidents from the time that she was an employee herself in this department, which was then called Recruitment and Advertising. 'Well, and since then the work load of the department has increased a lot, as today's agenda illustrates [...]' says meeting chairman Aristides, carefully putting an end to the discussion.

Aristides cannot bluntly ask his CEO Mathieu to leave; being up front about such an appeal would be impolite. He decides to give a hint in which the matter side, superficially seen, seems to be the most important, and which also fits in elegantly with the theme brought up by Mathieu.

1.2.5   Effectiveness of communication

Communication is only fully effective when sender and receiver both reach their goals. That can only be achieved if both sender and receiver are able and willing to cooperate. What does that imply for a communication message? Below we look at how effective communication can be facilitated for informative, instructive, persuasive, and motivating messages.

The effectiveness of informative communication
In most cases, communication has an informative goal at least to some extent. The sender wants to transfer knowledge to the receiver. The following conditions determine whether informative communication will be effective.
–   The information must be sufficiently *consistent with the receiver's prior knowledge*. The sender should not assume prior knowledge that the receiver does not

possess, otherwise the message may be incomprehensible. At the same time, however, the information must also contain some news, otherwise the receiver may quickly lose interest.

– The information must *meet the needs of the receiver*. No matter how interesting the senders themselves may find the information in their messages, if they do not include an answer to a question that is relevant to the receiver, the messages will have little or no effect.

– The message must be *well-structured*: It must have a clear organization. A good explanatory text, for example, progresses from easy to difficult and does not skip from one subject to another.

– The language used must *match the receiver's language skills*. Too many complex sentences and too many unknown words make it difficult for the receiver to understand the content. But texts full of short sentences and easy words may also be risky. Then there is a chance that the receiver does not feel he or she is taken seriously and loses interest.

– The information must *arouse sufficient attention*. Senders can capture and hold the receivers' attention by way of excitement, humor, a surprising twist, or a captivating style.

The effectiveness of instructive communication

The goal of instructive communication is to enable the receiver to carry out certain tasks such as operating a device, solving a mathematical problem, or completing a tax form. Instructive communication is effective when such a task is successfully accomplished. However, in addition to this requirement of effectiveness in a narrower sense, instructive communication also needs to meet other requirements.

– The communication must help to carry out the task in an *efficient* way, that is, with as little effort as possible. Efficiency is particularly important when it comes to tasks that need to be carried out as a matter of urgency, like emergency measures in the event of accidents.

– The message must provide insight into the *structure* and the *rationale* of the task. Receivers should not only be able to perform the task, they should also understand what they are doing.

– Often tasks have to be performed more than once. In such cases, the information provided should also be *learnable*. Instructions for using the calendar function of a smartphone, for example, must take into account that people will want to remember how to do that. They do not want to have to look up the instructions every time they want to enter a birthday of a new friend or colleague, for instance.

– The message should also *motivate* the receivers to carry out the instructions correctly, for instance by showing what can be gained or lost by either following or ignoring the given directions.

How can you ensure that an instructive message meets these requirements?

- The instruction should be *complete*. There should be no missing steps unless they are completely obvious, such as 'unpack the equipment before setting it up'.
- The instruction should have the right *level of detail*. Each step should be elaborated in such a way that the receivers can carry it out. The instruction should not be unnecessarily detailed, however, as this would make it less efficient.
- The steps should be given in the *order* in which they are to be carried out.
- The instruction should be *logical* in the eyes of the receivers. This makes them confident that it makes sense to follow the instruction meticulously.
- The language used and the illustrations provided should be so *clear* that the receivers understand exactly what to do.

The effectiveness of persuasive and motivational communication

An important characteristic of persuasive and motivational communication is that the goals of the senders and receivers, although often symmetrical, can still easily collide with each other. Of course, receivers often want to form an opinion or take a decision on a particular issue, but they rarely a priori want to conform to the sender's point of view. We all like to decide for ourselves what we think about something and what we want (or don't want) to do.

If receivers are confronted with messages that somehow conflict with their current opinions or behavior, they will easily ignore these messages or even develop a certain resistance to the goal of the sender and the messages that follow from this goal. There are many ways in which receivers can resist a sender's attempt at persuasion.

- Receivers can try to *avoid* messages with an unwanted appeal. For example, most newspaper readers do not subscribe to a newspaper with views they do not like, but instead choose to read a newspaper with opinions with which they usually agree. In this way, they avoid confrontations that could bring them out of balance.
- Receivers can *ignore* the persuasive or motivational character of the message. A lack of emphasis on the appeal makes it easy for the receiver to pretend not to notice it. A surgeon who reads in a complaints report that her patients often have to wait a long time because she is called away for consultation with colleagues, may interpret this remark as no more than factual information and thus ignore the motivational goal ('Please give higher priority to waiting patients').
- Receivers can *downplay* the authority of the sender, making it easier not to take the appeal side of the message seriously. 'The committee is now proposing that the Research and Development Department be reduced, but we must not

forget that the committee mainly consists of marketing people who have a lot to learn about research.'

- Receivers may *seek counterarguments* to justify their current behavior. 'Drinking may be bad for my liver, but do I not have the right to enjoy things that make life easier?' 'Research has shown that a daily glass of wine is good for the heart and blood vessels. And indeed, look what happened to your own grandfather. He loved a good drink and last month he turned ninety-four.'

How can senders convince receivers? It often helps when the appeal in the message is very clear. Otherwise, there is always a risk that the receiver will simply not understand what the sender is trying to convey. But clarity about the appeal side can also have an unwanted effect: Receivers may feel that their freedom is impaired. In that case, a negative reaction is almost inevitable. Showing respect for the receivers is important: The receiver should feel that the sender is someone who is helping them weigh their options, and not someone who is imposing his or her will or, worse still, someone with a hostile attitude.

Senders can further increase their chances of success by emphasizing the 'benefits' in order to offset the 'costs' for the receivers (giving up their own freedom to take a stand or to make a decision). To achieve that goal, the message should clearly explain the benefits the receivers will enjoy if they comply with the appeal. The following elements can help to convince the receivers.

- *Advantages of the new behavior.* 'Quitting smoking leads to better health.' 'This new production process leads to more profit.' 'Following these guidelines for using sources leads to a higher thesis grade.' If the sender succeeds in demonstrating that such consequences are to be expected, it is more likely that receivers will be prepared to reconsider their views or behavior.
- *Disadvantages of the current behavior.* 'Smoking can lead to lung cancer.' 'Continuing the present production process is likely to lead to a drop in profits.' 'Careless use of sources may inadvertently lead to plagiarism, which may result in study delay or even suspension.'
- *Norms and values.* 'A contribution to this charity expresses solidarity with people in need.' 'A vote for the Labour Party is an act of solidarity with the weaker members of society.' By linking the appeal to the norms and values that are important to the receiver, the sender increases the chances of success.
- *Ethos of the sender.* Receivers with a high opinion of a sender are more likely to be persuaded than receivers who have little respect for the sender.
- *Sense of community ('we' feeling).* The sender may show that the desired behavior is desirable for the group the receiver belongs to or wants to belong to. 'Intelligent and dynamic young people are now joining this new political party in great numbers!' Who would not want to be seen as young, intelligent, and dynamic?

Chapter 3 elaborates on arguments that can contribute to the persuasiveness of the message.

1.3   The self-expression side: the sender

In communication messages, the senders—willingly or not—provide information 'between the lines' about themselves and about the organization they represent. This self-expression side of a message is even more pronounced in oral communication than in written communication. Listeners not only hear what the speaker says, they also deduce information from the speaker's posture, movements, clothing, and use of voice. The conclusions that listeners draw from this information about the speaker often overshadow what they deduce from the words that are being uttered.

The following two letters from a municipal sanitation department illustrate how written messages, in this case from the municipality of New Aduard, also create an image of the sender. The municipality is formally represented here by city manager J.M.J. Johnson, who signed the letters. We do not really know anything about the real Mr. or Mrs. J.M.J. Johnson. Most likely he or she did not even write the letters; they may well have been written by one of the subordinates working in the sanitation department or perhaps in the communication office. The actual writer of the first letter may well be a very nice lady, and the actual writer of the second letter may be an unfriendly gentleman, and the same may be true for Mr. or Mrs. Johnson. What matters here is how the *municipality* presents itself in these messages. And that differs quite a bit in the two letters.

MUNICIPAL SANITATION DEPARTMENT
P.O. Box 20
New Aduard

To the residents of this building

Today a municipal official on duty established that, contrary to Article 13 of the Municipal Waste Collection Bye-Law, the contents of your household waste container exceeded the maximum permitted filling weight of 75 kg. Nevertheless, from the point of view of service, it was decided to accept the container. If in the future, however, your household waste container is not correctly presented, it will not be emptied.

Yours sincerely,

J.M.J. Johnson, City Manager

Letter depicting an official, formal, and authoritarian city manager.

MUNICIPAL SANITATION DEPARTMENT
P.O. Box 20
New Aduard

To the residents of this building

Dear Sir, Madam,

Earlier today, when we emptied your garbage container, we noticed that it was heavier than 75 kilos. This is not how it should be: Garbage containers that are too heavy may pose a risk to the health of our garbage collectors, and such containers also increase the risk of equipment failure. For your convenience, however, we have emptied your container. But could you please pay attention to the weight of your container in future? Should it happen again, then regrettably we will have no choice but to leave your container unemptied.

Kind regards,

J.M.J. Johnson, City Manager

Letter depicting a friendlier city manager (but perhaps perceived as a bit patronizing).

For specific groups of senders, such as politicians and media personalities, the self-expression side of their messages is so important that they receive special training that teaches them how to create and maintain the *image* they want to convey of themselves.

Other professionals, too, should not neglect the self-expression side of communication. If senders have built up an unfavorable image of themselves without realizing this, it may be quite harmful to the effectiveness of their messages.

Displaying dominance and creating a facade

Senders sometimes tend to exaggerate their strengths. They try to display their dominance by showing off their qualities, expertise, indispensability, or important relationships ('my good friend Professor John Hayes from Pittsburgh'). As a result, senders may spend excessive attention to complicated issues, or they may come forward with a pompous presentation of relatively unimportant details. In such cases, the need to adapt to the audience's interests is sacrificed for the sake of the sender's desire to brag.

Conversely, senders sometimes try to hide their weaknesses by creating a facade. People who feel they do not have enough knowledge of a certain topic can, for example, try to divert the conversation to subjects they think they have more to say about, or they may downplay the importance of the topic at hand. They may also take refuge in complicated sentences to hide that they really have nothing to say: a combination of displaying dominance and creating a facade.

> The possibility cannot not be excluded that one of the potential causes of the dioxin content in milk fat is the fact that the emission of the waste incineration plant is related to the aforementioned dioxin content.

Creating a facade? In any case, what the sender does here is no more than saying in a difficult and cumbersome way that the dioxin in the milk may come from the waste incineration plant.

'Avoid displaying dominance and creating a facade and just be yourself'. This could be an encouragement to only utter messages with a clear, self-expression side. Sometimes, however, it is desirable for senders to consciously choose what they want to show about themselves. If, for example, senders never show their strengths in a conflict situation, they run the risk of not being taken seriously and thus shooting themselves in the foot. Politicians and leaders, on the other hand, sometimes need to hold back a little because they have to consider conflicting needs and interests.

Communicative roles

In the two letters from the municipal sanitation department, the goal was to motivate the residents to reduce the weight of their garbage containers. The *communicative role* chosen by the sender determined the content and wording of the text. In the first letter, the city manager was presented as a sender who only wanted to provide information about the garbage weight regulation, while in the second letter the city manager was presented as a sender who wanted to persuade the receiver to adopt a different behavior.

A well-considered choice of a communicative role can have a major positive impact on the effectiveness of the communication. Senders who want to convince a skeptical audience are usually more successful when they present themselves as a neutral information provider than as an enthusiastic missionary or as an intrusive seller. If the audience is less skeptical, however, a certain level of enthusiasm may be quite helpful. In that case, senders acting as neutral information providers may raise the suspicion that they do not really believe in their own case.

- Neutral information provider
- Enthusiastic missionary
- Obtrusive seller
- Strict evaluator
- Helpful assistant
- Confident expert

Some communicative roles.

Effects of self-expression

Receivers are sensitive to the self-expression side of a communication message, and it often greatly influences their reactions. If senders succeed in creating a sympathetic, expert picture of themselves or their organization, receivers are more inclined to take their message seriously and are more likely to be persuaded and motivated. Senders who want to be successful should therefore pay sufficient attention to the self-expression side of their messages.

However, there are limits. Senders may not always be able to fully adapt to the taste of the receiver, nor is it always necessary to do so. It is essential that a sender is *credible*. Senders who demonstrate that they do not actually believe in their own story engender distrust. The same applies to senders who are ostentatiously playacting and who present themselves as more sympathetic or easygoing than they really are. Such behavior is often counterproductive, for the receiver is likely to take the sender and the messages less seriously.

1.4   The relationship side: the receiver

As simple as it may sound, the secret of effective communication mainly lies in the ability and the willingness of the communication parties to put themselves in the other's position. Successful communication parties understand how their messages may come across. They are able and prepared to take into account the possible effects of their messages before determining the content and wording of what they want to convey. They treat the other as they would like to be treated themselves.

> Now that you are retiring, various problems are likely to arise at home. What will you do with all your free time? Are you not constantly in the way of your wife? Fortunately, there is a solution. With the municipal senior citizens card, you can take part in all kinds of relaxing activities at a reduced rate. You can participate free of charge in the recreation afternoons, visit the museum at a reduced rate, and take part in the annual bus trips for the elderly. In short: We are here to help you do everything you have wanted to do for years but just did not have the time for.

From a brochure distributed by the municipality of New Aduard about its senior citizens card. The writer has apparently forgotten that there are also female citizens, and he or she has a strong view of what is going on in the reader's mind. Whether that view is correct is questionable. It is also questionable whether readers will appreciate the writer's prejudices. 'What I have wanted to do for years but just did not have the time for is no business of the municipality', many readers may think. By distributing this brochure, the municipality runs a serious risk of irritating readers and launching an unsuccessful information campaign.

Messages not only show something (and sometimes a lot) about the sender, between the lines, they also often reveal what the sender thinks about the receiver. In the example about the senior citizens' card, the writer's ideas about the readers are rather clear. But the relationship side of a message can also be more subtle. The way we address each other, for example, already indicates how we perceive our mutual relationship. Do we use first or last names? Do we use 'Mrs.' and 'Mr.'? The content of a message also often shows what the sender thinks about the receiver. For example, what kind of arguments does the sender think are fit to convince the receiver? And how much prior knowledge is assumed?

> Do you strive for a good future, a nice job, and a fine income? Then you should definitely register for our Communication Science program.

This message suggests that readers will mainly base their choice of an educational program on future perspectives.

> The field of communication is undergoing vast developments. Technological innovations are constantly leading to new forms of communication. If you are interested in this, our Communication Science program is right up your alley.

This message suggests that readers will mainly base their choice of an educational program on their curiosity and their interest in innovations.

> EORGPLUS uses advanced digital techniques to get the most out of your electronic organ. For example, you can manually adjust the speed and depth of the tremulant to your preferences. If you wish, you can also adjust the tuning of your instrument, and give voice to the old masters in a completely authentic way. You can opt for equal, midrange, Pythagorean, Werckmeister, Kirnberger, and Valotti & Young temperaments.

In this advertising brochure for electronic organs, it is assumed that readers have a lot of prior knowledge. They know what a tremulant is and are familiar with six temperaments, listed here without any further explanation.

What kind of assumptions about the receiver play a role in communication?
- Assumptions about the receiver's *prior knowledge*. Some things have to be explained, others may be familiar.
- Assumptions about the receiver's *language skills*. Senders who use difficult words and complicated sentences apparently assume that their receivers have no problem with understanding their messages. Senders who 'bend down' to their receivers and approach them with overly simplified sentences apparently assume that these receivers lack the language skills of a grown-up.
- Assumptions about the receiver's *norms, values,* and *preferences*. What does the sender apparently consider to be important in the eyes of the receivers, and what expectations does the sender have about the kind of arguments that will convince them? Senders' ideas about these topics are almost always reflected in the content and the tone of voice of their communication messages.
- Assumptions about the *relationship between sender and receiver*. Do senders feel they are positioned 'above' their receivers and therefore think they can call the shots? Or is it the other way around, and do senders put the receiver in the leading role? Or do senders perhaps place themselves and the receivers on an equal footing? Messages often reflect a sender's ideas about the parties' positions in the communication.

When we try to determine how a message reflects the sender's view of the receivers, we have to take into account that a sender may be playing a strategic game in which he or she deliberately attributes unrealistic characteristics to the receivers.

Then the purpose is to flatter the receivers, making them more susceptible to the sender's persuasive or motivating communicative goals.

Advertisements for sound equipment sometimes seem to be intended only for people with an expensive taste, who listen to opera music, buy design furniture, and also have a great understanding of topics such as noise reduction and frequency characteristics.

But such advertisements are, of course, also intended for people who mainly love Elvis Presley, who are already happy if they are able to configure the tuner's presets, and who put their hi-fi equipment on a simple bookshelf.

This way the advertiser attributes characteristics to the readers that most of them do not have. But the idea behind this is that many readers will appreciate being addressed as someone with an expensive taste and a good understanding of technical equipment. The ad is not so much about the kind of people the receivers *can* identify with, but about the kind of people they *want to* identify with.

A strategic game with the presumed prior knowledge and taste of receivers.

The intranet of the O'Hara software company publishes a monthly column by the owner, John O'Hara, on the ups and downs of the organization. The column always radiates a sense of enthusiasm and positivity. John O'Hara apparently assumes that all readers of his column are dedicated to the company with heart and soul. But does he really think that is the case? Probably not. He may very well be aware that there are occasional tensions and signs of dissatisfaction. Evidently, he tries to guide his readers into the role of an enthusiastic employee.

A strategic game with assumptions about the receiver.

'Would you perhaps have some time this afternoon to copy this report and send it to the members of the committee? I would be very grateful if you could do this before six o'clock.'

Mary Steinberg, the manager who addresses her assistant Florence Davids in this way, acts at first glance as if Florence is free to decide whether or not she will accept the request – as if Mary and Florence occupy the same position on the hierarchical ladder. Both Mary and Florence, however, know that in reality this is not the case. This request is not free of obligations; it is an assignment that must be carried out. Mary is probably aware that Florence likes to be addressed as if they were equals, and Mary probably also feels more comfortable this way. The suggestion of equivalence is beneficial for the working atmosphere.

A strategic game with assumptions about the relationship between the sender and the receiver.

Reactions of receivers to the relationship side of a message

In general, receivers are very sensitive to the way in which they are addressed. Two general human characteristics are decisive in this: the need for self-determination (our desire for freedom) and the need for appreciation (our self-esteem).

- *Need for self-determination.* We all want to decide for ourselves what to do and what not to do. We want to be free and not be bossed around. As a result, senders with a strong tendency to control their receivers can count on a lot of resistance to their messages.
- *Need for appreciation.* We all want others to judge us in a positive way. Nobody wants to be belittled or criticized. Senders who take an aggressive stance toward their receivers can also count on serious resistance to their messages.

The microwave

You can take the test immediately. For example, try to heat this morning's coffee. It will taste as if it has been freshly brewed.

1 Take a cup without gold or silver decor and place a spoon in it. Slide the grille in the oven on rack 1. Place the cup in the middle of the grid.
2 Press the MAX button.
3 Use the TIME SELECTOR button to set the time to 1 minute.
4 Press the START button.
5 After one minute, you will hear a signal that you can switch off prematurely, if desired, with the DELETE button.
6 The coffee is hot.
7 In addition to this example, you will find other examples in the table on page 4.

While you are quietly enjoying your cup of coffee, you read the *safety instructions* in the first part of this manual. They are very important.

From a microwave manual. The sender shows a strong tendency to direct the receiver's behavior. He or she tells the receiver exactly what to do. On reading the first sentences, the receiver may not yet find this a nuisance. After all, this is a user manual, and the sender focuses on receivers who do not yet know how this microwave works. Most receivers will appreciate a sender who clearly tells them what to do and when. On reading the last paragraph, however, many receivers may get irritated by the tone of the text. Now they are no longer being informed about how to operate the machine, they are being told how to read this text ('while quietly enjoying a cup of coffee'). And that is something receivers will want to decide for themselves. Here, the sender's directing behavior will go against the receivers' desire for self-determination.

In a newspaper interview, Frank Olsen, the former manager of a Danish Open Air Museum, expresses his annoyance at the behavior of Jesper Eriksen, one of his former colleagues. Eriksen was once invited to address an international group of managers of open-air museums. Olsen remembers very well how the ambitious Eriksen addressed those present at the meeting by saying: 'Ladies and gentlemen, you are the past, I am the future.' The attendees were shocked; this was how Eriksen apparently perceived their work and themselves. Olsen, too, felt very hurt in his self-esteem. After this public show of disdain, things never got better between Olsen and Eriksen.

A problematic relationship between communication parties.

1.5   Feedback

The preceding sections discussed all kinds of problems that can arise in communication: misunderstandings, goals that are not achieved, incorrect images that are created, and relationships that come under pressure. In order to address such communication problems, it is necessary for senders to clearly understand how the receiver perceives their messages. The receivers' responses to a message provide information to the sender about the way the receivers interpreted the various sides of this message: the matter side, the appeal side, the self-expression side, and the relationship side. This information about the effects of their messages that senders deduce from the receivers' reactions is called *feedback*.

1.5.1   Indirect and direct feedback

Feedback is a natural phenomenon in communication between sender and receiver. When people exchange messages in a conversation, for instance, they continuously also give and receive feedback, consciously or not. They give verbal reactions (using language) and non-verbal signals (nodding or shaking their head, for instance) that reveal how the messages of the other communication party came across.

Feedback as part of oral, spoken interaction is usually indirect. Receivers generally do not straightforwardly tell senders how they perceived their messages. They give such information indirectly, between the lines. We have already mentioned non-verbal signals. There are also the so-called *minimal reactions*, such as saying 'hmm' or simply saying 'yes'. Other responses may also contain indirect feedback. After a presentation, for example, there is often an opportunity to ask questions. From these questions, the speaker can sometimes deduce that certain parts of the lecture did not come across clearly or that some people were annoyed by an unfortunate remark the speaker made.

An obvious difficulty with indirect feedback is that the sender may sometimes find it difficult to interpret. How should one understand a smile from a listener in the audience—as a token of amusement or as a slightly mocking sign of disapproval? Or maybe it does not mean anything at all. For this reason, there is often a need for *direct* feedback in which receivers, be it at the sender's request or not, clearly express how they feel about a message. 'Sorry, but the arguments for your position are not yet clear to me', 'So you think I am angry with you now?', or 'From what you just said, I understand you agree with me on this subject. Is that correct?' Direct feedback is often necessary when there is a potential misunderstanding: Receivers can ask senders to clarify their message (on all four sides), and senders can then try to remove any ambiguities.

Direct feedback plays a particularly important role when communication itself is the subject of a discussion. This is called *metacommunication*: communication *about* communication. Situations in which a lot of metacommunication may be expected include performance reviews, evaluations of meetings, and review rounds to comment on a draft version of a text.

> An internship supervisor points out to a trainee that the funny emails that he regularly sends to her and the other colleagues of the department are not appreciated. People are annoyed that the trainee acts as if he has been working for the company for many years, while in fact he only started a couple of weeks ago.

An example of metacommunication.

1.5.2   Giving and receiving feedback

Giving feedback can be quite difficult. Especially direct feedback may be experienced as a criticism of the other person's way of communicating and may hence be perceived as a threat to his or her self-esteem. This threat may not only put the mutual relationship at risk, but there is also a chance that receivers of such feedback will shut themselves off. Their self-esteem prevents them from taking the feedback seriously. It is, therefore, crucial to present feedback as constructive, as a way of *helping* receivers of feedback to achieve their own goals even better.

– Make *a conscious choice about the message sides that your feedback will focus on*: the matter side, the appeal side, the self-expression side, or the relationship side. Do not be too quick with a reaction aimed only at the matter level or at the appeal level ('I do not understand what you want to achieve with the second paragraph'), while the real problems may be at the self-expression or at the relationship side ('You take a patronizing attitude, and you clearly underestimate your audience').

– Emphasize *positive feedback*. It may be tempting to criticize the weaknesses of the messages you are discussing—and thereby also the person responsible for those messages. But by honestly pointing out the strengths of the messages, and therefore also the strengths of the sender of those messages, you show appreciation for what is already good, and you pay respect to the receiver of the feedback. He or she is usually perfectly able to deduce from this feedback what apparently did not go well and what could therefore be improved. When the receiver of the feedback wishes to learn more about possibilities for further improvement, then that may be a good time to make specific comments that are perhaps a little less positive.

– Give *productive feedback*. Offer comments that the other person can act on. Do not limit yourself to generalities ('I must confess I found this story a bit boring'), but try to make clear what exactly is lacking ('In my opinion, a few more examples could be added here') and how things could be improved ('Maybe it would help if [...]').

– Give *feedback from your own perspective*; try not to blame the other person. 'Your way of speaking is really boring' is a remark that the other will perceive as an attack. He or she will probably start defending himself or herself or decide to plainly neglect the feedback. 'Sometimes I found it difficult to focus on what you were saying' sounds less threatening because it is about the person who is giving the feedback. In short, emphasize the self-expression side of your feedback, not the relationship side.

Receiving feedback is not easy either. As a receiver of feedback, you must try to suppress the tendency to regard the feedback as an attack on yourself as a person, even if the feedback was formulated in a negative way. It is wiser and more productive to see the feedback you receive as a tool that can help you to improve your messages and make the communication more effective.

– *Do not interpret feedback as a personal attack*. At least until proven otherwise, assume that the criticism relates to the message and not to you as a person.

– *Do not get defensive*. Try to take feedback to heart and carefully examine to what extent the criticism is justified and what you can learn from it.

– *Do not forget to listen carefully to what is* not *being said*. Suppose you gave a presentation and you receive many compliments for the visuals you used in your introduction. If, however, your listeners say nothing about the visuals you have shown in the other parts of your speech, this may suggest that they were less enthusiastic about those. The absence of such comments may be an indication that there is room for improvement.

– *Ask for more.* Try to prevent the feedback from being restricted to general, vague comments that do not tell you much. Ask for the exact meaning of what is being said.

– *Show appreciation.* Communication parties who give feedback also reveal themselves to some extent. They show how they have interpreted the message, and by doing so they run the risk of their weaknesses coming to the fore ('He didn't even understand that simple way of reasoning!'). Showing your appreciation and respect for feedback providers may lead to more specific and useful comments.

Direct feedback is of great importance for good communication. But such feedback presupposes a good, open, and honest relationship between the communication parties. There is always a risk of the feedback provider falling into the role of prosecutor and the feedback receiver falling into the role of victim. In such a situation you need to make an effort to improve the communication climate—preferably by exchanging clear but respectful metacommunication messages.

Key points

The four sides of a communication message
- Communication is a goal-driven process in which messages are exchanged between two parties: senders and receivers.
- Messages always have four sides: the matter side, the appeal side, the self-expression side, and the relationship side.
- Providing and receiving useful feedback is essential for full-fledged communication.

Matter side
- The matter side of a message concerns the actual subject and the factual information provided about this subject (see chapters 2 and 3).

Appeal side
- Messages are intended to inform, instruct, convince, motivate, or evoke feelings. These goals can often be combined.
- The communicative goals are to a large extent determined by the underlying goal.
- The goals of senders and those of receivers do not always match.
- Senders can purposely make their communicative goals unclear, for example to evade responsibility.
- For informative communication to be effective, alignment with the receiver's prior knowledge, information needs, and language skills is important, along with an adequate message structure and an interesting way of presenting the information.
- For instructive communication to be effective, completeness, level of detail, order of the steps, logic of the instruction, and clarity of the language and the illustrations are decisive.
- For persuasive communication to be effective, arguments based on advantages and disadvantages or based on norms and values are important. The ethos of the sender and the sense of community may also play an important role.

Self-expression side
- Senders sometimes convey a distorted picture of themselves by displaying dominance and by creating a facade.
- Senders often behave in accordance with a certain role that is determined by the organization they represent and by the goals they are trying to achieve.
- Essential for the receiver's evaluation of the sender is the sender's credibility.

Relationship side

– The relationship side reveals what the sender thinks about the receiver's language skills, prior knowledge, norms and values, and also about the relationship between the sender and the receiver.
– Successful communication requires that parties are able and willing to take the potential effects of their messages into account before determining the content and wording of what they want to convey. They treat the receiver as they themselves would like to be treated.
– Receivers may be expected to react negatively to messages that go against their need for self-determination or their need for appreciation.

Feedback

– Feedback is information about the effects of messages that senders can deduce from receivers' reactions.
– Feedback can be given either indirectly or directly.
– Good feedback is selective, positive, and productive and is given from the perspective of the feedback provider.
– When receiving feedback, it is important not to see it as a personal attack, not to become defensive, to also pay attention to what is not being said, to continue asking, and to show your appreciation for the person providing the feedback.

Eighteen years of age in New Aduard

Purpose of the assignment

You will practice recognizing different sides of a communication message and you learn to identify possible communication problems.

Subject matter

Section 1.1

Section 1.2

Section 1.3

Task 1

The mayor of New Aduard has written to some of the residents about the so-called *18-year-old regulation*. According to this new national regulation, from now on all citizens, male or female, are expected to take care of their own finances from the moment they are eighteen years old. This has serious consequences for childless couples of which both partners are unemployed. From now on they will receive a much lower social security benefit than they did before. The general idea is that not only a husband but also a wife may be expected to apply for a job and to earn a decent income.

1   Who do you consider to be the sender and the receivers of this letter?

2   Briefly describe the four sides of this message and indicate how much weight the sender apparently wanted to give to each of these message sides.

Task 2

Imagine that you belong to the target group of this letter. Please give your well-argued opinion on each of the four sides of this message. Ask yourself the following questions.

1   Matter side: Would the content of this letter be important and interesting to you?

2   Appeal side: How do you feel about the appeal that the sender addresses to you here? How do you feel about the way the sender supports this appeal? Why would you be willing or unwilling to comply?

3   Self-expression side: How do you feel about this sender? Sympathetic, reliable, sincere, credible?

4   Relationship side: How do you feel about what the sender apparently thinks of you? Is the sender treating you as you would like to be treated?

Task 3
Write a brief report on the positive and negative points you have noticed in this letter.

The letter

Dear Joan, Sandra and all other girls in New Aduard aged 15, 16 or 17 years,

A letter from the mayor especially for you! That is something unusual.

Perhaps you have already heard of the changes in our social security system.

What do these changes mean for you? Well, our parliament has taken a new decision about who can get a social security benefit from now on and who cannot. This has consequences for you too.

Imagine a couple, a man and a woman, living together. Perhaps they are married, perhaps not. Suppose now that the man is unemployed. This couple has so far been receiving a family allowance, whether or not the woman has a job of her own.

This will change soon, however. In the new situation, the family allowance will expire. The man will get a much lower allowance, just enough for himself. This couple can therefore no longer live off the benefit together. Just like the man, the woman is now also expected to go and find a job. An exception will, of course, be made for a mother with children. She can stay at home to take care of the children.

All well and good, you may think, but what do I have to do with this? Let me try to explain this to you. Everyone, including you and me, runs the risk of being unemployed and having to live off a benefit. That is why it is important for today's youth – and this also applies to boys – that they have enjoyed a proper education. Such an education increases the chance of finding and keeping a nice job and not becoming unemployed. That's why I think it is important that you know all of this.

If you have any further questions about this letter, do not hesitate to ask your class teacher or school dean. You can also call the town hall; asking questions is free. Please call between 9 and 12 am and ask for Mrs. Teresa Delaware (0345-52215).

I wrote this letter especially for you. But, of course, it is completely okay with me if your parents and your friends also read this letter. In fact, this is important information for everyone!

I wish you a good future.

The mayor of New Aduard

G.W. Barker

2 Structure

◀ *The Transept of the Mariakerk in Utrecht, seen from the Northeast*, Pieter Jansz. Saenredam, 1637. On the foreground some visitors and cripple beggars.

Just as churches–or indeed, any building–need a solid structure to remain standing, so too does a text need both a logical internal and a clear external structure if it is to reach its goals.

Risk analysis

In a risk analysis, risk is often calculated as the product of the probability of a certain accident happening and the severity of that accident (the consequences). When one has little experience in the field in which the risk analysis takes place, one constructs so-called error trees in which you examine what errors can occur in a certain system step by step, how big the chance is of this happening and what consequences they can have. Risk analysis is a branch of applied mathematics that has attracted increasing attention in recent years. Risk analysis is mainly applied in decision-making about industrial enterprises, such as in the field of nuclear energy, where the government wants to know whether the risks outweigh the—usually economic—benefits that can be gained from them.

This text is very hard to follow: It is an unstructured series of sentences.

Risk analysis is a branch of applied mathematics that has attracted increasing interest in recent years. Risk analysis is concerned with forecasting risks. Risk analysis is mainly used in decision-making about risky industrial enterprises, such as in the field of nuclear energy, where the government wants to know whether the risks outweigh the—usually economic—benefits that can be gained from them. In a risk analysis, risk is often calculated as the product of the probability of a certain accident happening and the severity of that accident (the consequences). When one has little experience in the field in which the risk analysis takes place, one constructs so-called error trees, in which you examine what errors can occur in a certain system step by step, how big the chance is of this happening and what consequences they can have.

There is an improved line of thought in the text now, but a special effort is still necessary to follow the text. Although the text has an improved internal structure, it is still difficult to see.

Risk analysis is a branch of applied mathematics that has attracted increasing interest in recent years. Risk analysis is concerned with forecasting risks. Good predictions are particularly necessary in decision-making in industrial enterprises, such as in the field of nuclear energy, where the government wants to know whether the risks outweigh the—usually economic—benefits that can be gained from them.

In principle, two methods of risk analysis can be distinguished. Often the product of the probability of a certain accident happening and the severity of that accident (the consequences) is simply calculated. But if one has little experience in the field in which the risk analysis takes place, the probability and the magnitude of the consequences

> cannot be expressed in numbers. Then we construct so-called error trees, in which we examine step by step what errors can occur in a certain system, what the probability is that they will occur and what consequences they can have.

The text is much easier to read now. The internal structure is made visible in an external structure: The information is divided into paragraphs and the connections between the sentences are made explicit.

The examples above illustrate that the structure of a text plays an important role when we communicate. A text does not consist of just any number of random sentences. There is a certain line in it that ensures coherence. The structure is brought about by three characteristics of the text.

– The text has one particular subject: the theme.

– The text consists of parts that are in a certain logical order: the internal structure.

– With certain words and other aids, it is made clear how the text is structured: the external structure.

All three examples meet the first characteristic: They are about one theme, 'RISK ANALYSIS'. But on the other two characteristics they differ. In the first example, both the internal and the external structure are missing. In the second example, an internal structure is present but it lacks an external structure. The third example has both an internal and an external structure. This combination makes the text easier to read and to understand.

Structure supports the processing of information

A well-structured text ensures that the information is presented to the reader in a clear way. The main points are clear, and the reader knows what to expect. A text with a clear structure is much easier to read than a long text with few signposting devices. A good structure helps the reader to understand a text better.

Reading a text is more than just perceiving a series of words and sentences. Readers are constantly processing the information that is presented to them. They wonder about the meaning of a word or try to find out what the writer means by a certain statement. They want to understand the text and are constantly looking for coherence. This is especially important if the reader needs to remember parts of the text, for example in the case of study material.

The internal processing of information in the head of a reader is a complicated procedure. Roughly speaking, readers have to create a mental picture of what the text means and the information it contains. Research has shown that creating such a mental picture is much easier if the text is coherent and if that coherence is made explicit through signposting (headings, signal words, etcetera).

Expectations also play a role in the processing of information. If, for example, the title of a text contains a question, readers will expect to find an answer to it. The same applies to a presentation. If a speaker indicates that he or she is presenting a proposal, the audience expects the speaker to tell them what the proposal is about, what it is based on, and why it is necessary to implement it.

A receiver-oriented text or presentation meets these expectations. From the structure of the text or presentation, the audience can determine what to expect and when to expect it.

A good internal structure and a clear external structure are essential for effective communication. If there is no structure in the text, the information is not conveyed and the goals of the text are not achieved. Writing is more than just producing nice sentences, and an oral presentation requires more than smooth talking. For business conversations, too, a good structure is essential. If you structure a conversation well, you ensure that your conversational partners do not deviate from the subject and that the conversation yields the desired results.

In this chapter, we will offer a number of tools that allow you not only to analyze the structure of messages you receive but also to improve the structure of your own messages. These tools are:
–   text schemata, also called 'building plans' (section 2.1);
–   set schemata, a very helpful special type of text schemata, also called 'set text schemata', 'standard structures', or 'fixed structures' (section 2.2);
–   general principles of organization (section 2.3).

These sections concern the *internal structure* of a text. The last section (2.4) focuses on the *external structure*, that is, the means by which a writer can make the structure visible. We limit ourselves here to the verbal, linguistic means of clarifying the structure. Visual resources such as layout, typography, diagrams, and tables are discussed in chapter 5.

The emphasis in the examples in this chapter is on written texts, for these provide the clearest insights if you want to understand structure. For more information on structure in oral communication, see chapters 9 and 10.

2.1   Text schemata

From an early stage in our education, we learn to create messages and the texts that embody them by first 'setting' a schema or structure for the ideas that we want to convey. We have a theme and we want to convey something about this theme, so we start by developing the main points regarding this theme. Such a text schema represents the internal structure of the text. For writers, a text schema serves as a tool for planning the content of a text and as a guideline for the actual writing of the text. For readers, a text schema can help to get a clear overview of the content of the text and may even act as a tool to evaluate the text. We can think of this powerful tool as the identification of a theme and the most important questions regarding the theme that we think the reader would like answers to.

2.1.1 The elements of a text schema

A text schema essentially consists of:
– the *theme* of the text;
– the *questions* that the text implicitly or explicitly addresses;
– the *answers* to these questions.

To make a well-organized text schema, you should briefly formulate the theme and the main questions of the text and only provide the essence of the answers (which we call *key answers*).

Of course, the main points or questions can be complex and can therefore be divided into sub-questions regarding sub-themes of the main theme. Therefore, for longer texts, you should also develop sub-questions. These are questions that you address in response to a key answer. The answers to these questions are also presented as key answers. To fully utilize the power of this instrument, three types of text schemata are distinguished.
– A *mini text schema*, only containing the theme and the main questions;
– A *short text schema*: a mini text schema, extended with the key answers to the main questions;
– A *detailed text schema*: a short text schema, extended with the sub-questions and the corresponding key answers.

In order to keep the text schema clear, it is a good idea to decide on some conventions regarding your notation. You can develop your own conventions, but here is a suggestion of how you could go about conventionalizing your text schema notation.
– Write the THEME in capital letters.
– Underline the main questions and end them with a question mark.
– Give the key answer directly below each main question and end it with a period. If there are multiple answers, number them.
– Underline possible sub-questions and place them further to the right than the key answer to which it belongs.
– Place a key answer to a sub-question directly below this sub-question; if there are more key answers to a sub-question, number them.

RISK ANALYSIS

What is risk analysis?
The branch of applied mathematics that deals with predicting risks.

Where is risk analysis applied?
Risk analysis is mainly used in decision-making about risky industrial enterprises.

How is risk analysis carried out?
1   By calculating the product of the probability of a certain risk and its severity.
2   By the construction of so-called error trees.

What are error trees?
In error trees, step by step, we check what errors can occur in a certain system, what the probability is that they will occur, and what consequences they can have.

What reservations should be made about the results of risk analysis?
1   The possibility of human error is often not considered.
2   The subjective experience of risks is not considered.

An example of a text schema. The theme of the text is 'RISK ANALYSIS'. This theme is in capital letters above the text schema. The text answers four main questions about the theme.

2.1.2   When is a text schema useful?

A text schema can help both the writer and the reader to understand the structure of a text.

For writers and speakers
If you are writing a text or preparing a presentation, you can use a text schema during different stages of the process.
–   *For collecting information.* If you are going to write about a complicated or unknown theme, it usually takes a lot of time to collect information. If you start by making a preliminary text schema, you will have an overview of the topics you need to find information about.
–   *For selecting information.* Once you start looking for information, you will encounter many things that are interesting but may not be relevant. The text schema provides you with a framework to assess whether the information you found is relevant for your text. Does the information fit the theme? Does it provide an answer to the main question and the sub-questions? Or does it raise new questions?

–   *For organizing information.* Once you have the desired information, it is important that you organize it in a logical way. In a text schema, you can determine the order in which you present the information and how you divide the text into chapters and sections.

–   *As a discussion document in consultation with a client or colleague.* If you need to write a text or give a presentation in a business context, it is helpful to determine each other's expectations during a preliminary meeting. On the basis of a text schema, your client or colleague can form an early impression of the text or presentation. You can then discuss whether the proposed text schema is indeed the desired structure for the final text or presentation. And if you are working with others on one piece, it is also useful to have a text schema. You can use the text schema to determine who works on which part and how the parts are related.

For more information on how to use a text schema in texts and presentations, see chapters 7 and 9.

For readers

A text schema is useful for various reading tasks.

–   *For summarizing a text.* In a business or education context, it is sometimes necessary to summarize the essence of a text (or a number of texts). By making a text schema of the text, you will have more insight into the main points. What is the theme exactly, and what questions does the text answer? You can use the text schema as a basis for a summary or literature report.

–   *For assessing a text.* If you need to give your opinion about a text or a draft of a text, a text schema can help you see the strengths and weaknesses of that text. A text schema can show you whether the text is well-structured. It is an instrument to (literally) point out the places where things go wrong. The text schema can also be a starting point if you want to establish whether you are missing information or have insufficient details, and if so, where that is the case.

–   *For commenting on a text.* If it is very difficult for the reader to make a text schema, this may point to an unclear theme, main questions that do not fit the theme, or answers that do not entirely fit the questions. In a review meeting, the text schema can then help you to indicate, in a well-supported way, where there is room for improvement and what the writer can do during the editing phase (see section 7.4). This way, the text schema that you use to evaluate a text (or a draft of a text) can in turn be used by the writer to make an improved version of his or her text or presentation. This use of a text schema is further explored in chapter 6.

2.1.3   Making a text schema

When you start analyzing an existing text or creating your own, you first need to determine the theme of the text. It is from this theme that you will determine the questions that you need to answer. This is sufficient when you are analyzing or producing shorter texts, but if the text is longer, for example a report, you should go into more detail about the key answers by dividing them into sub-questions and their key answers. When drafting your text schema, you should always keep the following questions in mind.
–   Do the questions fit the theme, or has another theme crept in?
–   Do the answers match the questions sufficiently, or does any question need to be worded differently?
–   Are all questions important (or important enough)?
–   Are the important questions raised?
–   Is there any information missing from the text?

This check helps you as a reader to assess the quality of a text and as a writer to plan a coherent text. In both cases, you concentrate on the content of the text: What information is given and how is it arranged? In the following sections, the steps to draw up a text schema will be discussed in more detail.

2.1.4   The theme

The theme indicates the subject of a text or part of a text. The subject of the whole text is called a text theme. Themes can also be distinguished at other levels in a text: a chapter theme, a section theme, or a paragraph theme.

For a text schema to properly indicate the coherence between the theme, questions, and key answers, the theme must be carefully formulated. A theme needs to:
–   be in the form of a noun, if necessary with one or more descriptors (additional words or phrases);
–   be as concise as possible;
–   indicate as precisely as possible what the text is about.

The last two requirements are sometimes contradictory: The more concise the formulation of a theme, the less precise it becomes, and the other way around. You often have to find a compromise.

– CERTIFICATION IS IMPORTANT FOR DIFFERENT REASONS
– THERE ARE A NUMBER OF ADVANTAGES OF A VISIT TO THE INFORMATION CENTRE

Incorrectly worded themes. These are sentences, not themes.

> – THE IMPORTANCE OF CERTIFICATION
> – ADVANTAGES OF A VISIT TO THE INFORMATION CENTRE

Well-formulated themes: phrases with a noun (importance, advantages) as core element, complemented by other descriptors.

> A periodic survey is useful for insight into quality assurance. This enables us to inform top management about the amount of money involved in quality assurance. This allows us to provide arguments for investing energy in improving the situation, or in other words spending money on preventive quality assurance. Moreover, such a study into quality assurance makes it possible to identify where immediate action is needed and to draw up plans for this so that unnecessary costs can be avoided. A third advantage of periodic research in this area is the possibility to oversee the effects of our efforts, so that we can find an optimal balance between prevention, consequence and inspection costs.

If we try to describe the theme of this paragraph, we immediately notice the conflict between conciseness and accuracy. A very concise description would be: 'QUALITY ASSURANCE'. But that is not precise enough because the text concerns only one aspect of quality assurance. A more accurate description is: 'THE THREE REASONS WHY PERIODIC RESEARCH INTO QUALITY ASSURANCE IS USEFUL'. But that theme is a mouthful: it is not concise enough. A good compromise is: 'PERIODIC RESEARCH INTO QUALITY ASSURANCE'.

2.1.5 The main questions

After you have determined the theme, you should indicate the main questions that the text covers. Main questions are questions that are directly related to the theme. When you make a text schema of an existing text, you will notice that the main questions are not always explicit.

There are a few requirements for the formulation of main questions.
– A main question should be an open question that starts with an interrogative pronoun, such as 'who', 'what', 'which', 'why', 'when', or 'how'. Avoid using specific questions that can only be answered with a *yes* or a *no*, or with a choice between two options. Such questions do not encourage you to further develop the content.
– Main questions should refer to the text theme (or a part of it). In this way, you make explicit connections with the theme. This will prevent you from addressing main questions that are not related to the theme.

– A main question must be formulated precisely. The main question should indicate as precisely as possible the information that the reader can expect to find. This increases the accessibility of the final text.
– Finally, you should formulate a main question as concisely as possible, as this makes a text schema clearer.

Again, the requirements of conciseness and accuracy can be contradictory. Try to seek an appropriate compromise.

In a text schema, the main questions are placed directly under the theme. You should underline them so that they are clearly distinguished from the (key) answers.

INTENSIVE SUPERVISION OF THE BANKING SECTOR
Should bank supervision be stepped up?
Yes.
     Why is that necessary?
     Because of risky activities with money from clients and because of the bonuses.

Unsuitable: This text schema uses a specific question that only allows for a yes or no answer, which makes a sub-question necessary.

INTENSIVE SUPERVISON OF THE BANKING SECTOR
Why is more intensive supervision necessary?
Because of risky activities with money from savers and because of the bonuses.

Suitable: This text schema (of the same text) is more concise because it immediately uses an open question, thereby forcing a detailed answer.

POOR MAINTENANCE OF THE NATIONAL ROAD NETWORK
What complaints are there?
What are local governments going to do?

Unsuitable: The main questions do not refer directly to the text theme.

POOR MAINTENANCE OF THE NATIONAL ROAD NETWORK
What complaints are there about the poor maintenance of the national road network?
What are local governments going to do about the poor maintenance of the national road network?

Suitable: Because the theme literally appears in the questions, it is clear what exactly the questions are about.

POOR MAINTENANCE OF THE NATIONAL ROAD NETWORK
What are the complaints about this?
What are local governments going to do about it?

Even better: Because the expressions 'about this' and 'about it' have been used, the main questions have become more concise.

The following example illustrates the need for careful consideration of the wording of the theme and the main questions. If the formulation of a theme is very concise, this may lead to longer main questions. Conversely, concise main questions may require a more elaborate theme. A good compromise between these extremes yields the most transparent text schema.

In recent years, the number of students between twelve and fifteen years who start smoking has risen sharply again. Furthermore, the number of older people who quit smoking has decreased. And this while quitting smoking actually only has advantages. First of all, it appears that 'quitters' feel much fitter than 'smokers'. In addition, they get a healthier skin color and their taste and smell improve again. Last but not least, their sense of self-respect improves.

This example text can be displayed in different ways in a text schema.

SMOKING
What are the benefits if one quits smoking?

Less suitable: Here the theme is very concise but not very precise, and the main question is very precise but also cumbersome.

THE BENEFITS IF ONE QUITS SMOKING
What are they?

Less suitable: Here the theme is very precise but cumbersome. The main question is very concise (and exact).

QUITTING SMOKING
What benefits does that have?

Well-suited: A compromise has been reached here between conciseness and accuracy of both the theme and the main question.

2.1.6   The key answers

The answers to the main questions in a text can be very detailed. In a text schema, however, you should only show the essence of an answer. You can omit the details, examples, explanations, nuances, and exceptions. What remains is called the key answer.

There are various points to consider when it comes to formulating key answers.
– The key answer must be in line with the question. The answer should not include more or less information than the question suggests. If, for example, the question is 'How can we best support project X?', it is not appropriate to include a proposal for raising money for projects Y and Z.
– The type of information in the key answer must also be in line with the question. A question that starts with 'why' suggests that the answer will cover causes, reasons, or explanations; a question starting with 'how' leads the reader to expect information about an approach, method, or guideline.
– Just like the theme and the main questions, the formulation of a key answer must also be concise and precise. Here, too, these requirements may be at odds with each other and often require a compromise.
– If a main question has more than one key answer, you should formulate them all in the same way. The answers should all be in the form of a theme, for example, or in the form of a single sentence. This way, the coherence between the key answers is strengthened.

Write down the key answers directly below the main questions that they belong to. If there is more than one key answer to the same question, you should number the answers.

STUDY LEAVE
How do you apply for it?
1   The application forms are available from the Human Resources Department.
2   Before you register, you must obtain permission from your immediate superior. Your immediate superior must also sign the form.
3   The form must be handed in to your head of department.

Unsuitable: In this part of the short text schema, the key answers are not well-formulated. Although it is clear from the information what needs to be done, the 'how' question is not answered here with a series of actions. Moreover, the second key answer contains two answers to the question.

STUDY LEAVE

How do you apply for it?

1   Ask your immediate superior for permission.
2   Get an application form from the Human Resources Department.
3   Fill in the form.
4   Have the form signed by your immediate superior.
5   Return the form to your head of department.

Better: Here, all key answers are formulated as actions. In addition, each key answer includes one action. The order of the steps has become clearer and the whole is formulated more clearly.

2.1.7   Sub-questions and further elaboration

For longer texts such as reports, you should include more information than just the main questions and key answers. The key answers then need further elaboration, explanation, argumentation, and illustration. These elaborations are the answers to questions about the key answer: sub-questions. In this case, the key answer functions as a sub-theme, even if it does not have the exact form of a theme.

You can then search for the key answer to each sub-question, rephrase the sub-questions for key answers, and so on. The process of making the text schema is always the same, but the details are more specific. You can repeat this process until you feel that the information is sufficiently detailed.

The same rules apply for the formulation of main questions and key answers to the sub-questions and their answers. A sub-question should also be an open question that starts with an interrogative pronoun. It must contain an explicit reference to the key answer on which it is based, and the formulation of the answer to the sub-question should be precise and concise.

The sub-questions appear under the key answers to which they apply but a little further to the right. The answers to the sub-questions are placed directly under the sub-questions. If there are multiple answers to one sub-question, you should again number them.

HOUSING SUBSIDY

What is meant by a housing subsidy?

A subsidy for meeting the costs of rent and energy consumption for people with low income.

   Which scheme should a housing subsidy replace?

   The rent subsidy.

       How does the rent subsidy work overall?

       Rent subsidy is granted if rent charges are high in relation to income.

What amounts are involved in rent subsidy?
Approximately one billion euros annually.

What argument is there for the introduction of a housing subsidy?
The system of rent subsidy no longer suffices.
  Why does the system of rent subsidy no longer suffice?
  The rent subsidy does not consider the increased energy prices.
    Why is it that energy prices have risen in this way?
    1   Because the government has set a 'political price' for fuel that is higher than the
        cost price.
        What does a 'political price' mean?
        1   The domestic price may not be lower than the export price.
        2   In the long run, the domestic price must be the same as that of paraffin, and
            not the much lower price of paraffin.
        3   The proceeds from the sale of fuel must help to eliminate the budget deficit.
    2   Because the government has decided to increase the VAT rate for fuel.

What are the objections to a housing subsidy?
1   An instrument of public housing policy would be misused.
    Why?
    A subsidy from the Ministry of Infrastructure and the Environment would be used to
    combat the effects of the policy on two other ministries, namely Economic Affairs,
    Agriculture and Innovation (the natural gas prices) and Social Affairs and Employment
    (the fall in income).
2   Certain groups of residents would be unfairly favored.
    Why?
    1   People in high-quality homes would have to pay about the same as people in
        much worse homes.
    2   Owners of their own homes, who also have high energy costs, would not receive
        subsidies.
3   It is hardly affordable.
    What justifies this answer?
    The rent subsidy is already too expensive.

What are possible alternatives to a housing subsidy?
1   A reduction in energy prices.
    How could this be done?
    1   By going back to the low VAT rate.
    2   By using the price of fuel instead of that of paraffin as the starting point.
2   An extra tax reduction for low incomes.

3 Extra incentives for the construction of cheaper and well-insulated homes.
   Why are extra incentives attractive?
   1 Housing quality will be the most important factor determining housing costs.
   2 There will be no 'sector blurring' because the policy boundaries of different ministries will be exceeded.
   3 The people with the lowest incomes will benefit the most.
   4 It is relatively easy to implement.
   5 It has favorable effects on employment in the construction industry.

Detailed text schema of a discussion paper. In the paper, the idea of a HOUSING SUBSIDY is contested in favor of a number of alternatives. The main questions and the corresponding key answers are against the left margin; the sub-questions with the corresponding answers are indented to the right. In this way, the hierarchy of the information in the text can be read from the left-right ordering in the text schema.

2.2 Set schemata

The content of formal texts is often determined in advance: The text must offer a solution to a problem, for example, or it must contain advice or an evaluation. This gives rise to a number of set schemata for a number of recurring broad themes. These recurring broad themes (problem, advice, solution, and so on) can be associated with their corresponding recurring set schemata. A set schema is a tool to help you structure a text or a section logically on the basis of a number of fixed questions.

Set schemata are mini text schemata with a limited number of fixed main questions on a broad theme. The questions are listed in a logical order.

2.2.1 When are set schemata useful?

Set schemata can be useful in structuring information both for writing and for reading a text. They provide writers with support in drafting a text (or part of a text) in an efficient way. Writers can use a set schema as a starting point for drawing up a text schema for their text. A set schema can help you to decide the order of the information, and it can also be used for drafting both an entire text and parts of a text.

Set schemata can also help readers—for instance when they are making a summary—by giving them insight into the essence of a text. Readers who are familiar with set schemata can recognize the structure of texts more easily, even if a text does not exactly follow the set schema. Set schemata can also be helpful when you are discussing a text, to see whether the information is complete and the argument makes sense.

Set schemata are not meant as a rigid set of rules. Even when you use a set schema, you should always keep in mind what your text needs. For certain texts or presentations, you may omit some questions or add others when needed. All kinds of variations on the set schemata are possible, including a different order of elements.

2.2.2 Problem schema

THEME: A PROBLEM, AN UNDESIRABLE SITUATION
What is the problem exactly?
Why is it a problem?
What are the causes?
What can be done about it?

The problem schema.

Possible applications of this schema
You can use the problem schema when you want to take a closer look at an undesirable situation without giving concrete advice or suggesting actions. The problem schema is also useful for situations in which it is more suitable to offer advice than to suggest solutions straightaway. The text begins with a sketch of the problem and ends with the solution in the form of an advice or request. This set schema can be combined with other schemata, such as the measure schema (see also sections 2.2.3 and 2.2.9).

The theme
The theme that is central to the problem schema is an unwanted, negative, or difficult situation such as 'UNEMPLOYMENT IN THIS COMMUNITY', 'DECLINING VISITOR NUMBERS IN OUR MUSEUM', or 'POOR HOUSING FOR INTERNATIONAL STUDENTS'. Such a problem can be the theme of the whole text, but it can also be the key answer to a particular main question. In the latter case, the problem schema forms the basis for one part of the text and the related questions function as sub-questions.

Not everything we would call a problem in everyday life is necessarily a suitable theme for the problem schema. Problems such as 'Who is responsible for the losses of the company' or 'Calculate the integral of this mathematical function' are not workable themes for the problem schema, even if you change them into the form of a theme ('THE RESPONSIBILITY FOR THE LOSSES' or 'THE CALCULATION OF THE INTEGRAL'). These problems are not the same as undesirable situations.

What is the problem exactly?

This first question in the set problem schema is meant to paint a picture of the problem and its context; it is called the *elaboration question*. The answer elaborates by giving information about matters such as the extent of the problem, the situation in which it occurs, and the people involved.

The elaboration question does not always have to refer to the theme as a whole. A text about 'THE BAD ECONOMIC CLIMATE IN OUR COUNTRY' can start with some information about the country (its location, population, history, and so on) before addressing the actual problem. Such information is often needed for the reader to be able to follow the rest of the text.

The extent to which you develop this first main question depends on the audience's prior knowledge. If they are already familiar with the problem, you can keep the answer to the first main question short. If the subject is new, you will need to be more detailed. The information you provide here can also add to the persuasive power of your text, for example if you want to convince your readers that something needs to be done about the situation. In order to encourage your readers to support your proposal or advice, it is important that there is no misunderstanding about the nature of the problem.

Why is it a problem?

There are often two main reasons why something can be a problem.

– The current situation has unwanted or negative consequences. For example, 'TAX EVASION' can be considered a problem as this leads to a reduction in state revenues and an increasing financing gap. Negative consequences can play a role both in the short and in the long term.
– The current situation goes against certain ethical, political, or moral standards and values. For example, you could also qualify 'TAX EVASION' as a problem because this behavior is contrary to standards of civil decency and honesty.

The answer to the 'why' question explains why you need to pay attention to the problem. It emphasizes why something should be done about it. You can also indicate who is affected by the problem. If you pay sufficient attention to the 'why' question, you can avoid reactions such as 'What are you worried about?'

Furthermore, in the answer to the 'why' question, you can indicate to some extent where the solutions may lie. Someone who considers tax evasion a problem because it reduces state revenues will seek a solution mainly through economic and legal measures. On the other hand, someone who finds ethical motives more important is more likely to seek a solution in a strengthening of tax ethics.

What are the causes?

In order to solve a problem, it is important to have a good understanding of its causes. Ideally, removing these causes should solve the problem. You should therefore include these causes in your text. It is usually not necessary to mention all the causes. You can, however, try to distinguish between main causes and secondary causes.

What to do about it?

In a professional context, this question is usually the most important. Sometimes a text only explores solutions without making a choice (you are then mainly engaged in descriptive work). More often than not, you will choose one of the solutions and present arguments as to why it is preferable to other possibilities. The text then takes on the characteristics of a proposal.

　　Solutions will often be in the form of ways to eliminate the causes of the problem. In that case, there is a link between the third and the fourth main questions. However, it is not always possible to eliminate the causes of the problem; in the case of long-term drought predictions or an ageing population, for example, there is little that can be done about the cause. You can only do something about such problems by fighting the consequences. In that case, there is a link between the fourth and the second main questions. Of course, fighting the consequences does not necessarily lead to a bad solution.

MOTION SICKNESS

What exactly is motion sickness?

1　Nausea, headaches, and vomiting while travelling.
2　It occurs mainly in children and in some adults.

Why is motion sickness a problem?

1　From a medical point of view, motion sickness is not a problem.
2　But motion sickness can spoil the journey.

What is the cause of motion sickness?

Incorrect functioning of the balance organ.

What can you do against motion sickness?

1　Take precautions.
2　Use medicines.

Set problem schema applied to a pharmacy information brochure. The theme of the text is a problem ('MOTION SICKNESS is an undesirable situation'), and the main questions are those of the problem schema. The key answers to the last main question can be worked out in detail in the text.

If you want to apply the problem schema in an advisory situation, it is important to pay close attention to the connection between the first and the last question. The answer to the last question should not be a reversal of the problem as described under the first question. For example, if leakage is the problem (answer to question 1), your text is not very persuasive if you suggest that the solution is to stop the leakage (answer to question 4). In order to prevent this, you should carefully consider the answer to the third question: What are the causes? In the answer to the last question, it must be clear that the solution will remove these causes. This way, you make logical connections between cause, problem, and solution, which has the effect of strengthening your advice (see the examples that follow).

LEAKAGE IN OUR FACTORY IN KOWARY

What exactly is the leakage?
1   Our factory in Kowary, Poland has storage vessels containing hazardous substances.
2   During the weekend it was reported that leakage is occurring.

Why is the leakage a problem?
1   The leakage can be a danger to public health in the area.
2   Some of the stored substances are highly corrosive and can damage pipes, aggravating the leakage.
3   An environmental scandal is bad for our image.

What is the cause of the leakage?
The storage tanks are not sufficiently insulated.

What can we do about the leakage?
Inform the management in Kowary that the leak must be stopped immediately.

Poor text schema derived from a set problem schema. In this example, the advice is hardly more than a rewriting of the problem—'it leaks'—immediately followed by the obvious measure 'make sure it no longer leaks'. This does not help the recipient, as it does not lead to a real solution of the problem. The reason is that the answer to the fourth question does not relate to the answer to the third main question.

LEAKAGE IN OUR FACTORY IN KOWARY

What exactly is the leakage?
1   Our factory in Kowary, Poland has storage vessels containing hazardous substances.
2   During the weekend it was reported that leakage is occurring.

Why is the leakage a problem?
1   The leakage can be a danger to public health in the area.

2   Some of the stored substances are highly corrosive and can damage pipes, aggravat-
    ing the leakage.
3   An environmental scandal is bad for our image.

<u>What is the cause of the leakage?</u>
The storage tanks are not sufficiently insulated.

<u>What can be done about the leakage?</u>
The existing tanks must be replaced by insulated storage tanks.

Better application of the set problem schema. In this example, the receiver is helped to move
forward. The most important link in this text schema, based on the set problem schema, is
that between the third and the fourth main question: from cause to solution.

2.2.3   Measure schema

THEME: A MEASURE, A PROPOSAL FOR ACTION
<u>What is the measure?</u>
<u>Why is the measure necessary?</u>
<u>How will the measure be implemented?</u>
<u>What are the effects of the measure?</u>

The measure schema.

Possible applications of this schema
The measure schema can be applied to all kinds of texts: descriptive texts, advisory
texts, petitions, and so on. The measure schema can also be useful for describing
and justifying decisions retrospectively, for example in reports. It can even be used
for texts that criticize certain measures. In these cases, the third main question
can be divided into questions such as 'How did they do it?', 'How could it have been
done better?', or 'How should it be done?' and 'How can we do better?'

The theme
As its name suggests, the theme of the measure schema is a specific measure: an
action or a proposal for an action. An example could be a 'recently introduced
reduction in working hours' or 'the proposed purchase of a new registration system'.
With some imagination, you can formulate many kinds of subjects as a measure.
For a text about an innovation in logistics, for example, you can choose the measure
'WORKING WITH A NEW LOGISTICAL APPROACH' as a theme. This will then
serve as a starting point for the measure schema.

What is the measure?

Similar to the problem schema, texts or parts of a text with a measure schema often start with the elaboration question. Here you provide preliminary information about the nature of the measure, the implementer(s), the scope, the reason why the measure is necessary, and so on. The guidelines in section 2.2.2 about this elaboration question for the problem schema also apply here. The question may relate to only part of the theme, and the question is only necessary if your readers are not yet fully informed.

Why is the measure necessary?

In most cases, a measure is proposed to achieve certain goals, solve problems, or meet a certain need. The importance of the 'why' question is obvious: You need to convince others that some effort is needed. In many conversations, it is precisely this question that is likely to be the subject of a major debate. If the need for the measure is undisputed, you can quickly deal with this question in order to switch to the 'how' question.

How will the measure be implemented?

The next question concerns the method of operation, the resources needed, and other aspects of implementation. Who does what, when, and how? The answer to this third question may overlap with the answer to the first question, the elaboration question. Usually, the method of working is discussed in general terms in the elaboration question and worked out in greater detail in the 'how' question.

What are the effects of the measure?

Here, the text should discuss the extent to which the measure is an appropriate response to the goals, problems, or needs raised in the second question. An example is a proposal to increase the number of student rooms in a city. The answer to the second main question discusses this goal in detail (how serious is the shortage of rooms, how many rooms are needed). The fourth question then gives an estimation of the expected results of the proposed action.

Possible side effects, both positive and negative, are often discussed here as well. A plan to increase the number of student rooms, for example, can lead to a better consideration of the needs of new students (positive side effect) but also to increasing prices because people will realize how high the demand is (negative side effect).

In some situations, it may be useful to change the order of the questions, particularly in the case of an unpopular measure or a far-reaching plan with negative consequences. In such situations, presenting a measure or plan straightforwardly can lead to resistance, while the plan needs support in order to work. In such a situation, it is often better to discuss the first two questions only briefly and then to switch to the third and fourth questions.

A brief explanation of the measure or plan is followed by a brief indication of its goal or goals. You should not defend the plan at this point but only briefly point out the common starting point. Next, discuss the consequences: first the negative effects and then the positive effects.

The advantage of this order is that you have every opportunity to pay attention not only to the matter side but also to the relationship side of the message. By first identifying the negative effects, you can address sensitivities and show sincere empathy for the negative consequences. If you then present the positive effects, there is a greater chance that people will support a sensitive measure or plan. Finally, you should discuss the implementation of the plan.

INCENTIVE FOR THE APPOINTMENT OF WOMEN

What does the incentive entail?

Companies receive ten thousand dollars if they appoint a woman to certain positions as a permanent employee.

Why is the incentive necessary?

Because men, even if they are equally suitable compared to women, still seem to have advantages, so that women are not chosen anyway.

How will the incentive be implemented?

1   The money must be requested via the HR officer.
2   The intention is that the money will be used to strengthen the position of women.

What effects should or could the incentive have?

1   More appointments of women.
2   Better career opportunities for women.
3   Possible improper use of the money.

Set measure schema applied to a letter sent to management by the Personnel and Organization Department of a large organization. The theme, 'INCENTIVE FOR THE APPOINTMENT OF WOMEN', is a measure; the main questions are those from the measure schema. In the final text, one paragraph was dedicated to each question in the text, except for the third. This question was answered in two separate paragraphs, each dedicated to one key answer.

COOPERATION BETWEEN DIVISIONS

What is the measure?

The divisions of the sales departments in the different provinces must work together.

Why is it necessary to implement the measure?

1 The common goal we pursue is better external accessibility.
2 Combining the expertise of division heads can create a single central structure that can better coordinate the work of the different divisional departments.

What are the effects of the measure?

1 Negative effects: some staff members have to be reassigned, the existing infrastructure has to change, one has to share one's own work and one's own approach.
2 Positive effects: effective management, collegial consultation possible, more efficient approach, learning from each other.

How will the measure be implemented?

1 Trial period after the holiday.
2 Work schedule is made in mutual consultation.
3 Evaluation after two months.

Set measure schema applied to a memo to staff about a sensitive matter: COOPERATION BETWEEN DIVISIONS. The expected effects precede the implementation here, and given those effects a 'yes, but [...]' strategy has been chosen: First acknowledge that there are negative effects, and then indicate what the positive outcomes would be.

2.2.4 Evaluation schema

THEME: A SITUATION OR CASE THAT IS ASSESSED
What are the relevant characteristics?
What are the relevant evaluation criteria?
What are the positive aspects?
What are the negative aspects?
What is the overall evaluation?

The evaluation schema.

Possible applications of this schema

The evaluation schema is appropriate when a case or particular situation needs to be evaluated or assessed rationally. This evaluation is based on facts and rules as well as norms and values. Examples are a meeting to discuss the value of a proposal or a review of a particular approach to a project.

The evaluation schema mainly aims for a neutral, formal approach. It starts with a discussion of the evaluation criteria, then investigates all sides of the case, and finally reaches a conclusion. This does not mean that you cannot present a definite evaluation at the end of the text. In practice, writers will often interpret the positive and negative aspects in such a way that the desired final evaluation is the logical result. Applying the evaluation schema does, however, show that you have considered the matter from different angles.

The theme

The theme can be any subject that needs to be evaluated. The evaluation schema can be used as a starting point for a whole text—for example for an advice based on an evaluation—or for the elaboration on a key answer within a text. For example, you can use the evaluation schema in combination with a problem schema to evaluate the advantages and disadvantages of a particular solution. The evaluation schema then fits into the fourth question of the problem schema.

What are the relevant characteristics?

The first question of this set schema is once more the elaboration question, which presents the theme of the text. The answer should describe the case or situation that is being assessed. This section will contain factual information: who/what, where, when, and so on. In the evaluation schema, you should pay special attention to those characteristics that are important to make a good judgment. A product assessment, for instance, includes information about the specific characteristics of that product, the price, where it is sold, and so on—in short, all the information that is really relevant to forming an opinion.

What are the relevant assessment criteria?

A formal review is generally based on certain standards and values. To properly understand a particular judgment, it is useful to know the norms and values that form the basis for the judgment. After all, different criteria can be combined or weighed differently. For example, in a discussion on the livestock industry, vegetarians may use very different arguments than environmentalists or agricultural economists, even though all three groups may have a similarly negative view on the phenomenon.

In practice, the evaluation criteria are not always explicit in the text. Once you start discussing them, you are also questioning them; you are, as it were, obliging yourself to demonstrate that these criteria are correct. And that is often difficult, even when it concerns less ideologically charged subjects. In the case of purely technical reports, for example about noise or air pollution, it often seems less problematic to establish criteria. In practice, however, you can have all kinds of discussions about such technical subjects and the related criteria.

It is even more difficult when assessment criteria are intuitive or concern taste and feeling. Consider, for example, an art critic (What are the criteria for a beautiful painting?) or a discussion about the decoration of the city center (What is beautiful and what is ugly? What is allowed and what is forbidden?). These examples show that the question of evaluation criteria can be very important when it comes to forming a balanced opinion.

What are the positive and negative aspects?

The answer to this question forms the core of the evaluation schema. Here you will find the arguments on which the writer bases his or her conclusion. These arguments are seldom neatly listed.

– Positive and negative aspects are often mixed in the text. In the analysis it may therefore be useful to change the structure of the text schema so that the positive and negative aspects are more clearly distinguished.
– It is not always clear whether the writer considers a certain aspect of the theme to be positive or negative. Sometimes this only emerges at the end (in the conclusion), but sometimes it is never really clarified.
– In most cases, both sides of the issue do not receive equal attention. Frequently, one side is extensively discussed, while the other side is barely explained. In these cases, it is often clear what the conclusion will be.

What is the overall assessment?

In this part, the text reaches a positive or negative (but often also mixed) conclusion resulting from all the points above. The arguments supporting this conclusion are often still explicitly mentioned. In texts and presentations, the answer to this main question often resembles a summary: The positive or negative aspects mentioned earlier are emphasized again, now directly as support for the conclusion.

The fact that the overall assessment is presented at the end of the set schema does not necessarily mean that the sender's opinion on the subject only becomes clear at this point. It can often be found at the start of the text or is revealed by the tone and the way in which the positive and negative aspects are discussed.

AUTOMATIC PARKING SYSTEM

What are the relevant characteristics?

1 An automatic parking system has sensors in the front and rear bumper.
2 The sensors measure the distance between your own car and the other cars. A computer calculates the required actions by the vehicle or driver.
3 There are automatic versions that park a vehicle without the assistance of the driver and there are semi-automatic versions that provide partial support to the driver. In the semi-automatic version, the driver operates the accelerator and brake pedals. In the fully automatic version, these actions are computer-controlled.

What are the relevant assessment criteria?
1 Ease of use.
2 Safety.
3 Price.

What are the positive aspects?
1 Convenience: The driver no longer has to perform this often difficult operation, which can be a great advantage for inexperienced drivers or drivers with physical impairments such as shoulder or neck injuries.
2 The system is adjusted so that the risk of damage to the front and rear of the car is zero when used correctly.
3 Safe parking limits damage.

What are the negative aspects?
1 The system can create a false sense of safety. There may still be obstacles to the side of the vehicle that the system does not register. The driver then risks damage to the vehicle.
2 In semi-automatic systems, it is not always clear to the driver how far the accelerator or brake pedals should be depressed. This can still lead to damage.
3 In the case of experienced drivers who have been driving damage-free for years, the additional cost does not automatically outweigh the avoidance of damage costs.

What is the overall assessment?
Automatic parking can increase the driving pleasure, and depending on the driving style it reduces damage when parking. Especially for people who have difficulty with this special operation, it can be a solution.

Set evaluation schema applied to a product in a car magazine.

2.2.5 Opinion schema

THEME: A CASE OR SITUATION ON WHICH OPINIONS DIFFER
What are the relevant characteristics?
What is the existing view?
What are the arguments for the existing view?
What is the alternative opinion?
What are the arguments for the alternative opinion?
What are the consequences?

The opinion schema.

Possible applications of this schema

Whereas the evaluation schema concerns a more or less neutral evaluation, the opinion schema is used when you want to present a strong opinion on a certain subject, especially when this opinion is opposed to a different, existing opinion.

The opinion schema is suitable for discussions that attack an existing opinion on a subject. There are two ways to do this: fight the opponent's arguments or present new ones. These two ways are both incorporated in the opinion schema, in particular in the third question and in the fifth question.

Situations in which this schema can be useful are meetings (in particular in the opinion-forming part) and public debates (in a submitted letter, for example, by a professional who responds on behalf of his or her organization to a document that was previously published in the newspaper).

The theme

The theme of the set opinion schema is an existing situation or matter on which there are different views. This schema serves to convincingly present an alternative viewpoint. Some examples include: 'PROHIBITION ON LARGE BONUSES FOR CEO'S', 'MONOLINGUAL TUITION POLICIES IN OUR SCHOOLS', or 'THE POSITION OF PRIVACY WITH NEW TECHNOLOGICAL DEVELOPMENTS'.

What are the relevant characteristics?

As in the case of the evaluation schema, the elaboration question concerns the matter or situation that the text discusses. Here you will provide as much factual information as possible.

What is the existing view?

The answer to this question contains a summary of the existing view. It will also clarify whose view this is, how recent it is, where this view has been put forward, and so on. Of course, it is not necessarily a single unified opinion; there can be various existing opinions.

What are the arguments for the existing view?

This question is actually a sub-question raised on the basis of the discussion of the existing view. It is, however, still included in this set schema because it is essential to the argument.

The question has several functions. First of all, the answer to it proves that the person who is arguing the alternative opinion has studied the other party's arguments in some detail. This not only expresses respect, it also makes writers or speakers more credible because it shows that they are not simply opposed to something. In discussions, this question can also be important to make sure that both sides have understood each other properly.

Writers can present the arguments for the existing view in a neutral way, but they can also attack them directly, for example by showing that they do not make sense, that they are outdated, or that certain things have not been considered. The choice of attacking these arguments now or later depends on the point of view of the intended readers of the text. If they adhere to the existing view, it is better not to attack them right away. If readers are neutral or also critical of the existing view, then an immediate attack is usually effective.

What is the alternative view?

The next step is to describe the dissenting or alternative opinion. You can do this by contrasting it to the existing view.

What are the arguments for the alternative view?

This question, again a sub-question, presents the arguments as to why the alternative view is better. You can use three types of arguments for this.
– Arguments showing that the existing view does not make sense (if you have not already shown this).
– Arguments showing practical or principled objections to the existing view.
– Arguments showing practical or principled advantages of the alternative view.

What are the consequences?

The conclusion of the argument is obvious: The alternative view is better. The function of this question about the consequences is to indicate possible next steps. This is essential if you want to avoid a deadlock, which is often the fate of discussions. This question ensures that, in addition to the disagreement, a compromise or constructive follow-up is in sight.

APPLICATION OF GPS IN THE CARE OF THE ELDERLY
What are the relevant characteristics?
GPS (Global Positioning System) is a technique that detects the location of a person or object. It can be used as a means of tracking down elderly people who lose their way, for example Alzheimer's patients.

What is the existing view?
GPS for the elderly is applauded.

What are the arguments for the existing view?
1 Following older people in this way increases their safety.

2   This form of supervision allows elderly people, particularly Alzheimer's patients, to live independently for longer.
3   Given the financial problems in elderly care, this is an effective and inexpensive solution.

What is the alternative view?
This application of GPS infringes on the privacy of the elderly and should therefore be used with the necessary restraint.

What are the arguments for the alternative view?
1   Tracking people via GPS is contrary to articles 12 and 14 of the Universal Declaration of Human Rights.
2   The elderly are less aware of the negative consequences and are entitled to protection of their privacy.
3   The use of GPS as support in elderly care also requires human assistance. If patients have lost their way, they will still have to be found and taken care of by someone.

What are the consequences?
1   Do not support the application of GPS blindly, but determine per person whether the advantages outweigh the disadvantages.
2   If the system is to be introduced at all, do it only on a voluntary basis.

Set opinion schema applied to an argumentative article. The arguments for the existing view are presented in a neutral way at first, but they are then contested (in the first and second arguments for the alternative view).

2.2.6   Action schema

THEME: AN ACTION TO BE PERFORMED
What is the purpose?
What are the conditions?
What are the steps?
How is the process evaluated?

The action schema.

Possible applications of this schema
The action schema is applicable to all texts that concern a certain course of action. Such texts can be informative or instructive. If it is an informative text, it should

describe how a process works; if it is an instructive text, it should give instructions on how to carry out a certain procedure (a task).

The theme

The theme of the action schema involves anything that can be done over a period of time. It can involve all kinds of tasks that people have to perform, ranging from 'ASSEMBLING A BOOKCASE' to 'WRITING A TEXT' or 'SOLVING A TECHNICAL PROBLEM'. It may also be a natural or mechanical process, such as 'THE FOOD CHAIN', 'THE HYDROLOGICAL CYCLE', or 'HOW A POWER PLANT WORKS'.

What is the purpose?

The purpose may vary from making a concrete product to operating an appliance, preparing a dish, or applying for a subsidy. The goal can also be more abstract: a good study result, increased communication skills, or a favorable election result.

The question of the purpose does not apply to all themes. Some processes have no direct goal ('THE WATER CYCLE', for instance, or 'THE LAW OF SUPPLY AND DEMAND'). The question of the purpose can then be replaced by the question 'Why is it important (to pay attention to it)?'.

What are the conditions?

This question clarifies the situations in which the action can be performed. If you want to assemble a bookcase, for instance, you need certain parts and tools.

What are the steps?

The answer to this question is divided into complex steps. You first portray the broad outline of the action, followed by a detailed description. The details do not necessarily have to be complete. In some cases, the course of action is first outlined in general terms, and then one or more steps are worked out in detail, while the other steps are not further discussed.

For this question, a writer will always work chronologically from beginning to end, sometimes dividing the process into main steps and sub-steps.

How is the process evaluated?

An answer to this question is particularly important when an action is complex or difficult to perform. In these cases, the person who carried out the instruction will often want to check whether he or she has made any mistakes. For example, an instruction in a statistics manual for calculating a correlation coefficient may report that the outcome should always be between -1 and +1. If it is not, something went wrong with the calculation.

DEVELOPMENT OF A STRATEGIC PLAN

What is the purpose of the strategic plan?

1 The strategic plan must lead to the best possible realization of the association's mission over the next five years.
2 The strategic plan must lead to a healthy financial basis for the association.
3 The strategic plan must become the guideline for the activities of the board.

What are the conditions for the development process?

1 The members must be actively involved in the preparation of the plan.
2 The plan must be feasible within the available budget.

How will the development take place?

1 During brainstorming sessions, the members, led by the board, will formulate the goals to be achieved.
2 Priorities are set during members' meetings.
3 A special working group will make an analysis of the strengths, weaknesses, opportunities, and threats.
4 The same working group will formulate a number of specific projects that are necessary to achieve the chosen goals.
5 The overall plan will be discussed during next year's members' meeting.

How is the process evaluated?

The board will monitor the progress of the strategy and report on this every year in the members' meeting.

Set action schema applied to a memorandum on the adoption of a strategic plan within a particular organization.

2.2.7 Design schema

THEME: A DESIGN OR DRAFT

What is the use?

What requirements does it have to meet?

What resources will be used?

What does the design look like?

How is the design evaluated?

The design schema.

Possible applications of this schema

The design schema is suitable for texts with a variety of subjects that discuss a draft or a concept that has been designed by someone. You can write such a text in advance (if the concept has not yet been realized but only exists on the drawing board or as an idea) but also afterwards, as a report and justification for the design and development. In either case, you can construct the text on the basis of the five main questions of the design schema.

The theme

The draft under discussion may, for example, concern a technical device or a computer program. Less concrete themes can also be seen as a design. For example, you can draft a regulation, a certain policy for an organization, or an educational program.

What is the use?

The importance of this question is obvious: The purpose for which something is designed determines the requirements, the means, and the final properties. This question therefore concerns information about the current situation and why it is unsatisfactory, as well as information about the desired situation. It may also mention the intended audience of the design, what it is for, and so on.

What requirements does it have to meet?

There are often primary requirements that must definitely be met as well as secondary requirements that are more or less desirable.

What resources will be used?

This section contains an explanation of the means by which the goals are to be achieved and the requirements that will be met. It also includes a justification of those means: They should be feasible, acceptable, effective, and efficient. In order to demonstrate this, the writer will often make a comparison with other alternative means. In this context, the text often also pays attention to the other criteria mentioned above that determined the choice of the means.

There should be a clear link between the answers to this question and the information given under the first two questions. After all, the chosen means are meant to achieve the goals and meet the requirements. Ideally, therefore, the text will clearly indicate the chosen means for each of the goals and requirements, or conversely, the means will be linked to the corresponding goals and requirements.

What does the design look like?

This question concerns the description of the design. This description is often incomplete because it is limited to those aspects of the designed device, policy, or program that distinguish it from similar designs.

How is the design evaluated?

This question describes the effects that the use of the design has or will have. A preliminary description will include expected results or will explain how the effects will be determined. If the description follows the implementation of the design, this main question may include the results of studies into the effectiveness of the design.

SALES COURSE FOR NEW EMPLOYEES

What is the purpose of the course?

1 Drawing attention to common presentation and sales problems.
2 Providing and discussing solutions to these problems.

What are the requirements for the course?

1 Practical orientation.
2 Connection with the other parts of the training program.

What mode of training will be chosen?

1 Especially self-training.
2 A lot of attention to problems that one has already encountered.

What will the structure of the course be?

1 General introduction to problems in sales situations.
2 Discussion of problems that the new employees themselves have already experienced.
3 Communicative behavior in the sales situation.
4 Legal aspects.
5 Discussion of and practice with some specific cases (to be determined).

How will the course be evaluated?

1 The judgement of the new employees themselves will be asked (immediately after the course and also two months later).
2 The managers of the new employees will be asked what effects they have observed.

Set design schema applied to a text about a sales course.

2.2.8 Research schema

> THEME: A PHENOMENON THAT IS INVESTIGATED
> What exactly was investigated?
> What method was used?
> What were the results?
> What were the conclusions?

The research schema.

Possible applications of this schema

The research schema can obviously be applied to texts that present some kind of research (see also section 8.3). These texts can be complete research reports but also passages in texts that summarize research or use research to support a particular position. In addition to research reports, you can also use the research schema as a template for describing a research plan.

You can often recognize the set research schema in reports and articles by the conventional section titles used: Introduction, Method, Results, and Conclusion (or Discussion).

The theme

The theme is a research object: something that was investigated. Research objects can vary widely, from 'TWELVE-YEAR-OLDS STRUGGLING WITH MATHS' to 'AIR POLLUTION DUE TO PETROCHEMICAL INDUSTRY' or 'THE ROLES OF INTERPERSONAL COMMUNICATION IN MASS MEDIA CAMPAIGNS'.

What exactly has been investigated?

This question clarifies how, within a certain theme, the researcher came up with a specific research question. Within one theme, different research questions are almost always possible, and the beginning of a research report usually explains the decision to examine a specific question. Research into the theme 'TWELVE-YEAR-OLDS STRUGGLING WITH MATHS', for example, can focus on the nature and extent of the problem (using a large-scale math test), the causes (using pupil observation), or the effects of possible measures (using experiments).

It goes without saying that you should always justify the choice of a particular research question. This is usually based on a literature review that concludes that this particular research question has not been adequately investigated yet, and that the research is of scientific or social importance. Research reports usually start with such a justification, while the precise research question only becomes clear at the end of this section. When you are reading research reports, it is often useful to search for the research question first, and only then to read the justification.

Occasionally the justification turns out to be unnecessarily detailed. Researchers sometimes try to impress their readers with the large amount of literature they have studied.

The question of exactly what has been investigated may also include the goal of the investigation: Why was this research performed? This information is particularly important when the research was commissioned by a client.

What method was used?

This section explains the type of research conducted such as an experiment, a survey study, an observational study, or a literature study. This indication of the research method is supplemented with further details. In the case of an experiment this might include information about the participants, the materials that were used, the task that the participants had to perform, and how the results were recorded.

What are the results?

This section concerns the data that are obtained from the investigation such as figures, answers to questions, or observed events, often summarized in tables and graphs. Many studies also analyze the data statistically in order to identify possible differences and interrelationships and to check whether the effects are not purely due to chance.

What are the conclusions?

This is where the answer to the research question is provided. It is important to distinguish between results and conclusions. The results are the data obtained from the study, which are often statistically analyzed. For example, the data could be responses in a survey, the number of faulty products determined in a quality assessment, the differences between groups in an experiment, or the quantity of toxic substances in the air. The conclusion is the statement or general rule that the researcher deduces from these results, for example: The majority is against a measure, the production process is not reliable enough, young females performed better than young males, or the air is hardly polluted by emissions.

Often the conclusion will be followed by a 'discussion part' in which the researcher addresses any questions that might arise from the results. The limitations of the methodology are also often discussed here. Traditionally, a research report ends with suggestions and questions for further research.

Recommendations are often also attached to the conclusions, linking the conclusions with the measures that should be taken in the researcher's opinion.

This final part of a research report may also be entitled 'Discussion'. If this final part is short, then the title 'Conclusion' or 'Conclusions' is best used.

EFFECTIVENESS OF INSTRUCTIONS IN THE FORM OF COMPUTER ANIMATIONS

What exactly was investigated?

The question whether instructions in the form of computer animations are processed quicker and better than traditional verbal instructions.

What method was followed?

1 Instructions were developed for concrete casting, one in the form of traditional verbal instructions and one in the form of a computer animation.
2 Permanent employees and casual workers performed a concrete casting task, half of each group using the verbal instructions and the other half using the computer animations.
3 Both the time for reading or viewing the instructions and the time for performing the task was measured.
4 After this, the participants filled in a questionnaire about their satisfaction with the instruction and their self-confidence when it comes to concrete casting.
5 The quality of the results was assessed by a jury of three experts.

What were the results?

1 All subjects made significantly fewer mistakes when they had seen the computer animation than when they had read the traditional verbal instructions.
2 Looking at the computer animation took more time than reading the traditional verbal instructions.
3 The casual workers who had seen the computer animation worked significantly faster and significantly better than their counterparts who had read the verbal instructions. For the permanent employees, no statistically significant difference was found here.
4 The participants who had seen the computer animation were significantly more satisfied with the instruction, and they also had significantly more self-confidence.

What was the conclusion?

In this context, computer animations are preferable to traditional verbal instructions.

Set research schema applied to a text about a study into different types of technical instructions.

2.2.9   Networks of set schemata

The discussion of the set schemata above may have given the impression that a text may only be based on one such schema. On the contrary, many texts are characterized by the fact that they have an entire network of set schemata as their text schema.

Just as the text theme determines the set schema in which the main questions fit, so a key answer to a main question can again be the starting point for a set schema that fits this key answer and includes new sub-questions. Each key answer to these sub-questions can in turn be the starting point for a set schema, and so on.

THEME: A MEASURE THAT WAS TAKEN
What was the measure?
[...]

Why was the measure necessary?
KEY ANSWER: A PROBLEM
   What was the problem exactly?
   [...]
   Why was it a problem?
   [...]
   What were the causes?
   [...]
   What could be done about it?
   [...]

How was the measure implemented?
KEY ANSWER: AN ACTION
   What was the purpose?
   [...]
   What were the conditions?
   [...]
   What were the steps?
   [...]
   How was the process evaluated?
   [...]

What were the effects of the measure?
KEY ANSWER: EFFECTS THAT WERE INVESTIGATED
   What exactly was investigated?
   [...]
   What method was used?
   [...]
   ONE OF THE KEY ANSWERS: THE MATERIALS THAT WERE DESIGNED FOR THIS STUDY
      What was the use?
      What requirements had to be met?

What resources were used?
What did the design look like?
How was the design evaluated?
[…]

What were the results?
[…]

What were the conclusions?
[…]

Set schemata applied in a network. This text schema is basically structured according to the set measure schema. However, the key answer to the second question ('Why is the measure necessary?') is the starting point for the set problem schema, while the key answer to the third question ('How was the measure implemented?') functions as the starting point for the set action schema. For answering the last question of the set measure schema ('What were the effects of the measure?'), the set research schema is used. And for partly answering the question from the set research schema about the method that was followed, the set design schema is used to discuss the way in which the research materials were developed.

2.3   General principles of organization

Text schemata (including set schemata) indicate the theme of the text and the questions and answers about that theme. A question can often have more than one answer. For example, a problem can have various causes, and a measure can have multiple effects.

You can follow different principles for organizing the information belonging to one question from the set schema. Four general principles used are space, time, the given-new principle, and hierarchy. Information that is organized according to these principles is in line with common thinking patterns and therefore helps readers to better understand the text. Sometimes such principles are not only useful for answering a particular question from the text schema, they are also applicable to the entire text. For example, there are texts that include only one main question related to the theme. The structure of such a text, then, is entirely determined by the organization of the key answers.

2.3.1 Four ordering principles

Space
Texts with questions such as 'What does it look like?' or 'What does it consist of?' often present answers that use the physical lay-out of objects as an ordering principle: from left to right, from close to far, from top to bottom, from east to west. In the following examples, you can use the ordering principle of spatial planning:
- a description of a device that covers all its components, from left to right and from top to bottom;
- a brochure on factory lay-out describing the various buildings from north to south and from west to east;
- a tourist guide that does not list the places of interest alphabetically but describes a route along various places of interest.

Time
Answers to questions such as 'How is the process going?', 'How did it happen?', or 'How did it come about?' are often presented in the form of a description of events or actions. It goes without saying that the best way to organize such a description is to use chronological order. If you want to deviate from this principle, you should add signposts so as not to confuse the reader (see section 2.4). You can also use chronology as a principle of organization in other situations, for lists of persons or objects that can somehow be placed in time. Some examples of time as an ordering principle include:
- an instruction manual that describes step by step how to operate a device;
- a brochure on the factory lay-out describing the various buildings in the order in which they were built;
- a list of the actors in a play in order of appearance.

Given-new principle
Given-new is an ordering principle that you can apply very often. A text organized according to this principle starts with information that the reader may already know and then offers something new. The idea behind this principle is that readers of a text are better prepared for the new information if they first read about something they are already familiar with. They will then be able to judge the new information in its context.

A bank brochure contains a paragraph entitled 'Mobile payments: What options' This paragraph first refers to the method used until recently to pay digitally: via a program on the client's computer. Only then is the newer method introduced: paying via a mobile phone. Next to this, the advantages of this newer method are discussed.

Application of the given-new principle in an informative brochure.

There are several variants of the given-new principle.

–   *From easy to difficult.* This principle is often used in textbooks and instruction manuals. The easy information is discussed first, after which the more complicated part follows.
–   *From general to specific.* Texts ordered by this principle first give the key answers that always or most often apply and that are important in almost all situations. Then it discusses the special issues that only apply in particular cases.

Hierarchy

Answers to questions in a text—about phenomena, objects, events, persons—can be ordered hierarchically into classes, sub-classes, and sub-sub-classes, demonstrated in the following examples.

–   After some general information, a brochure about the admission of foreigners discusses various types of foreigners (guest workers, refugees, illegal immigrants). One class is again subdivided (e.g. refugees = asylum seekers, recognized refugees, and asylum seekers who have not received a residence permit).
–   A geography book first lists the continents: Europe, Africa, Asia, ... after which the countries within Europe are discussed: Portugal, Spain, France, Luxembourg, Belgium, the Netherlands [...]. Within certain countries, the provinces are discussed.

2.3.2   Arrangement requirements

The requirements set out below are necessary to achieve a logical structure for the answers presented to the questions in a section of the text.

Ensure that for each text section only one arrangement criterion is used

You can often arrange information in various ways, depending on the arrangement criterion that you use. A common error is using two arrangement criteria simultaneously. This results in an illogical layout, creating overlap because of information that falls under both criteria.

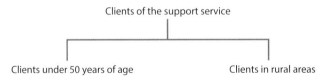

Poorly structured: not logical. People from rural areas can be younger than 50 years, so the categories overlap.

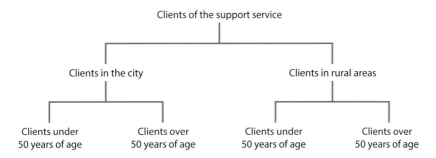

Better structured: This arrangement is more complex but also more logical.

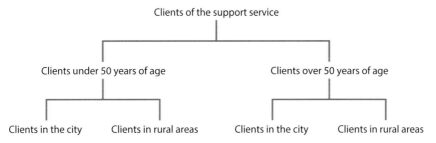

Also better: This arrangement is a variant of the previous one. The choice of variant would depend on the perspective that the text wants to convey: primary attention on the division along age groups or primary attention on the division along living areas.

Ensure that the arrangement covers all aspects

In practice, it is often very difficult to make a comprehensive arrangement of all the information you want to discuss, simply because reality itself is complicated. You can use an 'other/miscellaneous' category to deal with remaining cases.

Foreigners in Canada
- foreign workers
- tourists
- refugees
- illegal immigrants
- others

The category 'others' could include visiting academics, political asylum seekers, family members of foreign workers, and so on.

Ensure that the arrangement is clear and unambiguous

The arrangement criterion is the viewpoint that determines the ordering of information in a text. An example of an unclear arrangement criterion, at least for Westerners, is the following from ancient China.

> Types of animals: animals belonging to the emperor, embalmed animals, domestic animals, suckling pigs, mermaids, mythical animals, stray dogs, animals that rage like madmen, animals that cannot be counted, animals drawn with a fine brush of camel hair, animals that have just broken a jug, animals that look like flies when seen from afar.

This arrangement might be based on the importance attached to the different types of animals. With this extra information, the arrangement criterion may become a bit clearer, although it is not unequivocal: What one person finds important, someone else may consider unimportant.

Ensure that the arrangement is functional

A good arrangement fits the goal that the writer wants to achieve. If, for example, you write a note about the planned replacement of office chairs in an organization, you could arrange the current office chairs according to their original suppliers. It would be better, however, to order them by wear or ergonomic characteristics, so that you can determine the order in which they should be replaced.

Ensure that the categories are mutually exclusive

A clear arrangement means that information should belong in only one category. This may seem simple but it can prove to be difficult. For instance, if you divide addicts into alcoholics and drug addicts (and possibly other addicts, to make the categories exhaustive), these categories would not be mutually exclusive. After all, you can also categorize alcohol as a type of drug. And even if you do not, there are still people who are addicted to both alcohol and drugs.

2.4   External structure

At the start of this chapter, we made a distinction between the internal and the external structure of texts. Text schemata, set schemata, and other ordering principles concern the internal structure: They help you to select and organize information.

'External structure' is the overarching term for all characteristics and elements of a text that ensure that the reader of a text:
-   can quickly and accurately see what the text is about (theme, questions, and key answers);

- can clearly distinguish between primary and secondary issues (questions and sub-questions) in the text;
- can see the connections between the different parts of the text;
- can quickly find specific information in the text;
- can easily remember the content of the text.

A clear external structure is essential in professional communication. In a formal context, people often do not read a text from beginning to end but select certain parts. A manager who has to make decisions about finances reads a report differently than an expert who looks for certain specific results. Lack of time forces them to search only for the main message that is relevant to them. The division of a text into smaller parts, such as sections and paragraphs, can help a reader to do this.

A reader wants to understand the text. What is the advice based on? Why is your overall assessment negative? To find out, the reader looks for the coherence of the information in a text. If a writer has indicated the coherence clearly, it will be easier for the reader to understand the text (see also the examples at the beginning of this chapter). References, enumerations, signal words, and other ways of signposting can help make this coherence visible.

In this section we will discuss a number of structural elements that are important for written communication. Those for oral communication are discussed in chapters 9 and 10.

2.4.1   Text format

A text can be divided into a number of complete parts: chapters, sections (identified by a title and often a number), sub-sections (groups of paragraphs separated by a blank line or identified by a number), and paragraphs (groups of related sentences).

Whether a text includes all of these components depends mainly on the length of the text. A long text such as a book or a report usually contains all of them, while short texts such as letters only use paragraphs.

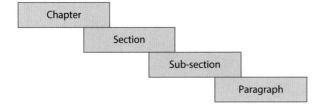

The layout of the text often corresponds directly to the text schema underlying the internal structure. Each chapter contains one main question, each section a key answer to that main question, each sub-section a sub-question to that key answer, and so on. But it is not always as simple as that. The external layout may also differ from the text schema. Often the main reason for this is that the arrangement is uneven if you stick to the text schema. Some of the main questions may need a less detailed explanation than others, so the chapters would be very unequal in length.

Not only the layout itself but also the titles of chapters, sections, and sub-sections (all of which are sometimes numbered) can help to clarify the structure. The title of the text reveals the theme; the titles of the sections can in turn show what the main questions and the key answers are.

You do not always have to formulate titles, sub-titles, and headings in exactly the same way as in the text schema. Besides their role in structuring the text (making the structure clear), they must be engaging and motivating; they should make the readers curious about the content of the text and keep them interested. If, for example, the theme in the text schema is 'ADVANTAGES OF A VISIT TO THE FUNFAIR', you could use a structuring headline saying 'The advantages of a visit to the funfair', followed by a headline listing the disadvantages. A more engaging variant would be, 'Do you know why you should go to the funfair?' And a more motivating headline would be, 'Come to the funfair on Wednesday and pay only half of the entrance fee!'

The text layout and chapter or section titles of books and reports are usually listed in a table of contents. These show at a glance the structure of the text at a glance. If the structure is clear from the wording of these titles, the table of contents will closely resemble a text schema.

2.4.2   Paragraphs

Paragraphs are units of text that are larger than a sentence and smaller than a section. They are the thought units of the text. In terms of content, a paragraph contains one main idea or one step in a line of reasoning that is worked out in some detail. Visually, a paragraph is recognizable because it starts on a new line, preferably indented. A good arrangement of the paragraphs is one of the most important ways you can support the reader in processing the text. There are a number of guidelines that help you to achieve this.

The size of a paragraph

The size of a paragraph can be a tricky problem for writers. Determining when to start a new paragraph is not always easy. There are three principles that can help you determine this.

- A new paragraph begins when you introduce a new sub-topic, a new argument, or a new sub-question.
- A paragraph should not be too long, but neither should it be too short. About ten lines of text is a good rule of thumb. For online texts, paragraphs should be shorter: around five lines.
- A paragraph should be longer than a sentence. It should contain a number of coherent sentences.

It should be noted that there are many exceptions to these three principles. They can, after all, sometimes be contradictory. If a paragraph becomes very short, you may want to deal with two sub-topics in one paragraph. If the paragraph becomes very long, it is often desirable to divide a sub-topic into two paragraphs.

Of course, you can also consciously achieve a special effect by deviating from these principles. A paragraph of one sentence, for instance, puts more emphasis on your words.

The bill to criminalize alcohol under the age of 18 gives a new impulse to the fight against alcohol abuse by teenagers. They risk a fine if they are found drinking at too young an age in any public space.

This bill is welcome at a time when the impact of drinking at a young age is slowly but surely affecting society. On the one hand, thanks to science we are rapidly learning more and more about the disastrous consequences of drinking for minors. It seriously affects the development of the brain, is harmful to various organs, and increases the risk of addiction in later life.

On the other hand, the extent of the phenomenon is becoming increasingly clear: 90% of all young people start drinking before the age of 18. Almost one in ten 12-year-olds drinks one to four glasses of alcohol during the weekend. At the age of 14, 16% drink five glasses or more. Some hospitals have special 'alcohol clinics' for the treatment of young binge drinkers. Most parents have no idea how serious this problem has become. According to research, adolescents drink three times as much as their parents think. Furthermore, sports canteens and cafés in particular appear to be hard learners. Although they risk hefty fines, they continue to sell alcohol on a large scale to minors.

The bill raises questions about its enforceability. The police do not always have the time to actually do the necessary checks at the bars of many cafés. But it does send out an important signal. Anyone who, at a young age, misbehaves under the influence of alcohol, gets involved in a fight, or ends up in hospital goes home with a fine simply because they were drinking unlawfully, and only then comes the added punishment for the bad behavior.

Society should not tolerate minors in a drunken state in public spaces.

In this text, the second and third paragraph belong together in terms of content: They give two arguments ('On the one hand, [...]'. 'On the other hand, [...]') for the position with which the second paragraph begins. Nevertheless, the author has decided to make two paragraphs of them to prevent one paragraph from becoming disproportionately long. The fact that the last paragraph consists of only one sentence gives it extra emphasis. This way it acquires the character of a somewhat emotional, hard-hitting final point that further underlines the argument.

The key sentence of a paragraph

A paragraph consists of a key sentence and an explanation of or elaboration on that sentence. The key sentence is the most important sentence of the paragraph and must be clearly recognizable to readers. That is why the following is important.

– Formulate the main idea of a paragraph as clearly as possible in a single sentence and use the rest of the paragraph to elaborate on this key sentence.
– Place this key sentence in one of the following positions (the so-called preferred positions):
  – as the first sentence, at the beginning of the paragraph;
  – as a second sentence, after a sentence that is clearly of a preliminary nature or acts as a link to the previous paragraph;
  – in the middle, marking a strong turn in the line of thought;
  – at the end of the paragraph, by way of conclusion.

It is very important that websites are designed in such a way that they are also easily accessible for 'digital risk groups' such as the illiterate, people with visual impairments, or computer illiterates. There are legal obligations for public institutions such as government departments and higher education bodies to present digital information, services, and educational resources in an accessible way, but accessibility of websites is also essential for the business community. Many organizations such as banks, health insurers, or public transport companies may have the intention to be accessible to people with disabilities, but in practice they fail to achieve this sufficiently. In doing so, they fall short in their social responsibility, and they run the risk of not reaching part of their target group.

In this paragraph, the key sentence is paramount. The rest of the paragraph explains why the accessibility of websites is important.

> The slogan 'Four in a row, cashier on the go' of a large supermarket chain does not always seem to apply. At several branches throughout the country, customers have complained that the rule is not being observed. Many customers complain that they often have to wait in a line with more than four people. To quote one shopping couple: 'Normally that's not that bad, but if the suggestion is that it's your turn soon, it's far from pleasant if you have to keep waiting.'

In this news item, the key sentence is in second place, after an introductory sentence that makes it clear to the reader that things are not going smoothly in the supermarket. After the key sentence, it is explained what exactly the problem is, and an example follows in the last sentence.

> The establishment of the head office in New Aduard had many advantages, such as its proximity to Lubinga Airport, the stock exchange, and the presence of a large number of advertising agencies. Moreover, the metropolitan image and the broad array of cultural offerings in the area are attractive to many of our employees. Nevertheless, the head office will return to Davistown, where our company originated and flourished. The lower house prices and the beautiful wooded and hilly surroundings are even more important to most employees than the cultural offering of New Aduard.

In this paragraph, the key sentence is in the middle. In the paragraph segment before the key sentence you find the arguments for a location in New Aduard, followed by the arguments to return to Davistown anyway. The word 'nevertheless' is very important in this paragraph as a signal that this is where the key sentence finds itself, indicating a strong turn in the line of thought.

> When it comes to research, most social science students think of empirical research in a laboratory, of test subjects who are confronted with decision-making tasks, of reaction time measurement and the like. But you can also do field research. This can consist of making observations or conducting surveys, verbally or in writing, with open or closed questions. You can also carry out desk research by studying literature, thinking about it, trying to make connections, or looking for explanations. No type of research can simply be judged as right or wrong: Everything depends on the purpose and topic of the research.

The paragraph has a climax structure. Three types of research are dealt with, and the key sentence at the end serves as a conclusion.

Visual marking of paragraphs

For the visualization of paragraphs, follow the guidelines below.

– Paragraphs always begin on a new line.
– The first line should ideally be indented to the right (use the tab key for this, not the space bar). Do not indent the text after a heading, after a blank line, or at the top of a new page.
– Preferably, do not use blank lines to separate paragraphs; it is better to use blank lines to separate groups of paragraphs that belong together.
– The previous rule does not apply to texts on the screen. In that case it is better, for visual legibility, to have a blank line after each paragraph.

2.4.3   Referential ties

Within a paragraph, the sentences should be clearly linked. This is the case, for instance, when two or more sentences deal with the same subject. You can make this coherence more visible with the use of referential ties: words or phrases that link a reference in one sentence to a reference in a previous sentence. There are three types of referential ties:

– a more or less literal repetition of words or phrases (or parts of phrases);
– synonyms for the word or phrase;
– reference words such as 'this', 'that', 'he', 'she', 'it', 'they', 'those', 'thereby', and 'there'.

Temporary work is becoming increasingly important. More than half of the vacancies nowadays involve some form of temporary work. These temporary jobs offer a good opportunity to gain experience. This provides an advantage for job seekers applying for permanent jobs. Employment offices are responding to this development. In order to increase the chances of job seekers, they collaborate with temporary employment agencies. However, this collaboration is under great pressure now that the government is making less and less money available for employment mediation.

In this paragraph, many references are used to make the relationships between the sentences clear: literal or partial repetition ('temporary work' mentioned twice; 'collaborate – collaboration'), synonyms ('temporary work' – 'temporary jobs'), and reference words ('this', 'these', 'they').

2.4.4 Signal words and phrases

Signal words and phrases show how parts of the text relate to each other. Make sure that each sentence within a paragraph is linked to other parts of the paragraph through the use of a signal word or phrase. The following table gives an overview.

Type of relationship	Signal words and phrases
Time (sequence)	thereafter, then, before, later, earlier, next day, one year earlier
Time (simultaneity)	then, at that time, while, at the same time
Place (elsewhere)	next to, above, along, further, adjacent
Place (same)	in the same place, there, exactly where
Whole-part	part of this is, this consists of, an aspect of this is
Part-whole	this belongs to, this falls under, this is a part of, this falls into, this is an aspect of
Announcement	the rest will be about […], hereafter we […], in the fourth part we […], subsequently we […]
Enumeration	1, 2, 3, 4, […], firstly, secondly, […], first of all, to start with, then, also, subsequently, finally, lastly
Contradiction	but, nevertheless, however, though, although, despite, on the other hand, in contrast to, opposed to this, albeit, on the one hand […] on the other hand […]
Comparison	likewise, compared to, in the same way, corresponding to, this resembles, similarly, just as
Illustration, example	for example, for instance, so, similarly, in other words, to illustrate, as an example, to give an example
Cause-effect(prediction)	therefore, because, for, since, as a result
Cause-effect(explanation)	therefore, because, for, since, as a result
Reason	because, therefore, for this reason
Argumentation (from argument to conclusion)	therefore, in short, it follows that, from this, it can be concluded that, leading to the following conclusion, in conclusion
Argumentation (from conclusion to argument)	because, since, as, an argument in favor of this is, my argumentation is as follows
Problem-solution	so, therefore, the solution is
Solution-problem	the underlying problem is that, this is caused by
Target-means	so, so that, in order to, to ensure that
Summary	therefore, in summary, in short, all things considered, concluding, in the end, by way of conclusion

Signal words and phrases showing how parts of a text relate to each other.

Lamination is the application of a thin layer of a metal or metal compound to another material by evaporation in a vacuum. Thin sides can be made in many ways: by crushing, rolling, or galvanizing. If one places high demands on the layer thickness distribution, structure, and physical properties of the thin layer, evaporation is an appropriate method.

In this paragraph, the coherence between the sentences is not clear because signal words and phrases are missing.

Lamination is the application of a thin layer of a metal or metal compound to another material by evaporation in a vacuum. Thin sides can *also* be made *in other ways*: *for example* by crushing, rolling, or galvanizing. *But* if one places high demands on the layer thickness distribution, structure, and physical properties of the thin layer, then evaporation is an appropriate method.

In this paragraph, the coherence between the sentences is made clear by the use of signal words and phrases ('also in other ways', 'for example', 'but').

2.4.5 Lists

A list can help to create a clear structure because of the following three characteristics.
– A number of elements are grouped together, revealing the conceptual coherence.
– The elements show parallelism: they are similar to each other.
– The bullet points or numbering make the structure clearly visible.

Lists are widely used in written reports and in slides for oral presentations. However, you should always check whether there is a more meaningful way to present your information than in a list.

To prevent a list from becoming a list of parts that have no clear coherence, pay close attention to the layout of the list.
– Always present the elements of the list in the same form. Either use full sentences for all elements, or list them all as noun phrases. Do not mix such forms.
– Start with a clear introductory sentence. Formulate the sentence in such a way that it fits all the parts of the list.

You can use three types of listing signs:

– letters, suggesting that the list is exhaustive;
– numbers, suggesting that the list is not only exhaustive but also that the order is important;
– dashes or bullets, which have a neutral appearance and do not suggest either exhaustiveness or a particular order.

> No subsidy will be granted if it concerns the improvement of homes that are not permanently occupied, such as holiday homes, or so-called second homes, and also not if it concerns improvements the cost of which is less than one thousand euros, unless the improvement is a toilet or a shower. Even if you install a central heating system, except in homes intended for the accommodation of the elderly or physically handicapped, you are not eligible for subsidy. Finally, homes that are demolished in the short term and improvements that only relate to the removal of technical defects that have arisen as a result of postponed or neglected maintenance are an exception to the subsidy scheme.

This paragraph indicates in running text the cases where no subsidy is granted for improvements to a home.

> No subsidy is provided for:
> a the improvement of homes that are not permanently occupied, such as holiday homes, or so-called second homes;
> b the installation of improvements the costs of which amount to less than one thousand euros, unless the improvement is a toilet or a shower;
> c the installation of a central heating system, except in dwellings intended for the accommodation of the elderly or physically handicapped;
> d homes that are demolished at short notice;
> e improvements that relate to the removal of technical defects that have arisen as a result of postponed or neglected maintenance.

In this version, a list is given that makes the content easier to process. Note the uniformity of the elements: The parallelism leads to a more coherent structure. The elements are marked with letters, suggesting that the list is complete but the order random.

2.4.6   Structure indicators

Structure indicators explicitly clarify the structure of a text by announcing what you will do, for example, or by looking back at what you have done. Particularly in longer texts, there are certain places where structure indicators play an important role (see also section 6.1).

– At the start of a text, you can give a guide to the structure that is to follow (a reading guide). For a longer text such as a report, this is usually included in an introductory chapter. Announcing what you will do is also appropriate at the start of a chapter or a long section.
– At the start or at the end of a section, you can provide a brief summary with one or more signposting sentences. This way, the argument provided becomes clearer for the reader.

> The structure of this article is as follows. In section 2 an overview will be presented of the state of affairs in writing education. Section 3 indicates what method of research we have used. A description of the results follows in section 4. Section 5 presents the conclusions. Finally, in section 6, we initiate a discussion about the problems in current writing education.

A reading guide to the structure of the article.

> In this memorandum, a number of frequently heard objections to the limited duration of students' enrolment are refuted. As we have shown in chapter 1, it is often claimed that students are no longer willing to take part in activities that do not earn them 'points' for their examinations, and that part-time studies are made very difficult. We have argued, however, that the first objection can easily be met by creating 'free space' in study programs, as described in chapter 2. The second objection can just as easily be overcome by creating sufficient possibilities for exemption, a proposal for which we have put forward good arguments and proposals in chapters 3 and 4.

Final summary of a memorandum. The content of the memorandum is summarized in such a way that it already leans toward the final conclusion. Note that this way of working is not necessarily objectionable. After all, the text is written to convince the reader that the proposed policy must be implemented.

Key points

A good structure is important to convey the referential message well. The internal structure records what units a text consists of, how they relate hierarchically to each other, and in what order they are offered. The external structure is the whole of verbal, linguistic elements and non-verbal, non-linguistic elements with which the internal structure is made clear to the receiver.

Internal structure

The internal structure of a text can be represented in the text schema. This consists of the theme of the text, the main questions, the key answers to those main questions, possibly sub-questions, answers to those sub-questions, and so on.

Set schemata are general mini-text schemata that can be used well in professional contexts for texts on certain types of themes and with a certain line of reasoning. Set schemata can also be combined well in a network that forms the basis for a text.
–   The set problem schema is suitable for texts in which one or more solutions to an undesirable situation are discussed.
–   The set measure schema is suitable for texts recommending and elaborating a particular course of action.
–   The set evaluation schema is suitable for texts in which the advantages and disadvantages of a particular case are weighed up.
–   The set opinion schema is suitable for texts in which an opinion is compared with one or more other opinions.
–   The set action schema is suitable for texts in which a process or procedure is described, with or without an instructional purpose.
–   The set design schema is suitable for texts describing a draft that has been developed, and which may or may not already have been put into practice.
–   The set research schema is widely used in texts in which research is presented; it may also be a proposal or a report.

The ordering of key answers can often be based on general ordering principles such as space, time, the given-new principle, and hierarchy.

External structure

To make the internal structure easily recognizable to readers without misunderstandings, writers use different tools. Important tools include the following.

– The text division into chapters, sections, sub-sections, and paragraphs.
– The structure of a paragraph, especially by using key phrases in preferred positions.
– Clear and unambiguous references in sentences.
– Clear signal words and phrases to indicate the relationship between sentences and larger text elements.
– Lists to mark equivalent elements.
– Structure indicators, especially the reading guide and the summary.

Assignments

Assignment 1: The mandatory language test

Purpose of the assignment
You will practice writing a text using different set schemata, and with different results.

Subject matter
Section 2.2

Tasks
In an increasing number of higher education programs, a so-called language test is taken in the first year to check whether students have sufficient command of English. This language test is about spelling, sentence structure, and knowledge of difficult words, among other things. Students must pass the test before the end of the first year, otherwise they will not be able to continue their studies.

Imagine that you have been appointed as a teacher in your study program. You have been asked to write a proposal to introduce such a test in this program as well. The proposal is intended for the management of the study program and also for the lecturers and students who together form the program committee. You can use various classification principles for the text, including the problem schema and the measure schema.

1   Formulate a short text schema for the proposal, based on the set problem schema. Think of the elements (key answers) that fit into this set schema.
2   Also formulate a short text schema based on the set measure schema. Here too, you should think of the necessary content yourself.
3   Determine which of the two text schemata you would find most suitable as a starting point for the proposal, and indicate why.

Assignment 2: Fear appeals to combat obesity

Purpose of the assignment
You will practice restructuring a paragraph.

Subject matter
Section 2.4.2

Tasks
The following paragraph outlines the reason for a study into the possibilities of using health education to combat obesity. The authors do not immediately address their topic but first introduce a case about overweight children before they mention the subject of their research (fear appeal messages) in the last sentence of the paragraph.
1   Rewrite the paragraph so that it starts with that subject.
2   Show with underlined signal words and phrases how you have ensured that it remains clear to the reader how the text elements relate to each other.

Text
In our environment, the number of overweight children has doubled in the last twenty years. Last year, one in seven children were too fat. Besides physical complaints, such as cardiovascular diseases, diabetes, and joint complaints, obesity can also lead to social-emotional problems. In this context, RERIS started a campaign in 2005 with the central message 'Don't think too lightly about obesity – Say no more often'. This message was conveyed with an illustration in which a baby's head with a slightly reproachful look in the eyes was mounted on an enormous, adult body. The intention of RERIS with this image was to frighten parents of young children in a way that might seem unrealistic but confrontational about the possible consequences of obesity. In this way, RERIS wanted to change the attitude of parents who do not yet take responsibility for this aspect of their children's health seriously enough. With this, RERIS chose to use what is referred to in the literature on health education as fear appeal messages: expressions that attempt to achieve a positive behavioral change in the target group by frightening recipients about the undesirable consequences of continuing their existing behavior.

Assignment 3: A minority majority

Purpose of the assignment
You will practice using referential ties and signal words and phrases to show the coherence in a text.

Subject matter
Section 2.4.3
Section 2.4.4

Tasks
The coherence between the sentences in the paragraph below (adapted from a text in *National Geographic*, July 2018) has not been made clearly visible, resulting in a seemingly incoherent text.
1   Add referential ties and signal words and phrases to this text to improve the coherence. Try to avoid monotony by using different connecting words.
2   For each connection, explain why you used it here.

Text
Latinos account for more of the nation's demographic changes than any other group. The Latino numbers are increasing. The United States will become a 'minority majority' by the middle of this century. The dramatic reordering of the nation's demographics has spawned anger and conflict. Some opportunistic politicians and media commentators have helped by portraying whites as victims in an increasingly diverse United States. Politicians and media commentators, including the President, cast Latinos as violent gang members, job stealers, and undocumented immigrants who come to the United States and have so-called anchor babies, children who are citizens at birth. Resentment about immigration helped fuel the political shifts. Most of the estimated 11 million undocumented immigrants in the US are Latinos.

Assignment 4: Primary school Desmond Tutu

Purpose of the assignment
You will practice giving feedback on the draft version of a text.

Subject matter
Section 1.5

Task
Imagine that as a student you are doing an internship at the Desmond Tutu primary school. Yesterday, during a team meeting, the teachers decided to temporarily change the school times because of the beautiful summer weather. A letter to the parents of the children must be sent out quickly. Paula Best, another intern at this school, was asked to take on this task and to write a draft for this letter. Paula has asked you to send her your feedback, hoping that the letter can be sent to the parents as quickly as possible.

Give Paula feedback on this letter, following the advice you find in section 1.5.

The letter

Dear parent,

The people of our village are enjoying the nice, warm weather of the last few days. Many of them go to the swimming pool or enjoy a walk in the shade in the park. But here at school it is not so nice. We are puffing from the heat.

As you probably know as an involved parent, most of our classes are north-facing and our windows can only be opened a little bit. That is why we are going to adjust the timetable from tomorrow morning on. We will switch to a schedule we developed for this kind of tropical weather.

Until further notice, school will start at half past eight in the morning and will continue until twelve o'clock. The lunch break will last until half past one and after that, only one more hour will be spent on teaching. At half past two school will be out, and from then on the children—and we too—can enjoy the nice weather.

We assume that you are happy for your children that we take this measure. If there are any difficulties, please give us a call. Perhaps something can be done to help solve your problem, but we trust that will not be necessary.

Warm regards,
The staff of the Desmond Tutu School

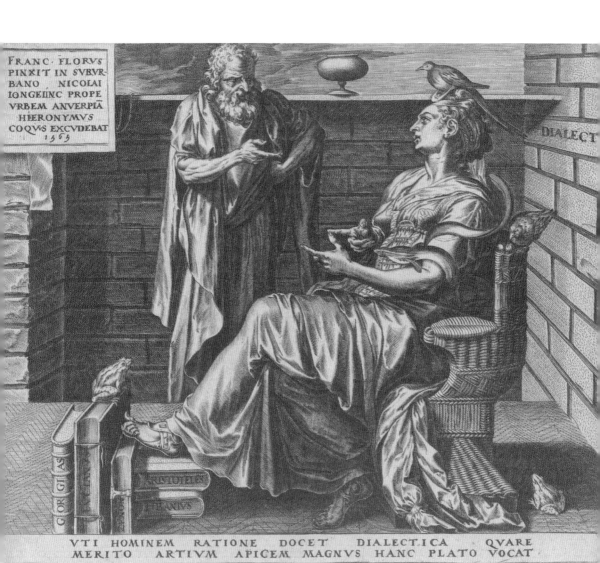

DIALECT

GORGIAS

ARISTOTELES

ZENO FABIVS

VTI HOMINEM RATIONE DOCET DIALECTICA QVARE
MERITO ARTIVM APICEM MAGNVS HANC PLATO VOCAT

3 Argumentation

◀ *Dialectica*, Cornelis Cort, 1565. Dialectica sits on a chair in a room with stone walls and argues with an old man. She counts her arguments on her fingers. On her head and on the back of her chair are birds, on the ground two toads. Dialectica has her foot on a pile of books by important thinkers. The caption reads: 'Dialectics teaches man reason. That is why Plato identifies her as the most important of the arts.'

This chapter provides you, like Dialectica, with a firm foundation in argumentation, based on classical teachings.

A plea for a vegan lifestyle

BENEFITS OF A VEGAN LIFESTYLE

Every year more and more people are making the decision to go vegan, and for good reason! There are so many amazing ways that veganism can improve our lives – fantastic health benefits, less stress on our environment, more efficient ways to use our resources, and many more!

There are so many unique reasons someone might choose to adopt a vegan lifestyle. When thinking about transitioning to veganism it's important to ponder your morals and the reasons why this lifestyle speaks to you. A big lifestyle change is easier to sustain if you wholeheartedly believe in your decision. Think about the standards you hold yourself accountable to, and what guides you as you decide what is right and what is wrong.

In the consumer culture we live in today we show support with money. Every purchase we make is like a vote of support. When we buy commercial products our money is voting in support of not only the product but also the practices and morals of the company. For this reason it's important to be an educated consumer so that with every dollar you spend, you're supporting something you truly believe in.

In October 2018, the website *www.ilovevegan.com* published a plea for veganism, part of which is shown above. As this example shows, communication is not just a matter of information transfer. When people or organizations communicate, they often try to make their message more persuasive by means of argumentation. Some arguments may appeal to one group of readers, while other arguments may be more convincing to another group. But without some form of argumentation, it is hard to persuade any audience. Argumentation is not only relevant to texts or speeches with a persuasive purpose. Argumentation can also be found, for instance, in texts with other main communicative goals, such as textbooks or instruction manuals.

At least two components are needed for argumentation: a position on a certain topic and arguments to support this position. Contrary to what people often think, this is not only necessary when you want to support an opinion. Argumentation is also used to support factual statements or encouragements to adopt certain behavior. We will return to that later.

Argumentation naturally plays a role in communication that has a persuasive goal, but that does not mean that persuasive communication always contains arguments. An election poster that proclaims in large letters 'Of course you will vote PPCT!' has a persuasive purpose, but the point is not argued: The poster provides no statements in support of its claim.

In this chapter, we will discuss a number of tools that will help you recognize and evaluate argumentation (or the lack of it). We will present these tools mainly as instruments that you can use to critically assess the argumentation in a message. But these instruments are also useful as a tool to anticipate criticism on your own messages and thus to enable you to speak or write more convincingly.

We will first discuss the role that argumentation plays in communication (section 3.1), after which we will explain in section 3.2 how you can recognize argumentation in messages (written texts, oral presentations, or contributions to a conversation) and how you can display the relationship between a position and its supporting arguments—in other words, the structure of the argumentation. In section 3.3, we will discuss the classic distinction between logically valid and logically invalid reasoning. In section 3.4, we will present a number of standard forms of argumentation and the critical questions related to them that can help you to form an opinion about the quality of a reasoning. Finally, in section 3.5, we will discuss a few examples of fallacies: forms of argumentation that seem reasonable but are not.

3.1   The role of argumentation in communication

Our government spends millions every year to promote healthy behavior, for instance on the efforts to combat alcohol consumption among young people. From a medical point of view, there are good reasons to discourage this behavior. Research shows that alcohol consumption at a young age causes damage to the brain, which leads, among other things, to a loss of concentration and learning ability, a loss of memory, and undesirable social behavior. Moreover, this brain damage is irreversible and leads to various disorders at a later age, even if the young person does not become a heavy drinker.

Both health educators and the government know that such rational considerations do not often convince young people, or at least do not deter them from drinking alcohol. Messages therefore not only include rational arguments, but also play on emotions, for instance by showing scary videos. The government also uses other means: higher prices of beer, wine, and other alcoholic beverages; a ban on selling alcohol to young people; and fines for young people who have alcoholic beverages in their possession.

Argumentation is not the only means of persuasion.

As this example shows, argumentation can be persuasive, but it is not the only option. Emotions, social pressure, legal regulations, rewards, and penalties can have the same effect, often even more. Apparently, mere facts presented in a logical structure do not always 'speak for themselves'. Why, then, do we attach such value to rational argumentation?

– Argumentation is the most democratic means of conducting a discussion. In a rational debate, everyone is equal: The person who presents the best arguments will win the debate. If we use social pressure, legal regulations, rewards, and punishment, then the most powerful person will win.

– No matter how important emotions are—without emotions there would be no love, art or religion—when it comes to forming opinions and making decisions, we would prefer not to base them on our emotions. We prefer to use our common sense to reasonably determine what we find convincing and what we find implausible.

3.1.1 When is argumentation necessary?

The basic principle of reasoning is that someone who claims something (the *proponent*) has to provide evidence to the other party (the *opponent*). In other words, the proponent takes the burden of proof upon himself or herself. That is a good principle, but it does not always apply to the same extent.

> Suppose Maria Vespinelli says something like: 'I don't like classical music.' Then Maria probably will not be expected to give arguments. There is no accounting for taste, after all. But sometimes arguments are necessary, for example if Maria actually wants to claim that it is right that she does not like classical music. That is a position that can be argued about. Or perhaps Maria recently claimed that she did love Mozart. If she now says she does not like classical music, she has some explaining to do.
>
> A similar case: If a manual for a printer includes the instruction 'Do not put more than 200 sheets of paper in the tray', there is no need to give arguments. The text is intended to instruct, not to convince. But if the writer of the manual is afraid that readers will ignore this instruction, he or she can decide to add an argument anyway: '[…] otherwise you may cause a paper jam.' In that case, the writer is not only providing instructions, but also has a motivating goal.

The burden of proof (the need to argue) is not always the same.

The presence of a disagreement

Argumentation is especially necessary when two parties each have a different view on a particular issue. One side is in favor of a particular position P, the other is against it or has no opinion. Argumentation is then meant to motivate the other party (and perhaps also the neutral listener or reader) to adopt position P.

If the parties already agree on a particular position, argumentation for that position is superfluous: Nobody needs to be convinced. Claims such as 'computers play an important role in daily life' and other truisms do not need to be argued. To give another example: Supporters of the Labour Party do not need to be convinced by the party leaders that the income inequality in the UK needs to be reduced. That is probably one of the reasons why they vote for the Labour Party. If an argument is still made, it is mainly meant to repeat the arguments eloquently and to confirm the views of the audience ('preaching to the choir').

In practice, it is not always clear whether or not there is a difference of opinion and how profound it is. Writers (or speakers) do not always know exactly what their audience thinks about a certain issue, and there may also be many differences within that audience. In such situations, the criteria mentioned below often play a decisive role in determining whether or not to use arguments.

Importance of the issue

The more important an issue is, the more important the argumentation becomes. As a general rule, someone who proposes to change the status quo has the burden of proof, not those who wish to maintain the existing situation. In the case of important changes, writers or speakers are expected to motivate their position. For issues of lesser importance, this expectation is generally lower.

You can often deduce the importance of an issue that arises at some point in a text or a presentation from the underlying text schema (see chapter 2). Answers to main questions generally require more argumentation than answers to sub-questions or to questions at an even lower level in the structure.

Ambitions of the sender

When senders want to convince others of their position, they can have different levels of ambition:
– to convince everyone that this is the only correct position (universal ambition);
– to convince their own group that this is one of the possible correct positions, and that it is at least reasonable to take it into account;
– to convince the other party that it is, at the very least, acceptable to take this position.

Senders who have universal ambitions must be confident of their position: This level of ambition requires very convincing arguments. Senders with a more modest level of ambition have a lighter burden of proof.

Conventions of conversation types and text genres

How heavy the burden of proof is also depends on the situation. During a debate in which the proponent and the opponent are facing each other, everyone will likely argue his or her position in detail and argue against the position of the other party. In an exploratory discussion that is aimed at exploring ideas in a more non-committal way, there will be fewer demands on the argumentation.

Various text genres also require different levels of argumentation. The need for argumentation that applies to one type of text does not automatically apply to another. In scientific publications, almost everything that is not generally known must be supported by arguments. For other types of texts, such as journalistic articles, this requirement is less strict.

3.1.2 The critical reader or listener

When you take part in a debate, you should carefully study the arguments of the other party to identify the points you can attack and disagree with. However, a critical attitude is also often needed in other situations. Managers and CEOs who have to make decisions on the basis of advisory reports have to pay close attention to the argumentation of the advice before they follow it. Students referring to publications in their thesis should carefully check how the authors arrive at their conclusions before they adopt them.

In practice, we are not always very critical. For example, there are types of messages we do not find important enough to examine critically (such as advertisements for products we will not buy), or we rely on the judgment of the person making the claims or on the medium through which the information reaches us (such as news on TV).

3.2 The structure of the reasoning

Before you can criticize a reasoning, you must first have a clear picture of how the reasoning exactly works. This is not always easy, because the conclusions and arguments are interspersed with other types of information, are not always expressed in a clear and concise way, or are sometimes not even explicitly mentioned. In this section we will explain how you can deduce the exact reasoning from a message.

3.2.1 Definition of position and argument

Argumentation consists of at least two elements: a position and an argument. We speak of a position when someone makes a statement that he or she tries to make (more) plausible to another party. It can be a factual statement, an opinion, or an encouragement.

- When you are judging a *factual statement*, you can say that it is correct (in accordance with reality), incorrect (not in accordance with reality), or more or less likely. Judgments on facts concerning the past ('Charles Darwin died in 1882') or on frequently recurring situations ('Darwin's theory of evolution still causes heated debates') can in principle be verified. You can establish whether or not these statements are correct. We cannot know beforehand whether statements about facts that will occur in the future are correct. Predictions can at the most have a certain degree of probability ('Discussions about Darwin's theory of evolution will continue for as long as mankind exists').

– An *opinion* reflects a judgment ('Darwin's meaning is greatly overestimated'). One party may try to convince the other party that their opinion is right and that the other party should therefore share it, but they can never prove that their opinion is correct. They can, however, prove that it follows logically from other opinions ('If you agree that Darwin did not really add anything essential to the work of his predecessors, then you also have to agree that his importance is greatly overestimated').

– In the case of an *encouragement*, one party tries to convince the other party to behave in a certain way ('You should definitely read *On the Origin of Species* by Darwin!'). Again, you cannot really prove the accuracy of this statement. Still, the encouragement may follow logically from arguments ('If you are as convinced of creationism as you say you are, then you should also examine the opposite position by reading *On the Origin of Species* by Darwin!')

There are many other terms for what we will call the *position*: an *assertion*, a *point of view*, a *standpoint*, a *claim*, or a *conclusion*. If writers or speakers first give their position and then the arguments, we use the terms position, assertion, standpoint, or claim. If the position follows after the arguments, the term conclusion may be used.

Arguments are those parts of the argumentation that serve to make the position more plausible or credible.

> Tickets for an André Rieu concert aren't too expensive at all. Have you seen how many people work at such a concert? And compare the price of a ticket for André Rieu to what you pay for a performance by Coldplay or Bruno Mars!

The position in the first sentence is supported by arguments in the second and third sentences.

3.2.2   Recognizing positions and arguments

In practice, it is not always easy to determine exactly what the position is that a writer (or speaker) is taking and what the arguments are.

The situation

The starting point is always what is discussed in the text: something on which there seems to be a difference of opinion. In an argumentative essay, a commentary, a review, or a reaction to a news item, the writer almost always adopts a certain position, preferably supported by arguments. Other types of texts, such as news items and instructions, usually do not contain the writer's position. News items may report on the opinions of other people, but news items themselves are not supposed to include a position.

Markers of argumentation

Positions are often marked by certain linguistic elements:

- words that make the meaning of a statement explicit: 'my position is that [...]', 'my view is that [...]', 'I conclude that [...]', 'my advice is to [...]';
- encouragements, commandments, or prohibitions: 'I recommend that you [...]', 'you should [...]', 'now it is important to [...]', or the imperative: 'register today!';
- value judgments: 'it is good/bad/shameful that [...]', possibly in the form of rhetorical questions: 'Isn't it fantastic that [...]?' Judgments can also be formulated 'casually': 'the disgraceful way in which [...]' (implying the position that something is disgraceful);
- signal words and phrases such as 'so', 'therefore', 'for this reason', and so on.

Arguments can also be marked by linguistic elements. This usually takes the form of signal words and phrases such as 'because', 'therefore', 'after all', or explicit statements such as 'the reason for this is [...]', 'this view is based on the fact that [...]'.

> The risks of carbon dioxide capture and storage are unknown, and there is a great deal of resistance to it among the local population. For this reason, there should be no underground storage of carbon dioxide in New Aduard.
>
> There should be no underground storage of carbon dioxide in New Aduard, because the risks of carbon dioxide capture and storage are unknown, and there is a great deal of resistance to it among the local population.

Two ways of expressing the same reasoning: 'arguments, therefore conclusion' and 'position, because arguments'.

Reformulating the reasoning

Sometimes the position and the arguments follow each other without markers, so it is up to the reader to infer that there is a reasoning in the text. If you are in doubt about whether or not there is some form of reasoning in the text, you can test this by trying to insert indications of argumentation, preferably in the form of distinctive signal words and phrases ('so', 'therefore', 'for this reason', 'because', 'after all', and so on). If that results in a meaningful passage, you can assume that there is indeed argumentation, and you immediately see what the position is and what the arguments are.

Edith needs to check whether she still has a paper version of the report. The digital file cannot be opened.	Edith needs to check if she still has a paper version of the report, because the digital file cannot be opened.	Edith needs to check if she still has a paper version of the report, so the digital file cannot be opened.
Two sentences that together may form a reasoning.	With the signal word 'because', it becomes apparent that this is indeed a reasoning, and that the first sentence is the position and the second sentence is the argument.	Inserting the signal word 'so' does not make sense here. The first sentence cannot be the argument and the second sentence cannot be the position.

Especially with longer texts, it is sometimes difficult to establish what the writer's position is and what the arguments for that position are. This may be because the arguments and sometimes even the position are left implicit, or because the text contains a great deal of other information apart from the positions and the arguments. Sometimes this information resembles argumentation, or the author discusses what he or she thinks of other people's position or arguments. This stratification may make it difficult to determine the position and the arguments of the text.

3.2.3 Supplementing arguments that are left implicit

Amanda (1):	I don't think our government will last much longer.
Burt (1):	What do you mean?
Amanda (2):	Well, the last few years we've seen a great increase in the number of highly educated people in our country.
Burt (2):	What does that have to do with it?
Amanda (3):	It happens everywhere: When the level of education increases, authoritarian regimes lose their power.

In this discussion, Amanda puts forward a position. Upon being asked by Burt, Amanda gives two arguments, which together with the position form the full reasoning.

How can only one argumentative statement already make the position of the writer or speaker credible? The reason is that the writer or speaker invokes a general rule. The writer or speaker shows (or at least suggests) that the specific issue that is being discussed is a special instance of a much more general rule.

This principle was already used in classical logic: 'Socrates is a human being' (factual statement), 'All people are mortal' (general rule), so 'Socrates is mortal' (position). The statement 'All people are mortal' forms the foundation of the reasoning. This foundation shows that the reasoning is not based on a random argument but on the application of a general rule. Unlike the ancient Greeks, we now usually formulate such general rules in the form of 'if [...], then [...]': 'If X is human, then X is mortal'.

A complete line of reasoning therefore consists not of two, but of three elements:
– a position;
– a given statement as an argument;
– a general rule.

A line of reasoning is rarely or never fully presented. Two elements are usually enough; the reader or listener is supposed to be able to add the third element himself or herself. That third element is, as it were, imbedded in the combination of the other two. We call this third element the *implicit element*. This is usually the general rule, but it can also be the given statement or even the position.

Reasoning	Implicit element
The head of department is not a trend-setter. He still uses a mobile phone that is three years old.	If someone uses outdated equipment, he is not a trendsetter. (The general rule)
If someone uses a mobile phone that is three years old, he is not a trendsetter. Therefore, the head of department is not a trendsetter.	The head of department is still using a mobile phone that is three years old. (The data)
The head of department still uses a mobile phone that is three years old. If you do that, you are not a trendsetter.	The head of department is not a trendsetter. (The conclusion)

Usually only two elements of the reasoning are mentioned. The third element remains implicit, but should be clear to a good listener.

3.2.4   The organization of the arguments

The arguments that form part of a reasoning can be organized in different ways.

Single argument
A position is supported by one argument, which is explicitly mentioned; the second argument (usually a general rule) is left implicit. This is the type of argumentation we have used in the examples so far.

Single argument.

> In higher education you no longer need to pay attention to spelling. After all, everyone who is a student in higher education has passed their school exams.

This reasoning uses two arguments. One argument is explicitly stated in the text (every student in higher education has passed their final exam in a secondary school); the other argument is left implicit (those who have passed their school exams have learned to spell so well that they no longer need to pay attention to it).

Convergent arguments
This structure includes multiple arguments in support of the position, which are independent of each other. Each argument supports the position by itself. The fact that there are several independent arguments that all support the position, makes the argumentation stronger. After all, if the other party is not convinced by the first argument, then there is a second, third, or fourth [...].

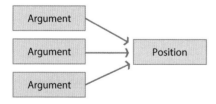

Convergent arguments (in this case, three arguments; it could also be two, or more than three arguments). Note that the absence of lines between the arguments shows that the arguments are independent of each other.

> We may as well stop using energy labels for houses. A recent study has shown that most homebuyers do not even care about a house's label. Moreover, any energy-saving measures that a homeowner has taken are hardly taken into account when the label is determined.

In this commentary on the energy label that the EU made compulsory for all houses that are on sale, the position is supported by two convergent arguments.

Linked arguments

In this structure, a combination of arguments supports the position. The arguments are therefore not independent of each other; they are linked. Only together do they form a good reasoning.

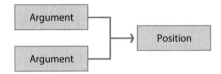

Linked arguments. Note that the lines between the two arguments and the position show that the arguments belong together and that neither can be omitted.

> The purchasing power of wages has increased by 60% since 1980. The purchasing power of the state pension has effectively remained the same. So clearly, the financial position of the elderly has relatively declined in the last 25 years.

This reasoning puts forward two arguments, both of which are necessary to draw the conclusion. Unlike in the previous example, they are not separate from each other.

Serial argumentation

Up until now we have only considered an argument as the element in a reasoning that supports the position. Often, however, the argument itself is also under discussion. If a reasoning includes an argument that is debatable, this argument in turn must be supported by a new argument. This results in a chain of arguments: serial argumentation.

The chain of arguments can quickly become longer than two. The argument that is meant to support the first argument may itself be called into question, so that it becomes another position that needs to be supported. And so it continues.

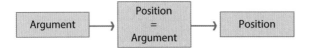

Universities quickly need additional funding for teacher training. Programs for teacher training may be expected to have far more enrolments than they had in previous years. After all, the government has made it much more attractive for students to become teachers when they have taken a teacher training after their Master's program. For example, they will earn more than in other professions, and they no longer have to pay back their study loan.

Example of serial argumentation for the position that universities need more funding for teacher training.

Networks of arguments

Combining the abovementioned basic structures in one argumentation results in complex argumentation structures. This can lead to whole networks of arguments and sub-arguments.

The government and the alcohol industry recently launched a campaign with the slogan 'No alcohol under eighteen'. However, young people under the age of eighteen can still easily obtain alcohol at supermarkets and liquor stores. Researchers at Berfelland University arrived at the same conclusion a few years ago, at a time when the age limit for buying alcohol was still sixteen. Moreover, parents often do not set clear boundaries. This is because they underestimate the problem and because they grew up in a free youth culture. The effect of signals from the immediate vicinity of young people is very strong and cannot be outweighed by the cooperation of popular artists or athletes in campaigns. Other research has shown, for example, that pop artists and athletes cannot substantially influence smoking behavior. Therefore, we have to conclude that a campaign such as 'No alcohol under eighteen' is as much use as sticking a plaster on a wooden leg.

A reasoning in which a network of arguments is used to argue that a proposed campaign will not succeed.

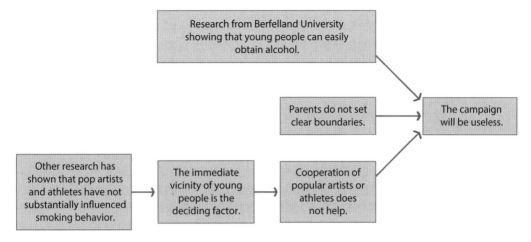

The example in a scheme. Note that the absence of lines between the three arguments for the position shows that these arguments are independent of each other.

3.3   Logical validity

Only when you have properly analyzed the structure of a reasoning can you make a well-founded judgment of its quality. Is the reasoning tenable? And is the conclusion correct? It is wrong to think that such judgments are always easy to make. Logic does teach us the difference between valid and invalid reasoning, but that does not say everything about the correctness of the conclusions. Logically valid reasoning with incorrect arguments can lead to both correct and incorrect conclusions, and the same is true for logically invalid reasoning with correct or incorrect arguments. The only thing that is certain is that the conclusion of a logically valid reasoning with correct arguments is always correct. See the following table.

	Reasoning is valid	**Reasoning is invalid**	
All arguments are correct	All birds have wings. Sparrows are birds. So, all sparrows have wings.	Birds have wings. Moose are no birds. So, moose don't have wings.	Birds have wings. Bees have wings. So, bees are birds.
	This conclusion is correct, as a valid reasoning with correct arguments must necessarily be.	This conclusion is correct.	This conclusion is incorrect.

	Reasoning is valid		**Reasoning is invalid**	
Not all arguments are correct	Birds have wings. Bees are birds. So, bees have wings.	Birds have wings. Moose are birds. So, moose have wings.	Sparrows do not have wings. Birds do not have wings. So, sparrows are birds.	Mammals do not have wings. Slugs do not have wings. So, slugs are mammals.
	This conclusion is correct.	This conclusion is incorrect.	This conclusion is correct.	This conclusion is incorrect.

Even if a reasoning is logically valid, that does not mean the conclusion is correct. And a logically invalid reasoning may also lead to a correct conclusion. But a valid reasoning with correct arguments always results in a correct conclusion.

What exactly do we mean by a valid reasoning? And what is an invalid reasoning? Below we will present four classical reasoning schemes. The first and the second are logically valid, the third and the fourth are not.

3.3.1   Two valid reasoning schemes

There are two valid reasoning schemes that are usually referred to by their Latin names: the *modus ponens* and the *modus tollens*.

Modus ponens
According to the modus ponens, confirmation of the cause leads to confirmation of the effect.

- A leads to B.
- A is the case.
- So: B is the case.

Logically valid — modus ponens.

When it rains, my garden gets wet. It rains. So, my garden gets wet.

Simple example of a modus ponens reasoning.

Modus tollens

According to the modus tollens, the denial of the effect leads to the denial of the cause. A modus tollens reasoning looks like this:

- A leads to B.
- B is not the case.
- So: A was not the case.

Logically valid — modus tollens.

When it rains, my garden gets wet. My garden is not wet. So, it did not rain.

Simple example of a modus tollens reasoning.

3.3.2 Two invalid reasoning schemes

Two reasoning schemes that are similar to the modus ponens and the modus tollens but that are logically invalid (and therefore called fallacies; see section 3.5), are *denying the antecedent* and *affirming the consequent*.

Denying the antecedent

In the case of denying the antecedent, denial of the cause (Latin: antecedent) wrongfully leads to the denial of the consequence (Latin: consequent).

- A leads to B.
- A is not the case.
- So: B is not the case.

Logically invalid — denying the antecedent.

When it rains, my garden gets wet. It did not rain. So, my garden is not wet.

Simple example of denying the antecedent. This reasoning is invalid. My garden can also get wet because I spray it with a garden hose.

Affirming the consequent

With affirming the consequent, the existence of the consequence (consequent) is wrongly taken as proof for the existence of the cause (antecedent).

- A leads to B.
- B is the case.
- So: A is the case.

Logically invalid — affirming the consequent.

When it rains, my garden gets wet. My garden is wet. So, it has rained.

Simple example of affirming the consequent. This reasoning is also invalid. Again, my garden can also get wet because I spray it with a garden hose.

3.4   Standard forms of argumentation

Here we will discuss a number of standard forms of argumentation: frequently used patterns of reasoning that are not always easy to trace back to one of the four reasoning schemes discussed in section 3.2.4. Each of these forms brings its own set of control questions that help you to make an adequate assessment of the reasoning and that may also help you to find arguments you can use to contradict your opponent in a debate. We distinguish four categories of forms of argumentation:
- *argumentation on the basis of regularity*: argumentation for prediction and explanation of facts (section 3.4.1);
- *argumentation on the basis of normative rules*: argumentation for opinions and encouragements (section 3.4.2);
- *pragmatic argumentation*: argumentation for means-end relations and comparison with alternatives (section 3.4.3);
- *unbound argumentation*: argumentation based on analogy, examples, and authority (section 3.4.4).

3.4.1   Argumentation on the basis of regularity

There are various situations in which you need to put forward arguments to support factual statements, especially when you are making a prediction about something that will happen or when you are trying to show on the basis of certain signals that something has happened: the reconstruction of a fact. In both situations, you appeal to the idea that there is a causal connection between two phenomena; a regularly occurring relation that means that one phenomenon (probably) causes or has caused the other phenomenon.

Predictions of facts

A predictive reasoning predicts the occurrence of an effect based on the cause. For example, mortgage interest rates have risen sharply in recent months (cause), so the housing market is set to collapse again (effect).

– A is the case.
– A (generally) leads to B.
– So: B is (probably) the case.

Standard form of predictive reasoning.

After every high-profile #MeToo case, we see an increase in the number of accusations. Female and male victims feel encouraged to reveal what happened to them. After the recent #MeToo case involving the famous actor John Smith, we will probably see another increase in the number of accusations.

Prediction of a fact.

– The famous actor John Smith was recently involved in a #MeToo case (A is the case).
– After every high-profile #MeToo case, there is an increase in the number of accusations (A generally leads to B).
– We may expect an increase in the number of #MeToo accusations (B will probably be the case).

The reasoning in a scheme.

You can assess the quality of a predictive reasoning with the help of the following control questions.
– Is A indeed the case?
– Have causes similar to A had effects similar to B in the past?
– Are there any other conditions for effect B to occur?
– Are there any special circumstances (in this case) that could mean effect B will not happen?

– Is A indeed the case?
  No, it was not. This is what happened: […].

- Have, in the past, causes similar to A always had effects similar to B?
  No, they have not. Compare: […].
- Are there any other conditions for effect B to occur?
  Yes, there are: […].
- Are there any special circumstances (in this case) which could mean that effect B will
  not happen?
  Yes, there are: […].

Possible counterarguments based on the control questions.

Reconstructions of facts

A reconstructive reasoning reverses the cause-effect perspective. In this case, the observation of a certain phenomenon is explained by the fact that the cause of that phenomenon must therefore have been present. In other words, a fact (in the past) is assumed to be true because it explains the phenomenon you are observing.

- A is the case.
- Phenomena such as A can be explained by B.
- So: B was the case.

Standard form of reconstructive reasoning.

Last week's information session on our study program attracted more people this year. So, the use of social media was successful.

The appropriate use of 'so' shows that this is a reasoning. The position ('The use of social media was successful') is supported by the implicit argument that this position is a plausible explanation for the observed fact ('There were many people during the information session').

- The information session attracted many people (A is the case).
- The increased interest can be explained by the use of social media (phenomena such as A can be explained by B).
- So: The use of social media was successful (B was the case).

The reasoning in a scheme.

The general control questions for reconstructive reasoning are as follows.
- Is it true that phenomenon A occurred in this case?
- Can you think of alternative explanations for phenomenon A?
- Did any other effects you could expect to follow from cause B also occur?

- Did A (the information session attracted many people) really occur in this case?
  No, it did not. This is what actually happened: [...].
- Are there alternative explanations for phenomenon A (the information session attracted many people)?
  Yes, there are such alternative explanations: [...].
- Did any other effects you may expect to follow from B (the use of social media was successful) also occur?
  No, they did not. This, for instance, did not happen: [...].

Possible counterarguments based on the control questions.

3.4.2 Argumentation on the basis of normative rules

Arguments about opinions or encouragements are not based on cause-effect relations but on normative rules. They do not state that something is the case but rather that we think about it in a certain way.

- *Opinions* (also called 'judgments' or 'evaluative positions') state whether something is good or beautiful, or bad or ugly. It thus concerns the evaluation of a phenomenon or an event. A reasoning that leads to an opinion therefore uses general evaluation rules.
- *Encouragements* (also: 'recommendations', 'advice', or 'deontic positions') concern whether or not something should be done. A reasoning that leads to an encouragement is based on rules of conduct. These can be laws or regulations, but also agreements or ethical standards.

Evaluative positions

Argumentation of evaluative positions is based on *evaluative rules* that express a certain opinion that another person does not necessarily share. Thus, when you assess the arguments for an evaluative position, you should critically consider not only factual knowledge but also taste, preferences, standards, and beliefs.

- A has characteristic(s) B.
- If phenomena or events have characteristic(s) B, evaluation C is appropriate.
- So: Evaluation C is appropriate for A.

Standard form of reasoning leading to an evaluative position.

The wonderful sales letter written by Nora Linde deserves everyone's admiration. The originality, the poetic style, and the good structure are unusually strong for a sales letter that concerns something as prosaic as a chipper.

Example of a reasoning based on an evaluation rule.

- The sales letter is original, poetic, and has a good structure (A has characteristics B).
- Originality, poetic style and a good structure make for an admirable sales letter (in the case of characteristics B, evaluation C applies).
- So: The sales letter is admirable (Evaluation C applies to A).

The reasoning in a scheme.

You can assess the acceptability of an evaluation reasoning on the basis of the following control questions.
- Does A indeed have characteristic(s) B?
- Is the evaluation rule (If B then C) acceptable?
- Are there perhaps other characteristics of A that should affect judgment C?

- Does A (the sales letter) indeed have characteristics B (it is original, poetic, and has a good structure)?
  No, it does not; for instance, A is not: [...].
- Is the evaluation rule acceptable: If B (if a letter is written in poetic style and has a good structure) then C (it is an admirable sales letter)?
  No, this rule is not acceptable, because: [...].
- Are there perhaps other characteristics of A (the sales letter) that should affect judgment C (it is an admirable sales letter)?
  Yes, there are: [...].

Possible counterarguments based on the control questions.

Deontic positions

Deontic positions are about questions such as: 'What should happen now?', 'What should we do or what should we not do?', 'What is or is not allowed?'. Deontic argumentation is based on *rules of conduct*. These can be formal laws or regulations but also agreements, customs, or norms and values. Deontic positions occur in different degrees.

- Something must be done (it is mandatory).
- Something may happen but it does not have to happen (it is allowed).
- Something must not happen (it is forbidden; it must be prevented).

- In situation X, A applies.
- If A applies, B must/may (not) happen.
- So: In situation X, B must/may (not) happen.

Standard form of reasoning based on rules of conduct.

The critical questions in this case are as follows.
– Is A indeed the case in situation X?
– Is the rule of conduct that is applied (if A then B) acceptable?
– Are there perhaps any special circumstances that make conclusion B less obvious?

In the last few months we hardly sold hardly any toys from our new collection. So, we will have to do market research.

Example of a reasoning based on a rule of conduct.

- Last week, we sold hardly any toys from the new collection (In situation X, A applies).
- If people do not buy toys from the new collection, we need to do market research (If A, then B must happen).
- Market research is needed (In situation X, B must happen).

The reasoning reduced to the standard form.

- Is A (last week, we sold hardly any toys from the new collection) indeed the case?
  No, it is not: [...].
- Is the rule of conduct that is applied—if A (people do not buy toys from the new collection) applies, then B (market research) must happen—acceptable?
  No, it is not, because: [...].
- Are there perhaps any special circumstances that make conclusion B (we need to do market research) less obvious?
  Yes, there are: [...].

Possible counterarguments based on the control questions.

3.4.3   Pragmatic argumentation

Discussions are often not limited to facts, opinions, or encouragements. They may contain several positions at the same time, particularly in the case of arguments about policy.

Means-end argumentation
A reasoning with a means-end argumentation argues that the end is desirable (an evaluation), that the means will lead to the intended end (a prediction), and that it would therefore be good to start using those means (an encouragement).

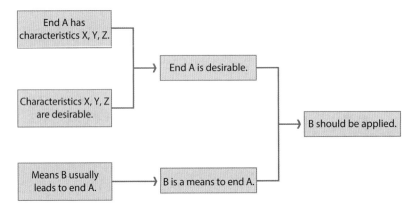

Standard form of means-end reasoning. The upper half of the argumentation leads to an opinion; the lower half leads to a factual statement. Opinion and fact together lead to an encouragement: the final (deontic) position. Note that the lines between the arguments and the positions show that the arguments belong together and that neither can be omitted.

It is very important that young people talk more about the risks of unsafe sex. When they see billboards about unsafe sex with puzzling texts and pictures, they will probably start a conversation about it. Therefore, our advice to the Ministry of Health is to place such billboards throughout the country.

Example of a means-end argumentation.

- It is desirable for young people to talk more about the risks of unsafe sex (A).
- Confronting young people with puzzling billboards on that subject leads to them talk more about it (B leads to A).
- Puzzling billboards about the risks of unsafe sex should be placed throughout the country (B).

The reasoning reduced to the standard form.

You can critically assess a means-end argumentation using the following control questions.

- Is end A really desirable? If necessary, divide this into sub-questions: Does the intended end really have characteristics X, Y, Z, and are those characteristics really desirable?
- Does means B usually lead to end A? Have similar means always led to similar ends in the past? Are there any specific circumstances that could prevent it from happening in this case?
- Are there any other side effects to the use of means B that renders it undesirable ('The cure is sometimes worse than the disease')?
- Are there any other means (alternatives) that are better than the recommended means B?

- Is end A (young people talk more about the risks of unsafe sex) really desirable?
  No, it is not, because: [...].
- Does means B (confronting young people with puzzling billboards on the risks of un-safe sex) really lead to end A (young people talk more about the risks of unsafe sex)?
  No, it does not, because: [...].
- Are there any other side effects to the use of means B (confronting young people with puzzling billboards on the risks of unsafe sex) that render it undesirable?
  Yes, there are: [...].
- Are there any other means (alternatives) that are better than the recommended means B (confronting young people with puzzling billboards on the risks of unsafe sex)?
  Yes, there are: [...].

Possible counterarguments based on the control questions.

Comparing alternatives

It is usually not enough to show that a particular means leads to an end, because there are often alternatives: means that may equally lead to the desired end. With pragmatic argumentation, therefore, you often have to demonstrate that the recommended means are better than the alternatives. You can do this:

– by demonstrating that alternative C is not effective: It does not (or not with certainty) lead to end A;
– by demonstrating that the recommended means B has serious advantages compared to alternative C;
– by demonstrating that alternative C has serious disadvantages compared to the means B.

Clearly, the last two possibilities mirror each other. When you are defending a position, you can choose either option.

Different criteria may play a role when you are comparing alternatives:

– *effectiveness criteria*: The recommended means B leads to a higher chance of achieving end A than the alternative means C;
– *efficiency criteria*: The recommended means B requires less time, money, or effort than the alternative means C;
– *ethical criteria*: There are certain ethical objections to alternative C, and there are no such ethical objections to the recommended means B;
– *undesirable side effects*: The alternative means C has certain undesirable consequences (for humans, animals, the environment, and so on) that the recommended means B does not have.

You can also use these criteria to check whether a comparison of alternatives in an argumentation is correct.

I propose to cancel the two-year teacher training at universities for students who have obtained their BA. It is much better if students with a BA diploma who want to become teachers first obtain an ordinary MA diploma in their own field, and then take teacher training for a year. This way, we can leave the existing MA courses as they are, and we only need to worry about restructuring the one-year teacher training courses. That will be enough work in itself. Moreover, we know from experience that students do not like it when they have to follow a two-year program that results in a single diploma, especially when it concerns a diploma that is only really useful if you want to become a teacher. If we want more university students to choose the teaching profession, we would do well to take their preference seriously.

Example of comparison with alternatives.

- We want more university students to choose to become academically schooled teachers (end A).
- The combination of a one-year MA program followed by a one-year teacher training program (means B) increases the chance that university students will choose to become academically trained teachers (end A) more than a two-year integrated teacher training program (alternative C).
- It takes less time and effort to restructure the one-year teacher training system (means B) than to start restructuring the two-year teacher training system (alternative C).

The reasoning reduced to the standard form.

- Is end A (more university students who choose to become academically schooled teachers) really desirable?
  No, it is not, because: […].
- Does the recommended means B (a one-year MA program followed by a one-year teacher training program) lead to a greater chance of achieving end A (more university students who choose to become academically schooled teachers) than the alternative means C (a two-year integrated teacher training program)?
  No, it does not, because: […].
- Does the recommended means B (a one-year MA program followed by a one-year teacher training program) take less time, money, or effort than the alternative means C (a two-year integrated teacher training program)?
  No, it does not, because: […].
- Are there ethical objections to the alternative means C (a two-year integrated teacher training program) that do not apply to the recommended means B (a one-year MA program followed by a one-year teacher training program)?
  No, there are not, because […].
- Does the alternative means C (a two-year integrated teacher training program) have undesirable consequences that the recommended means B (a one-year MA program followed by a one-year teacher training program) does not have?
  No, it does not, because […].

Possible counterarguments based on the control questions.

3.4.4 Unbound argumentation

In addition to forms of argumentation that are linked to a particular type of position (predictions or factual statements; opinions and encouragements; advice about policy), there are also some reasoning patterns that can be used for all of these types of positions. We will discuss these patterns in this section.

Analogy argumentation
A phenomenon or a situation can be compared to something similar. By doing so, senders try to show that what applies to one case also applies to another. In other words, they show that the two phenomena or situations are so similar that in both cases the conclusion must also be the same. This argumentation is called *argumentation on the basis of analogy* or *comparison argumentation.*

- A has characteristics X, Y, Z.
- B also has characteristics X, Y, Z.
- So: B resembles A (in relevant respects).
- C is the case for A.
- Therefore, C must also be the case for B.

Standard form of argumentation on the basis of analogy. The first two elements are in practice often left implicit.

I think it is an excellent idea of the Board of Berfelland University that students need to have obtained a certain number of credits in order to be allowed to continue their studies. I also believe that the requirement should be at 50 credits. After all, the University of New Aduard uses the same measure and both staff and students consider it completely normal.

Example of an analogy argumentation.

You can critically assess an analogy argumentation using the following control questions.
- Does B really resemble A (do A and B indeed have relevant characteristics in common)?
- Is C really the case for A?
- Is there a difference between A and B that is important in this particular case?

- Does B (Berfelland University) really resemble A (the University of New Aduard)?
  No, it does not, because: [...].
- Is C (both staff and students consider it as normal that students need a certain number of credits to continue their studies) really the case for A (the University of New Aduard)?
  No, it is not, because: [...].
- Is there a difference between A (the University of New Aduard) and B (Berfelland University) that is important in this particular case?
  Yes, there is: [...].

Possible counterarguments based on the control questions.

Example argumentation

Example argumentation is mostly useful for more or less general positions that concern a particular set or category of phenomena or events. The position is then supported by presenting one or more of these phenomena or events and identifying some of their characteristics. The sender then claims or suggests that those characteristics apply to the whole category.

- Characteristic A applies to X, Y, Z.
- X, Y, Z are representative examples of category B.
- So: Characteristic A applies to everything concluded in category B.

Standard form of example argumentation.

The National Educational Inspection identified major problems with three of our programs. These programs are mainly taught by staff members who were educated at the University of New Aduard. Apparently, graduates of the University of New Aduard are not equipped to teach at our university.

Example of example argumentation.

You can critically assess an example argumentation by asking the following control questions.
- Is A really the case for all examples mentioned: X, Y, and Z?
- Are X, Y, and Z representative examples of category B? (This is particularly important when only a few examples are given and B is a heterogeneous category of phenomena or events.)

- Is A (there are major problems) really the case for all examples mentioned (three programs mainly taught by staff educated at the University of New Aduard)?
  No, it is not, because: [...].
- Are the examples (these three programs) representative of B (all programs mainly taught by staff educated at the University of New Aduard)?
  No, they are not, because: [...].

Possible counterarguments based on the control questions.

Authority argumentation

Most of the knowledge we have, as well as many of our opinions and preferences, are not based on our own direct observation. Instead, they are based on statements by others whom we consider to be authorities to some extent, such as our parents, teachers, colleagues, journalists, or experts in a specific field.

Authorities can also play an important role in the argumentation of positions. If we think someone is sufficiently credible, we also tend to adopt their views: not only facts but also opinions or encouragements.

- Person (source) A claims that B is correct.
- Person A is credible.
- So: B is right.

Standard form of authority argumentation.

As mentioned in a recent article by three co-authors, the so-called *Extended Parallel Process Model* (EPPM) is a widely accepted theory that explains and predicts the effects of fear appeals: frightening messages in health communication.

Example of authority argumentation.

The quality of authority argumentation depends on the credibility of the source. The following control questions can help you to make a critical assessment.
-   Is it clear who source A is?
-   Did source A indeed take position B?
-   Does source A have expertise in the field of position B?
-   Is source A unbiased regarding position B?

– Is it clear who source A (three co-authors) is?

No, it is not.

– Did source A (three co-authors) indeed take position B (the EPPM is a widely accepted theory about fear appeals)?

No, they did not [...].

– Does source A (three co-authors) have expertise in the field of position B (the EPPM is a widely accepted theory about fear appeals)?

No, they do not, because: [...].

– Is source A (three co-authors) unbiased regarding position B (the EPPM is a widely accepted theory about fear appeals)?

No, they are not, because: [...].

Possible counterarguments based on the control questions.

3.5 Fallacies

In an ideal world, writers and speakers who try to convince others of their position would only use arguments that all parties consider reasonable. But in reality, this is not always the case. After all, someone who presents an argument has certain interests in mind. Writers and speakers who advertise a product or who try to convince others of their political view will, given their own interests, tend to steer the communication in a direction that is favorable to themselves without becoming unreasonable. This is called *strategic maneuvering.* In itself, there is nothing wrong with this. However, if in strategic maneuvering effectiveness becomes too prominent, it can lead to derailment of the argumentation. Sound arguments are then replaced by *fallacies*: argumentation that critical analysis can reveal to be unreasonable .

It is important that you are able to recognize fallacies and to distinguish them from reasonable arguments. Denying the antecedent and affirming the consequent—the classic invalid reasoning schemes discussed in section 3.3.2—are fallacies. We also speak of a fallacy if the answer to one or more of the control questions for a standard form of argumentation is 'no'. If, for example, you cannot affirm that a presented authority really has expertise in the field of the position that is taken (one of the control questions for an authority argumentation; see section 3.4.4), then you are dealing with a fallacy.

In this section we will discuss some other examples of fallacies. It is important to realize that fallacies are often presented in well-chosen formulations, which try to carry receivers along with the argument and may thus make them less critical. Such formulations will be discussed in section 4.4.

3.5.1 Evading or shifting the burden of proof

In section 3.1.1, we discussed the situations in which you have to support your position with arguments; in other words, where you have the burden of proof. Clever writers and speakers sometimes try to avoid this by suggesting that they do not have the burden of proof and that their position can therefore be unquestioningly accepted. This fallacy occurs in different forms.

–   The position is presented as self-evident, as if it is not open for discussion. The sender uses phrases such as 'It goes without saying that […]' or 'No sensible person doubts that […]'.

–   The sender guarantees the audience that his or her position is correct: 'You can rest assured that […]'. The sender thus presents himself or herself as an authority in the field. If the sender indeed is an expert, and if the control questions for this type of argumentation can be answered satisfactorily (see section 3.4.4), the sender is justified in doing so. But presenting oneself as an authority in the field can also be used as a rhetorical device that obscures the truth. Then it is a fallacy.

–   A third version is shifting the burden of proof to the other party; the one who doubts the position needs to prove why it is wrong. This mostly happens in discussions: 'I think we should implement this measure. If you disagree, tell me what is wrong with it.'

Punishments for serious crimes are clearly not severe enough. The vast majority of the population agrees on that. I invite anyone who thinks differently to explain how you can defend that murderers in our country are on average only imprisoned for six years, and those who have committed manslaughter only three years and four months.

Evading and shifting the burden of proof.

3.5.2 Simplifying the issue

Sometimes a writer or speaker misuses the charm of simplicity to suggest that a conclusion is very easy to draw, thereby portraying any further discussion as nitpicking. Simplification of the issue that is being argued is especially prevalent in the run-up to elections. By reducing complex problems to black-and-white issues, politicians can suggest that they are clear and decisive, in contrast to their opponents.

> The amount of traffic jams in our country is increasing every year, as is the length of the average traffic jam. It is clear what we need to do. If there is no road to drive on, there will also be fewer cars. A substantial increase in taxation, leading to higher car and fuel prices, is the only real solution. That may be painful for the ardent fans of this holy cow, but ultimately, we have no other choice.

The situation and the solution are presented in a very simple way, in spite of the complexity of the traffic problem that has been under discussion for many years. Many measures have already been taken (more asphalt, better public transport, rush-hour lanes), and these have had a real impact. The image that the sender creates of a growing problem is therefore not correct. The same applies to the image of the proposed measure as a very easy solution. It is not easy—if at all desirable—to substantially raise taxes without damaging the economy.

3.5.3   Distorting the other's reasoning

During a discussion or argument, one party may sometimes distort the arguments and positions of the other party to such an extent that they become completely different and easy to attack or refute. This form of argumentation is also called the *straw man's fallacy*. Sometimes the distortion takes the form of *generalization*. The other is then credited with a much more general position than what he or she actually proclaimed.

> A: Our country's asylum policy is less humane than we often think. Recent events reminded us of that. First, there was the deportation of underage asylum seekers, and then there was the fire at the detention center in our main airport. Clearly, our government could be more lenient by allowing minors to stay here for humanitarian reasons. And about the asylum seekers who survived the fire: You cannot simply send them back, as our government has done.
>
> B: What you are saying is that we should just allow everyone who is sick or sad to stay in our country. Then there will be no end in sight. Contrary to what you think, we cannot let half the world in.

Fragment from a debate in which B creates a straw man. B distorts A's reasoning by attributing a much more general position to A than A actually put forward.

Key points

- Argumentation involves a position (a factual statement, an opinion, or an encouragement) that is supported by one or more arguments. Argumentation is especially necessary when two parties each have a different view on a particular issue. Party A can then use argumentation to try to motivate party B or neutral observers to adopt A's position.
- Argumentation is the most democratic means of conducting a discussion. In a rational debate, everyone is equal: He or she who brings forward the best arguments, wins the debate. No matter how important emotions are, when it comes to forming opinions and making decisions, we do not want to be carried away by them. We prefer to use our common sense to reasonably determine what we find convincing and what we find implausible.

Analysis of the structure
You can identify a reasoning by looking at the situation ('Is there a burden of proof?') and at signal words and phrases. When in doubt, you can try to add signal words such as 'because' and 'therefore' and check whether this results in a sensible passage that does justice to the rest of the text. For a full understanding of the reasoning, you should add elements that are left implicit, consisting of:
- one or more statements or facts that are not disputed, or
- a general rule that is invoked, or
- the position that needs to be supported.

We distinguish four basic structures that describe the relationship between arguments and the position:
- single argument: one argument that supports the position;
- convergent arguments: two or more arguments that separately support the position;
- linked arguments: two or more arguments that are all necessary to prove the position;
- serial argumentation: arguments that support a position are in turn supported by new arguments.

In practice, these basic structures are often combined into a network of reasoning that can sometimes become complex.

Valid and invalid reasoning

The difference between logically valid and logically invalid reasoning is important. We distinguish four well-known reasoning schemes.

- Two of those reasoning schemes are logically valid: the modus ponens and the modus tollens.
- Two other reasoning schemes are logically invalid: denying the antecedent and affirming the consequent.

Standard forms of argumentation

- Standard forms of argumentation are patterns of reasoning that are often used. Each comes with a set of control questions that can help you form an adequate assessment of the reasoning. The control questions always concern the correctness of the presented facts and the general rule on which the reasoning relies.
- In the case of a prediction of facts, the general rule concerns a causal relationship. It is important that this relationship is valid. Is there perhaps an exception in the given situation?
- In the case of an explanation of facts, the general rule is also a causal relationship. It is then important to consider whether you can find another possible cause of the given fact.
- An evaluative position (an opinion) invokes an evaluation rule. In this case, you should ask whether that rule is generally accepted or whether this particular case presents an exception to the rule.
- A deontic decision (something should be done or something should *not* be done) appeals to a rule of conduct. Check whether this rule is generally accepted and applies in the given case, and whether the recommended behavior does not have any negative side effects.
- Pragmatic argumentation recommends a means for achieving a particular end. For a critical evaluation, assess whether the end is desirable, whether the means will lead to that end, and whether there are no alternative means that are more effective, efficient, or attractive. In addition, you should check whether the recommended means is ethically acceptable.
- Analogy argumentation argues that something that applies to one case must also apply to the other (comparable) case. As a critical evaluator, you should check whether the cases or situations that are being compared are sufficiently similar, and whether any differences are relevant in the given situation.

- Example argumentation uses one or more examples to make a general statement or rule plausible. In this case, you should determine whether there are sufficient examples and whether they are representative in the given situation.
- Authority argumentation uses a statement by an expert to support a position. To critically asses this, verify that the authority is indeed an expert, that the authority has really made the statement (in a relevant context), and that the authority is unbiased.

Fallacies

If writers or speakers consider effectiveness to be more important than reasonableness in their attempts to persuade others, this can result in a fallacy: argumentation that critical analysis reveals to be unreasonable. Examples are:
- evading or shifting the burden of proof;
- simplifying the argumentation;
- distorting the other's reasoning.

Assignments

Assignment 1: Positions, arguments, and structure

Purpose of the assignment
You will practice recognizing positions and arguments as well as the structure of the arguments.

Subject matter
Section 3.2

Tasks
Fragments A and B below contain different positions and arguments.
1   For each fragment, check what the positions and arguments are.
2   Display the structure of each reasoning in a diagram such as presented in section 3.2.4.
3   For each fragment, indicate whether it concerns a single argument, convergent arguments, linked arguments, or serial argumentation.

Fragment A
The Development and Research Department has done almost nothing in terms of product development for the last six months. Constant attention to product development is necessary for every company. Otherwise we will unavoidably lose to our competitors.

Fragment B
We need to make it clear to parents that they should not allow their children to watch violent programs. Last week, four children from the fifth grade got into a fight with each other after watching *Teenage Mutant Ninja Turtles IX* the night before. Violence on television has a negative impact on small children.

Assignment 2: Logical validity

Purpose of the assignment
You will practice recognizing whether a reasoning is logically valid.

Subject matter
Section 3.3

Tasks
Examine the following text fragment.
1   Which of the four classical reasoning schemes is this?
2   Is this a valid or an invalid reasoning?

Fragment
In recent years, management was always very silent prior to the publication of poor quarterly figures. They seemed to agree that, before telling us the bad news, they would say nothing, so we would remain calm. The figures for the fourth quarter will be announced soon and we have heard nothing yet from the management. There's no doubt about it: The new figures are bad again.

Assignment 3: Fallacies

Purpose of the assignment
You will practice recognizing fallacies, and you will be able to name them.

Subject matter
Section 3.5

Task
For each of the following fragments, identify which type of fallacy is being used.

Fragment A
Smoking cigarettes on streets nearby this hospital should be forbidden. Most staff members agree on that. People who feel differently cannot be taken seriously. They just want to maintain their own liberty to do as they wish at the cost of being a severe health threat to others.

Fragment B
Recently a website was launched that offers help to people who want to commit suicide. According to the founders, providing help to someone who wants to commit suicide will in many cases prevent them from doing so. That is an interesting proposition. They evidently want anyone who feels confused, depressed, or otherwise unhappy to seek help with suicide because this will lead to fewer victims. That is a completely ridiculous idea, of course.

4 Style

◄ *Girl in a large hat*, Caesar Boëtius van Everdingen, circa 1645-circa 1650. The half figure of a young woman stands against a light sky in bright sunlight. She is wearing a hat with a very wide brim, woven from stripes of pink and white cloth. This casts a shadow over the top half of her face; her eyes, beneath the hat's shade, are directed at the viewer. She wears a white satin robe, leaving the shoulder bare. A pink ribbon falls from the hat onto her bare shoulder, another wider ribbon of the same color serves as a belt. The girl is holding up with both arms a basket filled with violet plums. The horizon is quite low, so at the bottom of the picture only the tops of trees are visible.

Like the girl's hat that is both practical and beautiful, the stylistic choices you make as a writer may strengthen and embellish your text by making it more accessible, trustworthy and more pleasant to read.

The power of effective style choices

What Democrats Don't Get About the South

There is no accent quite like the Southern accent, and there is no Southern accent quite like the Southern politician's. Spend any time in the South—especially in the rapidly growing suburban and ex-urban South—and you'll hear the drawl. The men sound just a tiny bit folksier, as if your doctor would be just as comfortable plowing a field as he would be reading an X-ray. The women just sound nice, so that the same words you hear in daily life across the U.S. somehow come off kinder and gentler.

But there is nothing—absolutely nothing—subtle about the Southern politician's accent. No sir. To hear the Southern politician talk is to hear the backwoods come to the big city. Their past profession doesn't matter. Neither does their upbringing. There's something about runnin' for office in the South that exaggerates that drawl and drops those g's.

At its heart, Southern politics is cultural politics. That's because Southern politics isn't just about the South as it is—representing its concrete economic and religious inter-ests, for example—it's also about the South as it sees itself. The idea of the South is very important to the people of the South, and it has been for a very long time.

In 2018, the South sees itself as economically advanced but culturally traditional. It's proud of its industry and technology, but it's also proud of its faith and its families. The majority of the people don't hunt or fish or farm, but they feel connected to people who do. A Tennessee lawyer may never leave a paved road, but he'll drive a truck that can haul hay. Even people who don't own guns value the South's gun culture. They may not have a firearm, but they will not tolerate a government that restricts their ability to defend themselves.

That's the idea of the South in 2018. Southerners love God. They respect the traditions of faith and family—including manners and respect for elders. Southerners are connected to the land. They despise elitism. They're suspicious of government but not averse to its help. And they are definitely proud of their region and its way of life—even if its day-to-day reality is no longer so distinct.

Ideologically, it's a mess. Culturally, it's coherent […].

French, a lifelong Southerner, is a senior writer for National Review and a former major in the U.S. Army reserve.

Source: French (2018).[3]

Just as one can recognize a tune as belonging to a certain artist, you can hear the voice of the writer, David French, in this article published in *Time* (a magazine from the U.S.). You can feel that his heart is in the subject matter, and this actually is underscored by the subscript at the end of the article, identifying him as a lifelong Southerner. So, not only does he start building an argument for the understanding that politicians should show for the Southern voter, but by making the right style choices he creates a certain emotional layer in the text that actually strengthens his argument. How does he achieve this?

– First of all by engaging the reader '([…] and you'll hear the drawl')

– By choosing for a less formal, almost conversational style ('No sir')

– By using plain language, even though he may be arguing about rather complex abstract concepts, such as the typical Southern spirit and identity

– By using examples and clear oppositions to make his point ('the South sees itself as economically advanced **but** culturally traditional. It's proud of its industry and technology, **but** it's also proud of its faith and its families. The majority of the people don't hunt or fish or farm, **but** they feel connected to people who do. A Tennessee lawyer may never leave a paved road, **but** he'll drive a truck that can haul hay')

– By keeping it lively and retaining the attention of the reader, using—among other strategies—humor to get the message across ('There's something about runnin' for office in the South that exaggerates that drawl and drops those g's')

And these are only a few of the comments that one could make about this stylistically rich text.

3   French, D. (2018, July 26). *What democrats don't get about the South*. Retrieved from http://time.com/5349531/democrats-dont-get-the-south/

Style is about a distinctive, specific way in which things are done: the way someone dresses, how a house is furnished, how a building is designed, or how writers express themselves in a text. Style provides recognition. Tight and minimalist, baroque and colorful, or formal and informal: A style can fit perfectly into an environment or contrast with it. Choosing a certain style—and writing text is mainly about words and phrasing—therefore also means choosing a certain effect. For every writer (and speaker, of course) who wants to achieve his or her goal, aligning the style to the audience and the situation is essential. There are several reasons for this.

- A good style makes sure the message gets across, without readers wasting valuable time deciphering opaque prose.
- Style inspires confidence. If readers see that a writer attaches importance to consistency and precision in his or her text, they will be confident that the writer also attaches such values even to subjects that are not so easily understood by the readers.
- Style makes the world a little more beautiful. A sharp sentence, striking imagery, humorous note, or elegant phrase makes reading a pleasure for any reader. That may seem like an impractical consideration, but the trick is to hold on to the reader's attention and focus on the content of your message. An effective style entails the effective use of words to involve the reader—as in a conversation—in a subject. It is about *how* you present your content.

This chapter provides a number of tools for style analysis and writing texts in a style that suits your type of text, goal, and audience. We will discuss the issue of defining style and the dimensions associated with writing style (section 4.1). We will then look at how to write texts with a primary informative goal (section 4.2), with a primary instructional goal (section 4.3), with a primary persuasive goal (section 4.4), and with a primary motivational/affective goal (section 4.5). Note, however, that the suitability of the style elements discussed in these sections is often not limited to a single text goal, so that there will almost necessarily be an overlap between the different sections, with issues discussed in one also being applicable to others. For example, plain language is important in informative texts but also in texts with an instructive or persuasive goal. And an interesting style can serve not only a motivating purpose but also a persuasive goal. That is why some techniques are examined in several sections.

4.1   Formal versus informal style

It is difficult if not impossible to define style, as the voluminous literature on the topic makes clear. Apart from referring to the 'how' of presenting your content, as in the introduction above, a more productive strategy might be to refer to dimensions of style such as formal versus informal style, plain vs difficult style, lively vs heavy, bureaucratic style, informative vs persuasive style, and so on. What then makes it even more complex is that these dimensions also have a certain unidirectional overlap: The more formal a style, the more difficult it will be; the more informal a style, the more lively it will be; the most persuasive style is quite often not too difficult or too formal, and so on.

The difference between a formal and an informal style can best be illustrated by the difference in the following text fragments. The examples show the different versions of a paragraph from a document on the procedure for the payment of funds.

- Should the application form be submitted within ten days of receipt, it would be attempted to ensure that no delays would occur in the pay-out procedure thereof.
- Should you submit the application form within ten days of receipt, we will ensure that no delays occur in the pay-out procedure.
- If you submit your application form within ten days of receiving it, we will make sure that the money is paid out as soon as possible.
- Submit your application in time, and we pay out in a flash.

The first example is highly formal and also has a higher degree of difficulty. The examples then become less formal and less difficult, more lively and reader-orientated as you move down the list, with the last one clearly very informal (almost conversational) and in plain language.

The formality of a text can best be described as the distance between the writer and the reader: In a highly formal text, the distance between the writer and the reader is considerable; the text also has a stronger focus on the topic and the language is more difficult. In a highly informal text, the distance between the writer and the reader is small; the text also has a stronger focus on the reader and it is written in plain (often conversational) language. The question of formality or distance in a text is related to particular grammatical variables.

- The use of more formal, often old-fashioned or archaic words and phrases such as 'thus' (as opposed to 'so'), 'seeing that' (as opposed to 'since' or 'because'), 'endeavor' (as opposed to 'try'); 'at all times' (as opposed to 'always'); 'take into account' (as opposed to 'think about').
- The use of some form of address (for instance by using a person's name when directly addressing the particular person), such as the second-person personal

pronoun 'you' and its variants in some of the examples above, or the direct form of address in a letter.
–   The use of the passive voice in more formal texts, as opposed to the use of the active voice in more informal texts (see section 4.2.2)

   –   The service is offered so people can let their money work harder.
   –   We offer the service so people can let their money work harder.

The first sentence is the more formal of the pair, written in the passive voice. The second sentence is more informal because of the use of the active voice.

Formal texts are also characterized by jargon (see section 4.2.1) and longer and more complex sentences (see section 4.2.3).

4.2   Difficulty and the need for plain language

Usually you want to effectively communicate the actual content of the message (the matter side) to your target audience. That can go wrong in three ways.
–   *Misunderstanding.* The reader or listener thinks that he or she understands the content, but he or she misunderstands it; something else is meant.
–   *Difficulty.* The reader or listener must make an unnecessary effort to understand the text.
–   *Incomprehension.* The reader or listener has no idea what is meant.

In fact, many of the reasons why a text is incomprehensible can be traced back to one main problem: the so-called 'curse of knowledge'. Writers usually do not realize how much more they know about their subject than readers. They are so familiar with the subject and find many aspects of it so self-evident that it does not even occur to them to elaborate on those aspects, with all the consequences that might entail: Readers cannot create a representation of the content that the writer wants to convey in a crystal-clear way.
   How can you escape the curse of knowledge as a writer? The age-old advice 'Always keep the reader in mind' is less effective than it seems. After all, trying to stand in someone else's shoes does not mean that it will automatically become clear what that person does and does not know about a certain subject. But it is a good start to try and get the reader to look over your shoulder. Always keep in mind that your readers know much less about your subject than you think they know.

We will discuss four specific issues that are important in terms of improving comprehensibility. First, your choice of words is crucial. We then discuss three sentence structures that may influence comprehensibility: the passive voice, syntactically complex sentences, and the stacking of prepositional phrases.

4.2.1 Word Choice

Is a text or presentation intended for experts in a particular field or for lay people? The answer to this question determines what is plain language in the context of your text. An extreme degree of simplicity is not necessary in most professional texts. Too simple a language can even lead to you not being taken seriously or to the target group feeling patronized. For example, official documents require the use of formal language, so a very informal level of communication and corresponding word choice would be inappropriate. And technical terms are indispensable in technical reports. If you try to avoid or exaggerate them, you suggest a lack of expertise on the part of the reader. Your word choice can lead to incomprehension for various reasons:

- *a high level of 'clever' words or phrases:* words that sound learned and are often used to impress the reader, such as 'phenomenal' (as opposed to 'exceptional'), 'adroit' (as opposed to 'tactful'), 'insinuate' (as opposed to 'hint'), and so on.
- *a high level of 'officialese' or jargon*: words that sound more important than is actually necessary in the context; more often than not, these word choices simply try to impress the reader at the cost of the comprehension of the text (see section 1.3);
- *technical terms*: terminology that is known only to a specific public ('turbo-supercharger', 'papaveraceous', 'deictic'); for an audience that is not among the insiders, it is better to use simpler terminology; when a technical term is absolutely necessary, it might be a good idea to explain this term briefly and clearly;
- *secret language*: non-technical words, phrases, and abbreviations that are often used only within a certain group but are unknown outside that group;
- *unusual, self-conceived compositions* whose meaning cannot be directly deduced by readers or listeners from their constituent parts;
- *abstract and vague words*: words whose meaning everyone knows but that are so general that it is not clear what they mean in this context;
- *referential words or phrases* where it is not exactly clear what they refer to in the rest of the sentence or text; an accumulation of references sometimes presents readers or recipients with an insoluble puzzle.

Difficult wording	What is the problem?	Possible solution
The editorial team of the Journal would like to insist that authors state the level of significance applicable in their articles.	'Insist' may be too strong a word and an example of so-called 'officialese', with an unnecessary level of formality. 'Level of significance' is an example of jargon, but in this case it is appropriate.	The editorial team of the Journal requires authors to state the level of significance applicable in their articles.
For retail, good complaint management is of vital importance.	Marketing jargon that should not be used outside the world of marketing.	For the retail sector, a good complaints system is of vital importance.
It might be a good idea to adopt a 'zipping' policy at those traffic nodes where a double lane becomes a single lane.	Although we may understand the verb 'zip' and the noun 'policy', a composition such as zipping policy will not be clear in the particular context.	Where a double lane becomes a single lane, a 'zipping' policy might be a good idea: Motorists in the double lanes take turns to enter the single lane, just like the fastening technique in a zip.
[...] i.t.o. the policy this should not happen.	The use of an unusual abbreviation. The writer uses a kind of shorthand not clear to the average reader.	[...] in terms of the policy this should not happen.
There are a number of pitfalls that SMEs should avoid.	The abbreviation SMEs for small and medium enterprises may be known to specialists in economics but not necessarily to the layperson.	There are a number of pitfalls that small and medium enterprises (SMEs) should avoid.
Should the application form be submitted within ten days of receipt, it would be attempted to ensure that no delays would occur in the pay-out procedure thereof.	This sentence is very formal and creates a lot of distance between writer and reader. It has an official wordiness through the use of words and phrases such as 'be attempted to ensure' and 'thereof'.	If you submit your application form within ten days of receiving it, we will make sure that your money is paid out as soon as possible. Or perhaps even better: Submit your application in time, and we pay out in a flash.

Difficult wording	What is the problem?	Possible solution
Some groups in our society insist on discussing their elementary democratic rights.	Phrases such as 'some groups' and 'elementary democratic rights' are so vague that the statement becomes almost nonsensical.	People in our society who have been politically and economically disadvantaged insist on discussing elementary democratic rights such as the right to free speech and the right to property.
The chairman of the board criticized the decision of the CEO. He had a point, however.	The reference of the pronoun 'he' is not clear, since it can refer to both 'the chairman of the board' and 'the CEO'.	Though the director had a point, the chairman of the board insisted on criticizing the decision.

Examples of difficult wording influencing the level of understanding and readability.

4.2.2 Passive or active

The passive voice is recognizable by a 'grammatical move': the object in the active voice is elevated to the position of the subject, with the original subject of the corresponding active sentence being demoted in a prepositional phrase, or deleted. The passive voice is also characterized by the verbal phrase 'be + past participle'. The following example demonstrates this grammatical move:

Active voice:

> The director (subject) informed the department (direct object) of the new developments.

Passive voice:

> The department (passive subject) was informed ('be + past participle') by the director (original subject demoted in prepositional phrase) of the new developments.

or:

> The department was informed of the new developments. (the so-called agentless passive, with the original active subject—also referred to as the agent—deleted)

A text formulated mostly in the active voice would normally be easier to read and have a less formal or official character. This follows from the fact that sentences in the active voice are more direct and concise and have a more human look and feel because of the presence of the agents (most of which are human) in the subjects of the sentences. The passive voice, on the other hand, would normally be associated with more formal texts (scientific or bureaucratic texts being clear examples). But that does not mean that the passive voice should always be avoided. On the contrary, the passive voice can be very effective. However, a warning is called for: Three or more sentences in a row in the passive voice would quickly make the text detached and indirect, often more cumbersome and less concise than an active one, and also more difficult to process. Even worse, the passive voice often offers opportunities to hide, confuse, or obfuscate information. That may be useful for a writer with a hidden agenda, but it is annoying for the reader who wants to know what the writer is getting at. The passive voice may be useful:

– *to avoid an impolite or painful direct contact with the reader*: 'Unsolicited remarks are sometimes made about women [by men]'. You can easily omit the actor 'men' from this sentence, softening the blow, so to speak. This is sometimes useful for tactical reasons. In other situations, however, omissions are quickly made at the expense of the precision of the text. If precision is desired, choose an active formulation.

– *to leave open the question of who is responsible for what*: 'Financial cover will be sought'. You can apply the passive voice if you cannot or do not want to say who is responsible for what, or if the reader or listener does not need to know: 'Tickets will be sent to you next week'.

– *if you need to be vague about the content, in so doing leaving yourself with an escape route, or distancing yourself from the content*: 'She was considered to be the candidate with the best papers for the presidency of the US'. If you use the passive voice here, you can easily distance yourself from this opinion later. In an active variant such as 'I found her the candidate with the best papers for the presidency of the US', you have no escape route since you make it clear that this is your own opinion.

– *to ensure coherence with a previous sentence*: With a passive voice, you can create a link with the previous sentence by elevating the object to the first sentence position: 'According to the majority, the contribution of the opposition was nothing more than a useless motion. The motion was therefore voted down by the governing party.' The first sentence ends with a reference to 'the motion' and the first words of next sentence then lead with a reference to the very same 'motion', improving the coherence between the two sentences.

Active voice or passive voice?	Comments
Employees are required to adapt to the 24-hour economy.	By using the passive voice, the question remains as to who exactly requires adaptation. Moreover, the sentence shows a certain distance. The writer leaves it unsaid whether he or she agrees with the requirement. The wording is not optimally precise for the reader and the tone is detached.
One requires that employees adapt to the 24-hour economy.	Removal of the passive voice does not guarantee that it is clear who is responsible and whether the author agrees. Compared to the passive version of this sentence, the information is not more precise or less detached.
Employees are required to adapt to the 24-hour economy by the employers.	By adding the agent ('the employers') in the preposition phrase with 'by', the writer ensures that it is clear who is requiring the employees to make the adjustment. However, the passive wording makes the sentence cumbersome.
Employers require employees to adapt to the 24-hour economy.	This variant in the active voice is concise and clear.

The nuances in using different variants of the active or passive voice.

4.2.3 Complex sentences

A writer striving for maximum comprehension and readability will always carefully consider the length and complexity of his or her sentences. The following example illustrates the point:

There is a general perception that high interest rates are bad for the consumer, but this is not necessarily the case, because, although it is true that debt-ridden consumers will suffer when the interest rates go up, those consumers with no debts, but rather huge amounts of savings and other investments, will benefit from high interest rates, as they will receive higher returns.

The complexity of this sentence can simply be ascribed to its length, but in essence it is its structural complexity that adds to the difficulty of the sentence. The structural complexity of the sentence is partly due to the piling-up of sentences within a complex construction of co-ordination, which in turn is complicated even more by the presence of subordinate clauses. See the following fragment from the example:

There is a general perception [start of a subordinate clause:] that high interest rates are bad for the consumer [start of a coordinate clause:], but this is not necessarily the case [...]

The solution would be to split the sentence into two or more less complex sentences, improving the readability and comprehension of the message:

There is a general perception that high interest rates are bad for the consumer, but this is not necessarily the case. It may be true that debt-ridden consumers will suffer when the interest rates go up. However, those consumers with rather huge amounts of savings and other investments will benefit from high interest rates, as they will receive higher returns, especially if they have no debts.

In this case, the sentences are shorter, even though they still contain examples of coordination or subordination. This split into shorter, less complex sentences makes it easier to process the text fragment.

4.2.4 Prepositional phrases

Prepositions ('in', 'on', 'before', 'after', and so on) form the 'cement' between different parts of the sentence. They are of great importance for coherence and therefore for comprehensibility. In addition to the prepositions themselves, we also have so-called complex prepositional constructs such as 'with regard to', 'as opposed to', and 'within the framework of'. Prepositions add to complexity in the sense that they combine two concepts in one structure. So when one writes about 'the calm before the storm', two concepts—namely 'the calm' and 'the storm'—are joined by the preposition 'before'. And this is where the problems with difficulty or incomprehension start. When you start stacking a lot of prepositional phrases in one sentence, you tax the reader because for each preposition a relationship needs to be untangled. In these cases, some unstacking of the phrases is warranted, and where complex prepositional constructions are used, one should use a simple preposition where possible.

Stacked prepositional phrases	Comments	Alternative
The delay in the consideration by the Senate of the paper presented by the government on the new tax system even made the Prime Minister comment on the delay.	The sentence contains six prepositions ('In', 'by', 'of', 'by', 'on', 'on'), which makes it difficult to unravel (the sentence can hardly be read aloud without faltering).	The Senate has not yet considered the government's paper on the new tax system. This has made even the Prime Minister comment on the delay.

Stacked prepositional phrases	Comments	Alternative
We have taken note of your high level of concern with regard to the state of play in the market for cars.	In this case, the complex prepositional construction ('with regard to') can be replaced. The sentence structure is complicated even further by the stacking of five prepositions ('of', 'of', 'of', 'in', 'for').	We have noticed your high level of concern regarding the situation in the car market.

How to avoid difficult prepositioning constructions.

4.3   Instructive language

Instructions occur in all types of texts in which readers are told how to perform certain tasks. Typical examples are manuals and instructions for use, but there are also less obvious cases: a website indicating the route to a company for motorists and rail passengers, a staff announcement explaining how to apply for special leave, or an internal directive to deal with a student's complaint.

An instruction must be complete and clear, and the steps must be in the right order. The visual side is also very important. Especially with technical instructions and route descriptions, pictures are often much more effective and efficient than words. Just think of the complete visual installation instructions for furniture from a well-known Scandinavian company. But animations, videos, and comic strips also offer good opportunities for user-friendly instructions. As soon as there are also textual elements in the instructions, the wording is essential.

4.3.1   Imperative style and some of the alternatives

What does the standard wording of an instruction look like? Such a wording consists of an action verb in the imperative mode, denoting an instruction (or any other imperative language act, such as a command or request) expressing an action, followed by the object of the action and possibly a few other qualifications. With the imperative mode, you make it clear that this is an instruction. By putting the verb first, you emphasize the action that the reader should perform. Different variations are possible on this standard wording.

- When you want to indicate that there is no absolute obligation on the reader to carry out the instruction, you can use a verb such as 'can' or 'may'. In cases where the action denoted in the instruction is absolutely essential, corresponding verbs such as 'must' should be used to strengthen the instruction.
- *Descriptive phrases* are appropriate if you want to give less emphasis to the instructional character, for example because readers might perceive a direct instruction as patronizing or authoritarian.
- *The passive voice* is useful in cases where you want to leave the interpretation open regarding the actor of the action, or if the focus is not on the action but on another element in the instruction.

Remove the packaging.

Turn the volume knob counterclockwise until you hear a click.

At the yellow sign, go to the right.

Stir the sauce until smooth.

Straightforward instructions with a strong imperative mode plus qualifications.

Now remove the ink cartridges from the printer. These must be deposited in the special containers for chemical waste; they do not belong with ordinary waste.

The passive voice in the second sentence is appropriate because the emphasis is not on depositing as an action but on the place where it should be done. Moreover, the depositing does not necessarily have to be done by the reader of the instruction.

In the case of many html tags, you must fill in a color. This can be done in three ways.
- You fill in the English name of a standard color. The possibilities are here: Aqua, Black, Blue, Fuchsia, Gray, Green, Lime, Maroon, Navy, Olive, Purple, Red, Silver, Teal, White, Yellow.
- You click on the Color button. This will take you to the color menu, where you can double-click on the desired color. After this, it will automatically be entered in the tag.
- The third possibility is to indicate the color with a #rrggbb code, where rr is the amount of red in the color (from 00 to 99), gg is the amount of green, and bb is the amount of blue.

In this instruction, the verbs 'must' and 'can' are used to emphasize that there are different possibilities. Therefore, these sentences do not have the typical imperative structure and wording.

4.3.2 The details in an instruction

Instructions typically consist of a number of steps (often numbered) that the reader must perform in sequence. It seems obvious that each step would consist of one separate action. But there are a number of objections to this rule.

– If you were to stick to the rule, many instructions would result in very long lists of steps to be taken. These can be confusing and often discouraging for the reader.

– If readers were to perform the relevant action each time after reading the step, they would constantly have to 'switch' from the instruction to the task they are performing (for example, switching between reading the instructions for a device and looking at the device itself or switching between reading a recipe and paying attention to the dish to which the recipe applies). Readers can often very well read and remember different actions before they start making the switch between the instruction (or set of instructions) and the target of these instructions.

There are ways you can limit the number of steps, as can be seen from the following two examples.

1 Fold the paper in half, insert it into the machine, and press the ON button.
2 Wait for the paper to be completely shredded and press the OFF button.

Five actions have been reduced to two steps in the instruction. In principle, one could even consider giving everything in one step, but that is less logical because there is a difference in time between the two steps.

1 Make a sauce of four tablespoons of melted butter.
2 Add the crushed hard-boiled egg.
3 Add the boiling cream on a soft heat while stirring, but do not let it boil.
4 Add salt, pepper, and nutmeg to taste and pour over the asparagus.

In this recipe, a number of actions are 'hidden' in a few steps: the melting of the butter, the cooking and crushing of the egg, and the stirring. The addition of salt, pepper, and nutmeg is conceived as a whole, whereas strictly speaking it concerns three actions. This creates a structure of four main actions: making sauce, adding the main ingredient, binding, and seasoning.

4.4   Persuasive language

What style would you use to convince readers or listeners of the correctness of a position or of the desirability of a certain behavior? Much depends on the means you use to persuade your reader. Chapter 3 on argumentation discusses this at length. Now we will be examining how persuasion attempts can be reinforced with well-considered style choices.

4.4.1   Clarifying the reasoning

It is important that the content and structure of your argumentation are properly reflected. The content is made clear, above all, by the precise and clear formulation of the position (or point of view) you take and the arguments in support of the position. The position is most clear if you formulate it in the form of one sentence that is not too complicated. Keep in mind, however, that positions cannot always be formulated in a straightforward manner. Many positions are nuanced, with conditions and reservations. These nuances cannot simply be omitted, because then a critical reader or listener will soon be able to undermine the position.

> Climate change will have a major impact on Southeast Asia.
> – Southeast Asia is one of the regions where climate change will have a major impact.
> – Southeast Asia is one of the regions where climate change is likely to have a major impact.
> – It is not inconceivable that Southeast Asia is one of the regions where climate change is likely to have a major impact.
> – If current developments continue, it is not inconceivable that Southeast Asia will be one of the regions where climate change is likely to have a major impact.

A position that is formulated in an increasingly nuanced manner. The latter wording is so cautious that very little remains of the original position.

A simple, straightforward position is not always more convincing than a nuanced position with conditions and reservations. An audience that is already moving in the direction of the speaker is likely to appreciate a simple position. But an audience that is neutral or even has some doubts about its position is more likely to be convinced by a nuanced wording. However, whether you are putting forward a straightforward or a nuanced position, it is good to do so as clearly as possible. That always has a positive effect.

This also applies to the arguments you put forward, certainly if these are intermediate arguments in a chain reasoning. The argumentation itself is—from a purely rational point of view—most convincing if its structure is clear. With signal words (see section 2.4.4) you can indicate what the arguments are and how they relate to one another. Are you presenting a single argument, convergent arguments, linked arguments, serial argumentation, or a network of arguments (see section 3.2.4)? The easier it is for your readers or listeners to identify and understand the structure of your argument, the more convincing your argumentation will be.

> If current developments continue, it is not inconceivable that Southeast Asia will be one of the regions most likely to be severely affected by climate change. Indeed, the area already suffers from extreme weather conditions such as heavy rainfall alternating with long droughts, while at the same time governments are unable to take appropriate measures to combat their consequences (floods and food shortages). The latter is not possible in view of the poverty in the region.

The signal words 'if [...] (then) [...]', 'indeed', 'while', and 'in view of' all act as signals to highlight the structure of this reasoning.

> The proposal to employ specialists in hospitals is not a very good one. First of all, most of the freelance specialists will earn less than they currently do. It is therefore unprofitable for the specialists. Secondly, according to research, salaried specialists are less productive than their freelance colleagues. We will therefore need more specialists in the future. Thirdly, these specialists may lose their partnerships, while these partnerships may have a value for which young, up-and-coming specialists soon pay a lot of goodwill. The specialists will want to be compensated by the government for the loss of this goodwill. This means, therefore, that the government will have to provide substantial early-stage financing.

Although the signal words 'first', 'secondly', and 'thirdly' suggest that there are three arguments in favor of the position, the arrangement within the reasoning is illogical, as shown in the diagram below.

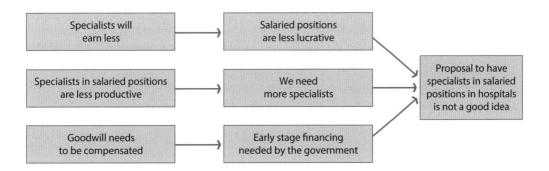

4.4.2 Nominalizations

Nominalizations are phrases consisting of nouns (often recognizable by a preceding article) that are derived from verbs. This can be done by:

- using the article 'the', followed by the present participle, for example 'the finding of' (from 'find'), 'the making of' (from 'make');
- using a suffix, for example 'management' (from 'manage'), generalization (from 'generalize'), 'development' (from 'develop');
- putting the nominalization in a verbal phrase such as 'take into consideration' (in stead of 'consider').

These nominalizations are powerful but risky stylistic mechanisms. They are risky because they can make a text rather cumbersome when overutilized, but they can also provide a desirable nuance to the meaning.

Unnecessarily cumbersome with nominalizations	Comment
The long wait for road traffic at the bridge came to an end: The royal couple performed the official opening of the new tunnel on Wednesday.	The phrases 'came to an end' and 'performed the official opening' make the sentence cumbersome. The phrase 'the long wait', on the other hand, is concise, compared to, for example, 'the long waiting times'.
Alternative wording	**Comment**
The long wait for road traffic at the bridge is over: The royal couple officially opened the new tunnel on Wednesday.	The sentence becomes more concise by replacing the undesirable nominalizations with ordinary verbal phrases.
Different meaning with nominalization	**Comment**
The Committee is responsible for the assessment of the works of art.	The nominalization specifies the meaning of this sentence: A committee is responsible for the assessment but it does not necessarily carry out the assessment itself. Rewriting the sentence in a more verbal style gives it a different meaning: 'The Committee will assess the works of art [itself]'.

Nominalizations: sometimes cumbersome, sometimes nuanced.

Nominalizations can have several effects that enhance the persuasiveness of the text. By using a nominalization you can:

– prevent the reader from feeling too directly addressed and confronted by the message. For example, 'The chance of contracting an STI through sexual contact is reduced by the use of a condom' sounds less threatening than 'You have to use a condom because then you have a lower risk of contracting an STI'.

– avoid giving the reader the idea that he or she is considered stupid. The warning on an ammonia bottle, for example, is 'Beware! In the case of internal use, seek medical advice immediately'. Would the wording be 'If you use this internally […]' then the reader would be addressed as someone who could possibly take it in his or her head to drink from an ammonia bottle. This can easily be experienced as insulting.

– avoid direct reference to an actor. 'After a purchase of two packs of Persil Color, you will receive a voucher of five dollars'. By talking about 'the purchase' (and not saying 'If you buy two packs'), and then writing 'you receive', the emphasis is on something that the reader will experience positively ('receive') and less on something that is likely to sound more negative ('buy', and therefore having to spend money).

– leave open the question of who is responsible for what: 'The search for financial cover will take some time'. Sometimes it is not yet known who is responsible; sometimes it does not matter. The reverse is also true: If senders want to address their receivers directly and place the emphasis on who is responsible for something, they should avoid nominalizations.

– place the emphasis on the action instead of on the performer. For example, in 'The realization of the plans for the introduction of the coming year is in the hands of the board', the emphasis is much more on the realization of the plans than in the case of 'The board must realize the plans'.

4.4.3 Suggestive style

With unchecked passing comments, one can make claims between the lines, expecting the reader to take them for granted without thinking. This gives the suggested position an almost self-evident character: It is not called into question.

> We have not reached an agreement in this afternoon's discussions. The intransigent attitude of the unions has forced us to break off the negotiations. For us, this is not doing good business. No further comment.

The value judgment that the unions are intransigent is presented as an adjective to the noun 'attitude' and can pass almost unnoticed, so that it is not immediately recognized as a position with the burden of proof. The word 'forced' is also suggestive of a position which is not necessarily valid without argumentation presented.

The use of so-called loaded language can also give a certain 'color' to the message, forcing the listener or reader in a certain direction or position without there being any proper arguments to justify the direction or position. Texts with loaded language are often more attractive than their dry, businesslike counterparts.

> Surveys by our institute among parents with children in secondary education showed that in the three years after 2000, the average cost of textbooks increased by between 70% and 90% for high school education. For college education—which accounts for 60% of all secondary education in the country—the increase was one hundred percent between 2000 and 2003.
>
> Is there any other sector where the market would absorb such a stranglehold policy? It is easier to drive up prices in education than anywhere else, because universities and colleges can prescribe books but do not have to pay for them, while on the buyers' side there is a cultural-psychological natural law that parents would rather cut back on anything else than the education of their children.
>
> In order to give this incredible, almost criminal price movement a semblance of justification, educational publishers invariably refer to continuous educational innovation plus the increasingly demanding consumers. I maintain, however, that for the largest part these inflated prices are pushed through to the advantage of only the publishers and their authors.

With the rhetorical question in the second paragraph (a question for which the answer is already suggested), and also with evocative words such as 'stranglehold policy', 'incredible', 'almost criminal', and 'inflated', the speaker sets the tone for the view that the power of the publishers of textbooks should be limited. (adapted from a speech by Frits van Oostrom in 2007)

4.4.4   Repetition and enumeration

An argument does not become more true or appropriate if it is repeated frequently. However, most people do appear to be sensitive to repetition. Advertisers and politicians know that only too well. By repeating certain words often, such words also work as a 'frame' for a certain phenomenon: They become inextricably linked to it. For example, qualifications such as 'our national pride' or 'the biggest grocer' become synonymous with certain companies, and 'mass immigration' and 'street terrorists' automatically become political problems for all parties to deal with.

A variant of repetition are enumerations in which variations on the same theme are, as it were, strung together, often as examples. Certain words are repeated, and the structure of the sentences often shows parallels. All this results in a 'constant hammering' that sometimes increases the power of persuasion even more than a literal repetition.

> While the world waited, Saddam sought to add to the chemical weapons arsenal he now possesses, an infinitely more dangerous weapon of mass destruction—a nuclear weapon. And while the world waited, while the world talked peace and withdrawal, Saddam Hussein dug in and moved massive forces into Kuwait.
>
> While the world waited, while Saddam stalled, more damage was being done to the fragile economies of the Third World, emerging democracies of Eastern Europe, to the entire world, including to our own economy.
>
> The United States, together with the United Nations, exhausted every means at our disposal to bring this crisis to a peaceful end. However, Saddam clearly felt that by stalling and threatening and defying the United Nations, he could weaken the forces arrayed against him.
>
> While the world waited, Saddam Hussein met every overture of peace with open contempt. While the world prayed for peace, Saddam prepared for war.

Extract from President George Bush's speech at the beginning of the first Gulf War, 17 January 1991. The phrase 'while the world waited' is repeated over and over again, after which Saddam Hussein's reprehensible actions are repeatedly mentioned, with reference to different examples of these reprehensible actions.

Special forms of the enumeration phenomenon are *bicolons* such as 'peace and quiet', and *tricolons* such as 'blood, sweat, and tears' (also see section 9.3.2) They give the text an emotional color that can strengthen its power of persuasion.

These conjunctions are often built up in an almost poetic way to strengthen the idea, as in the well-known phrase 'government of the people, by the people, and for the people' (Abraham Lincoln) or 'the wrong war at the wrong place at the wrong time' (John Kerry regarding the war in Iraq).

4.4.5   Irony and understatement

When something is formulated with irony, the letter and the spirit of the message differs, that is, there is some message hidden behind the literal message. It is assumed that the reader or listener will be aware of this. Understatements are a form of irony in which something or someone is deliberately presented as not being very important, while the opposite is meant. So one can say 'Aren't you funny today?!', meaning you are not funny at all. The different forms of irony and understatement, including humor, can strengthen the power of persuasion.

Of course, it is best to dismiss Mr. Jones. After all, he has contributed nothing to the development of our company. Yes, he made sure that we got out of the red and that turnover abroad doubled. But he didn't do anything else, did he? It is true that such a person deserves nothing but dismissal. Or are we going to keep him in service and put him in the spotlight today?

The speaker clearly does not think that Mr. Jones should be dismissed. On the contrary, by presenting the great merits of Jones for the company as little ones, the speaker emphasizes the paramount importance of those merits and provides a good prelude to the positive, almost festive suggestion at the end of the fragment.

4.4.6   Metaphors and other forms of non-literal language

Metaphors and other forms of non-literal language entail the use of words that are not to be understood literally but 'stand for' what is meant. The imagery created in this way often rests on a form of comparison: 'He is as stubborn as a donkey', 'She smokes like a chimney'.

If the comparison is not stated in clear terms ('Your argument is as clear as mud'), and if it remains implicit in part, then it is a metaphor. This way, someone can be 'attacked' personally in a debate (as if in a fight or a war), and the opponent can 'play the man' (as if participating in a sporting event). And when a speaker makes a speech to an audience that already agrees with him or her, the speaker is 'preaching to the converted'. An area in which metaphorical language abounds is sports reporting.

We are ready for war
The national football team has clearly set up their field of warriors to attack on all fronts. The choice of forwards and midfield players clearly indicate the intention of the coach to play an attacking game without creating too much space for effective counter-attacks from their old enemy.

The war metaphor is quite typical in sports reporting, as illustrated in this fragment with metaphorical references such as war, warriors, attack, fronts, counter-attack, and enemy. In this case, one would be justified in asking whether the use of metaphor is not overdone.

4.4.7 Oppositions

Your position can be strengthened when it is presented in opposition to another position, especially when that other position provokes a negative response from the audience. By presenting two positions in this way, you are strengthening the first at the expense of the second.

> It is not through discussion groups or the establishment of new committees that we can solve the problem of alcohol abuse among young people, but through immediate action. It is not by having another investigation carried out that we will tackle this growing problem, but by taking immediate measures. If we do not take action now, this problem will continue to grow and grow.

Immediate actions and measures are presented in opposition to 'weak' resources such as discussion groups, committees, and research.

4.4.8 Inclusive references: the 'we' feeling

There are several ways you can suggest that you and your opponents in a discussion actually agree because you belong to the same group. You create a sense of community: the impression that you identify with the group of your audience or opponents, that you feel yourself included in this group. In essence, then, you use the relationship side of the message to reinforce the appeal side. Especially when it comes to oral communication—where speakers and listeners have direct contact with each other—this can be an effective means of persuasion. The suggestion is that anyone who disagrees with the speaker's position would be left in the cold, that is, would not be considered a member of this in-group.

> We all want to be able to enjoy our old age. It is a good idea to make sure now that you are well prepared for your retirement. Request a free quote for our Old Age Policy.

The inclusive reference 'we' in the first sentence, reinforced by *all*, creates the feeling that we all (including the speaker/writer) agree with this position.

> Dear neighbors, don't you think that we should do something about the degradation of our neighborhood? You can make a major contribution to this yourself. Not only your neighbors, but you too are responsible for the fact that garbage bags are scattered across the streets, that waste paper blows through our gardens, and that discarded bicycles are left on the pavements. If you agree that this should no longer be the case, then you should do something about it yourself.

By using the direct form of address 'Dear neighbors', the audience is immediately involved in the subject of neighborhood degradation. This speaker also explicitly states that all those present are partly responsible for the problems. This is reinforced further by the inclusive reference in the phrase 'our gardens'. In this way the speaker tries to make those present more receptive to the specific proposals he wants to make later in his presentation.

4.4.9   Not convincing: inconsistent style

Stylistic inconsistency occurs when words and phrases are combined in such a way that they do not match in terms of tone. An obvious example would be to mix a style associated with spoken language with a style associated with written (often more formal) language. Such a 'break in style' can confuse the reader and is considered inappropriate. A break in style usually does not inspire confidence and so detracts from the power of persuasion of a text.

> The Board of Governors is of the opinion that the financial support of the program should be charged to the third stream of funding, on the understanding that the Board of Governors is not too stingy to cough up some funds themselves.

An example of inconsistent style in what should be a formal letter from a board: between more or less formal expressions such as 'being of the opinion' and 'on the understanding' and more informal expressions such as 'stingy' and 'cough up', normally associated with a more informal context.

4.5   Liveliness

Persuasive power requires more than just formal arguments and emotions, it also requires you to draw and hold the attention of the reader or listener. The most convincingly worded text will have no effect if the reader does not become engaged in it or if you lose the attention of the reader after a few sentences. That is why the use of a captivating, lively style is also an important contribution to a persuasive message.

4.5.1   Surprising and varied choice of words

Surprising terms attract attention, and people such as advertisers and politicians are eager to use them. Think about inventions such as 'selfie', 'Brexit', 'crowd sourcing', 'Brangelina', and so on. A surprise effect can also be achieved when someone uses a term in a context where it is unexpected or unusual.

Texts become boring when a certain word or name keeps returning. Writers and speakers can prevent this by using references to the word or name and by occasionally using descriptions or synonyms.

> I have serious complaints about Writewell. When I bought Writewell a few months ago, I was assured that with Writewell I could easily edit texts I had made with my previous program. But that is not true. After this disappointing experience with Writewell, I would like to discourage everyone from working with Writewell.

The fragment is monotonous because the name 'Writewell' is repeated over and over again.

> I have serious complaints about Writewell. When I bought this outdated word process-ing program a few months ago, I was assured that it would allow me to easily edit texts I had created with my previous program. But that is not true. After my disappointing experience with Writewell, I would like to discourage everyone from working with this 'old'-ware.

In this version, the repetitions have been replaced by references ('there', 'this', 'these') and other descriptive variants ('this outdated word processing program' and 'this 'old'-ware').

4.5.2   Variation in the sentence structure

On a sentence level, too, variation ensures that readers do not get bored. Sentences can be varied in a number of different ways.
- *Variation in the length of sentences.* Texts with only long sentences quickly become boring, texts with only short sentences are often considered too simplistic.
- *Variation in the types of sentences.* Occasionally, you may interrupt communi-cation by asking a question, by direct speech (a speaking person), or even by an exclamation or an incomplete sentence.
- *Deviations from the standard order in the sentence.* Almost every 'ordinary sentence' follows the order 'subject'-'verb'-'rest of the sentence'. However, in

English, as in many other languages, it is quite possible to put other parts of the sentence first and thus achieve variety.

Dr. Brocken described Mr. Tahamata's investigation as deficient and misleading. His objection did not concern the methodology used but the manner in which the conclusion was reached. He found that that was not acceptable.

All the sentences are declarative sentences following approximately the same word order.

Deficient and misleading. That is how Dr. Brocken qualified the research of Mrs. Tahamata. Did he object to the method that she had used? Not so much so, but rather to the way in which the conclusion was drawn. 'There's nothing good about that,' Brocken said.

This variant is more inviting because of the alternation of sentence types and the periodic deviation from the standard word order.

- The trade union movement will have to make even greater efforts than before to maintain employment in the coming years.
- In order to maintain employment, the trade union movement will have to make even greater efforts in the coming years.
- In the coming years, the trade union movement will have to make even greater efforts than before to maintain employment.
- Even more than in the past, the trade union movement will have to make an effort in the coming years to maintain employment.

The four variants each have a different order, so that the accent is placed on a different part of the sentence (the part of the sentence that comes first).

4.5.3 Comparisons

With well-chosen comparisons, you can enliven your style and clarify your intention. The effectiveness of comparisons is enhanced when you take into account the following.
- *Originality.* Cliché comparisons do not make your wording any more interesting.
- *Applicability.* The comparison must be in line with what you want to convey.
- *Moderation.* An accumulation of comparisons may distract attention from the actual subject.

Searching for information in your memory, how does that work? Suppose you enter an intricate office building like a stranger and you have to be in room A342. You first look for a floor plan to get an overview of the building as a whole: Where are the different wings? Then you try to find your way to the A wing. There you end up going to the third floor and finally you try to find the right room.

This is also how a search for information in your memory would go. First, you try to find the right entrance and get a picture of the systematics (the 'map'). Then you look for the part where the searched information should be (the 'wing' and the 'floor'). And finally, you look for the necessary record (the 'room').

Explanation of a (psychological) process using a comparison. It is not only the comparison itself that enlivens the text but also the order in which it is presented. The text does not start with what needs to be explained but with what is meant to be the explanation. As a result, the reader wonders where it is going—and is drawn into reading further.

4.5.4 Specific descriptions

Professional communication often deals with abstract issues such as policy objectives, implementation problems, technical developments, financial markets, or goods and services. By giving specific form to information about these abstract subjects, you can make your text more interesting. An effective way of doing this is to refer to people who carry out actions.

The confidence of customers in the protection of their privacy is an important condition for the success of transactions over the internet, both for the transfer of goods and for electronic services.

Abstract: This text deals with concepts such as trust, privacy, success, transactions, and transfer of goods.

If customers want to buy something over the internet or use services, they need to be able to rely on the supplier to treat their personal data confidentially, otherwise they will not do so.

Concrete: This text is about people (customers and suppliers) and about concrete actions such as buying and renouncing the purchase.

4.5.5 Storytelling

A specific way of concretizing is storytelling: You tell a story about persons and events—invented or not—to introduce or clarify a particular concept or phenomenon. This approach tends to work particularly well at the beginning of a text or oral presentation but also at the end of it (see also section 9.2.3). It is also effective as an advertising tool to promote a product or service.

Since time immemorial, we have been telling each other stories to entertain each other, to make something clear to each other (sometimes indirectly), and to convince each other of something. A good story can also reduce the potential resistance of the reader or listener to a certain message. No wonder, then, that storytelling is being used more and more in professional communication.

What does a story need? The story must, above all, evoke human interest: It must be about people and about human concerns, problems, and feelings. A story is really effective when the readers or listeners forget the real world around them for a moment and identify with one of the main characters, look through this character's eyes, and feel this character's emotions. No matter how different stories may be, there are only a few basic patterns. One of them is the classic heroic story; an effective way to help build a convincing story. The main character has a certain mission. He is encountering obstacles in fulfilling this mission, but help is coming. At a certain point there is a turning point for the better, and the story ends with a positive result.

In a formal, businesslike text or presentation, there is not always room to tell a detailed story. But you may be able to create human interest with a few strokes of the pen. The following example from the website of *Smile Train*—an organization helping children born with a cleft palate—shows what you can achieve with this technique. A whole section of the website is devoted to storytelling in order to promote the good work that the organization does.

> Peter Strachan, the son of Jacqueline and Richard Strachan, was born in London with a cleft lip and palate. The Strachan family entrusted Peter's cleft treatment to Evelina London's South Thames Cleft Team, who helped ease their fears via sound medical advice and experience.
>
> When Peter was two years old, the Strachans moved to Bermuda, where finding information about cleft treatment was much more difficult. Jacqueline remembers, 'We were unable to find any information about cleft lip and palate or anything to do with facial differences and support surrounding that. It was really frightening, and we felt very alone.' Fortunately, Jacqueline and Richard were eventually referred to the cleft team at Boston Children's Hospital by a family on the island whose son had received excellent cleft care there.

Over the next several years, Boston Children's Hospital provided Peter with a variety of needed surgeries and other cleft treatments, including tubes for his ears, extensive jaw and nose surgeries, and speech pathology. To keep Peter positive through the 10+ procedures, Jacqueline and Richard created themes for each of his hospital stays, which included filling his room with decorations and themed gifts from friends.

As the family prepared for an upcoming bone graft surgery, Jacqueline had trouble finding information on post-recovery diets. 'What few recipes we found seemed very unhealthy. I'd heard that many of the children hated the post-op food and lost a lot of weight after surgery,' Jacqueline recalls. She decided to create her own nutrient-dense, blended-food recipes from scratch to keep Peter healthy. The standard was that they had to be nutritious, easily eaten, and most importantly pass Peter's taste test. The experimental recipes worked, and Peter never lost a pound.

On a holiday break from school, Peter decided that he wanted to create a cookbook to share his mother's post-operative recipes with other families who were affected by clefts. Peter, Jacqueline, and friend Sharron Hawker remade Peter's favorite recovery recipes, with Peter tasting each one to ensure that it was as good as he remembered. When the cookbook was finished, Dr. John Meara, Plastic Surgeon-in-Chief at Boston Children's Hospital, was so impressed that the recipes now serve as the inspiration for a new after-care cooking package.

After receiving amazing feedback about the cookbook, Peter took on the task of creating Facial Awareness Connection for Everyone (FACE) Bermuda—an association with the goal of providing information for people who are affected by facial differences on the island. Peter wrote to 70+ island medical practitioners to help shape the FACE Bermuda website and Facebook page. Richard commented, 'The feedback on the site has been amazing, and a few children have shared their own struggles with us via the Facebook page.'

Peter then created a GoFundMe page, which has raised more than $9,000, a portion of which was sent to Smile Train. Peter had decided to include Smile Train in his fundraising efforts because a nurse he had interviewed for his website was a big supporter and introduced him to Smile Train's global work. Peter really connected to the idea that children worldwide deserve equally incredible comprehensive cleft care. Peter said of his accomplishment, 'I feel great pride in that, with my fundraising, I have changed people's lives forever. Changing the quality of their lives is a great thing to do.'

A story told on the website of *Smile Train* (www.smiletrain.org). The story is presented in a way that advertises the cleft advocacy role that *Smile Train* plays, while at the same time showing the power of an individual's role in this regard.

4.6   A final word on correctness

The issue of correctness (correct grammar, correct punctuation, correct spelling) will not be dealt with in full here. There is extensive literature on this issue, and some good references are presented in the last part of this book, entitled *Suggested readings.*

From a stylistic point of view, it is important to stress the effect of correctness on a text. A badly edited text will always create a negative look and feel and will adversely influence the readability of the text and the reader's appreciation of the text as the following example illustrates.

> The issue of correctness (correct grammar, correct punctuation, corect spelling) will not dealt with in full. there is an exxtensive literature on this issue and some good references presented in the last part of this book, entitled sugested readings.
>
> From a stylish point of view it is important to stress the effect of correctnes on a text; A badly edited text will always cre-ate a negative look and feel and will adverselly influ-ence the readibility of teh text and the readers appreciation of the text as this example ilustrates.

Poor editing equals bad image.

Though this may seem obvious, the final editing of a text is of the utmost importance—even the best writers among us will make mistakes.

Key points

Style matters in communication. A good style ensures that the message gets through to the public. Moreover, an appropriate and carefully constructed style inspires confidence in the audience/reader. And finally, style can make reading or listening a pleasure for any reader or listener. A choice of words that fit the context and the communicative goals ensure that readers and listeners are and remain involved in the subject of the text or presentation. A good style is created by the well-considered use of techniques to increase comprehensibility, instructive force, persuasiveness, and attractiveness.

Formality
It is important to choose the appropriate level of formality for the specific message and its context, and to be wary of:
- difficult words;
- the passive voice;
- complex sentences;
- prepositional phrases.

Plain language
It is important to avoid incomprehension and misunderstandings. Tune the content of your message to the reader's knowledge. Remember that the reader always knows less about your subject than you think. Moreover, the reader should not have to make much of an effort to understand the content.
- When choosing a word, it is important to avoid highly formal bureaucratic language, unfamiliar technical terms, secret language, unusual abbreviations, abstract and vague words, and unclear references.
- The passive voice is useful for expressing 'distance' from the content of the text and for ensuring that sentences fit together properly. However, avoid an accumulation of sentences in the passive voice.
- Avoid long and complex sentences.
- Avoid sentences with stacked prepositional phrases.

Instructive language
Instructive texts must be effective and efficient, provide insight into the logic of the instructions, be convincing, and be learnable. As far as the wording is concerned, this means:
- a preference for action verbs in the imperative mode;
- a limit to the number of actions per step in the instruction.

Persuasive language

For the persuasiveness of your text, it is important that:

– your position and your arguments are clearly formulated;
– the structure of the argumentation has been made clear with the relevant signal words and with a proper arrangement of arguments.

Improved persuasion can also be achieved with:

– nominalizations, to avoid resistance on the part of the receiver;
– suggestive wordings;
– repetitions and enumerations;
– irony and understatement;
– metaphors;
– oppositions;
– inclusive formulations, to create a 'we' feeling.

It is better to avoid breaks in style.

Liveliness

To hold the attention of the reader or listener, it helps to:

– use a surprising and varied choice of words;
– create variety in the sentence structure;
– use comparisons;
– develop detailed descriptions of abstract phenomena.

Assignments

Assignment 1: A medicine insert leaflet

Medicine insert leaflets (those informative and instructive leaflets that accompany your medicine) are notoriously formal and difficult to read.

Purpose of the assignment
You will practice evaluating the level of formality and difficulty in the text fragment. You will also practice reformulating the fragment in order to make it more accessible to the average reader.

Subject matter
Section 4.1
Section 4.2

The text fragment
The following text fragment is taken from a medicine insert leaflet for *Cataflam D* tablets, a medicine used to combat muscular pain, rheumatism, gout, and a number of other related conditions (leaflet as published by Novartis South Africa).

Cataflam D tablets should preferably be taken on an empty stomach. *Cataflam D* tablets should be dropped into a glass of water and the liquid stirred to aid dispersion before swallowing. Since a proportion of the active substance may remain in the glass after swallowing, it is advisable to rinse the glass with a small amount of water and to swallow again. The dispersible tablets must not be divided or chewed.

Tasks
1   Assess the level of formality and difficulty in the text with reference to style mechanisms that might have a bearing on these dimensions of style.
2   How would you improve the style with reference to this formality and difficulty of the text so that it becomes more reader-focused and readable?

Assignment 2: A difficult sentence

Purpose of the assignment
You will practice identifying the factors that contribute to the difficulty of sentences. You will also practice providing solutions to the difficulty of such sentences.

Subject matter
Section 4.2

The example sentence
A demonstration included in a 2014 Ted Talk given by sports journalist David Epstein showed that if Owens had run on the same surface as Bolt, Owen's best time in the 100 meters (10.2 seconds)—accomplished shortly before the 1936 Olympics—could have been within one stride of Bolt's performance in the 100 meters (9.77 seconds) at the 2013 World Championships.
Source: Brennan (2018).[4]

Tasks
1   Why should this sentence be deemed to have an unacceptable degree of difficulty? Can you identify the phenomena contributing to the difficulty?
2   How would you improve this sentence to increase its readability?

---

4   Brennan, C. (2018, July). How technology and smarts help athletes push the limits. *National Geographic Magazine*. Retrieved from https://www.nationalgeographic.com/magazine/2018/07/

Assignment 3: A creative exercise

Purpose of the assignment
You will practice applying stylistic techniques that add to the liveliness of a text and improve its persuasiveness.

Subject matter
Section 4.5

The tasks
1   Create a case for the advertisement of a winery and its products. This entails that you consider things such as the name of the winery, the location of the winery, the characteristics that one would associate with a good winery, the products (the different wines) of the winery, and so on.
2   Write an advertisement for the winery and its products, keeping in mind that you have to draw and hold the attention of the reader and actually sell the winery to the reader, keeping in mind that you only have the power of words and no support from graphical material.

a b c d e f g h i j k l m n
o p q r ſ s t u v w x y z.

A B C D E F G H I K L M N
O P Q R S T U V W X Y Z.

a b c d e f g h i j k l m n
o p q r s ſ t u v w x y z.

A B C D E F G H I J K L M N
O P Q R S T U V W X Y Z.

a b c d e f g h i j k l m n o p q r s ſ t u v w x yz.
A B C D E F G H I J K L M N O P Q R S T U V W X Y Z.

a b c d e f g h i j k l m n o p q r s ſ t u v w x y z.
A B C D E F G H I J K L M N O P Q R S T U V W X Y Z.

5   Visualization

◄ *Alphabets in different fonts*, attributed to Johannes Condet, 1781. Illustration for the *National A-B book, for Dutch youth* by J. H. Swilden. Below, a vignette with a ship and powder kegs. Publisher: Willem Holtrop.

In order to make your text both attractive and effective, it is important that you choose the right form of presentation for your message from the plethora of visual and graphical possibilities available to you.

A picture sometimes says more ...

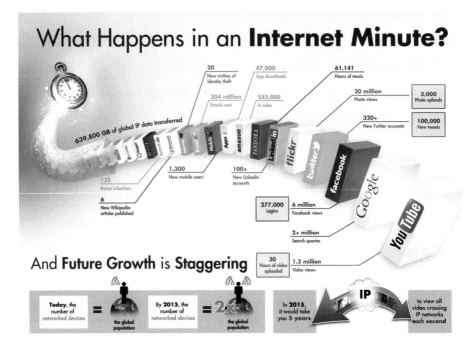

Source: Intel Free Press.[5]

Infographic with visual display of the huge information output on the internet.

The internet has been part of our lives for so long now that we might just have forgotten how powerful this system is, and to some extent also how scary. This infographic (from 2011) paints a dramatic picture by starting the stopwatch with the question 'What happens in an internet minute', and then visualizes the rather dramatic set of answers as a stream flowing from the stopwatch. It demonstrates the huge capacity of the internet and—equally so—it hints at the huge capacity needed to accommodate this output. By following the 'stream' one discovers that during this minute mentioned in the question, the following has happened: 639.800 GB of data transferred, 61.141 hours of music downloaded, 20 million photo views, 277.000 logins and 6 million views on Facebook, 30 hours of video uploaded from YouTube with 1.3 million video views, and more. Keeping in mind that this graphic was from 2011, and that it predicted that within four years (in 2015) the number of devices linked to the network would be twice the global population and that it would take you five years to view all video crossing IP networks each second, one comes to understand the wonderful power of this infographic to make a lot of facts visually appealing and easy to grasp. It demonstrates the power of visualization in communication, where not only the graphics speak to the reader, but where the text also becomes part of the picture.

5   Retrieved from https://www.flickr.com/photos/intelfreepress/6780720740/sizes/o/in/photostream/

'Tell me about it and I will forget it. Show me and I will remember.' The difference between verbal and visual communication may not always be this clear, but there is some truth in this statement. Information transmission happens not only with the spoken or written word but also with images and through the form in which writers and graphic designers present their text and images. A good visual presentation is not a luxury but a necessity in professional communication. Text, image, and design reinforce each other. Design, illustrations, and infographics help to get the message across.

Especially if your text has an informative or instructive goal, the design of the text must first and foremost be clear and help to guide the reader to the desired outcome. It is important to have a well-balanced approach to the use of the different elements: headings, running text, numbering, tables, illustrations, and so on. The design must support the reader's understanding through the effective use of text, graphics, and typography.

If your main communicative goal is to persuade or motivate your reader, then other considerations also apply. The image can attract attention and fascinate your reader, it can arouse emotions, and it can persuade and motivate. The target group also influences design choices. Many people like a quiet and clear design. But a publication aimed at young people can bear a busy, daring formatting perfectly well. If the message needs to stand out, a striking, different form can contribute to an effective transfer of information.

Good graphical and typographical design is a profession. For a professional design, you need specialists such as graphics designers or illustrators and professional typographers. But you can easily apply a number of basic principles for text formatting and image use in your own word processing environment.

Criteria for good design

In professional communication, three design criteria are essential.

- *Clarity.* With written text, it is important that the reader can easily read. Font choice, line length, and line spacing are some of the important elements in this case.
- *Structure.* Make sure that the parts are evenly distributed, correctly positioned, and marked, to give the text a strong external structure. This allows the reader to more easily discover and follow the big picture.
- *Appearance.* The design should be in line with the self-expression side and the relationship side of the text. A sleek, businesslike design characterizes the writer (or the organization) as professional and serious. An artistic design radiates that an organization is modern or fashion-conscious. A 'screaming' design evokes the atmosphere of a low-cost fighter. And in all cases, the design should make the reader feel at home with the appearance of the document (the relationship side).

Judgments about design are often based on intuition and taste, especially when it comes to appearance. It does not, however, have to stop there. There is certainly a discussion to be had on the basis of insight and rational arguments. In this chapter we will first discuss a number of basic principles that can play a role in such a discussion. After that, we will look in more depth into the choices of fonts and layout (typography). We then discuss how certain types of information can be transmitted not only in words but also in images (the visualization of the content). At the end of the chapter we will give some advice on the use of illustrations.

5.1 Basic principles of design

5.1.1 Principle of foreground and background

When we observe something, we always distinguish between information in the foreground (which we focus on primarily) and in the background (which we pay much less attention to). In a good composition, it is clear what the foreground is and what the background is, so that the viewers (readers) can divide their attention properly. We are familiar with the picture (seen below), in which we can recognize not only the vase but also two faces in profile, depending on what we see as foreground and what we see as background. It is almost impossible to see both figures in the drawing at the same time. This optical effect can be cleverly used in a design, but it can also lead to unintended reactions, depending on the intention with which the viewer looks at the image.

Rubin's vase: Different interpretations are possible, depending on what the viewer sees as the foreground and the background.

Choose the contract that suits you best

You can downgrade or upgrade at any moment

	Basic	Standard	Premium
Price after your free period ending on 22-11-18	€ 7,99	€ 10,99	€ 13,99
HD available	×	✓	✓
Ultra HD available	×	×	✓
Number of screens you can use simultaneously	1	2	4
Watch on your laptop, TV, telephone, and tablet	✓	✓	✓
Unlimited films and series to watch	✓	✓	✓
You can cancel at any time	✓	✓	✓
First month free	✓	✓	✓

Source: https://www.netflix.com/getstarted (Dutch version, translated into English).

In this advertisement the middle cube and the column below that cube draws the viewer's attention: They are in the foreground. The advertiser sends the potential customer directly to one of the options.

5.1.2 Principle of simplicity

When considering simplicity in the design, think about the adage 'less is more'. At the same time, consider that details are needed to be able to make a clear distinction between what is important and what is less important. If too much is left out, there is a danger that everything will seem to be of equal weight. The art of good design is to determine which parts are needed and which are not (on a page, on a website, and so on).

A good criterion for simplicity lies in the grid of imaginary horizontal and vertical lines that needs to be drawn on a page or a screen to place all the surfaces and boxes. The fewer lines in such a grid, the greater the simplicity.

Source: Advertisement in *Blue Chip*, 2018.[6]

This advertisement has a very simple grid, dividing the page horizontally into two areas. The top 40% of the page is filled with a photograph with some text in the photograph announcing the topic of the advertisement. The rest of the page is divided in two parts, the left of which contains only the logo of the company, while the right part contains the body text of the advertisement. The text is limited and printed in a large font, increasing the readability. There is a lot of white space in the advertisement, increasing the simplicity of the layout.

6   *Blue Chip: The South African Journal of Financial Planning*, 68, June 2018, p. 9.

5.1.3 Principle of proximity

What belongs together should be together. That prevents a lot of misunderstandings. As a reader, you will certainly be familiar with situations in which people sin against this rule of thumb.

– An illustration is not positioned with the text to which it belongs, perhaps it is even placed on the next page.
– The text is interrupted by images in such a way that you no longer know where to read on.
– The illustrations have no captions because they would disrupt the page image—or so the (false) argument goes.

Often it is not even aesthetic reasons that lead to an unclear relationship between text and image but rather purely practical reasons, such as a lack of space for an illustration on the page where it actually belongs.

A lack of space or surplus space on a page is often solved by removing or inserting white space, as a result of which certain text elements are placed closer to each other or further apart. If this is done in an ill-considered way, it can have far-reaching consequences for understanding the message.

– Principle of foreground and background
– Principle of simplicity
– Principle of proximity
– Principle of sameness
– Principle of symmetry

Normal interpretation: The five principles belong together.

– Principle of foreground and background
– Principle of simplicity
– Principle of proximity

– Principle of sameness
– Principle of symmetry

The same list with an additional white line. This layout (wrongly) suggests that two groups of principles should be distinguished.

5.1.4   Principle of sameness

When two elements have the same form, readers almost automatically assume that they belong together and that they form a single group. The reverse is also true. If elements have different forms, readers assume that they differ from each other and that each performs its own function. On a page with circles and squares, readers immediately distinguish two groups: a group of circles and a group of squares.

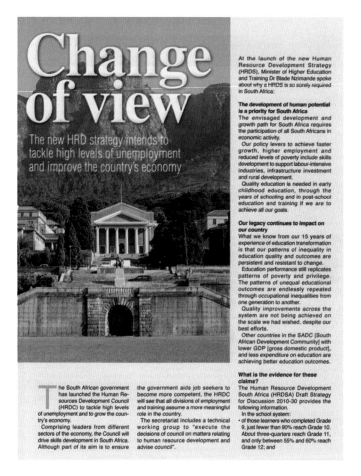

Source: First page from article in *Achiever*, 2010.[7]

The title of the article 'Change of view' and the streamer 'The new HRD strategy [...]', both included in the picture make this page look more interesting. The intention is to draw attention and to tempt the reader to immediately read more.

---

7   *Achiever: Advanced Education for Industry in South Africa*, 33, June 2010, pp. 34-35.

If various elements on a page have the same form but deviate from the standard form in which the (body) text is presented, readers assume that the deviating elements have a special function. Think, for example, of text boxes that are placed in the current text, with tips or anecdotes. Also think of so-called streamers or blurbs: very short texts of two or three lines that are placed in the columns or even in a graphic such as a photograph as a separate text segment, printed with a larger font. With a teaser, you can draw extra attention to the content of the body text and enliven the presentation. A teaser often contains a conclusion or a quote or some other 'juicy bit' from the content.

Different text elements can be designed in a variety of ways, for example with
- the same font, but different from the body text (for instance for headings);
- the same position relative to the margin, but different from the body text (examples);
- the same color or background color (warnings). Sometimes these deviating designs are conventional. Everyone knows, for example, that an underlined text on the computer screen is a hyperlink. Anyone who underscores 'normal' text or marks hyperlinks differently quickly creates confusion for the computer user.

TIP	**Merit bursary**	**Calculator**
Ensure that you apply for a student grant on time. Submit your application at least three months before you start your studies.	– basic bursary + student travel allowance – supplementary bursary **Loan (different options)** **College credit (different options)**	On our website you will find an online calculator to help you determine the amount of financial support you are eligible for and the amount of your loan at the end of your study.

These three text blocks in a folder about study grants seem to include action-oriented tips for the reader. However, the block in the middle does not give a tip but contains a list that is intended as an explanation. By choosing the same form (dark block with white fonts), the designer sins against the principle of similarity. This can cause the reader to become confused.

5.1.5   Principle of symmetry

We experience symmetrical images as a unit, even when they are at a distance from each other. Symmetry provides balance and harmony. Most people prefer symmetry to asymmetry: in faces, in layout, in images. This is important to take into account as a starting point, not as an absolute rule. There is nothing wrong with a deliberate deviation from symmetry, as long as it is not a question of sloppiness. An asymmetric design provides more space for loose or unexpected elements, which often creates a more interesting or exciting image than a completely symmetrical image. On the other hand, symmetry can also have a very strong effect.

A strong application of the principle of symmetry: the Taj Mahal in India.[8]

---

8   Retrieved from https://commons.wikimedia.org/wiki/File:Symmetry_of_the_Taj_Mahal,_Agra.jpg

To illustrate the principle of symmetry, above we have reproduced three pages from two different reports. For our purposes here, it does not matter if you are unable to read these texts. It is the visual impact that counts; what the text says is less relevant here. The top page is symmetrically arranged (up to and including the location of the graphic), which creates a harmonious effect. The second page has a more surprising, asymmetrical design. There are three columns; the introductory text at the top is running across two columns, and the columns are unevenly distributed because of the placement of the graphic. The use of white space increases the readability of the text. The layout of the third page is less successful. It shows the body text in strictly symmetric design, but the headings of sections are presented flush left, therefore in an asymmetrical design. The line width is large and the text is justified to the right margin. As a result, there are some ugly gaps between the words.

5.2   Typography and layout

The typography of the text is very important for the accessibility of the information in the text. Choosing suitable fonts, making decisions about issues such as line length and spacing, and deciding on the layout of different text elements are not easy tasks. There are so many options—just think of the variety of fonts—many of which are available through standard software. Companies and organizations usually have a house style, which prescribes which typographical choices should be made for which applications. But if you do not have to work within a certain house style, it is by no means always clear in advance what options are more or less suitable.

The layout of a page or a screen shows where the different parts start and end and how they relate to each other. A good layout is therefore one that clearly distinguishes the parts from each other and organizes them in a transparent way in relation to each other. In section 5.2.1 we will be looking at font choices, while sections 5.2.2 to 5.2.4 deal in more detail with the page layout, the line layout, and the layout of special text elements.

The following typographical terms are commonly used (see the illustrations that follow for clarification of some of these terms).

-   *Font*: The font is the specific appearance of a font denoted by a name, such as Helvetica, Arial, Georgia, or Times New Roman. A font can appear in different variants, such as regular (also called upright roman), *italic*, **bold**, or ***bold italic***. These variants together form a so-called font family. These variants are also referred to as the 'weights' of a font, referring to the fact that the line thickness or weight of the font can vary (lighter in the case of *italic*, heavier in the case of **bold**, for example).
-   *Font size*: The font size is often expressed in points (pt). Depending on the font type and context, a font size between 9pt and 12pt is often a good choice for your layout.
-   *Serif* versus *Sans Serif*: Serifs are those little 'hooks' at the end of a line in a font form (see illustration). Times New Roman is a clear example of a Serif font, whereas Calibri is a clear example of a font without serifs, or a Sans Serif font.
-   *Lower case* and *upper case*: Lower case refers to the non-capitalized letter of a font, upper case refers to the CAPITALS OF A FONT.
-   *Counter*: the enclosed (almost circular) spaces in some fonts such as o, a, e, d and g; in different fonts of the same size this part of the font body may differ in size, creating an illusion that some fonts are larger than others (see illustration).
-   *Baseline*: the line on which the body of a font such as 'a' or 'x' rests.
-   *Mean line*: the line indicating the top of a font such as 'a' or 'x'.

- *Cap line*: the line denoting the top of the CAPITALS OF A FONT.
- *Ascender*: The fontline of a font such as 'h' or 'k' rising above the mean line.
- *Descender*: The fontline of a font such as 'p' or 'y' stretching below the baseline.
- *x-height*: The x-height is the height of a lower case font such as the 'a' or the 'x', between the baseline and the mean line. It does not include the ascenders or descenders of fonts such as 'h', 'k', 'p', or 'y'.
- *Leading* or *line spacing*: The line spacing or leading is the distance between the baseline of one line of fonts and the baseline of the following line of fonts.
- *Line gap*: the gap between the lowest point of a descender and the highest point of an ascender on the next line; this gap must be such that these descenders and ascenders do not touch.
- *Page area*: the full page, that is, the print area plus all the margins.
- *Print area*: the area covered primarily by the print of the body text.
- *Margins*: The margins are the white spaces above, below, to the left, and to the right of the print area.
- *Body text*: The body text is the main text—in contrast to other parts of the text such as titles, headings, and teasers.

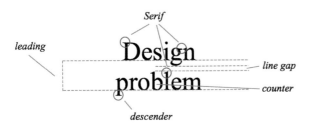

Illustration showing the leading, the line gap, the serifs, the descender, and the counter.

Illustration showing the x-height, the ascender, the cap line (also defining the top of the ascender), the mean line, and the baseline.

font size

Design

Illustration showing the font size.

broad   broad   *broad*   **broad**

Times New Roman | Arial | Bodoni MT | Bernard MT Condensed
(all 20 pt)

Illustration showing the effect of different counters. Here you see four different font types, all in the same font size. However, because of the differing counters, they appear to have different sizes: The Bernard MT Condensed font looks larger than the Bodoni MT font, and so on.

5.2.1   Font selection

A good choice of font, combined with other aspects of typography such as line spacing, is essential for the design of the text. The choice of a font is decisive for the following reasons.

–   *The legibility of the text.* If the fonts are too small or too large, too thick or too thin, if the lines are too close to each other or too far apart, or if they are too long or too short, the legibility quickly decreases.
–   *The look and feel of the text.* Some fonts have a refined, friendly look, while others are more rugged or even aggressive. There are traditional and modern fonts, business and informal fonts. Special screen fonts have been developed for almost all fonts, so that the fonts are also shown sharply on the screen.

Times New Roman is a typical example of a Serif font. Times New Roman fonts have small horizontal dashes at the ends. It is a popular font with a somewhat traditional or formal look and feel.

Arial is a typical example of Sans Serif. The fonts do not have dashes at the ends and therefore have a more modern look and feel.

Comic Sans was designed as a font for informal documents. The font quickly became popular, but there are also many opponents. Surprisingly, this font helps students to remember information more easily. The theory behind this is that because it is more difficult to read due to the playful forms, children's brains must work harder to decipher what is written, with the effect that they remember the content better. It is, however, not a good font to use in more formal and serious texts. It is not called Comic Sans for nothing.

Fonts differ in appearance.

Choosing a font allows you to support the content of a text element. The best choice in a given situation depends on the goal of the text and on the context. A few rules of thumb are given below.

– The body text is often best presented in a more classical font.
– To create a contrast between the headings and the body text, you can use a Sans Serif typeface for the headings and a Serif typeface for the body text.
– In instruction texts such as manuals and forms, the combination of upright roman (regular typeface, not **bold** or *italic*) and *italic* is often useful to ensure that the instruction is clearly distinguishable from other text elements.
– In the case of magazine-like texts, the style often supersedes legibility: Here designers often experiment with less classical fonts for a trendy effect. In a professional context, trendy fonts are usually not a good choice, since you wish to create a more 'serious' look and feel.

In standard software, often no more than three weights of a font are available: regular (upright roman), **bold**, and *italic*. This is usually more than sufficient to distinguish text elements from each other. For example, for main headings, you may want to use **bold** in a larger font size, and for subheadings the **bold** variant of the font size you are using for the body text. If you need additional heading levels, think of *italics*. Do not allow yourself to be tempted to stack font attributes such as **bold + underlined** or *italic + underlined*. This gives a crowded and messy effect. For example: In the current text, *italics* is generally suitable for displaying titles and names. You can also use *italics* for long quotations (which must always be put in quotes) and to give a word extra emphasis.

5.2.2   Layout

The most important principle to adhere to when considering the layout of your document's pages is that you treat the text as a graphic. The reader sees the text first, which creates a first impression of its look and feel, and only then does the reader start reading the text. The following two examples illustrate this principle. The difference in layout and the effect that the layout may have on the reader is rather obvious (here it is not about being able to read the text but simply about 'seeing' it).

Without having to read these texts, it is immediately clear that the layout of the first text is more interesting and enticing than the layout of the second text.

The page format or layout is the layout of a page with the purpose of adequate visual presentation of the information. The setting of the interaction between text and graphics, the margins, column widths, and line spacing form the basis of a good page layout.

Do not be afraid of white space: It gives 'air' to the text and often makes the page more readable than if it is overcrowded. The print area should not fill the page area. As a principle, one could start experimenting with a print area that does not fill more than 60% of the page area.

Most word processing programs offer the possibility of defining formatting profiles. This determines the characteristics of each text element that will follow: title, main heading, sub-headers, body text, lists, quotations, and so on. You can also determine their position on the page, the font and font size, and possibly other characteristics such as text color, bullets, and lines.

An underlying pattern, also called a template or grid, is an important tool to build up balanced pages in a consistent way. A grid is used to divide a page or screen into spatial planes or units. These units are used as a tool to place headings, text blocks, and images in the design. In principle, each element has to be placed flush with one of the underlying help lines of the grid.

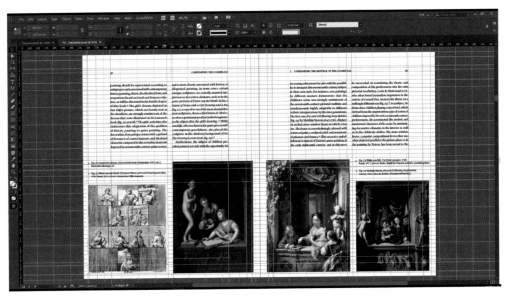

A grid helps to consistently create pages or screens.

5.2.3   Line format and white space

White lines and indentation

The white space on a page or screen plays an important role in the perception of coherence. Readers almost always interpret horizontal separations such as a blank line or a horizontal line as a sign that something new will emerge. If there are text elements next to each other, readers assume that they are connected in one way or another. Moreover, readers usually expect that the most important parts are on the left and the less important parts are on the right. A rule of thumb for the distribution of text elements across a page is therefore: Use horizontal separations to mark new units and use vertical separations to mark coherence and hierarchy.

When choosing mechanisms of separation, it is important that the design makes clear how strong or weak the substantive coherence is between the various text elements. The most important means that can be used here are the following.

–   *A new line* is the weakest mechanism of separation: A heading at a lower level in the information hierarchy is presented directly above and flush left to the corresponding text passage and a new paragraph begins on a new line directly below the heading. For paragraphs without a white line above it, you can always have the first line indented to make sure the beginning of the paragraph is highlighted.

On this page, the three blank lines create horizontal separations, in each case indicating the start of a new information item.

The extra white space to the left adds another dimension: The parts that are indented are apparently subordinate to the rest of the text block.

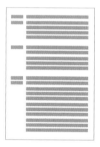

In addition to horizontal divisions, there is now also a vertical division. The horizontal arrangement makes it clear what belongs together. The vertical arrangement suggests that the elements to the left (headings positioned in the margin, for instance) are at a higher level of information than the elements to the right.

The hierarchy of the headings is marked here by the level distribution. The main heading is farthest to the left (and is therefore the most important) and is isolated by extra white from the text that follows. With this distribution of levels, it is not necessarily vital to make the main head larger than the subheadings, which are flush left with the body text.

- *White space* (*white line or white column*) separates text passages from each other but at the same time suggests a certain coherence.
- *Marking by means of a different font, color, or grid* isolates a text passage from the rest of the text and indicates that it is either of special importance (as in the case of a warning) or should be regarded as a non-essential addition (as in the case of an example).
- *Headings* indicate that a new part of the text is being discussed. They should be clearly separated from the foregoing text.

- *Lines* create a strong separation. It is therefore recommended that you use them economically.
- *A new page* is the strongest separator. New parts of a report and new chapters should preferably start on a new page, on the right side of an opened book/magazine.

Justification

The question of whether the text should only be left justified or completely justified (with straight left and right margins) is a matter of taste. Complete justification gives a symmetrical effect, with a quiet, traditional look. But if the line length is too short, the spaces between words can become excessive and uneven, often resulting in a lower level of readability. It can also result in rather unsightly cases of hyphenation. It is therefore important to correct the hyphenations manually where necessary. Left-aligned text gives an asymmetric image, making this style look a little more dynamic and modern.

5.2.4   Special text elements

In addition to the body text, there are many other special elements that you need to design effectively. Below we will discuss the most important: headings and subheadings, and special and separate segments of text.

Headings and subheadings

Headings and subheadings are important mechanisms denoting the structure of a text. They act as entrance mechanisms to the text, helping the reader to find and structure information. The headings and subheadings provide content that describes what the following section will be about, and they motivate the reader to browse through the text.

Headings and subheadings also denote different levels in the hierarchy of information (as suggested by the terms *heading* and *subheading*). The different levels can be denoted by numbering (for example 5.1, 5.1.3, and so on) and by a choice of different fonts, font sizes, and **bold** or *italic* print. The unnumbered heading of the section you are reading now ('Headings and subheadings') is of a lower level in the hierarchy compared to the heading above it ('5.2.4 Special text elements'). This heading is of a lower hierarchical level than the next heading above it ('5.2 Typography and layout'), which in turn is of a lower hierarchical level than the title of the whole chapter ('5. Visualization').

The following design principles guide the design of headings and subheadings.

- Headings and subheadings are usually placed above the text passage to which they relate, but they can also be placed next to the text passage in the left margin, which makes them stand out and makes it clear that they are important.
- If headings and subheadings are numbered, it may help to place the numbers in the margin so that readers looking for specific sections can find them easily.
- The level of the heading or subheading must be reflected in the design. Apart from their position and the amount of white space surrounding it, the font type and font size are suitable mechanisms for this. At the lowest level, it is sufficient to use headings of the same size as the body text, preferably using **bold** or *italic* print. The higher the level, the more appropriate it is to have a different font type and especially a larger font size. It is wise not to have too many different designs (a rule of thumb: Each subsequent level should be 20% larger than the previous one). A design for headings and subheadings that is too varied can create a chaotic effect and detract from the coherence of the text.
- A heading or subheading should be closer to the text it relates to than to the previous text.
- It is not a good idea to print the headings or subheadings in ALL CAPS. This makes them more difficult to read than when using lowercase fonts.
- It is not customary to have a full stop at the end of a heading or subheading.

Separate segments of text

In addition to the body text and headings, a text may contain additional text segments. Sometimes this concerns information that is of minor importance (such as examples and definitions), sometimes it concerns information that requires extra attention (such as a warning or a summary). In both situations, good design can help to clarify the status of such elements and draw attention to this special status. If a passage is less important than an ordinary text, the following possibilities exist.

- Separate the special text element from the body text with white lines before and after.
- Use a different font type or smaller font size for the text element (about 80% of the body text).
- Provide the text element with a short heading in which the nature of the passage becomes clear (*definition*, for example, or *example*).

If a text element is more important and requires more attention than the normal text, then there are the following possibilities.

- Use a larger or **bold font**. However, do not use **bold print** for more than two lines of text, as this will create a busy look and feel.

– Mark the passage by putting a frame around it or by placing a grid behind it (possibly with color).
– Make sure you have a clear heading that emphasizes the importance of the text element in question.
– DO NOT CAPITALIZE LONG PASSAGES. THE TEXT MAY ATTRACT MORE ATTENTION, BUT IT MAKES THE TEXT LESS READABLE: READERS MUST MAKE MORE EFFORT COMPARED TO TEXTS IN SMALL PRINT (WHEN QUICKLY SCANNING THE LETTERS, THEY LACK THE GRAPHIC 'TEXTURE' PROVIDED BY ASCENDERS OR DESCENDERS IN SMALL PRINT). THERE IS A GOOD CHANCE THAT READERS WILL NOT TAKE THAT EFFORT. MOREOVER, A TEXT THAT CONSISTS ENTIRELY OF CAPITALS FEELS TO THE READER AS THOUGH HE OR SHE IS BEING SCREAMED AT.

5.3 Visualization with graphics

A picture sometimes speaks louder than a thousand words, so the saying goes. But for this to happen, the picture (which in a professional text is often a graphic) must be well-chosen. The best kind of graphic to use depends very much on the information you want to present and the goal you want to achieve.

5.3.1 Numerical information

The following table lists five options for displaying numeric information.

Type of information	Example	Type of graphic
Absolute approximated (rounded) values; not a large number of values	Average income in different age groups	Bar chart
Proportionality	The material costs were distributed as follows: 34% equipment, 29% maintenance, 22% materials, 10% shipping costs, 5% insurance.	Pie chart. But take note: Pie charts only work well in cases where you do not have too many values and when the depicted values differ enough.
Exact values (a few values depicted)	The test results for the three components were 3.66 for the first component, 5.22 for the second and 8.48 for the third.	Bar chart with the values depicted on each bar

Type of information	Example	Type of graphic
Exact values (a large number of values depicted)	Public transport timetable: complete statistical data	Table
Trend	Voltage slowly increased from 6V to 14.6V.	Line graph

Options for visualizing numeric information.

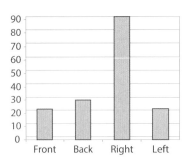 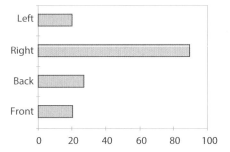

Bar chart (different options).

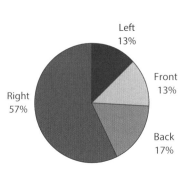 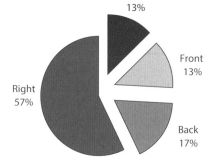

Pie chart (different options).

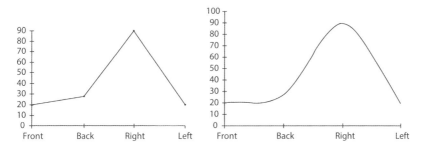

Line graph (different options).

5.3.2 Logical relationships

The following table lists five options for displaying logical relationships.

Type of information	Example	Type of graphic
Part – whole	X consists of […], comprises […], is composed of […]	Exploded drawing showing details as required
Interdependency	Modem 385 requires option XB, which in turn needs upgrades 34C and 34D. Instead of 34D, 34C can be used, and model 387 can also be used as a replacement for model 386. However, model 386 and upgrade 34D are not compatible.	Organogram
A simple list of rules or instructions	You can save your text in three formats: text only, text and graphics separately, and text and graphics integrated.	Simple list of the items; simple graphic showing the choices (with captions); a table of the rules or instructions
A complex list of rules or instructions	If […] and […], then […] unless […] or else […]	Flowchart
Comparison of properties or characteristics	There are five climate types that are characterized by certain properties.	Table

Options for visualizing logical relationships.

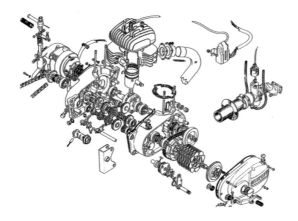

Exploded drawing showing which parts a technical apparatus consists of.[9]

Organization chart: The structure of an organization is shown schematically.

Age	Phase	Description(approximate)
0-1 years	Oral	Needs focus on oral satisfaction and persons who provide it.
1-3 years	Anal	Control of the anal sphincter is a source of pleasure and frustration at the beginning of toilet training.
3-6 years	Phallic	The Oedipus complex: desire of the parent of the opposite sex and anger towards the parent of the same sex. Fear leads to identification with the parental value system and development of the superego.
6-12 years	Latency	The sexual needs of the child are relatively controlled. Energy is spent on school and playing.
12-17 years	Genital	Development towards adult sexual relations: Many previous conflicts arise again.

Comparative table. A table can help to compare the properties of certain phenomena (in this case, the psychosocial stages according to Freud).

9   Retrieved from https://commons.wikimedia.org/wiki/File:Bultaco_engine_exploded_view.jpg

5.3.3   Processes and procedures

The following table lists five options for displaying processes and procedures.

Type of information	Example	Type of graphic or text design
Series of actions with a fixed order	First […] then […], then […], then […], and finally […].	Numbered list; where necessary with illustrations
Series of actions without a fixed order, but all mandatory	Before you start, you need to have […].	Checklist
A series of simple, stand-alone decisions	Error messages, malfunction warnings	Table of decisions
A (complicated) network of simple, interconnected decisions	If […], then do […], and then […]. But if […], then do […]; else do […].	Flowchart

Options for visualization of processes and procedures.

If PROGRAM is set to	If PROCESS is set to	If ONLINE is set to	Then proceed as follows:
TTA	OK	YES or NO	Click on PROCEED
TTA	ERROR	YES	Click on WAIT
TTA	ERROR	NO	Ask for assistance
ERG	OK	YES or NO	Click on PROCEED
ERG	ERROR	YES	Click on WAIT
ERG	ERROR	NO	Click on RESET

Decision table. The reader can find instructions on what to do under certain conditions.

5.3.4 Physical objects

The following table lists options for displaying physical objects.

Type of information	Example	Type of graphic
The shape of a simple object	A part of a device	Photo
The shape of a complex object	A complex device with many parts	Line drawing
Spatial relationships in two dimensions	The university is located between X and Z, east of the motorway.	Map
Spatial relationships in three dimensions	The on/off button is located on the back of the device, top left.	Line drawing
Certain people	The director of the company	Photo
Non-defined persons	Everyone, the average student, any computer user	Slightly abstract drawing, cartoon
Locating a part of a device	The sensor to the left of the line, about 4 cm from the corner	Three-dimensional drawing with magnification
Detailed representation of the construction of a device (possibly combined with a procedure)	Remove the lock nut from the shaft, remove the valve and slide the sleeve over the shaft up to the transverse legs.	Exploded line drawing with explanation and arrows
How a device works in principle	This is how your espresso machine works.	Drawing showing a cross-section with captions

Options for visualization of physical objects.

5.4 Graphic design

Choosing the right type of illustration is the first step towards effective graphic design. But after making the choice, a bad design can still throw a spanner in the works. Below we will present a few principles for the design of the most common types of illustrations. On the internet you can also find a variety of applications, sometimes free of charge, sometimes for a fee, that allow you to easily design your graphics. It is worth exploring.

5.4.1 Tables

A table consists of (horizontal) rows and (vertical) columns. The intersection of a row and a column is called a cell. When designing a table, you must ensure that the reader is able to find data as easily and accurately as possible. As a writer, you can do this as follows.

– Provide each row and column with a title or heading.
– Provide a logical arrangement of rows and columns. Possibilities are, for example: an alphabetical order or an order from large to small.
– If there are many rows, insert one line white after every five rows. This makes searching easier.
– Be sparing with lines in your table. It is not necessary to completely delineate all cells in your table. As an example: Use lines between the head of the columns and the figures and not more. If necessary, add a line if two parts really have to be well separated.
– Record any units (%, kg, and so on) in the header of a row or column so that you do not have to repeat them in each cell.

Tables are easy to create with the tabular function of the word processor you use, or with a spreadsheet program. The latter is particularly useful if you want to calculate totals, percentages, and so on in the table. A spreadsheet program offers the possibility to do that automatically.

Number	Course	Course	Number
11	HLF	HLF	11
15	PTT	PTT	15
18	FQRA	FQRA	18
28	ATC	ATC	28
31	RKTVV	RKTVV	31
103	total	Total	103

The arrangement of rows and columns in the left-hand table is useful for readers who want to know which courses are more or less common. The arrangement in the right-hand table is better suited to readers who want to know how many people have followed a certain course. Note that the arrangement in the left-hand table is not suitable if the total is to be included: The reader will expect the word 'total' to the left, and not to the right of the corresponding number.

Course	HLF	PTT	FQRA	ATC	RKTVV
Number	11	15	18	28	31

The orientation of the table can also be different: The columns become rows and the rows become columns.

Temperature	Volume		Temperature (°C)	Volume (cm³)
100 °C	300 cm³		100	300
200 °C	310 cm³		200	310
300 °C	319 cm³		300	319

Give the units in the header of the column, as is done in the table to the right.

5.4.2 Graphs

A graph shows the relationship between two variables. One variable is plotted on the x-axis (from left to right) and the other variable on the y-axis (from bottom to top). Which variable one should plot on the x-axis and which on the y-axis is not a matter of chance or personal preference. For example, in the case of a graph expressing the growth in numbers of participants in a sporting event, the years in which the event was organized make up one variable and the number of participants the other. The number of participants depends on the year in which the event took place, and not the other way around. Therefore, the number of participants is called the dependent variable, and the year is called the independent variable. The independent variable is usually plotted along the x-axis and the dependent variable along the y-axis.

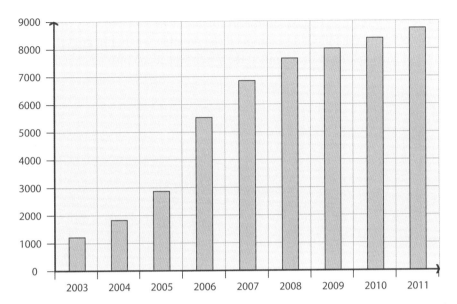

The independent variable (the year in which the event was held) is on the x-axis; the dependent variable (the number of participants) is on the y-axis.

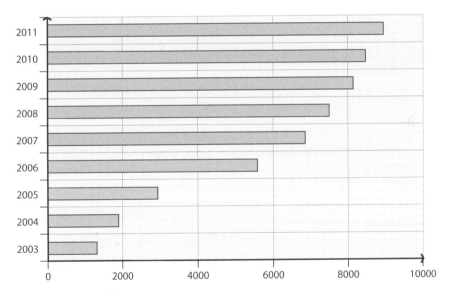

The dependent variable (number of participants) is on the x-axis; the independent variable (the year in which the event was held) is on the y-axis. This choice results in an unconventional chart, which can put readers on the wrong track.

The selection of units on the axes is important for the image created by the graph. Note the effect in the following example if the possible maximum growth in the number of participants in the event on the y-axis was 18000 instead of 9000.

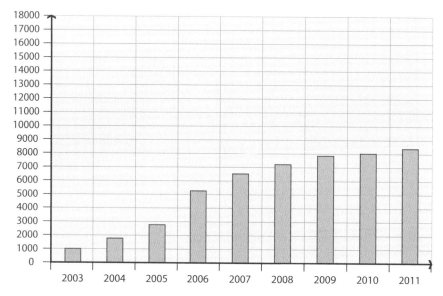

Graph with the same information as the previous page, but now depicted in such a way that the growth in the number of runners appears to be considerably smaller.

5.4.3 Flowcharts

Flowcharts can be used to show phases in a process or tasks that need to be performed. A flowchart consists of blocks in which text is placed, connected with lines and arrows. The blocks can display certain terms or parts of a whole. The lines show the connections. Flowcharts primarily have a clarifying function.
- Flowcharts should not be too complicated and should not contain too much information.
- The texts in the blocks should be as concise as possible.
- The structure of the information must be logical and transparent: from left to right and from top to bottom.
- In some disciplines, it is common practice to use certain forms with conventional meanings. For example, in technical flowcharts, ellipses are used for the start and the finish, windows for questions and for splits in the route, parallelograms for operations, and so on. Such conventions are important if you are writing

for specialists, but they may be unnecessarily complicated if you are writing for lay people.

– If you feel the need to explain how the reader should read a flowchart, you should ask yourself whether it does not complicate rather than solve the problems of understanding.

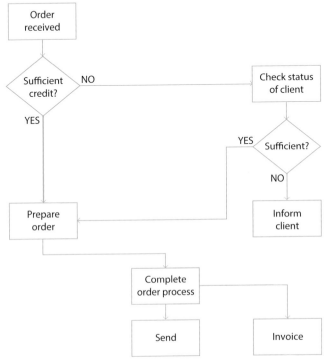

Flowchart. The reader can see how a process is going or how a task has to be carried out.

5.4.4 Images

A document that consists solely of text often looks rather boring and inaccessible, no matter how well written it may be. With an image—a well-chosen photo or drawing— you can make your text more attractive, clearer, and more convincing. If you want to inform your target group about a new type of aerodynamic crash helmet for cyclists, then it is obvious to combine the text with a photo of this crash helmet (whether or not on the head of a cyclist, for example during a spectacular descent). You might also add a drawing that clarifies the characteristics of the crash helmet. In the case of images with a clarifying function, the reader must be able to understand what the image represents quickly and easily. For images with an attention-drawing or aesthetic function, other requirements apply, such as artistry, atmosphere, and originality.

A striking newcomer to professional communication is the photo strip (also known as a photo story). It consists of a series of images with short captions that tell a story (also see section 4.5.5 *Storytelling*). In recent years, the photo strip has been used, although on a limited scale, to inform the public about health and other issues. A photo strip can be an effective means of transferring knowledge and influencing readers' behavior, especially if the target group consists (in part) of low-literate people.

Source: Koops van 't Jagt (2018, p. 142).[10]

This short photo strip aims to convince readers that you are not stupid if you do not understand a doctor's jargon and ask for an explanation. On the contrary: Often experts themselves do not realize that to a layperson they sound like they are speaking abracadabra.

10   Koops van 't Jagt, R. (2018). *Show, don't just tell: Photo stories to support people with limited health literacy* (Doctoral dissertation). Groningen: University of Groningen. Retrieved from https://www.rug.

Key points

Good visual presentation helps to get the message across effectively. Good legibility, a recognizable external structure, and an appearance that fits the target group and the goal of the text are of essential importance. The quality of the design is determined by five principles:

– principle of foreground and background;
– principle of simplicity;
– principle of proximity;
– principle of sameness;
– principle of symmetry.

Font selection
The choice of the font affects the legibility and appearance of the text.
– For the body text (the main text), it is better to choose a classical typeface.
– Allow the headings to contrast with the body text, for instance by using **a bold font**, a larger font, or a different font type.
– Do not use trendy fonts in a professional context.

Page layout
– Balance the placement of headings, text blocks, and images.
– Create horizontal white space on a page or screen to display individual units.
– Create vertical white space (for instance with indented text) to make hierarchy visible.

Graphics
Information that is ideal for visualization:
– numeric information: graph, table;
– logical relationships: drawing, table;
– processes and procedures: list (with images), checklist, flowchart;
– physical objects: drawing, photo, photo strip.

nl/research/portal/publications/show-dont-just-tell(0a7be685-b2ef-40f1-92a5-7740cc36c19e).html. The photo strips in this dissertation were developed for the EU research program IROHLA (FP7/2007-2013; n° 305831)by Ruth Koops van 't Jagt in collaboration with Ype Driessen.

Assignment

Speed limit table

Purpose of the assignment
You will practice presenting numerical or other research data in a table.

Subject matter
Section 5.3
Section 5.4

The text fragment
Where on rural roads there is no sign indicating that a special speed limit applies, the following maximum speeds shall, as a general rule, apply to motor vehicles: (a) on highways 130 km/h, (b) on motorways 100 km/h, (c) on other secondary roads 80 km/h. In addition, there are speed limits for certain categories of vehicles. For example, passenger cars with single-axle trailers on highways and motorways may not exceed 80 km/h, and with twin-axle trailers 80 km/h on highways and 60 km/h on all other roads. Motorcycles with trailers may not be ridden faster than 80 km/h. For trucks and buses without trailers and for buses with single-axle trailers, the maximum speed on all roads is 80 km/h, with the exception of secondary roads, where it is 60 km/h. For trucks and buses with a two-axle trailer, the maximum limit is 80 km/h on highways and 60 km/h on all other roads.

Tasks
1   Display the information in this text in a table. Present the data in such a way that you can easily see the maximum speeds per type of vehicle.
2   Imagine you have to make an overview for speed checkers on highways, motorways, and secondary roads. They must be able to see quickly when the speed limit of 80 km/h applies and when the speed limit of 60 km/h applies. What would such an overview look like?

6   Reading and summarizing

◀ *Still life with books in a niche,* Barthélémy d'Eyck, 1442-1445. In the middle a pencil case, on the right a round and a rectangular box. Upper part of the left side panel with the prophet Isaiah, in the Museum Boijmans-Van Beuningen in Rotterdam. The right side panel is in the Royal Museum of Fine Arts of Belgium in Brussels, the middle panel with the proclamation is in the church of Ste. Madelaine in Aix-en-Provence.

With the overwhelming abundance of written knowledge that is available nowadays, you need to use practical strategies to select and summarize the information that is relevant to you.

Microsoft: Concentration decreases because of technology and social media

The average attention span for the notoriously ill-focused goldfish is nine seconds, but according to a new study from Microsoft Corp., people now generally lose concentration after eight seconds, highlighting the effects of an increasingly digitalized lifestyle on the brain.

Researchers in Canada surveyed 2,000 participants and studied the brain activity of 112 others using electroencephalograms (EEGs). Microsoft found that since the year 2000 (or about when the mobile revolution began) the average attention span dropped from 12 seconds to eight seconds.

'Heavy multi-screeners find it difficult to filter out irrelevant stimuli—they're more easily distracted by multiple streams of media,' the report read.

On the positive side, the report says our ability to multitask has drastically improved in the mobile age.

Microsoft theorized that the changes were a result of the brain's ability to adapt and change itself over time and a weaker attention span may be a side effect of evolving to a mobile Internet.

The survey also confirmed generational differences for mobile use; for example, 77% of people aged 18 to 24 responded 'yes' when asked, 'When nothing is occupying my attention, the first thing I do is reach for my phone,' compared with only 10% of those over the age of 65.

And now congratulate yourself for concentrating long enough to make it through this article.

Source: McSpadden (2015).[11]

Our concentration is waning. According to the *Microsoft* study referred to in this article, we are so obsessed with portable technology, social media, and an abundance of information that it is difficult for us to focus on something for a long time. Indeed, we now apparently have a shorter attention span than a goldfish. At least that is what the Microsoft study, conducted among 2,000 Canadians, says.

We are confronted with such a great amount of information—both solicited and unsolicited—that we can hardly process it without losing track. Someone who does not know how to select and organize properly will almost literally fall victim to the enormous range of informative texts, images, and videos. Each one of these items may be interesting or useful in itself, but taken together they form such a large pile of food for thought that we are barely able to consume it in a healthy way. This not only concerns information on social media. It also applies to the literature that you have to process as a student to properly prepare for your classes, successfully pass your exams, or write a good literature review for a thesis. Business professionals, whatever their specialization, are also faced with a huge amount of information, for instance when they have to conduct research, write a report, or give a presentation for their colleagues.

A well-chosen approach to the variety of sources you are confronted with, will help you to deal effectively with all the information you will find. Good reading and summarizing skills are indispensable for this purpose. Good reading and summarizing skills also form the basis for your own well-developed messages, both oral and written. This chapter will show you how best to strategically read and summarize information, especially from texts relevant to your own particular purposes. We will discuss two diffferent ways of doing this.

In section 6.1, we pay attention to ways of reading and summarizing while following a text's original structure. This is a method of processing information that uses the content and structure of the text as the starting point. You start by quickly reading through the information as it is presented to you, and then you carefully read and summarize those parts of the text that are most relevant to your own goals. Section 6.2 deals with restructuring reading and summarizing. In this case, you do not follow the content and structure of the text, but instead allow your own questions to determine the way you read it.

After you have read and summarized a text that is important to your goals, you will often have to incorporate its content into your own text. How do you correctly present the content of other texts without risking accusations of plagiarism? And

11   McSpadden, K. (2015, May 14). *You now have a shorter attention span than a goldfish*. Retrieved from http://time.com/3858309/attention-spans-goldfish/

how do you format your quotations, citations, and bibliography correctly? These questions will be discussed in more detail in chapters 8 and 9, which deal with various types of writing tasks that you may need to perform.

6.1   Structure-based reading and summarizing

Many readers tend to read all texts from start to finish. But this is often an inefficient approach: You may already know large parts of the content, or you run the risk of missing the general point of the text. Good readers therefore adapt their way of reading a text to the goals they want to achieve in each particular case. Sometimes you only need to have a general impression of the content of the text. At other times, for example when you are studying for an exam, you have to thoroughly read the text or at least parts of it.

Our advice is therefore to read a text in two rounds. Start with a cursory review of the entire text to get a general impression of its meaning. If you want to study the content in more detail—either the whole text or parts of it—then you can carefully read the relevant sections.

6.1.1   Cursory reading: a brief summary

A cursory reading means that you concentrate on the main points of the text. You try to determine the theme of the text (or the passage), the main questions, and the key answers to the main questions. Using the term we introduced in section 2.1, you could say that you concentrate on the elements of a short text schema. At this stage you pay as little attention as possible to details, examples, and nuances. A cursory reading of the text is important to:

- get an impression of the *content and structure* of the text (this is often enough);
- get an idea of the *goals* of the text (informative, instructive, persuasive, motivating);
- gain insight into the *value* of the text (news value, depth);
- understand the *usefulness* of the text for your own purposes (will I benefit from it for my research, my advice, my report?);
- identify areas for *further examination* (for example because they contain new information or questionable views).

First orientation
Before you start searching for the theme and main questions, you first need to determine what kind of text you have in front of you. Then you will know, to some extent, what to expect with regard to content and meaning, as well as how much

effort and time it will take to read the text, the problems you can expect, and the help offered by the text. The orientation phase is concerned with the following points.

–   *Text type.* A didactic text from a textbook probably contains many structure indicators (headings, summaries, diagrams) and explanations (definitions, examples). A research report in a scientific journal usually follows the conventional structure for reports on research, and a text that contains many arguments is an argumentative essay.

–   *External structure.* Is the text clearly divided into separate parts (chapters, sections, paragraphs)? Do the sections have titles or headings? Do all sections start with a brief introduction? Are there any summarizing sections? If a text contains many structure indicators, a cursory reading takes less time.

–   *Additions.* Does the text contain figures, diagrams, tables, definitions, formulae, a register, a glossary, a list of abbreviations, footnotes, or endnotes? These are often the signs of a complicated, sometimes technical text. Reading such a text will require a great deal of effort, especially in the stage of careful reading; you should therefore take enough time to read it.

In search of text theme, main questions, and key answers

After the first orientation phase, you should look for the specific elements of the short text schema: the text theme, the main questions, and their key answers. You should realize that it is usually easier to determine the theme and the key answers than the main questions, simply because the theme and the key answers are in most cases mentioned explicitly, although not always in the shortest possible format. The main questions, however, are usually much less explicit: The reader often has to infer them himself or herself by identifying the necessary link between the theme of the text and the key answers that the text explicitly presents.

#MeToo

The original purpose of 'Me Too' as used by Tarana Burke in 2006, was to empower women through empathy, especially young and vulnerable women. In October 2017, Alyssa Milano encouraged using the phrase as a hashtag to help reveal the extent of problems with sexual harassment and assault by showing how many people have experienced these events themselves.

After millions of people started using the phrase and it spread to dozens of other languages, the purpose changed and expanded, as a result of which it has come to mean different things to different people. Tarana Burke accepts the title of the leader and creator of the movement but has stated she considers herself a worker of something much bigger. Burke has stated that this movement has grown to include both men and women of all colors and ages, as it continues to support marginalized people in marginalized

> communities. There have also been movements by men aimed at changing the culture
> through personal reflection and future action, including #IDidThat, #IHave, and #IWill.

After *Wikipedia (English)* (2018).[12]

This short text clearly presents the evolvement of different purposes of the #MeToo movement
in the course of time. However, the question that links 'the #MeToo movement' (the text theme)
with its different purposes (the key answers) is left implicit. This question has to be inferred
by the reader by analyzing the logical structure of this text: 'How has its original purpose
evolved in the course of time?'.

> THE #METOO MOVEMENT
> How has its original purpose evolved in the course of time?
> 1 First: Empower women through empathy.
> 2 Then also: Help reveal the extent of problems with sexual harassment and assault.
> 3 Now also: Support marginalized people in marginalized communities.

Short summary, including the main question that was left implicit in the text.

When you are determining the text theme, the main questions, and their key
answers, it is helpful to pay attention to *structure indicators*. Structure indicators are
parts of a text that clarify the structure of the text as a whole (see also section 2.4.6).
You can often already make a short text schema of the text on the basis of these
structure indicators. The most important structure indicators are:
– the title;
– an added summary or abstract;
– the table of contents;
– the introduction (especially its beginning and its end);
– chapter and paragraph titles, subtitles, headings;
– concluding passages;
– (for a book) the text on the front or back cover.

Furthermore, you may profit from *signal words or phrases* in the text and from
words or phrases the writer puts in *italics* or **bold**. Also useful for discovering the
text theme, the main questions, and the key answers may be the so-called *preferred
positions* in the text as a whole or in parts of the text. Preferred positions are the
places where the most important information can usually be found: the beginning
of a certain part of a text, or the end of it. When you are reading cursorily, the first
and last paragraphs of a section or chapter are particularly important.

12   *Wikipedia (English)* (2018). Retrieved from https://en.wikipedia.org/wiki/Me_Too_movement

Sometimes a section at the start of the text serves as a kind of appetizer, such as an anecdote, an example, or a quotation. At the end of a text, writers can make an elegant connection with the appetizer the text started with, or they end with a cliché—'there's still a lot of work to be done', for example. In these cases, the second or penultimate part of the text often serves as the preferred text location.

To demonstrate the process of cursory reading and working toward a short summary, we use an example text that is shorter than most texts you might read in practice but still shows the most important elements that can help with cursory reading.

Materials for artificial implants

Introduction

Surgical treatments in hospitals often involve the removal of a diseased part of the human body. A well-known example is the appendectomy, which is the surgical removal of an inflamed section of the intestines. But it is also possible to surgically add something to the human body to replace or support a sick organ. Such an 'addition' is called an implant. Well-known implants include leg prostheses, heart valves, and dental implants.

In this article we focus on the materials used for *artificial implants*. We first distinguish the types of implants; then we describe the *requirements* for artificial implant materials; and finally we briefly go into the research on these materials.

1 Types of implants

Depending on the kind of material that is added to the body, we can distinguish two types of implants: those using living material and those using artificial materials.

Implants of *living material* may come from the patient himself or from a donor. Living material originating from the patient himself can be used, for instance, to restore the blood supply to the heart by adding pieces of vein from the patient's leg. A major advantage of this method of implantation is that the body will not reject the material, because it is familiar tissue.

When a donor supplies tissue or an organ, we speak of a transplantation. Good results have already been achieved with the transplantation of kidneys, especially if the patient and donor are related. The advantage of transplants is that the procedure is, in principle, possible with very complex body tissues (such as kidneys). The disadvantage is that sometimes the body rejects the implants. It is for this reason that heart and skin transplants have not always led to long-term success. A second disadvantage of this procedure is that it depends on a donor, whose organ has to be removed very quickly after his or her death. This raises not only medical but also ethical issues.

Non-living, *artificial material* can also be used for implants. The search for suitable artificial implant materials belongs to the field of biomedical sciences. The mechanical side of the problem concerns the shape and consequently the strength of an implant.

A very large and well-known area of the implantation of artificial materials is dentistry. Until recently simple fillings, together with the placement of dentures and crowns, were the most common dental interventions. But now there are also so-called dental implants. Dental implants are artificial roots made of titanium that are fixed into the jawbone and on which the dentist places a crown, bridge or overdenture.

Another example of an artificial implant is plastic suture that is used to temporarily close a wound until it is healed. The suture does not have to last for a long time. Internal sutures are therefore made of a special plastic that does not leave behind any foreign material after it has decomposed.

Finally, orthopedics use larger constructions that need to have a long life span, such as a hip replacement or knee joint. Other orthopedic applications include bone plates, pins, and screws. These standard components serve to surgically reattach bone parts after a fracture so that it heals more quickly.

2   Requirements

The materials used for artificial implants have to meet strict requirements. We distinguish between *technical requirements*, which concern the function of the implant and its construction, and *biological requirements*, which relate to the functioning of the implant in the human body.

2.1   Technical requirements

When choosing the material for a part of a machine or something else, a manufacturer considers the material properties that are necessary for the part to properly function. For the design of a door hinge, for instance, properties such as strength, corrosion resistance, wear resistance, and appearance are important. The weight is not as important in this case, and electrical conductivity does not play any role in determining the most suitable material for its purpose.

The manufacturing method also places demands too on the chosen material. Depending on the design, a material must be easy to cast or weld, or it should easily bend into a certain shape without breaking. Another requirement may be how easy it is to drill into the material. For each component of the final product, the manufacturer has to make a choice by comparing material data. Costs often play a major role in the decision.

The design of implants also entails a consideration of suitable properties. However, in this case the costs are not as important. After all, the enormous costs of the surgery and aftercare in the hospital overshadow any costs of the implant. And of course, it concerns people's health, and so in principle only the best is good enough.

2.2 Biological requirements

The additional material requirements that the human body imposes on an implant are summarized with the concept of biocompatibility. A material is biocompatible if:

– the body is resistant to and accepts the material, and
– the material is resistant to the body environment.

The first requirement is met if a material is non-toxic and does not cause a rejecting reaction in the body. Toxicity can lead to dead tissue. Usually this will be near the implant, but body tissue can also die in other places if the material is spread through solution or corrosion. A rejecting reaction occurs when the surrounding tissue is resistant to the material but does not accept it. In this case, the body will try to remove the implant. Symptoms that can occur as a result of this are a fever, an inflammation on the spot, an allergic reaction, or the development of a tumor. When an implant is accepted, it will be encapsulated with a thin layer of connective tissue. If the material is in permanent direct contact with blood, as is the case with a heart valve, it also needs to meet a special requirement: It must not cause the blood to solidify.

The second required characteristic of biocompatible material is that it must be resistant to the body environment. For metals, this means they must be corrosion resistant, because bodily fluids are as corrosive as seawater. Plastics, in most cases, should not break down over time. If they do need to, as is the case with biodegradable sutures, the duration of the degradation process must be known.

3 Research

The discussion of the requirements above shows that a great deal of research is necessary to design suitable implants and to enable their application. This research requires close collaboration between physicians and technicians and is referred to by the term *biomedical engineering*. Biomedical mechanical engineering and biomedical chemistry are particularly important.

The first discipline focuses mainly on usable constructions for artificial implants (joint replacements, for instance); the second discipline focuses mainly on research on usable materials for artificial implants.

An example from the field of biomedical chemistry is research on the biocompatibility of certain materials. This research is partly carried out through animal testing. The material is implanted in the form of powder or plates in rats, for example. The researchers then monitor the reaction of the surrounding tissue of the rats by studying microscopic preparations. If the researchers kill a number of rats once a month and examine their tissue, the course of the reaction over time becomes visible. The presence of certain cell types reveals the nature of the reaction. The researchers can observe the deterioration of the material by examining the presence of small amounts in the surrounding tissue. Very small concentrations can be determined through spectrochemical analysis.

This type of research has revealed that some materials do cause dead tissue when they are implanted in powder form, while plates made of the same material do not lead to any problems. This shows that the wear of an artificial joint can pose a greater threat than the artificial implant itself.

How may this example be read cursorily?
- *First orientation.* The text offers you a lot of support for cursory reading: It is divided into fairly short units with numbered headings, and there is a clearly structured introduction section. The text is about a technical subject, but there are no formulas, diagrams, or tables that indicate that the information is highly complex.
- *Searching for the text theme.* The text theme is already mentioned in the title. The emphasis in the final paragraph of the introduction points in the same direction and a quick consultation of the subheadings and the end of the text removes any doubt: The text is about MATERIALS FOR ARTIFICIAL IMPLANTS.
- *Searching for the main questions.* The introduction, including the signal words 'first', 'then', and 'finally', and the subheadings already give a lot of clues.
- *Searching for the key answers.* You can already find the key answers to the first main question in the introduction and in the first paragraph of section 1 (preferred position). In section 2, the first paragraph provides the key answers to the second main question: the distinction between technical and biological requirements (again in *italics*). Those answers are also marked by the headings 2.1 and 2.2. The key answers to the third main question are somewhat more difficult to find, but they are still in a preferred position. The last two sentences of the first paragraph of section 3 mention the two types of research: biomedical mechanical engineering and biomedical chemistry.

The outcomes of cursory reading can be presented in a short text schema such as the one below.

MATERIALS FOR ARTIFICAL IMPLANTS
What types of implants are there?
1   Implants of living material.
2   Artificial implants.

What are the requirements for the material of artificial implants?
1   Requirements of a technical nature.
2   Requirements of a biological nature.

What kind of research is conducted on these materials?
1 Biomedical mechanical engineering.
2 Biomedical chemistry.

Short text schema of the text about artificial implants.

After cursorily reading the text, you can already write a short summary of the text based on the text schema. Of course, such a summary cannot be very extensive because you have not yet studied the text accurately enough for that. This short summary is based on the short text schema. It states what the theme is, what the main questions are and what the key answers are to those main questions. When writing the short summary, you can choose between two formats (see also section 8.1.2).

– With a *direct summary* (also called an *informative summary*), you choose the perspective of the author of the original text. Your summary is a shortened version of the text as presented by the author.

– With an *indirect summary* (also called an *indicative summary*) you write a text from your own perspective as a reader. It is a text about the text you have read. Characteristics are phrases such as 'This report concerns' and 'The author claims that', and indications of the text structure such as 'In the first paragraph' and 'In chapter 7'.

There are two types of implants: implants from living material and artificial implants. The materials for the latter sort are subject to both technical and biological requirements. Research into artificial implants is divided into biomedical mechanical engineering and biomedical chemistry.

Direct (informative) short summary of the text on artificial implants.

In this text on artificial implants, the author first makes a distinction between two types of implants: implants from living material and artificial implants. In section 2, she explains that the materials for artificial implants are subject to both technical and biological requirements. Finally, in section 3 she describes two disciplines of research into artificial implants: biomedical mechanical engineering and biomedical chemistry.

Indirect (indicative) short summary of the text on artificial implants.

The distinction between direct and indirect is not just a formal issue. When writing a direct summary, you identify, as it were, with the writer: You give an unfiltered representation of what is in the text. The more distant, indirect form offers more possibilities to show any doubts or criticism you may have. By alternating both perspectives within one summary, you create the opportunity to show where you do and where you do not doubt the reliability of the content.

> Many texts are difficult to read. This is because many writers do not know that their texts are difficult, and because writers often do not know how to make their texts easier. But according to the author, there are also writers who could formulate less complex sentences but simply don't want to. These writers, as this text claims, consciously choose to adopt imposing or facade behavior with all the harmful consequences that this choice entails.

Change between direct and indirect form in a short summary. The phrase 'according to the author' suggests that this point is new and that the preceding point was already generally known. The formulation 'as this text claims' suggests that the person who wrote this summary considers the statement that follows here to be a position that can be discussed.

6.1.2   Careful reading: a detailed summary

If you read a text (or part of it) carefully, you try to find out what sub-questions result from the key answers, how those sub-questions are answered, what sub-questions result from those key answers, what their key answers are, and so on.

You can read a text carefully in different ways, depending on the amount of detail you need. Your goal determines how thoroughly you should read the text. If you want to do well on a literature exam, you should naturally study each text very carefully. If you only need part of the information, it is better to read the relevant parts of the text carefully and to read the rest of the text only cursorily.

Method
Always start with a cursory reading of the text. You will then know the theme, the main questions, and the key answers to those main questions. It may also be wise to make a general outline of the text for yourself on paper (or on screen) in the form of a short text schema. This will help you follow the general thrust of the text when you are reading carefully.

The best way to read carefully is by working *top-down*. Try to divide the text into parts that coincide with one of the key answers from the short text schema. You can use any of these key answers as a theme of a text section. You can now analyze this part of the text in roughly the same way as you did the text as a whole. In your detailed analysis, you can also use structure indicators and preferred locations.

If this does not work, or not entirely, you can use the *bottom-up* method. In this case, you treat the paragraphs as units in your careful reading and try to determine the essence of each paragraph. This can be a question (or sub-question), but it can also be a key answer (or sub-key answer) that is discussed in more detail with explanations, examples, or arguments.

In practice, the top-down approach is usually the fastest method. However, in order for this approach to work, the text must be well-structured and contain sufficient structure indicators. Not all texts meet this condition—far from it. You will therefore often have to apply the bottom-up approach.

We will not discuss the top-down approach further here. This method is the same as the one used for a cursory reading; you simply apply it to smaller parts of the text. In the next section, we will discuss a number of options for the bottom-up approach. After that, we outline some of the problems that may arise when you are reading a text carefully.

In search of the paragraph theme

When you are looking for the theme of a paragraph, you should naturally start by asking yourself: 'What is the paragraph about?' To find out quickly, you can often use two tools: preferred positions and references.

As noted above, preferred positions are those places in a text that often contain the most important elements, such as the theme and the key answers to the main questions. In general, there are three preferred positions where you have a good chance of finding the theme:
- the first sentence of the paragraph;
- the second sentence of the paragraph, if the first sentence is of an introductory nature;
- the last sentence of the paragraph: Here the text often reaches a conclusion on the basis of examples or arguments.

Message designers working in the field of mass health communication have to overcome some great challenges when trying to develop effective persuasive messages. To give one example: The behaviors that they have to target are frequently performed automatically and unconsciously, making it difficult to get recipients to even contemplate changes. Many health messages also have to compete with commercial messages that point in the exact opposite direction and that may be much more attractive to the recipients. And finally, there is barely any research available that really helps in determining the most effective content and format for health communication messages.

The theme of this paragraph, 'challenges for health communication message designers', can be found in the first sentence.

The behaviors that message designers working in the field of mass health communication have to target are frequently performed automatically and unconsciously, making it difficult to get recipients to even contemplate changes. That is one example of the great challenges that health communication message designers have to overcome when trying to develop effective persuasive messages. Many health messages also have to compete with commercial messages that point in the exact opposite direction and that may be much more attractive to the recipients. And finally, there is barely any research available that really helps in determining the most effective content and format for health communication messages.

The theme of this paragraph, 'challenges for health communication message designers', can now be found in the second sentence.

The behaviors that message designers working in the field of mass health communication have to target are frequently performed automatically and unconsciously, making it difficult to get recipients to even contemplate changes. Many health messages also have to compete with commercial messages that point in the exact opposite direction and that may be much more attractive to the recipients. And finally, there is barely any research available that really helps in determining the most effective content and format for health communication messages. These are some examples of the great challenges that health communication message designers have to overcome when trying to develop effective persuasive messages.

The theme of this paragraph, 'challenges for health communication message designers', can now be found in the last sentence.

Apart from preferred positions, *referential ties* in the text (see section 2.4.3) may also be helpful to find the theme.

Prolific pills, a sex stimulant that was available for a long time, contain 0.2 mg of the artificial hormone silbestrol, better known as DES. According to the instructions, a 'frigid woman' had to take two pills with every meal to be more sexually stimulated. The capsules were available in sex shops but could also be ordered by mail. Prolific pills were, for instance, included in the catalogue of a shipping company for sex products. It was revealed only much later that the pills could pose a major risk to an unborn child during a pregnancy.

The first sentence of this paragraph contains two possible themes: 'prolific pills' and 'the artificial hormone DES'. The second sentence refers back to 'prolific pills' by repeating the word 'pills', and in the third sentence by the synonym 'capsules'. A quick check for the remainder of the text shows that 'prolific pills' is indeed the theme of this paragraph.

Prolific pills, a sex stimulant that was available for a long time, contain 0.2 mg of the artificial hormone silbestrol, better known as DES. DES has many side effects and is carcinogenic. About forty years ago, DES was used to prevent miscarriages. It has also been used for the treatment of breast cancer and prostate cancer, for disruptions of the menstrual cycle, and to combat the symptoms of menopause. By now, it has been discovered that DES can cause great damage to an unborn child during a pregnancy. The organization of the so-called DES daughters has made sure there is more public attention for this topic. No doctor will prescribe DES nowadays.

The first sentence of this paragraph is the same as in the previous example and therefore contains two possible themes: 'prolific pills' and 'the artificial hormone DES'. Now, however, the second sentence does not refer back to the pills but to 'the artificial hormone DES' by means of a literal repetition. Checking this with the remainder of the paragraph confirms that the theme of this paragraph is indeed 'the artificial hormone DES'. Halfway through the paragraph, it is referred to with 'it' and in the last sentence the word 'DES' is literally repeated.

In search of the questions and the key answers in a paragraph

Once you have found the theme of a paragraph, you can try to identify the questions and key answers. You can once again make use of the two tools mentioned before: preferred positions and signal words. In addition, you can look for all kinds of graphical signals:

– *signal signs*: letters, numbers, bullet points;
– *deviating fonts*;
– *text size and formatting*: **bold**, *italic*, color;
– *layout*: wider margin, different line spacing.

Combining small parts to form a larger whole

When you are reading a text using the bottom-up approach, it is not sufficient to only find the themes, questions, and key answers in the separate paragraphs; you must combine this information from the different parts to form a larger whole. Before you can do this, you first need to determine the themes of the individual paragraphs. Then you can search for the common factor among these sub-themes in order to find the theme of the whole text.

Just as you can combine paragraph themes to find the theme of a larger text section, you can also determine the theme of an entire text by searching for the themes of all the separate sections of a text and combining those themes again.

The current exams at secondary schools often cause psychological problems among pupils. The main cause of this is that they have to work under great pressure during their whole last year at school. This constant pressure to perform well leads to nervousness, insomnia, and sometimes even disinterest, which has a negative impact on the results.

Another objection to the current exams concerns the regulations. Firstly, the results seem rather unreliable, as many teachers tend to increase the prior grades of their pupils to such an extent that they achieve the required average even if they fail their final exam. On top of this, often the timing of the resit is an obstacle for pupils who apply to a higher education program that preselects its students during the summer.

The theme of the first paragraph is 'psychological problems of exam candidates' and the theme of the second paragraph is 'the regulations of final exams'. What these two themes have in common is that they are both objections against the current final exams (note the word 'another' at the start of the second paragraph). This, then, is the theme of the entire text passage.

The detailed summary

You can make a detailed summary on the basis of a detailed text schema. This will include not only the text theme, the main questions, and the key answers but also the sub-questions, the key answers, further sub-questions, and so on (see also section 2.1).

As with the short summary, you can choose to use the direct form (an informative summary). Such a summary is written from the point of view of the author of the text. You can also write the summary in an indirect form (an indicative summary). Then you use the reader's point of view.

Another choice that you have to make concerns the level of detail of the different passages of the original text. It is important that you summarize the passages that are relevant to you in more detail than the parts of the text that are less relevant. This may mean that you make a short summary for some parts of the text while providing a detailed summary of other parts. The detailed summary can give you or others a brief but sufficiently precise overview of the content of the whole text or its relevant parts.

MATERIALS FOR ARTIFICAL IMPLANTS
What types of implants are there?
1   Implants of living material.
2   Artificial implants.

What are the requirements for the material of artificial implants?
1   Requirements of a technical nature.
    What are they?
    1   The material must suit the function of the implant.
    2   The material must be easy to process.
    3   The material does not have to be cheap.

2 Requirements of a biological nature.
   <u>What do they mean?</u>
   1 The material needs to be biocompatible.
      <u>What does that mean?</u>
      The body must be resistant to the material.
         <u>What does that mean?</u>
         1 The tissue should not die.
         2 The implant should not be rejected.
   2 If the implant is in permanent contact with blood, it should not cause the blood to
      solidify.
   3 The material must be resistant to the body.
      <u>What does that mean for metal implants?</u>
      They should not start to rust.
         <u>What does that mean for plastic implants?</u>
         In most cases, these should not break down.
            <u>With what exception?</u>
            Material that only has to function temporarily, such as suture.

<u>What kind of research is conducted on these materials?</u>
1 Biomedical mechanical engineering.
2 Biomedical chemistry.

Text schema of the example in section 6.1.1. The answers to the second main question are plotted in detail here.

First, this text presents a distinction between two types of implants: implants from living material and artificial implants. After that, the author states that the materials for artificial implants are subject to both technical and biological requirements. As far as the technical requirements are concerned, the material needs to be suited for the function that the implant will perform, and it needs to be easy to process. The author considers the costs of the material to be of little importance. A biological requirement is that the material is 'biocompatible'. This means that the body must be resistant to the material and that the material must be resistant to the body. If the body is not resistant to the material, tissue will die or the material will be rejected. If the material is in permanent contact with blood, an additional requirement applies: It should not cause the blood to solidify. Metal implants should not corrode. Also, in most cases plastics should not break down, with the exception of material that only has to function temporarily, such as suture. In the last section of the text, two areas of research into the materials for artificial implants are mentioned: biomedical mechanical engineering and biomedical chemistry.

An indirect or indicative detailed summary based on the previous text schema.

6.1.3   Critical reading: a critical summary

Properly reading a text is not simply a matter of seeing and understanding, you also have to form judgments about the written message. Good readers therefore also read critically. There are four aspects of a text to guide you in this.
– *Completeness*: Is the issue dealt with in enough detail?
– *Relevance*: Is there no superfluous information in the text?
– *Accuracy*: Does the information in the text correspond with reality?
– *Credibility*: Are the claims that need to be supported well-argued?

The criterion: context and goals of the text
It is not fair to judge a newspaper article as if it were a scientific report or to expect an Italian travel guide to offer viewpoints on the merits or problems of the country's current government. Before passing a judgment, you should therefore first consider the communicative goals of the text and the context in which it is supposed to be used. You can find the starting points for this in chapter 1.
– Start with the *underlying goals* of the text. What was the production context? What is the intended audience? What problems is the text meant to solve?
– What are the *communicative goals* of the text? Is the text mainly meant to be informative, instructive, persuasive, motivating, or affective? And was that an apt choice, given the text's underlying goals and its context?
– Consider in this round *all four sides* of the communicative message. Besides the goals (appeal side) and the information (matter side), you should also pay attention to the question of how the sender presents himself or herself in this context (self-expression side) and how the sender apparently sees the relationship between sender and receiver (relationship side).

This reflection on the goals and the context not only serves to clarify the requirements that you can reasonably expect a text to meet. The four text aspects mentioned above (completeness, relevance, accuracy, and credibility) also make you aware of what the writer might gain by omitting or 'coloring' certain information in order to achieve his or her goals. This, in turn, will help you to identify possible shortcomings of the text.

Assessing completeness and relevance using a set schema

No text can cover all the questions that can possibly be asked about a subject. Writers always have to make a selection. The critical reader must assess whether the writer of a text has made a good selection in the given context. There are different strategies to determine this.

-   You can compare the content and structure with a set schema (see section 2.2) that fits the context. If certain elements from that set schema are missing, this could be a point of criticism. Remember that it is only a *possible* point of criticism: In certain contexts, elements from a set schema can be omitted without causing problems.
-   If the text contains important elements that do not fit the set schema, you may wonder whether they are necessary in this context. If that is not the case, this may once again be a possible point of criticism.
-   Check whether the classification of the key answers meets the arrangement requirements set out in section 2.3.2. Is the classification clear, logical, and exhaustive, or can you reasonably criticize it?
-   Make sure that all the important key answers are sufficiently substantiated with arguments. Section 3.1.1 describes when argumentation is necessary. Check for each standpoint whether they meet this requirement.

Imagine you work for a small non-profit organization and you receive a draft memorandum concerning the purchase of a new computer network that connects all PCs, notebooks, and iMacs of the employees both in their workplace and at home. You are asked to comment on the draft memorandum.

The draft memorandum consists of an introduction followed by four sections. The first section contains a brief summary of previous discussions about the desirability of further automation in the organization. The conclusion based on these discussions is that there is broad support for the introduction of a new network. The second section outlines the requirements for the network configuration, including a new server. This is followed in the third section by an overview of the hardware and software currently on the market, and the fourth section presents the final proposal: to purchase a BOA-file server with the FL-MAIL software package.

In order for you to be able to give good comments, you should first examine which set schema is the most obvious choice for this text. There are two candidates: the set measure schema and the set design schema. The first is particularly suitable if the readers still need to be convinced of the importance of the measure, in this case the introduction of a new network. The set design schema is more suitable if the emphasis is more on the question of what the configuration will look like: the requirements and the implementation. Since there already seems to be a consensus on the decision to create a new network, the most obvious choice in this situation is the set design schema.

When you compare the structure of the draft memorandum to the set design schema, you will notice that the first four questions of the set design schema are indeed dis-cussed but that the last question is not addressed. How will they (retrospectively) check whether their decision was the right one?

This point could be elaborated on in the memorandum, or perhaps a section should be added that outlines how the functioning of the new network will be evaluated after some time. You can send this critical comment (along with any other comments) back to the writers.

The completeness of the text can be critically assessed on the basis of a set schema.

Assessing accuracy and credibility

Accuracy and credibility are important considerations not only for the key answers as such, but also to assess whether a key answer is a good answer to the question. When assessing a text, you should take both of these aspects into account.

If a text addresses the question 'What are the causes of excessive drinking among young people?' and one of the answers is that parents barely know what their children are drinking, critical readers should then ask themselves two questions: 'Is it true that parents barely know what their children are drinking?' and 'Does the parents' knowledge of their children's drinking affect the children's behavior?' (By the way, research indicates that the answer to both questions is no).

It is essential to critically assess not only the key answer but also the relationship between the key answer and the theme addressed in the main question.

How can you, as a critical reader, judge the *accuracy* of the factual information in the text?

– Check whether the information in the text corresponds to your own knowledge of the subject.
– Determine whether you can consider the writer a reliable source of information.
– If you are in any doubt, use the internet to check the information. Of course, that is still no guarantee: There is a lot of nonsense on the internet. However, if multiple (independent) sources provide the same information, it is more likely that the information is correct.

Credibility is not so much concerned with the factual information of the text but more with the positions taken by the writer. In chapter 3, you will find many starting points for a critical reading in this respect.

– Identify the disputable statements that the text needs to prove.
– Check whether these statements are supported by arguments. Are there any statements that the writer presents as indisputable facts even though they are actually positions?
– If the text contains arguments, map out the structure of the reasoning as accurately as possible (see section 3.2).
– Check the forms of argumentation that are used and assess the quality of the reasoning (see section 3.3, section 3.4, and section 3.5).

Systematically assessing accuracy and credibility is a complex and time-consuming task, especially if you are not (yet) familiar with the subject of the text. It is therefore better to focus on those parts of the text that are crucial for:

– the goals of the text in the given context (when a writer presents an opinion on proposed measures, for example);
– your own goals and reasons for studying the text. If you want to use the text as a source for your own argument, concentrate on the elements you want to use in your text.

The critical summary

A critical summary can be based on either a brief summary or a detailed summary. It always includes one additional element: your judgments on the completeness, relevance, accuracy, and credibility of the text as a whole or of certain passages.

The indirect form is often the best choice for a critical summary. This will allow you to clearly distinguish between what the writer of the text claims and how you, as a reader, respond to it.

This text first explains what football hooliganism is and how it relates to other forms of vandalism. It then outlines the scale of the problem, both in terms of the number of victims (especially among the vandals themselves) and of the material damage caused by football hooliganism. *The writer seems to underestimate this material damage. It is also striking that there is no mention of victims among the police and stadium attendants, of the nuisance to the residents of the neighborhoods where the vandals go before and after the match, and of the damage to the club's image and the image of sport.* The text ends with a plea for a form of summary judgment which has already been used in other countries for a long time but is still waiting to be introduced in our country. The author predicts that the introduction of a special football law such as the one in England will lead to a significant reduction of vandalism in and around stadiums.

However useful this plea for our football law may be, it is a pity that the text does not address the underlying causes of football hooliganism. The risk therefore remains that a special football law will be no more than symptom control and that the underlying problem of disrespectful immorality, coupled with discrimination and destructiveness, will resurface in another way.

Critical summary. For the sake of convenience, the comments of the person who wrote the summary in this example are in *italics*. Note that the critical summary ends with arguments that support the criticism of the shortcomings of the text. This makes the critical summary more convincing for outsiders than if the commenter would only have identified omissions.

6.2   Restructuring reading and summarizing

When you read a text cursorily or carefully, as outlined in the previous section, you follow the structure of the text. You read the text from beginning to end and try to translate this into a text schema or a summary that corresponds to this structure. However, there is also a reading strategy that allows you, as the reader, to choose the way in which you summarize a text. In that case, you do not follow the text's original structure but restructure it to fit your goals.

Restructuring reading means you use the information in the text for your own purpose: You select and restructure the information so that it fits into your own new text. You choose your own perspective, you select the questions and key answers that are important to you, and you organize those questions and key answers so they fit within the structure of your own text. You make your own text schema, possibly on the basis of one of the set schemata from section 2.2. In doing so, you are *tilting*, as it were, the information you have found in the literature.

You can apply restructuring reading (and summarizing) to one text but also to several texts on a certain subject. The latter is useful when you write a literature review, either as an independent text or as part of a thesis, a research proposal, or a policy text.

Imagine you are preparing for a meeting in which you will discuss a proposal to establish a new Master's program in Arts and Culture. You receive a detailed report on the interest of prospective students, on the opportunities for graduates on the labor market, and on similar study programs at home and abroad. There is, of course, also a proposed study program and a good section on the contribution that this new Master's program will make to the profile of your academic institution.

You can obviously read this report from start to finish, following its structure. However, while preparing for the meeting, it may be more useful to focus on the pros and cons of the proposal. These are the matters that you will discuss during the meeting. The advantages and disadvantages of the proposal are not neatly listed in a specific section of the report. That means you will have to collect them from different parts of the report. By doing this, you select information from the text and organize it into a new structure.

An application of restructuring reading.

Maisie Brown is preparing a course intended for writers of user manuals and instructions. For one of the classes, Maisie wants to discuss the subject of flowcharts. She starts looking for literature about flowcharts and finds a good, classic article about a study on the effects of flowcharts.

Maisie reads the article, which clearly follows the set research schema, from start to finish, and records the information from the text in a short summary based on a text schema following the same structure as the text. She describes what was investigated, what the reason was for the research, what method was used, what the main results were, and what conclusions could be drawn on the basis of those results.

This approach leads to an excellent summary, but Maisie realizes that for the people who follow her course, the set measure schema would be more relevant. After all, her principal goal is to advise the students to use flowcharts and to show them how best do it. Information about the reason for researching the topic and about the method is not really important for them.

Maisie therefore selects the information that is important for the students and re-structures it according to the set measure schema: What is a flowchart, why does she recommend it, what should it look like, and what kind of effects do flowcharts have? Here, too, she makes a certain selection of the information but at the same time restructures it: The same information is now read, summarized, and presented from a different angle.

Another application of restructuring reading.

6.2.1 Working with a literature matrix

Restructuring reading is almost inevitable when you have to read different sources on the same theme and summarize your findings in one text. This is the case with exams but also when you are working on a thesis or other writing tasks in an educational or professional context.

In such cases, it is best to rely on a structure of your choice and use the various sources to find answers to the questions in your structure. For example, if your text investigates a particular problem, you can use other sources to identify causes and solutions and put these in your own text schema under the relevant questions (see section 2.1). You can also organize the most important findings from your sources in a table: a literature matrix. In this literature matrix, the rows would list the sources where you get your information from and the columns show the sub-themes (key answers to main questions and sub-questions; see section 2.1.7) that are relevant to your subject. It might even be better to *tilt* this literature matrix so that the sub-themes are in the rows and the sources in the columns, and use this as a basis for your text schema.

© European Union, 1995-2015.

Student Yolanda Rodríguez Alonso is graduating on a subject that caught her interest partly due to her own smoking behavior. She has been smoking for a long time—too long, she thinks—and that means she keeps encountering anti-smoking warnings on cigarette packages, with texts such as: 'Smoking leads to lethal lung cancer'; 'Smoking ages your skin' and 'Smoking can lead to a slow, painful death'. For a couple of years now, there are also photographs on the packages she buys, clearly intended to be frightening. Some photos are very explicit and confrontational, while others are less explicit and more subtle (such as a wrinkly apple). But all contain a warning. Yolanda obviously knows that those texts and those photos are on the packages she buys, but she doesn't really see them anymore. She ignores them and she doesn't let her behavior be influenced by them, at least not consciously.

For her thesis, Yolanda wants to investigate whether the scary pictures in these warnings actually have any effect, and if so, how. Her supervisor sends her two articles, both on another health topic (HIV/AIDS), in which she finds some information about the effects of scary pictures in information material. Through *Google Scholar* she finds two other articles on the subject, in this case not warnings about HIV/AIDS but about the risks of sunbathing.

The question Yolanda is now faced with is how she can organize the information from the four articles in such a way that she can create a good literature review about scary pictures. This chapter will form the basis of the research she wants to do about her own health theme (smoking), with her own questions and her own participants.

She is aware that a literature review should be more than a summary of a series of articles that she has read. It should be a logically constructed text that presents the information from the consulted literature as a theoretical framework for the question that will be central to her research. The literature chapter should convince the reader that there is still an important question about health warnings that is left unanswered by previous studies, and that it is a good idea for Yolanda to start working on that particular research question.

The first thing Yolanda does is to reread the four articles carefully, because she doesn't want to overlook anything. At the same time, she is already focusing on the issue that is most interesting to her: In which cases did the use of scary pictures have an effect? It is not always immediately clear where she can find this information in the articles. But if the authors of the articles have kept more or less to the set research schema (and this is usually the case for research articles), then the introduction, the results, and the conclusion will probably provide the information that Yolanda is most interested in: research data about the effects of scary pictures in health warnings. Yolanda writes down the most important findings from the articles in a literature matrix, with the sources in the rows and the relevant sub-themes in the columns.

	Health theme of the warning	Country where the research was carried out	Kind of pictures that were investigated	Effect found on
Article 1: Dryers (2003)	HIV/Aids	South Africa	explicit pictures	– belief that the threat is real – belief that the threat is real to the test subject – level of fear
Article 2: Huige (2005)	HIV/Aids	The Netherlands	explicit pictures and less explicit pictures	for explicit pictures: – level of fear – tendency to ignore the message for less explicit pictures: – no effects found
Article 3: Rural (2006)	sunbathing	Australia	explicit pictures	– belief that the threat is real – intention to change behavior
Article 4: Perez (2010)	sunbathing	Spain	explicit pictures and less explicit pictures	for explicit pictures: – level of fear – actual behavior for less explicit pictures: – no effects found

Example of a fictitious literature matrix.

Based on this literature matrix, Yolanda could now choose to make a text schema for her chapter in which she first discusses the information from the article by Dryers, then the information from the article by Huige, then the information from the article by Rural, and finally the information from the article by Perez.

But it is much more insightful for the reader, and much better for a logically constructed argument that leads to her own research question, when she tilts the literature matrix. She would then organize the information from the articles along the lines of one of the sub-themes she found in all articles: the effects they discovered of the various types of scary pictures in health warnings. Yolanda's text schema will then look like this:

EFFECTS OF SCARY PICTURES IN HEALTH WARNINGS
<u>What types of scary pictures should we distinguish?</u>
1   Explicit, confrontational pictures.
    <u>What do these pictures appear to have effects on?</u>
    1   On the belief that this is a serious threat.
        <u>What research has shown this?</u>
        1   Research by Dryers (2003) on health education about HIV/AIDS, carried out in South Africa.
        2   Research by Rural (2006) on warnings against excessive sunbathing, carried out in Australia.
    2   On the conviction that this threat also applies to the participant himself.
    <u>What research has shown this?</u>
    Dryers (2003).
    3   On the level of fear that the participant experiences.
        <u>What research has shown this?</u>
        1   Dryers (2003).
        2   Research by Huige (2005) on health education about HIV/AIDS, carried out in the Netherlands.
        3   Research by Perez (2010) on health information about sunbathing, carried out in Spain.
    4   On the tendency to ignore the message.
        <u>What research has shown this?</u>
        Huige (2005).
    5   On the intention to change one's behavior.
        <u>What research has shown this?</u>
        Rural (2006).
    6   On the actual behavior.
        <u>What research has shown this?</u>
        Perez(2010).

2 Less explicit pictures.
   <u>What do these pictures appear to have effects on?</u>
   No effects of these pictures were found.
   <u>In which studies?</u>
   1 Huige (2005).
   2 Perez (2010).

Text schema for a literature chapter based on a tilted literature matrix.

With this text schema based on a tilted literature matrix, Yolanda is able to convincingly present her own research question. She can demonstrate that her research will focus on an aspect that has not yet been investigated in previous studies, or on an issue that the sources disagree on. For example, she could focus on the question of how to prevent someone from ignoring the explicit, confrontational pictures on cigarette packages (an undesirable effect that was only found by Huige). But a tilted literature matrix also offers good ways to show a link between previous research and a theory or perhaps even multiple theories about the phenomenon central to that research.

In this case, Yolanda can show that the research results of the four articles perfectly fit a theory on the effects of frightening messages, or 'fear appeals', that was developed in the second half of the twentieth century in the United States. According to that theory, a message that is meant to be frightening only achieves the desired effect on behavior if the people who are confronted with it are convinced that it is a serious threat that also applies to them. Only then will they be anxious, and only then might they change their behavior. How they will do this depends on several factors, according to the theory. If they think that they cannot defend themselves against the threat, they will ignore the message; they will bury their heads in the sand, so to speak. Only if they are really afraid and if they think that they can change their own behavior will they take the warning as it is intended and eventually—if circumstances allow—behave differently.

The results from the articles that Yolanda has studied fit well with this theory. Pictures in health warnings can only be expected to have an effect if people really become frightened. This explains why the less explicit pictures in Huige (2005) and Perez (2010) did not have any effect. The theory also describes the results of the studies on explicit, confrontational pictures. Some of these results concern the conditions under which messages that are meant to be frightening can have an effect (the threat must be considered serious; people confronted with it must feel that it applies to themselves; they must experience real fear). The other results concern the different types of effects that can occur (burying their heads in the sand, developing the intention to change their behavior, and ultimately implementing actual behavior change).

Most importantly, Yolanda has now also found a suitable theoretical framework for her own study. The theory predicts that the explicit, confrontational photographs on cigarette packages will lead people who are afraid of not being able to stop smoking to bury their heads in the sand. On the basis of this prediction (hypothesis), Yolanda can start her own research.

When you work with a literature matrix, you can create your own line of reasoning, which is more than a list of fragments that happen to have ended up in the same section. After all, you work on the basis of your own text schema (see also section 7.2.3). An additional advantage of using your own plan is that it usually makes it easier for you to identify any inconsistencies or incompleteness in the literature you have read. This approach distinguishes advanced and successful readers from their less skilled peers. After all, you are the one who decides the form in which you process and organize the information, without relying on the more or less random form in which your various sources present the information. The restructuring activity itself also helps you to better understand and remember the information. This makes the extra effort and time it will take, certainly in the beginning, more than worthwhile.

Key points

Reading Strategies

−   Cursory reading focuses on the main lines of the text. The result is a short text schema (theme, main questions, and key answers) that forms the basis for a short summary.
−   When reading carefully, you also try to find out what the sub-questions are in the text (or part of the text), how those sub-questions are answered, what the answers are for those sub-questions, and so on. The result is a detailed text schema that can form the basis for a detailed summary.
−   When reading critically, you assess the information in the text for completeness, relevance, accuracy, and credibility.
−   In the case of restructuring reading, you select and restructure the information in the original text or texts so that it fits within the structure you want to use for your own text. You create a literature matrix that you tilt, as it were, so that you are able to base the text schema for your own text on it.

Types of summaries

−   A direct, informative summary is written from the perspective of the author of the original text.
−   An indirect, indicative summary is written from the reader's perspective. The indirect form makes it possible to distance yourself from the original text and to insert your own comments on statements in the text.

Assignment

Influence of social media

Purpose of the assignment
You will practice reading and summarizing a longer text.

Subject matter
Section 6.1

Tasks
Below you will find an article published on the website of the Huffington Post.
1   Make a short text schema of this article.
2   Based on this short text schema, write a direct, informative summary.
3   Make a detailed text schema of the text.
4   Based on this detailed text schema, write an indirect, indicative summary.
5   Which set schema do you recognize in the structure of this text?
6   What main questions from this set schema are missing? How would you evaluate
     that?

The text

Influence of Social Media on Teenagers

The influence of social media on adolescents and teenagers is of particular importance, not only because this particular group of children is developmentally vulnerable but also because they are among the heaviest users of social networking. According to a report by Common Sense Media, 75 percent of teenagers in America currently have profiles on social networking sites, of which 68 percent use Facebook as their main social networking tool.

While social networking undoubtedly plays a vital role in broadening social connections and learning technical skills, its risks cannot be overlooked. The lack or difficulty in self-regulation and susceptibility to peer pressure makes adolescents vulnerable to such evils as Facebook depression, sexting, and cyberbullying, which are realistic threats. Other problems such as social network-induced obesity, Internet addiction, and sleep deprivation are issues that continue to be under intense scrutiny for the contradictory results that have been obtained in various studies.

The American Psychological Association defines bullying as aggressive behavior by an individual that causes discomfort to another. Cyberbullying ranges from direct threatening and unpleasant emails to anonymous activities such as trolling. 32 percent of online teens admit to having experienced a range of menacing online advances from others. While direct unpleasant emails or messages are the most straightforward form of cyberbullying, they are probably the least prevalent in that only 13 percent of surveyed youngsters admitted to receiving threatening or aggressive messages. Even forwarding a private note to a group without permission from the sender is often perceived as cyberbullying; Pew research found that 15 percent of teens were disturbed and uncomfortable about having had their private message forwarded or posted in a public forum. Pew also found that nearly 39 percent of teens on social network have been cyberbullied in some way, compared with 22 percent of online teens who do not use social networks. Trolling, the act of deliberately inflicting hatred, bigotry, racism, misogyny, or just simple bickering between people, often anonymously, is also pervasive in social networks. If you thought Trolls lived under bridges, 28 percent of America lives there, it seems.

A very important cause for cyberbullying is the anonymity possible on the Internet. According to Stopbullying. gov, two kinds of people are likely to be cyberbullies — the popular ones and those on the fringes of society; the former resort to such activities to stay popular or to feel powerful, while the latter troll to fit into a society or to get back at a society that excludes them. The National Council on Crime Prevention found from a survey that about three out of four victims of cyberbullying eventually trace the identity of the cyberbully, and so the anonymity may not be as safe a net as the bully believes. The cyberbully is often a friend (if they can be called that without insulting the word or sentiment) or someone they know from school or outside. Only 23 percent of the victims reported to have been bullied by someone they don't know.

Cyberbullying appears easy to the bully because they do not see their victims' reactions in person, and thus the impact of the consequences is small. In reality, however, the consequences can be life-altering to the extent that the victims could go as far as taking their lives or becoming psychologically distressed enough to require medical intervention. The ironically individualistic nature of social networking activities makes it difficult to recognize a victim of cyberbullying, but tell-tale signs include avoiding or being anxious around the computer or cellphone and sudden changes in behavior patterns.

Sexting, the action of sending sexually revealing pictures of themselves or sexually explicit messages to another individual or group, is another common activity among the teen community in social media. A nationwide survey by the National Campaign to Support Teen and Unplanned Pregnancy found a shocking 20 percent of teens participating in sexting. While teenage boys resort to sending sexually explicit or suggestive messages, teenage girls are more likely to send inappropriate photos of themselves, mostly to their boyfriends. However, the permanence and pervasiveness of the internet makes it a fertile ground for spreading such information to the extent of getting viral—17 percent of sexters admittedly share the messages they receive with others, and 55 percent of those share them with more than one person. Beyond the personal trauma and humiliation that sexting may cause, there are judicial ramifications as well; some states consider such activities as misdemeanors while many group sexting under felony.

'Facebook depression', defined as emotional disturbance that develops when preteens and teens spend a great deal of time on social media sites, is now a very real malady. Recent studies have shown that comparisons are the main cause of Facebook depression; the study showed that down-comparison (comparing with inferiors) was just as likely to cause depression as up-comparison (comparing with people better than oneself). However, there are contradictory reports as well. Another study showed that Facebook makes us happier and increased social trust and engagement among users. Given that our brains are wired to connect, it seems logical to expect that social networks, by enabling sharing, could cause a self-reinforcing sense of psychological satisfaction. These studies show that the effect of social network on well-being hinges on how social networks are used—whether to connect or to compare.

Other risks of extensive social networking among youth are loss of privacy, sharing too much information, and disconnect from reality. The digital footprint is a permanent trail that users of social media, indeed of the Internet itself, leave the moment they sign into any service.

The digital footprint, by its permanence, can have serious repercussions in future, in both professional and personal areas of life. It is important to know that every activity online—posts on social media accounts, comments left on various sites, tweets, retweets, and +1s—through years can contribute to the digital footprint. Another serious risk is the amount of information shared on social network sites. LexisNexis and Lawers.com surveyed 1,000 Americans and found that half of them divulged too much personal data online. What is more worrying is the fact that 44 percent of them believed that the information they posted on sites like Facebook, LinkedIn, or MySpace were being used against them.

Adolescence is the time to spread wings and take the tentative first flight out into the world, and parents and caregivers must be part of the process. In the domain of social networking, this entails parents becoming educated about the advantages and disadvantages of social networking and themselves joining social network site—not to hove, but to be aware of the activities of their teenage wards. It is essential that parents are aware of and monitor privacy settings and online profiles of their wards. Open discussions about social network protocols and etiquettes would go a long way in establishing global digital citizenship and healthy behavior.

Source: Ramasubbu (2015).[13]

13   Ramasubbu, R. (2015, May 26). Influence of social media on teenagers. *Huffington Post*. Retrieved from https://www.huffpost.com/entry/influence-of-social-media-on-teenagers_b_7427740

7 Writing—the process

◀ *A writer trimming his pen*, Jan Ekels (II), 1784. The writer sits at a table by the window. Above the table is a mirror showing the man's face. On the table is an inkstand, on the right a coat is draped over the chair.

Like the young man who has set up his writing desk and is preparing the tools he will need, all good writers need serious preparation. And just as the writer in the painting can see his own reflection in the mirror, all good writers figuratively reflect on their work by continually analyzing and evaluating the writing process.

What writers have to say about the writing process

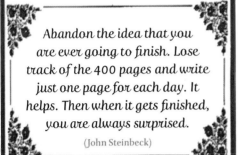

Abandon the idea that you are ever going to finish. Lose track of the 400 pages and write just one page for each day. It helps. Then when it gets finished, you are always surprised.

(John Steinbeck)

If you want to be a writer, you must do two things above all others: Read a lot and write a lot.

(Stephen King)

Style ought to prove that one believes in an idea; not only that one thinks it but also feels it.

(Friedrich Nietzsche)

By using stale metaphors, similes and idioms, you save much mental effort, at the cost of leaving your meaning vague, not only for your reader but for yourself.

(George Orwell)

The writer cannot make the seas of distraction stand still, but he [or she] can at times come between the madly distracted and the distractions.

(Saul Bellow)

You can't wait for inspiration. You have to go after it with a club.

(Jack London)

The quote by John Steinbeck must be quite intimidating to those of us who need to start writing a long, complex text. But there is something positive in his words: If you want to write something worthwhile, it is essential to start from the assumption that writing is a continuous process. However, if you think about the writing of a text as a once-off action—that is, that you sit down and write the text in one sitting—your writing will not be as good as it should or could be.

Good writers understand this truth, and therefore understand the need for effective planning, proper research, and lots of reading (King). They also appreciate the importance of thinking about the pitfalls (Nietzsche and Orwell); rewriting again and again and again (King), editing and being edited; dealing with distraction and writer's block (Bellow); and finally understanding that writing hardly ever is about inspiration but rather about perspiration (London).

This chapter is about the writing process of longer and more complex texts such as reports, theses, and articles. The central question of this chapter is: How do you write a long text? In chapter 8, we will discuss in more detail the characteristics of the distinct parts of such texts, in particular those of research reports.

Although many people are daunted by the prospect of writing a longer text, it can be an instructive and even pleasant activity. The process often turns out to be the best way to acquire in-depth knowledge of a subject. Still, if you have to write long texts, it is important that you learn how to work in a systematic way.

It starts with understanding that writing is a *process*: Each writing project can be divided into a number of phases. These phases can help you keep track of your progress while you are working on the text. To provide you with some practical guidelines, we offer various concrete tips and suggestions for you to successfully complete all the phases. At the end of this chapter, we will discuss some tried and tested solutions for writing problems. First, however, we briefly discuss the different phases in the writing process.

Phases in the writing process
There are a number of main activities that are always part of the writing process:
– *Preparing*: establishing the point of departure of the text and developing a plan or schedule for your writing;
– *Determining the content*: generating, searching, and selecting content;
– *Writing*: elaborating the content into a full text;
– *Editing*: checking and improving the text at the level of the content on the basis of your own or another's judgment;
– *Finalizing*: checking and improving the text at the level of language use, spelling, and punctuation, and formatting the text according to specific requirements.

The picture below shows that these main activities are best understood as successive phases in a project, although writers sometimes return to an earlier phase at a later stage, depending on their way of working or the nature of the project. For example, writer X may find out during the *writing* phase that he lacks crucial information, so he must return to the phase of *determining content*. It is also possible to skip ahead to another phase, although this will usually concern a minor intervention. Writer Y, for instance, may have an excellent idea for a title during the preparation phase, even though she would normally determine the title during the final phase. After making a note of her idea, she will return to the preparation phase.

The number of times that writers return to an earlier phase or move forward to a later phase may depend on their preference and style of work. However, a lot of switching between the phases may also indicate a lack of control during the writing process. If you have a plan, you reduce the risk of problems caused by switching between phases, and you also make the project more manageable. Making a plan and sticking to that plan is something that you should continue doing throughout the writing process, unlike once-off actions such as determining the topic of and basic approach to your text. Nonetheless, because planning is part of the initial preparation, we will introduce this topic in the next section.

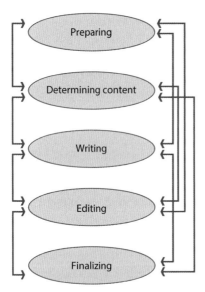

Activities in the writing process.

7.1   Preparation

Thorough preparation is half the battle won. Although this takes a lot of work, it makes the writing of the text much easier. The preparation phase can be divided into two steps: orientation and planning. During the orientation phase, you focus on the question of what you want to achieve with the text: What is your goal and who is your target group? How and to what extent you focus on these matters largely depends on the type of text you have to write. Planning involves setting deadlines for your own work and input from others, as well as continuously adapting and specifying the phases of the writing process. Below we will discuss these two aspects of the preparation phase in relation to each other. It may also be useful to take a look at section 9.1, which deals with the preparation of an oral presentation. Many of the steps that will be discussed in that section correspond to the preparation phase of a longer text.

7.1.1   Orientation

During the writing process you should always keep in mind what you want to achieve with the text and who your intended audience is. Although this is often already clearly described, especially for fixed assignments, it is always useful to familiarize yourself with your writing goal (or goals) and audience (or audiences) before you start writing. Only then will you be sure that you have a clear view of what you actually have to write.

Consider the goal of the text
A text is never written just for the sake of writing it; there is always a reason. Always try to find answers to the following questions.
– What problem or event is the motivation for writing the text?
– Who is involved and in what role?
– What is the background?
– What is the text supposed to contribute, for instance to the solution of the problem, or what role does it play in a particular process?

> A decision has to be made about new network software in the company. The Information Centre has established that the old software no longer suffices. The decision must be taken officially by the management, but the one who is actually responsible for it is the ICT manager.
>
> Three quotations were issued by suppliers for software and hardware, in consultation with the Infrastructure Department. An advisory report is requested in which the three quotations are compared and in which a proposal is made for the decision to be taken.

The reason for an advisory report in a company.

If you are still not sure what form your text should take, it is often useful to ask yourself the following questions.
- What do you, as a writer, want to influence: the reader's knowledge, skills, opinions, behavioral intentions, or emotions?
- What topic is your communicative goal related to?
- Who are the readers with whom you want to achieve your communicative goal?

For the consideration of your goals, the self-expression side and the relationship side of your messages (see chapter 1) are essential. For example, you should always show that you understand what you are talking about (self-expression side) and that you appreciate the needs of the client and the intended reader (relationship side): The text should not be too difficult, nor should it be too simple or too intrusive. In addition—and this is especially important if you have a persuasive or motivating goal—you must show goodwill towards your readers and address them honestly and openly.

Familiarizing yourself with the audience

A text may be meant for one person or for several persons or groups. Target groups can be homogeneous, which means that readers have roughly the same background. Often, however, target groups are heterogeneous in certain respects, meaning that the readers in these groups may have different levels of knowledge, needs, or perspectives.

A primary school's school work plan serves as an aid in planning education, with the teachers forming the target group; they will read the text with a view to implementation. However, the plan also serves as a justification for the way a school teaches; the reader dealing with this goal is the inspector of primary education; he or she will read the text with a view to assessment. Furthermore, a school work plan often serves as a means of providing information about the approach used at the school; in this case, the target group consists of the parents of the present pupils and any future pupils. They will read the text to gain knowledge, and to consider their options when it comes to the choice of school for their children.

A school work plan serves different purposes and target groups. In this case, difficulties may arise, for example, from the use of educational jargon. This is not a problem for the teaching team and the inspection team. On the contrary, the educational jargon makes it easier to indicate precisely what one is aiming for. But that jargon makes the text inaccessible to most parents. However, if one writes the text without jargon, there is a risk that the teachers and the inspector are not satisfied, because the text makes an 'amateurish' impression.

Besides the readers from your target groups, people who do not belong to the intended audience might also read your text. A practical text such as a school work plan, for instance, may be read by a journalist who writes an article about the differences between the primary schools in the area, by municipal councillors wanting to know more about the state of cultural (or multicultural) education, or by publishers of educational material who want to know whether they can sell this material to the school.

Unintended readers are also referred to as *shadow readers*. Although such shadow readers and their aims do not determine the content of a text, it is still wise to take them into account. In the example of the school work plan, you may want to leave out information you do not want the press to have, choose terms that appeal to politicians, or mention that there is no budget for new resources.

It is important to know your readers so that you can write your text based on their level of knowledge, needs, and perspective. In most cases, you can find relevant information about your readers in the following ways.

– *Put yourself in your readers' position*. What would you consider important or relevant information if you were them, and what would your opinion be? As long as you avoid taking yourself as the norm ('the reader is just like me'), empathy is a good guide for writing a text.
– *Follow good examples*. You are probably not the first person to write a text for your particular target group. You can, therefore, search for successful examples that you can follow. If you work for an organization, you may find good examples in the archive or by asking your colleagues.
– *Consult experts*. Talk to people who know the target group. They can predict how the readers will respond to your material and what the pitfalls are.
– *Read external sources*. Sometimes you can find background information about your target group in literature or on the internet (the company's website, for example).
– *Interview members of the target group about the subject of your text*. A few informal discussions may already reveal a great deal about their knowledge, interest, opinions, and sensitivities.

It can be useful to create a so-called *persona* based on the information you have gathered: a well-described but non-existent reader with his or her own biography and context. You can use this fictional reader in a thought experiment to test your text and to help you empathize with your target group.

 This is John Edison, personnel advisor at the Institute for Technology. John is a widower and lives alone. He studied law and then ended up in human resources. His task is to advise the director on hiring new staff; on terms of employment, salaries, and other rewards (bonuses); on performance and appraisal interviews; on conflict resolution; and occasionally on dismissal of staff members. In addition, he supports staff members in their career planning and the drafting of their Personal Development Plans, tasks that have consistently exposed John's more sensitive side without detracting from the principled way in which he has done his job over the years.

John has been doing this work for almost twenty years with great pleasure and to the satisfaction of the management. He views his job as that of compliance when it comes to employment conditions and remuneration, but without compromising the more human aspect of being fair in everything that he does. That is why he is a declared opponent of inconsistencies in awarding bonuses and other forms of reward. In recent years, this has regularly brought him into conflict with other department heads who have a much broader view of this, but John has consistently stuck to his principled way of doing his job.

The John Edison in this example is a persona, a prototype of a (non-existent) reader. This persona could, for example, be used when developing a brochure for a course on 'compliance in human resource management' or a course on 'dealing with difficult people' (such courses do exist). The technique for formulating personas (as realistic as possible, sometimes even with personal details and a photo) comes from the information technology industry. People there are meant to always have a specific idea of whom the program is intended for during the design of a computer program. Usually, different personas are created. In some companies, their descriptions and photos are even hung up on the wall to constantly remind employees of the customers for whom they work. If you write extended texts (a book, a website, or a complicated report, for example), or if you write a text together with others, it can be rewarding to invest in developing personas as a method of empathizing with your target group (or groups).

7.1.2   Planning

Already during the orientation phase, you determine the basics of your text with regard to goals and target groups, possibly based on the preconditions of your particular assignment. These basics will determine the actions you will need to perform during the writing project. The goals of the text, the target groups and the actions that need to follow can be recorded in a formal *writing plan* at the start of your writing process, a plan which will guide you through the process and which is particularly useful if you want to discuss the process with others. You should keep track of the actions to be taken for the whole duration of the project, using it as a tool as you write.

Drafting a writing plan

A writing plan serves as a roadmap for your writing process, but it can also serve as a basis for discussing your work with supervisors, clients, and colleagues. Determining the goals of your text and the target groups that it will be addressed to, can be aligned with the actions you need to perform during the writing project. This will allow you to check that what you aim to do corresponds to what they have in mind. In addition, they can comment on your ideas, offer advice, and maybe find problems that you did not see.

A writing plan is also useful if you have to work on a piece with other writers. Then it also functions as an agreement: You agree to work with particular goals, for a particular target group, and on a fixed time schedule. This way, everyone knows what kind of text you will write. A writing plan should at least contain:

- the reason for writing the text and the underlying goals;
- a description of the target group and the subject, and the preconditions of the project;
- the general content: an initial text schema with a preliminary description of the theme, questions, and key answers that need to be addressed;
- an overview of planned intermediate products and agreements that are or must be made with others.

Even if a writing plan is not necessary—for example because the assignment and preconditions are crystal clear—it is still useful to write down the goal of your project somewhere (for example, on a post-it you put on the edge of your computer screen) in a single sentence, possibly expanded with a few keywords.

Policy report on the international exchange of students

Arguments for the policy position
- International orientation is important for our educational programs.
- The ministry now provides a subsidy for international exchange.
- It is essential for the image of the university to be seen to be participating in international exchange.
- It is a drawing card for new students.
- The institutional and business environments place a high premium on graduates with international experience.

Communicative goals and audiences
- *Management*: persuading them of the importance of student exchange and motivating them to free the necessary budget for the initiative.
- *Teaching staff*: motivating them to establish the necessary contacts that would facilitate the student exchange.
- *Students*: informing them of exchange opportunities in the future.

Self-expression side
- The university should be presented as a dynamic, active, and internationally orientated institution.

Characteristics of the audiences
- *Management*: strongly focused on managerial and financial aspects; interested in initiatives to attract more and better students.
- *Teaching staff*: interested in international exchange; might present some opposition to change in the workspace.

- *Students*: enthusiastic about international exchange; need more information on the cost and the impact on their studies.

Timelines
- First version completed within four weeks and ready for discussion with management committee.
- Second version completed within eight weeks, ready for discussions with the Board.

Content: initial text schema with theme, questions, and key answers (where already available)
- Theme: international student exchange
- Why exchange of students and teaching staff? Most important arguments: European unification, internationalization, demands from the professional environment, drawing card for new students
- What models of exchange? Summer schools, exchange in specific modules, internships.
- Subsidy possibilities?
- Which international institutes?
- Integration of exchange with student's study program?
- What kind of support for exchange students?

Format and style of report
- Internal report distributed via e-mail and intranet. Clear structure; keep it short and sweet.
- Not too formal style; keep it lively for the sake of the persuasive goal of the report.

Example of a (brief) writing plan. Backgrounds to this case: You are the coordinator of the Business Administration program of a university of applied sciences, and the board asked you to write a policy note about the exchange of international students. In a conversation with the board, the various motives for intensifying this exchange were discussed. The board attaches importance to such a policy being supported by the entire university community: the board, lecturers, and students. Coincidentally, a circular from the Ministry of Education was received about a subsidy scheme for international educational contacts. The results of the discussions and of the necessary thinking end up in this writing plan, which you will go through once more with the board member who is in charge of educational innovation before you actually start writing.

Developing and managing the writing plan

A text must be well constructed, but it should also be finished in time. It is therefore indispensable to have a workable plan that includes all your tasks—one that makes sense and that you actually use. However, during the preparation phase you should not make your plan too detailed. It is important that it develops along with your project, for the following reasons.

– At the start, you often do not know what the finished text will look like, nor do you know everything you need to do to achieve it.
– In the course of your writing process, you may discover that your original plan is less feasible or that your task is more complicated than you thought.
– Most writers underestimate the time they need to finish writing; they hardly ever finish sooner than they thought.
– In a group project, you may be dependent upon others for parts of the final text. In many cases, other people also need more time than you thought.
– Finally, keep in mind Murphy's Law: Everything that can go wrong will go wrong at the most inconvenient moment.

Although your plan is for your personal use and needs to be flexible, it is important to set some hard deadlines for your interim results. These may include:

– the date you must reach an agreement on the writing plan with your client (content and structure);
– the dates by which certain parts of the document must be finished in terms of content;
– the date you must send the first complete version of the text to the client, or to others for comments;
– the date you need to have received the comments so you can start revising the text;
– the date on which the editing must be completed and the final version of the text (language, spelling, punctuation, design) should be ready.

You can, of course, add these deadlines to your writing plan and make a note of them in your diary. However, your writing plan is for your own use and will consist of a list of specific tasks that will lead to the products required by the deadlines. That is why the personal part of your planning is more like a detailed to-do list in which the correct sequence of actions is particularly important.

Elements of your personal planning

Your writing plan can be divided into three parts: a to-do list, possibly a log, and the increasingly elaborate text schema for your content. These documents develop along with the writing process and help you to carry out the project effectively and efficiently. The first two parts are discussed here; the text schema has already been extensively introduced in chapter 2 and will also be discussed in section 7.2.3.

Using a spreadsheet program for your planning can be useful. You can create a spread-sheet for each part of your planning. This has several advantages.
– You have all the information conveniently arranged in one place.
– With the many table functions in such programs, you can easily add sequential numbers, dates, keywords, and the like to the information for easy retrieval.
– If you decide to tabulate your text schema, you can add new columns per text item with information about that item. See the example in section 7.2.3.

Put your planning in a spreadsheet program.

To-do list

Each of the main activities of the writing process mentioned in the introduction of this chapter consists of a large number of actions and tasks. For example, in the *determining content* phase, you may need to search for a source that explains a key term, or during the *editing* phase you may need to remind reviewers to return their comments. Each substantial writing project comes with loose ends, all of which you can manage in a to-do list.

Especially during the writing phase, a general writing plan will often no longer suffice, and you will need to divide the work into smaller tasks. This is when a to-do list becomes indispensable. For example, if you initially planned to write chapter 1 in week 26 and only later decide that this chapter should consist of four sections, you may want to specify which section you will write on which day of the week. Because the planning becomes more and more precise, it will also be easier to see the data you need (for example, information from the secondary sources) and when you need them. This way, you can coordinate different tasks more easily, and you will also discover obstacles at an early stage. Here are some tips on how to make the best use of a to-do list.
– Make sure that your to-do list matches your preliminary text schema.
– Make a distinction between the main ideas or arguments in the text and the actions required to work out these ideas or arguments. Try to be as specific as possible: Provide details on how you want to achieve your intermediate goals.
– Determine when, where, and how you should perform a particular task. It may be useful to start with the tasks that require you to call people, for example, or to visit a certain location. For each task you write down, consider whether you have everything you need to carry it out at that moment in your planning. If not, you will know what other tasks you need to complete first.

—   If possible, provide the estimated time needed to complete each task. If you
    have many similar tasks, it can be useful to write down how long it took you
    to complete them so you can improve your estimates.
—   Mark the tasks that you need to perform to deliver an intermediate product.
    From this, you can estimate how much time you will need to meet the final
    deadline.
—   Finish every working day by updating your to-do list. Always ask yourself the
    same questions: What have I done today? What new tasks have emerged in the
    course of the day? Are all the tasks that I listed but have not yet undertaken
    still relevant?

Log

Writing is often a lonely activity. You have to make many decisions on your own
during the writing process. Sometimes these decisions follow from a clear assignment
or from a relatively specified list of tasks, but sometimes you will make decisions
based on a sudden insight while you are writing. Unfortunately, such insights may
disappear after a night's sleep or they might relate to changes that you will only
come to at a later stage. To make sure that you do not forget why you have given
yourself certain tasks, consider making a short note in a log at the end of every day.

Keeping a log is not about remembering your tasks—after all, you have your
to-do list for that. In your log, you record your view of the project as it develops over
time. If you later return to your log notes, you will remember why you made certain
choices at an earlier stage. In addition, keeping a log forces you to articulate your
choices, forcing you to carefully consider your decisions. In this way you become,
as it were, your own sparring partner.

7.2   Determining the content

In the preparation phase, the contours of your text will have emerged: its goals,
target groups, the primary content elements, and a rough outline. The next step is
to determine the content of the text.

Depending on the subject, the complexity of the task, and your familiarity
with the topic, the emphasis will be on generating, collecting, selecting, or only
structuring the material. If you already know a lot about the subject, you can start
filling in the parts of your text schema sooner. If the subject is relatively new to
you, then the phase of finding content is necessary.

Finding content works both ways: You can enlarge your text, but you can also
scale it down. Sometimes you have to search very broadly to generate or collect
more information that may be useful. Other times, you have to go into detail,

focus, select information, and, following that, also delete some information that might be irrelevant. A good, credible, and convincing text does not mean including everything you know about the subject but rather making a well-constructed text.

7.2.1 Generating ideas

To start with, you can generate your own ideas for the content of the text by asking yourself what you already know and think about the subject. There are various techniques to get an overview of your own knowledge and ideas. Below, we discuss the two most important ones: brainstorming and mind mapping.

Brainstorming

Brainstorming is a creative technique for coming up with many new ideas about a subject very quickly. The characteristic of this technique is that critical reflection is kept to a minimum. Although brainstorming sessions usually take place with more than one person, it is also possible to do it individually. Sometimes that even works better.

Brainstorming is very simple. Taking turns, participants mention a word or an idea that spontaneously comes to mind about the subject of the brainstorming session. These ideas are noted down on a blackboard, sticky notes, or a screen so that everyone can see. There are four rules for a brainstorming session to be successful, that is, to produce as many ideas as possible.

- *Do not criticize ideas.* Any idea can be put forward. Later on in the process there will be time for scrutiny and criticism.
- *Put forward as many ideas as possible.* The more ideas, the better. The idea is that this makes it likely that there will be something useful among them.
- *Look for wild ideas.* Unexpected associations may later lead to original perspectives.
- *Combine the results.* Earlier suggestions may lead to new ideas. That is why all ideas must be visible to all participants.

Brainstorming is not limited to words, phrases, sentences, and questions; it can also include drawings, sketches, or diagrams. Technicians often do this: Leonardo da Vinci's brainstorm sketches are each worth a thousand words! Your drawings do not have to be beautiful. If necessary, they can be clarified with a word or a color-coded symbol.

Result of an afternoon's brainstorming, using sticky notes.

Mind mapping

Just like brainstorming, mind mapping is a way of coming up with wide-ranging ideas, but mind mapping is less disorderly and free. You can also use mind mapping to organize the material generated during brainstorming. The emphasis with mind mapping is on identifying the relationships between the ideas and the subject, and between the ideas themselves. A mind mapping session goes as follows:

– You write the subject of the mind map in the middle of a paper, board, or screen.
– You write down related concepts or ideas around this and connect them to the subject with a line.
– You name the relationship indicated by the line, such as cause, reason, means, end, simultaneity, opposition, and so on.
– You can expand a mind-mapping session by taking concepts or ideas that have come up and making them the center of a new map.

There are various software packages available for mind mapping that can help you keep the results clear and ordered. One disadvantage of these programs is that they may hamper the spontaneity and speed of the creative process, especially if the participants are not familiar with the software.

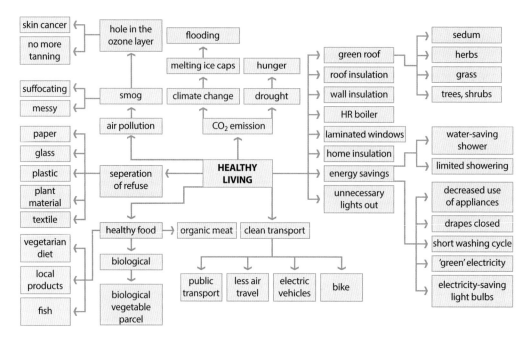

Example of a mind map in which the relationships have not been defined yet.

7.2.2   Collecting material

Whereas with brainstorming and mind mapping you take ideas from your own memory or imagination, you can also collect material from external sources.

Some writers try to find out everything there is to know about their subject. They collect piles of literature, talk to as many people as possible, and consult databases and search engines on the internet until they drown in the information, lose their grip on the subject and do not reach the actual writing phase. This is obviously not the right approach.

It is through effective selection that the master reveals himself. You must be selective when you collect information. That is why it is important to have a writing plan at an early stage.

It is useful to formulate specific questions to which you try to find answers in the literature or elsewhere. It can also be helpful to think of keywords that will help you find literature about your subject in bibliographies and catalogues. The results of your brainstorm and mind map sessions can help you find the right documentation questions and keywords. You can collect new information in a number of ways. Here are some possibilities.

- *Archive research.* You consult material that is already held in the organization's archive or in another archive.
- *Literature research.* You consult previous publications on the subject (professional literature, research reports, the internet).
- *Interviews.* You talk to people who are involved in the subject of your text, or to experts.
- *Empirical research.* For example, you can conduct a survey or set up an experiment to collect your own data.

Apart from literature research, we will not be elaborating on these methods, as that would take us too far from the subject of this book. However, you can find references to useful textbooks in the last part of this book, entitled *Suggested readings*.

Searching for literature

If you want to support your discussion of an issue with well-founded arguments, literature research is one of the most important methods of obtaining information. There are different types of literature you can consult.

- *Primary scientific literature*, such as scientific journals, monographs, conference papers, and dissertations. These sources represent the state of the art in theory and research but are generally not aimed at practical solutions to problems. You can use them when you are conducting research or when you want to dive deeper into a certain subject.
- *Secondary scientific* or *professional literature*, such as textbooks, advice literature, and professional journals. In these sources you will usually find solid but accessible information, often in the form of overviews of theories and research results.
- *Official documents*, such as policy documents, reports, and papers from research and consultancy firms and agencies.
- *Mass media*, such as newspapers and magazines, websites, blogs, and radio and television programs. These sources often provide good starting points to explore a subject, but it is sometimes difficult to assess their quality. This is much less the case for quality newspapers than for the internet, which has a lot of information based on rumors, fantasies, and hearsay. Always try to verify any information you find online by using one of the other types of sources.

It is always wise to check the accuracy and completeness of the information you find. Find out what data and sources the authors rely on, identify points of discussion and disagreement, and look beyond the first publication you find. Such checks not only improve the credibility of your material, they might also lead you to discover discussions and differences of opinion that are an interesting subject for your own writing project (for more information on critical reading, see section 6.1.3). How can you find suitable sources? That depends on the type of information you need.

– An online encyclopaedia is useful for your initial familiarization with a subject. Many people use the well-known, very extensive, and constantly growing *Wikipedia*. This source allows you to quickly find the most important relevant facts and sometimes provides links for further information. Keep in mind, however, that the information on *Wikipedia* is not always reliable. This is sometimes mentioned on the page itself, and sometimes you should take a look at the so-called talk page of an article to avoid copying incorrect information. If you want to be more confident of the quality of the information and it is not a problem if the database is smaller, you may also take a look at the *New World Encyclopedia*. This source can also be consulted online free of charge, and it has the advantage of being maintained by certified experts.

– *Google* (or other search engines) is also a useful tool to explore a subject. *Google* provides an easy way to search for specific information (names, dates, places, quotations, definitions). However, because *Google* does not distinguish between reliable and unreliable information, it is crucial to look beyond the first search result. Check multiple sources (websites) and make sure that they provide the same information without copying each other. Keep in mind that if you consult *Google* with the same search query a second time, the results may be different, since *Google* modifies them based on your search history.

– If you are looking for scientific publications, it is best to work with academic databases such as *Scopus*, *Web of Science*, or *Picarta*. The articles are often available digitally, but in order to read them you must have an account, so access to a university library is often necessary. You can also use *Google Scholar*, but there you will only be able to download publications that are accessible via the internet. It will also show unpublished reports and papers, and it is not always clear how reliable these are.

Selecting literature to read

A day in a good library or behind a computer with an internet connection quickly delivers more sources than you will actually be able to read. You will therefore have to select which publications you are going to study. At a later stage, you must choose which publications you will actually use to write your text (see below). The following rules of thumb may help you to identify the publications that are worthwhile and the ones that are less important.

– Try to find out more about a particular publication than its title (many articles contain abstracts and keywords). With this additional information, it is easier to decide whether or not you should read the publication.

- Check whether specific titles, names, or terms are often mentioned in other publications; these are probably important.
- If the title or summary of the article indicates that it is an overview of research (literature review), it is often useful to study this source.
- The internet often yields details about recent books. Some publishers and bookshops publish informative reviews and reader responses.
- Information about authors and where they work is also often available on the internet. This information can give you an impression of the credibility of the source.

7.2.3   Selecting and structuring

When generating ideas and searching for material, a broad approach is generally taken: You collect content for your text. In the process, you will already be discarding many things because they do not fit with your goals and your target group, or because they are not sufficiently reliable or interesting. In the final step of the content determination phase, you should be more rigorous in determining what material you will eventually include in your text.

You should also structure your information during this phase. The structure of your text should match your goals and the preconditions. A useful tool in this regard is the literature matrix discussed in section 6.2.1. In this table, your sources should be shown in the rows and the relevant sub-themes in the columns. Based on this literature matrix, you can then create your own text schema, as shown in the example in section 6.2.1.

Prescribed format: templates
An important question at this stage is whether the text you are going to write needs to adhere to a format prescribed by your field of expertise, your organization, or client. Such a format (also called a 'template') prescribes which parts (or chapters) the text must consist of, which information belongs to which parts, and sometimes even how long the parts should be. Not every prescribed format will be equally detailed. There may be only limitations on the 'macrostructure' of the text (the structure of the text in general, that is, the prescribed chapters or sections), while you may be relatively free to determine the 'mesostructure' (the type of content within each chapter or section).

Use of set schemata and ordering principles
If you are free to choose the structure and type of content of your text, you can use one of the set schemata or ordering principles from chapter 2 as the base for your text schema, depending on your needs. But realize that when you choose a certain

set schema, you also choose a specific perspective. A text with a set problem schema, for example, will have different accents compared to a text with a set measure schema or a set design schema. The suitability of possible set schemata as the base for your text schema depends on your goal and target group.

Your text schema is not just a roadmap through your own text. With a few minor adjustments, you can make this document the basis of your entire writing project. It may be helpful at this stage to arrange your text schema in the form of a table. Keep the following points in mind.

–   Make room for main questions and sub-questions by giving each one its own column. This clarifies the hierarchy of your text schema. Alternatively, use a tab for each new element so that the question structure takes the form of a hierarchical table of contents.

–   You can choose to work out the key answers in detail and place them in the next column, adjacent to the corresponding question. This way, they show a summary of the content of each part of your text. You can also choose to place the key answers under the corresponding question so that they fit into the hierarchical table of contents. With the latter option, you will have to significantly shorten the answers in order to keep the table orderly.

–   For many writing tasks, you have to keep to a maximum length. For example, a text should be between 3 and 5 pages long or should not exceed 10,000 words. A useful step in planning a text is therefore to divide the number of words over the different parts. In an extra column, you can indicate how many words you wish to dedicate to each part.

–   You can also create a column of relevant literature. In this column you would indicate for each item what publications you have found or still need to find for this part of the text. This information will also allow you to update your to-do list by showing when to read what before you can write a specific part.

–   If you use a literature column, you also create reading goals for yourself because you know exactly why you will consult new literature. This way, you can save time by limiting yourself to the passage (or passages) relevant to your goals.

–   A literature column also allows you to determine whether you have collected enough information for each item.

–   In addition to a literature column, you can create another column with references to other sources, such as documents, interviews, or notes you have previously made. The more specific your notes of what you need from the source are, the more useful the table will become. Think of page numbers, moments in an interview, and so on.

–   To keep the table concise, you should give each source a unique number.

The role of secrecy in religious movements

No.	Content	Length	Literature	Interviews
1	Why has it never been systematically examined before?	(600)		
1.1	It was considered unworthy	200	Wallach (2008) Johnston (2012, p. 12)	
1.2	It would not be researchable	400	Johnston (2012, p. 14)	Miriam
2	Where does the renewed interest in the subject come from?	(700)		
3	How does secrecy manifest itself in religion?	(550)		
3.1	Certain knowledge is not shared	250	DeBoer (2003, pp. 23-58) Alkemade (1991)	
3.2	Certain rituals are not accessible	300		David
4	What reasons do believers themselves give for secrecy?	(500)		
4.1	Knowledge is dangerous for the uninitiated	150	DeBoer (2003, p. 25)	Peter Kevin
4.2	Rituals do not work with strangers	150	Falkirk (2002)	Nora Ralph
4.3	The secret lies in the experience	200		Grant Nora
5	What unforeseen consequences does confidentiality have in practice?	(550)		
5.1	Suspicion of family members	250		Frieda
5.2	Suspicion in society	300	Lee (2006)	Joshua Miriam

Fragments of a text schema in tabular form. The first column, 'No.', contains the planned chapter and section layouts. 'Content', the header of the second column, refers to the elements from the text schema that have been greatly shortened here and can therefore be used as parts of a table of contents. The questions and answers have been put together for this purpose. The planned number of words is shown in the fourth column (with subtotals for specific parts in brackets). 'Literature' and 'Interviews', the headers of the last two columns, refer to the two types of sources that have been—or have yet to be—consulted for this research.

Working with the text schema and the literature matrix

Once you have determined the macrostructure, it is time to include the meso-structure in your text schema. This involves writing down the key answers to the main questions and asking the sub-questions resulting from these main questions, which in turn require new key answers, and so on. This way, you expand the text schema as much as necessary to get a clear picture of the content and structure of the text that you have to write.

By drafting a text schema and working it out in more detail, you can also identify any problems you may encounter during the actual writing. Do you know enough about each of the key answers to make it a relevant and engaging part of your text? Do you have enough arguments to support your views? If you have created a literature matrix (see section 6.2.1), this is a good time to take another look at it.

Depending on your preference and the nature of your writing task, you can arrange the information according to the prescribed form of your text or let the information you have found dictate the form. In both cases, your literature matrix shows which reading tasks you must perform. It also allows you to expand your text schema with the necessary information for each main and sub-question and key answer. Sometimes you will have to move back and forth between the literature matrix and the text schema until you are sure you have all the information you need. At that point, the literature matrix loses its function and the text schema becomes the starting point for the writing phase of your project.

7.3   Writing

Once you have a writing plan, enough information, and a text schema for your content, you can start writing. But do not expect the text to write itself after you set pen to paper.

– You should take a pause in the writing process from time to time to review what you have written and reflect on what you need to do next. Without such interim planning, you may jeopardize your own progress.
– It is wise to plan on having several writing rounds in which you generate different versions of your document. Not even the most experienced writers can do everything right at once. A text of some size and depth must be written in multiple cycles, each of which leads to a new version.

Every writer comes up with new ideas during the writing process. It is only once writers have started writing that it becomes clear what they actually know and think about various issues. In the course of writing their text, they will come up with new arguments both in favor of and against the position they have taken. Writing thus has a conceptualizing effect: In the process of writing, writers develop new ideas. Conversely, in the process of writing, writers start to doubt their original ideas, arguments, or chosen text structure, which can be equally useful.

It would be unwise to suppress those new ideas just because they are not part of your planning. Then you would not benefit from the thought process that is an inevitable part of writing. If time allows—and time is often the most critical obstacle—you should seriously consider following up on these new ideas. This will improve the quality of your final text. Park the new ideas in your to-do list until the right moment to use them. Once you have written down an idea in that list, it is no longer a loose end in your head and you can continue working.

7.3.1 Writing the first version

During the first round of writing, you should concentrate on the content and not let yourself be distracted by problems that you can solve later. It is crucial that you continue to focus on sharpening the content and structure while leaving considerations of form, style, and language aside for the moment.

During this first round, you can leave out some parts of the text such as the foreword, the summary, and so forth. When you start writing the introduction, you can include a description of your goal and announce what you will discuss in the text, but you should probably postpone writing an opening that is meant to catch the reader's attention until the next round (see section 8.1.5).

7.3.2 Writing subsequent versions

The first round of writing mainly concerns the translation of the text schema into coherent prose. The result is often a very rough version of the text. In the following writing rounds, you will make the necessary additions and changes. Your planning documents help you to adjust your plans efficiently and effectively.

Each time you finish a section or chapter, you should return to your text schema to check whether it still corresponds to what you have written. Sometimes you may need to revise your text, but it is also possible that you need to change the text schema because you find out that the original layout is not workable. In any case, make sure that there is a close relationship between your text and the text schema. Use your to-do list to add new ideas that you wrote down earlier. If you add a new idea, do so in an appropriate sequence of actions: first a round of reading, then incorporating the idea into the text schema, and finally adding it in a writing round.

For your interim revisions, you should shift your attention from the macrostructure to the mesostructure of the text. You are no longer just looking at the order in which you present the information, you should also focus on an *appropriate degree of specificity*. It is at this stage that you will add details, explain concepts, and clarify the relationships between the ideas in such a way that the reader can easily follow your argument, yet does not feel patronized. We will discuss this in more detail below.

Working out further details

It is possible that the text in development resembles one of the set schemata from section 2.2. If, for instance, one of your key answers concerns an undesirable situation, you can further elaborate on it with the questions from the set problem schema. If it concerns a certain action, the set measure schema can serve as a starting point for further elaboration, and so on.

If there are points of view in the draft version of your text on which opinions differ (and on which your readers may have a different view), you may want to look for additional arguments. The fixed forms of argumentation and their corresponding control questions from section 3.4 can offer useful starting points in this respect.

You can also use so-called topical questions to identify any gaps in the content of your text. Topical questions are very general questions on a wide range of subjects. With each of these topical questions, check whether the answer would make your content clearer and more convincing.

What is it?	How does it happen?	Who said it?
What kinds are there?	Who does it?	How is it financed?
What are its characteristics?	When will it happen?	In whose interest is it?
What does it belong to?	What parts does it consist of?	Why?
How many are there?	What is the cause?	Despite what?
What does it look like?	What is the result?	For what purpose?
Where is it happening?	What are the disadvan-	What is the result?
How does it differ from the	tages?	What are the benefits?
rest?	What does it cost?	What does it show?

A list of topical questions.

Explanation of concepts

In the first round of writing, you may have used terms that are not immediately clear to the reader. During a later round of writing, you should check whether the message could be conveyed without using these terms. If this is not the case, you need to provide an explanation. Sometimes a short, casual explanation is enough, while in other cases a more detailed explanation is necessary. If you are writing for your colleagues or peers, take care not to explain jargon that is already known to them.

In a note on an import ban on endangered species, reference is made to the bearded bird. In order to ensure that such a statement is not completely lost on the reader, it can be mentioned by way of explanation that this is a tropical woodpecker species. More information here would only derive from the argument.

In a note on the revision of a study program, it is proposed to introduce an interdisciplinary management project in the last year. If this is a new concept, a fairly detailed explanation will be required: One of the goals of the text is, after all, that the readers get to know the concept.

A report on office ergonomics can start with a detailed definition of the term 'office'—not because the reader would not know what a desk is but because the characteristic properties and function of the desk form the starting point for the content of the report.

Different functions of explanatory notes on terms lead to different requirements.

Explanations differ in how explicit they are. To introduce an explicit explanation, you will often use signal words and phrases such as *by this I mean* or *this is referred to as*. Such signal phrases give the text a didactic character. This is appropriate for textbooks and manuals, but for other types of text, you may want to use a more implicit explanation.

The wall of a cell forms a semipermeable membrane. Some substances can pass through it, while others are stopped.

By a semipermeable membrane is meant a membrane through which some substances can pass, while others are stopped. An example of such a semipermeable membrane is the wall of a cell.

The first explanation is less explicit than the second explanation.

You can also change the *order* of the concept and its explanation. In more or less didactic texts, the usual order is concept – explanation. For other text types, it is usually better to reverse this order.

A semipermeable membrane is a membrane through which some substances can pass, while others are stopped. An example of such a semipermeable membrane is the wall of a cell.

Cells are surrounded by a thin membrane through which some substances can pass, but others cannot. Such a membrane is called a semipermeable membrane.

The first example starts out with the technical term; the second example has it at the end.

The best way to explain a concept depends on the nature of the concept itself and on the target audience of the text. The context of the term within the text is also important. If you use the term *methanol* in a text on automotive fuels, your explanation can focus on its qualities as an environmentally friendly alternative to petrol. If you use the same term in a text about the chemical industry, it would perhaps be better to characterize it as a particular hydrocarbon compound.

Making leaps explicit

When you try to read the first version of your text from the perspective of your audience, you may find that at some points the connection between two messages is missing. As the writer, you know how you moved from one point to the other, but the reader does not. When you revise the first version of your text, you should repair such 'leaps' in thought.

> **Plastic: not so fantastic**
> We like to brag about being so environmentally conscious. We have all been collecting our plastic separately for years with the 'Plastic Hero' bags, to prevent it from ending up in the environment. Nine million German people are already participating. Yet plastic 'soup' is still increasing in our seas and oceans. This is partly due to so-called microplastics in skin care products. Something really needs to be done about that!

To understand why microplastics are released into the environment, the reader must consider that these plastics are flushed through the drain unseen when using certain products. Furthermore, the text does not say what needs to be done about these microplastics. In an improved version, the author could motivate the reader to buy other products or to call for a ban on the production of microplastics.

Introducing unexpected information

News value is one of the most important elements that make a text interesting and useful. On the other hand, unexpected new information may confuse readers and even lead to misunderstandings, especially with quick or careless readers, who will not read what is written but what they expect to be written. For this reason, good writers explicitly indicate when their information or opinion differs from what the reader may expect and why this is the case.

> To find out the attitude of the test subjects towards pedophilia, we had them write a free essay on this subject.

> How have we tried to determine the attitude of the test subjects towards pedophilia? It is customary to interview subjects in such situations. However, we did not do this in this case. We feared that it was difficult for people to express themselves about this taboo

subject to interviewers. To avoid the immediate confrontation with an interviewer, we
had the test subjects write a free essay on the subject.

The first statement would probably be a little out of the blue, and it might be advisable to
introduce and justify it, as in the second statement.

7.3.3 Checking the whole text

With each new version, your text grows through the addition of details, explanations,
examples, and arguments. However, you always need to check whether your text
is growing in *a healthy way*. To find this out, it is useful to check your text at the
end of each writing round by printing the text and updating your text schema and
to-do list. For large writing projects, it can be helpful to use a logbook to keep track
of important changes and your reasons for making them, but for short reports that
would be overdone. The following questions can help you to identify any difficulties
at this stage.

- *Is the main point of the text still clear?* Do the text schema and the text still
  correspond with each other, or are they very different? Find the explanation
  for any differences between them, then determine the best remedy for your
  writing plan: adapting the text to the text schema, or vice versa.
- *Have all additions been put in the right place?* Sometimes you have added an
  explanation that should appear earlier in the text. The important question is
  always whether the reader has enough information at every point in the text
  to understand what you have written.
- *Is there overlap or repetition?* Perhaps certain points recur two or three times, or
  you unnecessarily repeat an argument. Sometimes this means that you should
  dedicate a separate section or paragraph to this recurring subject.
- *Are there any contradictions?* While working on the text, you may have made
  a statement at one point that contradicts another claim elsewhere in the text.
  This will probably not apply to your main argument, but when it comes to the
  details, it may happen to even the best writer.
- *Is the added information functional?* Do all of your additions contribute to the
  ultimate goal of the text, and do they correspond to the needs and interests of
  the reader? After a writing round, you sometimes are in dire need of a round
  of deleting. However, do keep a copy of all your deleted material; you will not
  be the first person to eventually need previously deleted material, only to find
  out you did not save it.

Deleting

The preceding sections focused heavily on ways to enrich the content: additional information to make the text more informative or persuasive. In practice, however, it is often necessary to delete parts so your text does not become too long. Readers often have little time, and clients sometimes impose strict requirements concerning the maximum length of a text.

Deleting is not the most fun part of the writing process. You have made a great effort to gather interesting information, find good examples, and put forward strong arguments—and now they have to be discarded. *Kill your darlings*, as they say. One consolation is that your readers are now more likely to read the whole text instead of stopping halfway through due to time constraints or boredom.

At the same time, deleting can also feel liberating: If you create some breathing space in your text, this will make later revisions easier. And if you have kept your writing and editing strictly separate, you will only need to delete raw material, which is easier to discard than polished pieces.

If you have to delete parts of your text, look for the following things.
– *Unnecessary explanations.* You can often limit the explanation of difficult terms and unknown concepts to what is strictly necessary. In a specific context it may be enough to explain that a *Flarf* is a kind of poem, without having to discuss its characteristics. In some genres, you can use footnotes and endnotes for such digressions.
– *Unnecessary examples.* If you give two examples of something, you may want to delete one. Also, sometimes a brief list of examples can be clearer than one detailed example.
– *Over-argumentation.* This can take two forms. In some cases, you may have given arguments for points of view that will encounter little or no resistance from readers. In other cases, the argumentation may be so detailed that it seems to be completely 'closed off'. In both cases, you can try to tone it down and decide to select only the strongest arguments.
– *Unnecessary attention to other viewpoints.* It can sometimes be convincing to pay attention to other points of view or alternative solutions to a problem. But then you also have to give counterarguments and show that your views or solutions are better. This takes up a lot of space in the text. Perhaps it is possible to focus primarily on your own view of the matter and not, or less, on the views of others. It may be sufficient to note that there are other points of view, which you can refer to in other sources.
– *Explanatory notes to illustrations.* Many writers tend to repeat information from pictures or tables in their text. This is not always necessary.

End of the writing phase

If you change the structure of the text, the text schema will also have to be changed. You go back and forth between your 'blueprint' and your 'construction site'. Because of the close relationship between the text schema and the text, you will only finish the writing phase when the structure is finished. At that point, you can put your text schema aside, and it is time to edit the text.

7.4 Editing

In the first round of writing, you will take a broad approach by focusing on content only. In the later rounds of writing, you will increasingly take an in-depth approach by emphasizing details. During the editing phase, you approach the text from a height, so to speak. In this phase, you adjust your text in such a way that it becomes a neat end product. Your attention now shifts from the levels of the macro- and the mesostructures to the level of the 'microstructures'. You focus on style, clarity, completeness, consistency, and also correctness of language, spelling, and punctuation.

The starting point for the editing phase is your final text and the updated to-do list, but you can also use the comments you have received from others during the review process. In a professional work environment, texts seldom go directly from the writer to the audience, and in educational situations too, peers and supervisors will read your text while it is in development. Your work will benefit from the fresh perspective of others, so if your project does not include a review round catered for by others, you may want to consider asking people for their comments yourself. In this section, we first consider the review process before discussing the editing of the text. The entire review process is about feedback that others give and that you receive. You can find more information about giving and receiving feedback in section 1.5.

7.4.1 The review process – giving the text to others

Think carefully about whom you ask for comments

Depending on your situation, you can ask for comments from people who are involved in the project that your text is concerned with, such as a client, supervisor or—as is often the case—colleagues who are used to evaluating texts. You can also ask for comments from different types of experts.

- *Experts in the field.* These are people who understand the subject, for instance those who helped you gather information.

- *Other experts.* In some cases, you might want a lawyer to take a look at your text or someone who knows the target group well (an information officer or a marketing expert, for example).
- *A language expert.* It is often a good idea to send your text to an editor whose job it is to scrutinize grammar, spelling, style, and punctuation. If you are writing in another language, asking a native speaker may be a good idea.
- *Someone from the audience of the text.* Research has shown that experts can give good feedback but that they do not always look at the text from the perspective of the actual audience of a text. This is why it is useful to have your text read first by a potential reader.

It is not a good idea to ask too many people to comment on your text. Reviewing a text takes time and effort, as does processing the reviewers' comments. You should try to keep the goodwill of the people in your network by not taxing them too much, especially if you need their help more often.

Make sure the reviewers receive a final version of the text

If it is not possible for you to deliver a complete text in time, you should indicate what you are still going to add to the text. For example, mention that you will add an illustration, elaborate on a certain passage, or use another quotation from literature.

Allow sufficient space for your reviewers to write down comments (a left margin of 5 cm is a good idea). The neater the text looks, the more seriously the reviewers will work on their task. Sometimes reviewers prefer increased line spacing (one and a half or two). This is less important if the reviewers comment on a digital version of your text.

Reviewing on screen or on paper?

There are many advantages to commenting on texts on a computer. It is faster and cheaper; texts can be sent and received at one click, and it is better for the environment if you do not use paper and ink. Word processing software also offers many advantages for reviewing. Reviewers can make visible changes to the text, add readable comments, and highlight parts that need attention with colors. You can even combine the comments from different reviewers in a single document. And once you have all the comments, you can simply 'accept' any additions and proposed changes so that you do not have to retype them yourself.

Be aware that not everyone reads as well on the screen as on paper. There are also people who simply do not like it. It is therefore proper to always ask the reviewer if they want to receive the text digitally or in print.

Let the reviewers clearly know what you want from them

The review process is only useful if you have a version of the text that you think is already up to scratch content-wise. That does not mean that reviewing always takes place at the end of the entire writing process. In many cases, texts can already be read by others at an earlier stage. Depending on the timing of the review, different types of comments are useful. Should the reviewers pay attention to all aspects of the text or only to the subjects they have expert knowledge of? Should they only pay attention to the content or also to language and style? You should be very clear about this when you ask reviewers to comment on your text.

Deadlines for reviewers are often a point of debate. It is difficult to insist on urgency, especially if they are busy, but sometimes you have to. If it is not too rude, mention a precise date that you want to receive the review, or if that is not feasible for them, simply ask for a timely response.

If you write a text with other people, it is useful to agree on interim deadlines to present the documents to each other for a review. By doing so, if necessary in multiple rounds, you make sure that the text sections fit each other both in style and in content.

7.4.2   The review process — using feedback

After you have sent your draft text to a number of reviewers and received their feedback, you can incorporate their comments and suggestions into your text for the last phase of revision. When processing their feedback, it is useful to keep the following points in mind.

– Always be grateful for the comments you receive and resist the temptation to start a discussion with the reviewer. You can assume that your reviewers want to help you and that they are serious, sensible readers. In the end, you are the one who determines which comments to take into account and which ones to leave aside.
– Sometimes reviewers give contradictory feedback. Some people want you to pay more attention to a certain point, while others think you can leave it out. Some find the style of your text too formal; others find it too popular. Be aware that you cannot follow all feedback.
– Try not to consider only their suggestions for improvement but also to find out what problems the reviewers may have experienced with the text as a whole. Distinguish the problems they identify from their suggestions for improvement. The better you understand their reading problems, the easier it is to create a good revised version.
– Consider the importance of each comment. Does the reviewer think that a specific change is absolutely necessary, or is the comment intended as a suggestion? In the latter case, it is of course easier to ignore the comment.

–   Also consider the formal role that the reviewer plays in the production of the text. You should obviously consider comments more seriously if they come from your client, your teacher, or someone else who has to approve the text at a later stage.
–   Many writers tend to accommodate all comments by adding something to the text. If a reviewer identified a problem, they add a more detailed explanation instead of using other terms. If a reviewer did not find a certain statement convincing, they add arguments, while perhaps the whole statement could be deleted from the text.
–   Finally, consider whether the proposed changes are feasible. If a reviewer highlights a problem with your content that you cannot really resolve, you will need to discard the comment. Also, if a reviewer's suggestion would take too much time (for example, rewriting an entire chapter), that could be a reason not to use it.

7.5   Finalizing

After you have processed the last comments—and if they do not lead to a new round of writing—it is time to finalize your text. You are now going to finish the text completely. Your attention will now shift for the last time from the content to presentation. Print your text before you finish it; you are less likely to overlook anything if you read it on paper.

Preparing the final version of a text involves a variety of aspects, such as style, grammar, spelling, punctuation, consistency, and design. It is therefore advisable to read the text two or three times, each time shifting your attention to a different aspect. We will discuss three rounds of editing in the recommended order. For large projects it can be useful to make an overview of how you spell certain terms, the headings you use, and the layout rules you follow. Such an overview is called a style sheet. Also think about the language and genre conventions. Many disciplines have their own reference style, title descriptions, prescribed structure, and so forth. Your text must adhere to these conventions and look 'right' in order to be accepted at all.

Format and structure
In the first round of final editing, you will focus on the format and structure of the text. Is it clear to the reader? To answer that question, pay attention to the following aspects.
–   The *division of the text into parts. Do the chapters, sections, and paragraphs adequately reflect the structure* of your argument? Do the headings cover the content? Is the hierarchical structure correct?
–   The *transitions between the different parts* of the text. Does every sentence build on the previous one? Is it always clear why a new subject is introduced?

Is new information adequately explained, without assuming prior knowledge with the reader?
–   The *use of signal words and phrases* (see section 2.4.4) and structure indicators (see section 2.4.6). Have you made sufficient use of tools such as preferred positions, references, signal words, and so forth, so that the relations between each of the elements you introduce are clear to the reader?

Style

In the second round of final editing, you will be focusing on the style of the text. Now that the content of the text is fixed, it is important to check your word choice and sentence construction (see also chapter 4). Keep the following aspects in mind.
–   *Comprehensibility*. Make sure your text is easy to follow. Formulate precisely, use the active form where possible, do not make your sentences too long, and use clear examples. If necessary, use a dictionary. Bullet points sometimes make for a more concise formulation than a 'continuous' text and are ideal for readers who are in a rush. However, bullet points are not accepted in every genre, so it is wise to exercise caution.
–   *Persuasive force*. Make sure that not only your arguments but also your choice of words show that you support your own story. Be careful with adjectives. *Show, don't tell*: Do not merely say that something is the case, but show it.
–   *Consistency*. If the dictionary shows several options for spelling a word, or if a word is not in the dictionary, choose one spelling and stick to that throughout the entire text. If you have chosen a particular term, continue to use it unless you explain that the synonym you use means exactly the same thing.
–   *Conciseness*. If sentences start with 'in other words' or 'that is to say', this usually means that the previous sentence was not clear enough and should perhaps be deleted. Moreover, the first sentence of a text passage may be no more than an introduction to the second in which you really come to the point. This first sentence could then be deleted.
–   *Readability*. Make sure the text is easily accessible. Use jargon sparingly and give examples. Alternate longer sentences with shorter ones. If you describe actions, you can often do so more concisely with the instructive style.

Correctness

Of course, your text must be written in correct English without any spelling errors, and punctuation must be correct (see the references presented for chapter 4 in the last part of this book, entitled *Suggested readings*). As already mentioned in section 4.6, a poorly edited text will negatively influence its readability and the reader's appreciation.

Layout

After checking and where necessary improving the format, structure, style, spelling, and punctuation of your text, it is time to work on the layout. Your text should look good. This takes more time than you may think, but it is time well spent: Neat texts are read more carefully and often taken more seriously than messy texts. A neat text shows that you put some thought into the communication and that you take your audience seriously.

Many organizations have a house style that you need to adhere to. This includes guidelines on font, font size, and page layout, for instance, and possibly also on administrative codes needed to archive a text. A good house style presents a uniform and solid impression to the outside world. Of course, this only works if everyone in the organization adheres to the guidelines. You can include this house style in your style sheet so you can consult it throughout the writing process.

If you do not need to use a house style, you must make your own decisions about the layout of your text. Word processing programs offer specific style libraries or templates especially developed for various types of text to help you with this: from reports to forms, and from letters to instructions. Do keep in mind that these templates are often typically American and that they sometimes come across as old-fashioned or ostentatious from a European perspective. In section 5.2 you can find instructions on how to customize these templates to fit your own ideas and tastes.

You should always check whether you have numbered the pages, whether the numbering of your headings is correct, and whether the headings have a consistent layout. Also check whether figures are in the right place and whether they all have a caption and a number. Tables should all have a heading and a number. Ask yourself if your text is properly aligned and does not contain double spaces or unnecessary hard returns. Finally, make sure there are no 'widows' or 'orphans' in your text: sole lines that are on the previous or next page of the paragraph to which they belong, or lines that appear on an otherwise blank page.

7.6   Solutions to writing problems

Some say that writing is mainly a matter of inspiration. We could have started this chapter with the wise words of the British writer William Somerset Maugham: 'I only write when inspiration strikes. Fortunately it strikes every morning at nine o'clock sharp.' Writing is thus primarily a matter of discipline and hard work (more perspiration than inspiration). This holds true not only for novelists but certainly also for business writers. Writers who have trouble *starting*, *continuing*, or *keeping track of* their writing can often use some help.

In this section we will discuss various ways to make the writing project as pleasant and efficient as possible. We have already touched upon some of these ways, but we now treat them in greater detail in the context of writing problems and their solutions. Every professional writer can benefit from these guidelines.

7.6.1 Start writing

A large writing project often takes at least a few weeks and requires your attention on a wide variety of aspects as well as input from others. It is therefore no wonder that many people experience writing as stressful and tend to postpone it. Still, it is wise to simply start writing, if only to avoid increasing pressure at the last minute. But how do you get started?

Good planning is half the work

In section 7.1.2, we emphasized that before starting the process of writing, it was important to come up with a complete, achievable, but also flexible writing plan. In that section, the relation between your planning and your task was central. However, it is also important to consider your planning in relation to your other daily activities.

– *Protect your free time*. It may sound odd, but if you have a tendency to postpone tasks, it is a good idea to plan your free time first. These are the parts of the day and week that you do not work on your project. This way, you ensure that you have enough time to relax.

– *Be realistic*. It is imperative to make a realistic estimation of the number of hours you will actually be able to spend on your project. You often have less time than you would like. Before you start a project, keep track of how many hours you spend each day on activities that you cannot put on hold for the duration of your project. Then you will know how much time you will have left for writing.

– *Plan from end to beginning*. People who experience writing problems often postpone their work until just before the deadline, wrongly assuming they still have enough time to complete their tasks. It is therefore a good idea to start your planning from the deadline and work backwards in time from there. You can then easily identify intermediate steps and divide the project into small, manageable pieces. Instead of working towards the end goal from the start, you will learn to focus on sub-tasks. Reverse planning can thus help you to feel less stressed.

– *Plan as precisely as possible, but no more than that*. Control freaks tend to make a very detailed planning before they are sure that they will actually take each of the steps. Such a planning gives a false sense of safety and will only cause stress. You should plan in detail only those specific activities that are part of your current writing phase or that you are certain you will need to carry out at a later stage.

Create a pleasant workplace

People often tend to overlook one of the most obvious ways to increase your productivity: the workplace. This is not merely a spacious desk and a comfortable chair.

– *Keep your workplace neat and tidy.* Make a good habit of cleaning up your workplace at the end of a working day. This not only makes for a nicer working environment; it also obliges you to tie up all the loose ends of the day. Opened books and websites often indicate an incomplete action and can distract you from your work. Notes on napkins and such are often not yet included in your log or to-do list, and empty plates and cups create a restless atmosphere in which to work.

– *Make sure you have good working materials.* Do not keep working on a broken chair or with a malfunctioning computer. If you want to work comfortably, you need to be able to rely on your writing tools. Make sure everything is in a decent condition and that you have enough material at hand (paper, paper clips, and such).

– *Make good use of your computer.* In addition to good writing software, you can install other programs on your computer to support your work. There are also many websites to help you out, such as digital dictionaries, encyclopedias, and to-do lists. There are even programs that can keep track of the time you spend working.

– *Avoid distraction.* Some writers cannot resist the temptation to surf the internet aimlessly. If you tend to do that, it might be a good idea to temporarily disconnect from the internet. The same applies to your smartphone. Not everyone is as easily distracted, so make a realistic assessment of your own situation and take appropriate measures. Having social media open on your browser is not a good idea. Also consider whether you work best with or without background music.

Take yourself seriously

Many writers who experience problems are very self-critical and blame themselves for everything. However, postponing is not a sign of laziness but simply an unproductive way of dealing with stress. To reduce tensions in a more productive way, it is vital that you do not set the bar too high. Make sure that you can keep the agreements you made with yourself. Keep in mind the following points in mind.

– *Learn to start.* The beginning is always tricky, but if you set modest goals for yourself, it will be easier. If you are really having problems starting, agree with yourself to begin each day with your writing task and to not work on it for more than, say, 30 minutes. After those 30 minutes, you can reward yourself with a fun task or a short break. If you can complete the 30 minutes of work without interruption, you can schedule the next 30 minutes for that day. There are no strict obligations or goals except that you work continuously for 30 minutes.

– *Learn to stop.* If you agree with yourself to always work for short periods, dare to stop on time. Use your working time to work, but then also really use your free time for leisure. You can only enjoy your free time if you do not feel guilty about your work. If you can do this, you will be able to start working afresh on your next shift.

– *Keep your tasks manageable.* When you make a schedule, you are bringing together two things: the tasks belonging to your writing project and the time you have to perform these tasks. It is tempting to combine the two immediately, but it is often wiser to do so gradually. You should first establish the right order of these tasks because there is always more than one possibility. Then you know which step to take at any given moment, so your list of tasks remains concrete. Only make a note in your calendar of a specific task if you know exactly how long it will take and that you can actually finish it at the specified time. In other words, take agreements with yourself as seriously as agreements you make with others, or do not make them (or not yet, at least).

7.6.2 Continue writing

For some writers, beginning is not a problem, but problems arise when they are actually producing the text. If you stare at an empty screen for a long time puzzling over your writing task, you cannot say that you are not working. But neither can you say that your work is productive. How can you prevent such writer's block?

– *Remove any mental obstacles.* There are quite a few prejudices about writing that can demotivate you. It is sometimes said, for instance, that good writers start writing straight away and put everything on paper without mistakes. Although routine certainly helps with writing, when it comes to more complex writing tasks *everyone* needs a good plan—if not on paper, then at least a mental one. You should also keep in mind that your text cannot always meet the highest standards.

– *Build a routine.* The best way to prevent writer's block is to write every day. This way you keep your metaphorical pen sharp and make sure that you do not associate writing only with that one daunting project but also with blogs about your daily life, a review of a recently read book, or perhaps even a tweet about the state of the world. Whatever you write, make sure that at least part of your writing activity is dedicated to yourself so you do not experience too much stress when you have to write for work or for your university studies. You can also create a routine by writing at a fixed moment during the day. Choose the time of day when you are most productive, and reserve this time to work on your project. During these hours, you are not available for meetings, colleagues, or tasks other than writing.

– *Keep writing and editing strictly separate.* Writers often make it difficult for themselves by needlessly burdening their writing phase with editorial work. If you are constantly thinking about how to correctly formulate a sentence, what word to choose, or how to spell an unusual term while you also need to generate the right content, the pressure to do it all right at one go can be paralyzing. You should therefore limit yourself to the content when you are in the writing phase and vice versa: Once you have arrived at the editing phase, really limit yourself to editing. If you postpone editing until the end of your writing process, you will also be less attached to the unpolished versions of your texts, and it will be easier to rewrite or even delete parts of them.

– *Freewriting.* One method of keeping writing and editing separate is freewriting. If you turn off your 'internal censor', you can overcome writer's block more easily. Freewriting helps you to generate content without having to think about the final form in which you will present the information. You can freewrite about anything, from a very specific part of your project to a general summary of the whole.

– *Work on well-defined tasks.* It is important that you do not start a writing session until you have a clear idea of what you are going to do. You should be mainly concerned not with the goal but with the tasks you need to perform to achieve that goal. If you know exactly what concrete actions you have to take, it will be easier for you to actually do it.

Freewriting is a unique technique for generating content. In a short period of time (10 minutes, for example), you spontaneously create a text with complete sentences on your subject, trying to incorporate all your previous ideas. Freewriting works just like other techniques to come up with a broad variety of ideas, but it also has a structuring effect. By producing a coherent text, you express your ideas in sentences instead of keywords, thus forcing you to put your ideas in a certain order. Do keep in mind, however, that the outcome of a first freewriting session is not a rough draft of your text but only a source of inspiration meant for personal use. The rules are simple.

– Agree with yourself beforehand how long your freewriting session will be and set a timer. We recommend no more than 10-15 minutes per session.

– Do not rush to produce a lot of content but keep a steady and constant pace.

– Write continuously, without stopping to think or correct errors.

– If you cannot think of anything during the writing process, write down that you have no new ideas. The most important thing is that you do not stop writing.

- After the writing session, summarize the ideas you generated and how they are connected, then start a new session on the basis of that summary.
- Throw away the results of previous free-writing sessions after using them for a summary. You are only sharpening the pen; you are not yet writing a presentable version of your text. It is only when a version emerges that shows the contours of an acceptable text, after perhaps three free-writing sessions, that you can use it as a starting point for the content of your real text.

How freewriting works.

Enough is enough

Many writers find it difficult to finish their text. They keep on finding new possibilities to improve it, which means that they will never finalize their text. To guard against this tendency, keep in mind the *Pareto principle*: With many activities, 20% of your time and effort accounts for 80% of the result, while the other 80% of the time is spent on the remaining 20% of the result. In other words, effective writing also means knowing when to stop. Remembering the following principle might help the stopping process: There is no such thing as a totally perfect text.

7.6.3   Keep track

Apart from problems with getting started and staying the course, some of the biggest problems in writing projects are the following.

- *Not knowing what to do.* If you have not developed a task-oriented plan, you may get off to a slow start, do unnecessary things, and generate many loose ends that you have to tie up later.
- *Taking too long searching for material.* Some people keep looking for new material. There is almost always more relevant material than there is space in your project. For this reason, you should be very specific about what you search for, always check that you are not collecting more of the same, and ask yourself whether your continued search is not secretly a form of procrastination. Another pitfall is that you do not keep track of what you have found. When you need material that you found earlier, you may waste a lot of time searching for it.
- *Worrying about the project.* If you do not delimit your tasks properly, you may start to worry about everything that you are unable to address at that point. This is often the result of poor planning: you may have overplanned or not made your planning clear enough.

A flexible and task-oriented writing plan can help you avoid these problems. Such a plan will help you to get started, to keep working, and to eventually to stop. The basic idea is always to take all the 'loose ends' out of your head and put them on paper. You can then start working undisturbed on the tasks belonging to the current phase of your project. Here we briefly summarize once again all the documents that can help with your planning.

– *Writing plan*. The writing plan allows you to keep an overview of the basic conditions of your project and your overall planning. This planning is not too precise, but it does show the amount of time you think you need and the specific intermediate steps (deadlines).

– *Text schema* and *literature matrix*. The text schema and the literature matrix show how you want to construct the text, what information you want to provide where, and how many words you want to spend on each part. Ideally, you should work from your literature matrix to your text schema and from your text schema to your to-do list, although the reality is often different.

– *To-do list*. Your to-do list is meant to serve as a daily document that helps you to perform your tasks each day. In addition, you can also put activities in your to-do list that you think of while working but cannot carry out immediately (because they belong to a later phase, for example).

– *Log*. You can use a log to keep your pen sharp and to record all your decisions and thoughts about the project. This will later help to remind you why you took certain steps earlier in the project. You can also include notes about previous versions of your work.

– *Style sheet*. If you have to work with difficult style conventions for a large writing task, you can create a style sheet. Update this with your chosen solutions to problems concerned with style, spelling, numbering, punctuation, and such, so that you have a complete document at the end of the writing phase that you can use for the final editing.

Key points

— Writing in a professional context is a form of systematic problem-solving.
— The main activities in the writing process are: preparing, determining content, writing, editing, and finalizing. The sequence of the activities in the process is not fixed in advance. Where necessary, the writer will anticipate later phases and return to earlier phases.

Preparation

The preparation for a writing assignment includes both familiarizing yourself with the target group and planning the writing process.

Orientation

— When orienting yourself towards the goal, determine the reason why this text should be published, or what your assignment is.
— When you analyze the target group, determine who the readers will be and make an estimate of their level of knowledge, their needs, and their perspective.

Planning

— Create a writing plan with a description of the reason and the underlying goals of the text, the target group and the subject, the overall content, and the specified preconditions.
— Your planning is the translation into actions of the starting points you defined during the creation of your writing plan.
— Make sure that your planning is effective and flexible; in fact, your planning is a detailed to-do list, where the correct sequence of actions is especially important.
— Consider whether you want to keep a logbook in which you explain choices you have made before and where you reflect on your writing process.

Determining the content

As you determine the content, you will successively generate ideas, collect material, and select and structure the available information.
— Generate ideas by means of a brainstorming or mind mapping session.
— Collect material by means of archive research, literature research, interviews with experts, and your own research.
— Select and structure the information on the basis of a template or with the aid of set schemata and ordering principles.

Writing
– Write longer texts in several rounds, generating a new version with each round.
– During the first round, put the main lines on paper without worrying too much about details and external structure. At this stage, it is important to translate your text schema into running prose.
– In later rounds, supplement the first version by applying set schemata where appropriate or by asking topical questions. Explain difficult concepts, explain leaps of thought, and introduce unexpected information.
– Work back and forth between your text and your text schema in such a way that the two remain in harmony; this way you stay on course without losing flexibility.
– Check if the result still has a clear structure and if all information is still relevant.
– Delete unnecessary explanations and examples, excessive argumentation, needless attention to other points of view, and unnecessary explanations of tables and images.

Editing and finalizing the text

Editing
– Think carefully about who you ask for comments: Advice from content experts, language experts, or someone from your target group can each contribute in their own way to the quality of your final text.
– Make sure you offer a suitable version of the text to be edited. Also think about the desired format (electronically or on paper, depending on the preferences of the reviewer or yourself) and provide clear instructions on what you expect from your reviewers.
– Always show your appreciation for the feedback you receive.
– On the basis of the feasibility of the recommendations, the weight given to the recommendations by the reviewer, and the extent to which the reviewers agree with each other, determine for yourself whether and how you follow up each comment.

Finalizing
If the text is satisfactory in terms of content and structure, pay special attention during the final round to:
– the external structure (such as titles, numbering, headings);
– the style;
– the correctness of language, spelling, and punctuation;
– the design (typography, layout).

Solutions for writing problems

- Always start writing as early as possible with every writing project.
- Make sure you coordinate your writing planning for large projects with your other activities: Reserve enough free time, don't overestimate the number of really productive hours in a day, and don't plan for more than you can achieve.
- A good working environment promotes productivity. Therefore, make sure you have a tidy workplace, have good working materials, make optimal use of the possibilities of your computer, and avoid distractions.
- Take yourself seriously. Don't be too critical of yourself and try to start on time and stop on time.
- Keep the writing and editing processes strictly separated.
- If you get stuck, use freewriting as a technique to generate content.
- Work on clearly defined tasks and don't be too perfectionistic.

Assignments

Assignment 1: Generating ideas

Purpose of the assignment
You will practice generating and structuring your own ideas for a text.

Subject matter
– Section 7.2.1
– Section 7.6.2

Tasks
1   Choose a subject for an essay—a short, argumentative text, with space for the author's own insights. Some suggestions: *Young people on the streets, The younger generation and the church, Same-sex marriage, Freedom of religion, Living in fear because of crime, Euthanasia.*
2   Hold a brainstorming session and a mind mapping session on your own for one of these subjects.
3   Hold three consecutive ten-minute freewriting sessions, each based on the results of the previous task. After the first session and the second session, use up to five minutes to read your text and determine what the line of your argument is; use that line of argument as the starting point for the next session.

Important
This is purely a matter of practicing material generation. Normally, you would not start writing without first making a text schema for the content of your text. The freewriting task here is intended as an exercise to work out the relationship between the terms mentioned in the brainstorming and mind mapping sessions. Freewriting can also be used after you have created a writing plan and text schema; it is then used to prevent writer's block.

Assignment 2: Creating a retrospective writing plan

Purpose of the assignment

You will practice critical thought by making such a plan and experiencing the usefulness of a writing plan by looking back on an earlier writing project.

Subject matter

Section 7.1.2

Tasks

1 Select a project you have completed previously (a project report, essay, or research report, for example).
2 Make a writing plan for this project that you think meets the conditions set out in this chapter.
3 Based on this retrospective writing plan, note what you would do differently from what you did at the time.

Assignment 3: Working on a new writing project

Purpose of the assignment

You will practice working on a writing project in phases and reflecting on it.

Subject matter

– This assignment relates to the whole of chapter 7.
– Pay special attention to section 7.1.2

Tasks

1 Choose a future project, or a project that has just started, and start working on it according to the suggestions in this book. While executing the project, go through the whole of chapter 7.
2 Create a logbook to write down your thoughts on how to apply all the suggestions: comments, criticisms, and tricks you teach yourself.

8 Writing—reporting

◄ *Office of the notary*, Jan Woutersz. Stap, circa 1629. A clerk or accountant is negotiating with a man with a money bag on the left and a woman with a boy with a flute on her lap on the right. In the middle a table with a cash book and some coins. In the background a bookcase and sealed documents on the wall.

Just like the cash book in this picture, a report is often relevant for different stakeholders and interested parties with varying backgrounds; therefore it is important that you provide all relevant information in a clear and effective way.

A text with consequences

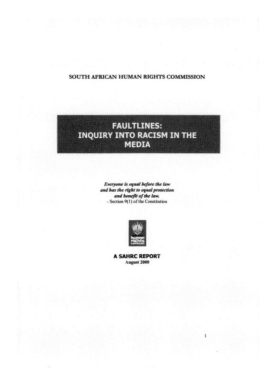

SOUTH AFRICAN HUMAN RIGHTS COMMISSION

**FAULTLINES:
INQUIRY INTO RACISM IN THE
MEDIA**

*Everyone is equal before the law
and has the right to equal protection
and benefit of the law.*
- Section 9(1) of the Constitution

A SAHRC REPORT
August 2000

Professional reports play an important role in our society. Although by no means all reports are eye-catching or accessible to the general public, their findings can have a major social impact. Reports can contribute to changes of direction in a particular company, lead to policy measures by the government, or influence the decision-making behavior of individuals.

What makes reporting a challenge is that there are often multiple stakeholders and interested parties. The report *Faultlines: Inquiry into Racism in the Media* published in 2000 by the South African Human Rights Commission demonstrates this point. This famous report was extremely important for a number of stakeholders, including the government, the human rights fraternity, the media, and those who had suffered because of racism in the media. It was a highly controversial report, widely discussed in media all over the world, and it had a huge impact on society as a whole. The variety of reactions to the report demonstrates how challenging it is to accommodate all the stakeholders and interested parties.

Reports are longer texts—ranging from a mere five pages to as many as hundreds of pages—that are usually not intended for a single person but for an organization (or a part of an organization). Reports are usually printed in larger quantities, and often several people work together to produce a single report. In education, reports are sometimes written by one person and assessed by one or more persons.

Reports come in all shapes and sizes. In practice, however, there are no clear boundaries between the different types of report. And what is called a memo in one organization can be called a strategic plan elsewhere.

Various types of reports also play a major role in higher education. In this case, reports are usually called assignments and, especially for larger projects, research reports, theses, or dissertations. In academic research and in an educational context, reports often take the form of a scientific article in which a theory is developed or tested. Some research reports also have an application-orientation, meaning that the research leads to recommendations to be applied, for instance by the client for whom the research was done.

Analytical report	Project plan
Policy memorandum	Proposal
Discussion note	Thesis
Feasibility study	Dissertation
Inventory	Grant proposal
Annual report	Test report
Research report	Progress report
Draft report	Work plan

Different types of reports.

In view of the variety of types of reports, it is impractical to provide separate guidance for each type. We therefore limit ourselves to discussing the common components of a report and their functions. We will do this in section 8.1, dealing specifically with the cover and title page, summary, foreword, table of contents, introduction, titles and headings, conclusion, notes, bibliography, and appendices.

In section 8.2 we will discuss the use of references. This relates to the references in the body text, the entries that should be included in your bibliography, and the structure of the bibliography itself.

In section 8.3 we will take a closer look at one genre in particular: research reports. For graduates in higher and academic education, the thesis or dissertation is the final and paramount instrument by which they are assessed. What does a crystal-clear and well-founded research report look like? There is no single answer to that question. After all, there are many conventions for research reports within university programs, organizations, journals, and even disciplines. The type of study that was performed (qualitative or quantitative, observational or experimental) also determines what the report will look like. Nevertheless, a set of 'common denominators' does exist for the research report. We will discuss its structure (based on the set research schema), its individual components, and the use of language, and we will show a sample report.

Finally, in section 8.4 we will discuss two common types of reports: the short report and the portfolio. Most organizations have various types of short reports. They are often texts of no more than five pages, written for internal use. Such reports often contain the practical results of previous research and are intended as a starting point for the implementation of a particular measure that has been decided upon. We will conclude this chapter with a discussion of the portfolio, a form of self-reporting that plays an increasingly important role in both educational and professional contexts.

8.1   Components of a report

In this section we will discuss the most common parts of a report in their most logical order. Note, however, that the order in which we discuss the parts here may differ from the order prescribed in your organization. In this case, follow the prescribed order. It is also important to note that not all the items discussed here may necessarily appear in all reports. Therefore, before you start, check carefully which parts you should and should not include.

8.1.1   Cover and title page

The *cover* (or cover page) of the report contains the following elements in a clear layout.
–   The author's name; if a report is written on behalf of an organization, the author's name is often omitted, and the organization's name is given.
–   The title and subtitle of the report; the subtitle is sometimes omitted.
–   The name of the organization with its logo.
–   You can also provide the date of the report (the exact date, the month and the year, or the year only); usually the date is presented on the title page.

With a carefully designed cover (beautiful illustration, color, solid paper) in the house style, report writers present themselves and their organization professionally to the readers.

The *title page* is the first right-hand page of the report and serves as a starting point for the reader to be able to make a full bibliographical entry of the publication (see section 8.2). The cover information is repeated and supplemented on the title page. The title page contains:

- the title and subtitle;
- the name(s) of the author(s);
- the name of the client(s) and the organization; in the case of a thesis: the name of the institution and the program; sometimes the name of the place is also given;
- where appropriate, the ISBN (International Standard Book Number: a unique code for a book publication) or the DOI (Digital Object Identifier: a unique code for a file on the internet);
- where appropriate, the number of the report;
- where appropriate, the date of publication (possibly only the year).

Example of a cover.   Example of a title page.

8.1.2   Summary

A summary that precedes the main text has four functions (on the functions of a possible review in the final section, after the main text, see section 8.1.7).
- It explains the title so that readers who have become interested on the basis of the title can see whether the report is really worthwhile for them.
- It is an abridged version of the text for people who do not have time to read the entire report and still want to have an impression of its content.

–   It provides an overview so that readers who will read the report will be able to better follow the structure of the report.
–   It serves as a memory aid so that readers who have read the report can more easily remember at a later date what it contains.

The summary comes immediately after the title page. You can choose from three different types.
–   An *abstract* gives a very brief account of the most important points in the report.
–   A *direct* or an *indirect summary* is longer and goes a little deeper into the content.
–   In a *management summary*, the emphasis is on the recommendations or issues that may govern the decision-making process that emerge from the report. This can be the basis for a new report in which these recommendations or issues are worked out in detail. A management summary, as the name suggest, would typically have the organization's management as its audience.

Abstract

In an abstract, one should make clear:
–   what the framework is in which the report was written (the reason);
–   what the theme of the report is;
–   what the main questions are;
–   what the most important key answers to these questions are.

Abstracts need to have a certain independence from the main text: The reader should be able to read this text on its own. Abstracts are often consulted separately from the report. Often they serve as introductory texts for reports that are published online. They are also used in announcements of meetings such as conferences and symposiums where the report in question will be discussed, or in announcements to advertise the publication of the report. The length of an abstract is usually about 150-200 words. Some journals and documentation systems have strict word limits; longer abstracts are not processed. Therefore, keep to the prescribed size (use your word processor's word counter).

In this report it is made clear that the accessibility of the public services of the municipality of New Aduard leaves something to be desired. In chapter 2 you will find the results of a citizens' survey, which shows this. In chapter 3 it will therefore be proposed that 100,000 dollars be set aside each year for the necessary adjustments over the next three years. This will be financed from the extra income that can be expected from the increase of the relevant budgets.

This abstract suggests that the readers have the report in front of them. It should be possible, however, to read the abstract separately from the report.

The accessibility of public services of the municipality of New Aduard leaves something to be desired. This can be deduced from the results of a survey of citizens. It is therefore proposed to allocate 100,000 dollars per year over the next three years for necessary adjustments. This will be financed from the extra income that can be expected from the increase of the relevant budgets.

This abstract is independent from the report, since it does not contain references to the report itself or references to the chapters, for example.

Commissioned by the Municipal Information Service, University of Applied Sciences is conducting a series of studies into the relationship between the municipality of New Aduard and its residents. This report focuses on a survey of public services. Interviews and a survey investigated how citizens come into contact with the municipality and what they think of the services provided. The research participants appear to be satisfied with the public services but find it difficult to call on them. Shame plays a role in this, but the limited opening hours also discourage many citizens from visiting in person. It is striking that the announcements in house-to-house magazines are very well read and highly appreciated, but that the same information made accessible on cable and internet is hardly known. The study concludes that the communicative attitude and quality of service are sufficient, but that the organization can be improved in terms of opening hours.

This abstract is much more suitable for readers who do not know the report or who do not have it at their disposal. The theme is better introduced, and no reference is made to parts of the report.

Direct or indirect summary

Just like an abstract, a summary briefly shows what can be expected of the main text. However, a summary is much longer. One can take two possible approaches to the summary. One option is to write a *direct* or *informative summary* containing information about the main issues in the text as presented by the author. A direct summary is therefore primarily writer-orientated. The other option is to present an *indirect* or *indicative summary* which indicates the main issues that the report deals with without necessarily offering any further discussion. An indirect summary is therefore primarily reader-oriented. It is a text about the report text, using phrases such as 'This report is concerned with', 'The question is asked whether', and so on. The distinction between direct and indirect summaries has already been discussed in section 6.1. In a summary that is published at the front of a report, a *combination* of these forms is also possible. In such cases, it would be useful to take into account the following recommendations.

–   Be informative about the main issues. Summarize the most important infor-
    mation in the report so that the main line is clear.
–   If side issues are discussed in the report itself, be indicative about them in
    the summary: Just announce that they are being dealt with and do not reveal
    what is being said about them. Also indicate the chapters in which some of
    the information can be found, particularly in long summaries. For the sake of
    clarity, use not only the numbers but also the titles of the chapters.
–   Follow the order of the sections in the main text, and also show this in the
    layout (new paragraphs or blank lines where a new chapter in the publication
    starts).

Just as with an abstract, readers must always be able to read the direct or indirect
summary without having the main text of the report at their disposal. Therefore,
do not refer to any further information, diagrams, tables, or illustrations in the
main body of the report and do not use any terms that readers cannot understand
until they have read the publication. Leave out such concepts or explain them.

> Commissioned by the Joint Health Service, a study has been performed into the needs of
> elderly people for information about health problems and available facilities. The study
> was prompted by the Elderly Association's observation that relatively few elderly people
> in the northern provinces make use of the available care and financial facilities.
>
> The survey was performed using a telephone survey. A total of 350 elderly people
> aged between 65 and 84 living independently, from six different municipalities, were
> asked to participate in the study. In the end, just over 200 surveys were useful.
>
> The investigation led to a number of significant results. It was found, for example, that
> one-third of older people feel that insufficient information is provided about health and
> facilities and that more than half of those surveyed need more information. In particular,
> more information is needed on ageing, care services, healthy behavior, and financial pro-
> visions (see Table 6 on page 18). Furthermore, it turned out that most elderly people see
> their GP as the most suitable person for providing information. After all, contact with the
> general practitioner is often easily and familiar. In addition, the social worker, the Elderly
> Association, and the Foundation for the Welfare of the Elderly are mentioned as suitable
> information providers.
>
> On the basis of these results, it is recommended that a further training program be set
> up for general practitioners and social workers. In addition, targeted campaigns should
> be used to draw the attention of older people to the right ways to obtain health informa-
> tion. In addition, municipalities can proactively inform older people about the available

facilities. Finally, it is recommended that a follow-up survey be performed to assess the satisfaction of older people with the services on offer.

Example of a direct summary. There are no references to the chapters, but that is not a problem in the case of such a short summary. One problem, however, is the reference to the table on page 18: The summary must be legible without the reader having to look inside the report.

Management summary

A management or executive summary is often used when the management of an organization has to make decisions on the basis of a report. The emphasis is therefore on the recommendations that are made. The point that a report usually ends with is key to a management summary. The structure is as follows.

– First, you summarize in one paragraph the theme and the reason for the report.
– This is followed by the recommendations. If the list is long, restrict it to the essentials: the matters of principle on which a decision must be taken.
– You then outline the recommendations by setting out the main arguments discussed in the report. These are the most important findings when it comes to a research report, but the arguments can also be derived from professional literature, for example.
– You end with the most important consequences of the recommendations, for example the costs you foresee, the specific measures to be taken, or the effects to be expected.

A management summary should be concise (maximum 500 words). In many organizations, the rule is that the management summary must fit on one A4 page.

The management of an organization takes many decisions on the basis of a management summary. That is sometimes frustrating for authors of a report. They do their best to write a thorough report, but the manager involved only reads the management summary. Would it not have been better if the rest of the report had remained unwritten? Of course not. Other stakeholders in the organization will read the rest of the report. The report is intended to prevent decisions from being taken without thorough consideration; these considerations can be found in the report.

In smaller organizations and in higher education, it also happens that report writers are asked to elaborate on the recommendations from their report. Such elaborations are often described in a separate implementation plan, which does not form part of the report.

Reason
The quality plan BGM ('Better governance in your municipality') stipulates, among other things, that there is room for improvement in the services provided by the Municipality.

In this context, the Faculty of Communication of our university conducted research into citizens' experiences and their satisfaction with these services.

Recommendations
- Extend the opening hours of the municipal services; preferably open on two evenings.
- Allow the extended opening hours to take effect on 1 May next.
- Close down the public services on Monday mornings.

Motivation
With our interviews and the survey, we investigated how residents come into contact with the municipality and what they think of the services. The residents appear to be satisfied with the public services but find it difficult to call on them. Shame plays a role in this, but the limited opening hours also discourage many citizens from visiting in person. It is striking that the announcements in house-to-house magazines are very well read and highly appreciated but that the same information made accessible on cable tv and the internet is hardly known.

Consequences
- The estimated cost of opening on two evenings is 75,000 euro per year, of which approximately 25,000 euro can be recouped by closing services on Monday mornings. The number of visitors is minimal on a Monday morning.
- In order to be able to implement the extended opening hours on 1 May next, consultations with the relevant service committees must be held in the short term.

This management summary is intended for the executive of the municipality. The most important points are marked with headings so that the reader can immediately see what the most relevant aspects are. The recommendations are listed with separate bullet points.

8.1.3   Preface and cover letter

The *preface* (also referred to as the *foreword*) usually is a personal part of the report in which you can discuss the reason or motivation for writing about the particular topic (for example: 'With this research we address one of the most important problems with governance [...]') or how you came to address the particular issue (for example: 'During the implementation of the policy we realized that there were still some outstanding issues regarding financing that we needed to understand more fully [...]').

Furthermore, the preface is the best place to thank persons or bodies who contributed to the report (such as experts who helped you on your way or test subjects who participated in the study). You can also say something in the foreword about the process that ultimately led to the report.

Foreword

In March 2015, Mr. Jones contacted the Department of Information and Policy at Berfelland University of Applied Sciences as part of the project *Information for the Elderly*. His request was for a study to be performed into the elderly's need for information about care facilities. This first contact led to the internship assignment that I have worked on in the past six months and of which you will find the set-up, results, and conclusions in this report.

The research is part of the project *Information for the elderly*. This project started in January 2015 at the request of *Care for the Elderly*, a partnership of fifteen healthcare institutions in Berfelland. The aim of the project is to improve information for the elderly. The project consists of three successive phases:

- making an inventory of the current information activities of institutions and organizations in Berfelland;
- conducting a survey among older people of their wishes and needs with regard to information;
- drawing up and implementing integrated information plan for older people.

The first part of the project, making an inventory of current information activities, has now been completed (Williams, 2015). This research report is a report of the second part: the research into the need for information.

It would not have been possible to perform the study described here without the kind cooperation of the more than 300 elderly people who took part in the survey. Thank you very much.

22 September 2018
Max Williams

Example of a preface or foreword.

Cover letter

As explained above, a preface or foreword creates an opportunity for a personal introduction to a report and to the context in which the report was produced. Sometimes you might need a more formal approach, especially in the professional context where there might be less need for this personal touch. One option that you then have is to produce an accompanying *cover letter*. The cover letter is usually issued separately from the report. The letter 'presents' the report to the reader. It usually contains:

- the actual offer ('We present this report to you [...]')

– a brief reference to the reason for the report;
– where appropriate, a word of appreciation to people and organizations who have made an important contribution;
– a brief indication of the role the report plays in a process ('This report is intended as a prelude to the discussion about / as a starting point for decision-making about / as a justification for the activities to [...]').

Cover letters are also often used when a report is submitted as an article to a magazine for publication. In such letters you might state that the article was written by yourself, indicate that the article has never been published or offered before, and state that the research on the basis of which you wrote this article was conducted in accordance with ethical guidelines.

8.1.4   Table of Contents

With a short text, you do not need to create a table of contents, but with a longer text (from about ten pages), this is certainly necessary. A well-designed table of contents contains:
– the numbers and titles of chapters and sections;
– all the other components of the report except the cover, the title page, and the table of contents itself (but including any preface and summary);
– the numbers of the pages where the items in question begin.

Make sure that your table of contents is as clear as possible, for example by indenting sections and sub-sections from the left margin and placing a blank line between the larger sections. Only with a good layout will the table of contents help you to read globally and to effectively find your way through the document.

   If you have sufficient skills with the word processor, you can create a table of contents automatically. However, you should take a critical look at the layout. Sometimes it is very messy (many `different` fonts, lower case and CAPITALS, upright roman, *italics* and **bold letters**, uneven indentation). In this case, it is worth simplifying the standard style or correcting the layout by hand.

List of illustrations
A list of illustrations appears mainly in technical or scientific reports. Such a list is useful if there are many drawings, maps, and so on in the report. The list includes the number of the illustration, the title (exactly as it appears in the text), and the page number. If you have numbered tables and figures separately, create one list for the tables and a separate one for the figures.

Table of Contents

Example of a table of contents. Note the simple typography: The arrangement of chapters and sections is indicated by indentations, not by deviating fonts. The page numbers are immediately behind the sections, to make it easier for readers to find what they are looking for.

Glossary

Glossaries, or lists of abbreviations and symbols, are also found mainly in technical and scientific reports. If you use many abbreviations, symbols, or technical terms that your audience may not immediately understand, explanatory lists are appropriate. You can process them into a single list, but you can also split this list if it becomes too long.

8.1.5 Introduction

A good text does not begin directly but has an introduction. In the case of short texts, such an introduction need not contain more than one or a few opening sentences, but in longer texts, the introduction can develop into a separate introductory chapter of the text. The introduction has three functions:
–   to draw the reader's attention;
–   to motivate the reader;
–   to prepare the reader for what is to come.

In books and long reports, introductions would ideally also provide a brief overview of the chapters and any important sections in the chapters that you might want to draw the attention to. For such introductions, the third, structuring function is usually more important than the other two.

To fulfill its three functions, an introduction section may contain:
–   an opening;
–   an explanation of the goal;
–   necessary preliminary information;
–   a look ahead at what is to follow in the text.

Opening

The first sentences of your opening should hit the sweet spot immediately. You have only a few moments to draw the reader's attention and to motivate the reader to immerse himself or herself in your document. In the introductions of separate parts of the text (chapters and longer sections), a separate motivational opening can usually be omitted, but it is certainly not prohibited.

There are more ways to write an attractive opening than we can discuss here. We therefore suffice with a number of examples (with explanations) of a number of tried and tested strategies. More examples can be found in section 9.2.1.

Wisse Dekker, former Philips CEO, had the habit of surprising applicants with a request the moment he entered the room. He invariably asked them to tell a story. In this way, he believed he could test the responsiveness of applicants. It was not a brilliant method, but in any case better thought out than the average, often chaotic job interview. In this booklet we give tips to anyone who has to do job interviews as an employer but has not been trained in this.

An *anecdotal opening*. The writer uses an event (in this case, a true one) to introduce the subject. There must be a lesson to be learned from the anecdote that is important for the topic. Many readers appreciate an anecdote, especially if they 'know' one of the main characters.

In March 2015, a judge fined Pharrell Williams and Robin Thicke close to 7 million Euro for allegedly plagiarizing Marvin Gaye's song *Got to give it up* with the release of their song *Blurred Lines*. The problem with this kind of thing is that every song from a certain genre by definition has some resemblance with other songs that also belong to that genre. In addition, mutual influence and inspiration are the sources of the development of music. Indeed, all culture exists by the grace of imitation and transformation. How does that work? In this article we discuss the question of cultural transfer.

The writer makes use of a *topical case* to attract the reader's attention. This is usually an effective method, but it can be difficult to divert attention from the appealing opening to the perhaps much duller actual subject. You should also bear in mind that most topical cases will not stay topical for long. So for a text that needs to last longer, this type of opening is risky.

'Whoever reads this is crazy' has been written in large letters on the side wall of the town hall since October last year. This does not apply in any way to the reader of this memorandum. The scale of vandalism in our city has reached such proportions that municipal intervention is urgently required.

The *surprise opening* is the start of a municipal policy document on combating vandalism. The aim is to surprise the readers by a statement they cannot immediately place. In this case, the readers are also directly involved in the opening sentence. Partly because this is very unusual in official texts, the writer did not use the second person form of address 'you' ('this does not apply to you'), but the more distant third person ('the reader').

How unique is the earth? In order to find the answer to this question, astronomers search the sky for 'exoplanets': planets orbiting other stars. Since the discovery of the first exoplanet in 1992, researchers have found dozens of those planets, at all kinds of distant stars.

 With the launch of the Kepler satellite in 2009 by the American space agency NASA, research gained momentum. As early as 2011, the researchers of the Kepler mission announced that they had discovered no less than 1,268 possible planets. And for the first time it became possible to determine the atmospheric composition of a small exoplanet from the Earth, the GJ 1214b. An enormous breakthrough, because planets themselves do not give light and therefore cannot be observed directly. In January 2015, it was announced that the star EPIC201367065, which is 150 light years away (astronomically quite close), has at least one planet with earthly characteristics.

American and German scientists studied the GJ 1214b with the help of the European giant telescope in Chile. A super-sensitive spectrometer has been installed on that telescope: HARPS. Recently, version 3.5 of the HARPS Pipeline was installed on the telescope. This version has a number of improvements compared to the previous one. One of these is the use of the measured extraction profile (FF frame) instead of the analytical profile. The effects of this are discussed in more detail in this report […].

Here, a so-called *funnel opening* was used. The writer starts with a very general phenomenon (what astronomers search for in the universe) and through a roundabout technique comes to the actual topic of the text: a relatively small aspect of the more general topic (a specific improvement in the new release of the HARPS Pipeline). Such an opening is an effective way to show the practical or social relevance of a rather specialist topic. The 'funnel shape' (moving from the more general to the more specific) is often found in introductions to scientific articles.

At the meeting of the council on 12 October, the response to the management team's proposal for a far-reaching decentralization of powers in the field of personnel policy was very varied. In particular, the plan to shift responsibilities for education and training from the education officer to the heads of department raised serious questions. The management team promised to review the policy on this point.

This internal memo examines in more detail the considerations that the management team had for decentralization on this point as well.

Opening of an organization's internal memo. The *reason for writing* the text is highlighted here. In situations like this, that is very often a good choice. After all, this reason is the most important motive for readers to read the memo.

Main goal of the text

An introduction should make clear what the main goal of the text is and why this goal is relevant. This information allows readers to determine what to expect and whether the text is useful to them. In an introduction to a part of a text (a chapter or a longer section), the goal statement must make it clear what the position and relevance of that part of the text is relative to the whole. The goal statement must then also bridge the gap between the previous part(s) of the text and what is to follow.

Note that the goal of the text should be presented in terms of what the readers may want to do with the text and not what the writer's purpose has been. For readers it is not really interesting to know what you want to achieve as a writer. Much more important is the usefulness of the text for the readers. Goals that explicitly arise from self-interest ('With this article I want to convince people that the budget of my department should be increased') contain an all too direct appeal and therefore evoke resistance (see also section 1.2, about the appeal side of a communication message). At most, it is possible to present such a goal as a conclusion: 'With this report I also wanted to make clear the need for an increase in the budget of this department [...]', but very often it is wiser to leave it to the reader to read between the lines regarding the self-interest of the writer.

> The guidelines in this brochure are intended to create the necessary unity in the ordering procedures within Telemax Ltd. This will make it easier to check orders from suppliers and the internal control of the handling of orders.

The goal is to instruct the personnel of a company. It prescribes exactly how to proceed when ordering goods from other companies. A disadvantage of this goal statement is that this goal appear to be mainly important for management (unity and control) and less so for the staff members for whom the brochure is intended.

> The guidelines in this brochure are intended to help you order goods from third parties efficiently and without problems. The established procedures make it easier to act appropriately in the event of problems with orders or their internal handling.

A different goal is set for the same brochure. The focus is now on the importance of the guidelines for the reader: They serve as support and as a means to solve problems. Such a goal statement, written from the perspective of the reader, invites the reader to engage with the text.

> The proposals in this memo are meant to serve as a basis for discussions on the restructuring of the internal service. They are not intended to be the last word from management, but they do make it clear within which framework one has to work. The memo must therefore be seen as a starting point for a process of consultation and decision-making.

Here the goal indicates what function the text should play in a decision-making process.

> For example, in Chapter 3 we highlighted the main advantages of an international exchange program. This does not mean that there are no challenges. A good exchange program requires a great deal of preparation and organizational measures. In this chapter we take stock of the situation. On this basis, an action plan can be developed, if the main conclusions of this report are supported.

Goal statement in a chapter of a report. This statement also links up with previous chapters, thus clarifying the broad thrust.

Looking ahead and highlighting the internal coherence of the text
A good introduction also creates an opportunity to announce what the theme of the text is and what issues will be addressed. It is useful to indicate in which sections the various main questions are dealt with. Such a 'look ahead' not only announces the content, but it also provides an explanation of the chosen structure. Unlike when enjoying a novel, readers do not want to be surprised, especially if you have chosen an unusual structure for your text.

In this report we discuss the development of a cooling system for magnetic field measuring devices. In section 1 we explain why such a system is necessary. In section 2 we discuss the requirements for the system, after which the design itself is explained in section 3. Finally, in section 4 we discuss the set-up and results of a number of tests that were carried out with the developed equipment.

An introduction presenting the structure of what is to follow. This presentation is rather limited. Not much more is offered than a table of contents in prose.

This report reports on an evaluation study in which the central question was the extent to which the introduction of the new telephone switchboard may be regarded as successful. This question is explained in more detail in Chapter 1. Interviews were conducted with the staff members involved in the introduction of the new switchboard. In addition, a survey was conducted among a number of staff members to determine the extent to which they were familiar with and made use of the new functions made possible by the new switchboard. Staff members were also observed when working with the new equipment. These research methods are explained in Chapter 2.

Chapter 3 summarizes the information from the interviews and the survey. The results of the observations are described in Chapter 4. From the observations it becomes clear which functions are used a lot, and which functions are used less or not at all. Chapter 5 then analyses the operating instructions. This includes an examination of the extent to which the problems identified in Chapters 3 and 4 are related to deficiencies in the instructions for use. In our conclusions and recommendations (Chapter 6), we therefore propose improvements to the instructions for use.

In this overview of the structure of a report, the veil is lifted. Not only the main questions mentioned but also a number of sub-questions are announced. Readers often appreciate such a 'dressed-up' overview: they are let in on everything the report covers and become curious about what else will be discussed.

In Chapter 1 we will introduce the project as a whole. We give a brief description and explain the motives that led to the project.

We then discuss the sub-projects in five chapters (Chapters 2 to 6). In each of the chapters we will discuss the goals, the proposed working method, and the time schedule. In Chapter 7 we will suggest an evaluation procedure at the end of the project.

This plan still lacks a budget for the project as a whole and for the individual sub-projects. A provisional budget will be submitted separately and will be further elaborated once an agreement in principle has been reached on the project.

An overview of the structure of the document, but with a difference. This overview makes it clear that Chapters 2 to 6 together fall under one main question. The third paragraph provides a special explanation of coherence: it justifies why an obvious part of the text is missing.

What does not belong in the introduction section?

Sometimes writers give information about personal backgrounds at the beginning of a text, for example about the history of the text or about the time and effort it took to write. The writer might also like to thank people who helped him or her. However, such statements do not belong in the introduction section but in a preface or foreword (in the case of a book or thesis), or in a footnote or endnote (in the case of a journal article; see also section 8.1.8). In most business reports, this kind of personal information is omitted altogether.

8.1.6   Titles and headings

The titles of a text, chapters, and sections—and any other headings or subheadings in the text—have three main functions.

– *Structure.* The titles should help the reader to follow the main thrust of the text. They should make clear what the text as a whole is about and what is dealt with in each section.
– *Selection.* The titles should help the reader to search for and select information. The headings should allow readers to determine whether or not they will or should read the relevant section of the text and to identify the information they need for their purpose.
– *Motivation.* The titles must motivate the reader to read the text or at least certain parts of it. The motivational function may sometimes be at odds with the structure function and the selection function. An example: The title *OJ who?!* may be highly motivational, but unless there is a subtitle warning you that it is a report about the general knowledge of students (not knowing who OJ Simpson was) the title will not help the reader to understand what the topic

is. Titles and headings can help to draw the attention of the reader and to make the reader curious, but one needs to align this function with the other two.

The importance of these functions depends on the goal of your text or the passage concerned. For a textbook, the emphasis will be on the structural function. In the case of a manual for a computer program, the selection function will be important. In marketing or recruiting texts, the motivating function will have the upper hand, although this function is also found in more formal texts such as articles in scientific journals.

Title of the text

The structural function of a title requires that the topic of the text be found (almost literally) in the title and that the title also indicates what kind of text it is. At the same time, the selection function is best met when a clear presentation of the topic and the type of text provide the reader with an initial indication of the usefulness of the text.

In order to achieve a motivating effect, the title must also stimulate curiosity. If the theme and the type of text are worthwhile for the target group, it is sufficient if they are clear. But something extra can be done. A title that stimulates curiosity, that typifies the theme, or in which rhyme and rhythm play a role will be more effective in attracting the attention of readers.

Often a combination of a main title and a subtitle is chosen, one of which mainly has a structural function and the other a motivating function.

The JPS Total Fund: The difference between paying taxes and receiving money.

A title from the world of advertising. The main title indicates the theme; the subtitle gives a curious characterization of the theme.

Hyperventilation, a breathtaking phenomenon: A systematic review of the research

The ambiguity of 'breathtaking' in the main title attracts the reader's attention. The subtitle makes it clear what kind of text this is: a progress report on research into hyperventilation.

Titles of chapters and sections

Chapter and section titles may also have both a motivating and a structuring function. Business texts (notes, reports) usually focus on the structuring function of these titles. The title should make it clear what question or key answer you are dealing with in the text passage that the title belongs to. The structuring effect of titles for passages of text can be further enhanced by three interventions.

- Number the chapter and section titles in such a way that the structure of the text is clear. Do not go beyond three levels, otherwise the whole system will become confusing. Preferably use Arabic numerals (1, 2, 3, 4, [...]) and not Roman numerals (I, II, III, IV, [...]).
- Give the same form to subtitles that are on the same level: use a question, a message, or a free selection of words, and do not use these forms interchangeably. In this way, you ensure unity of the whole.
- Use the terms you use in the titles as much as possible also in summaries and references in the text. If, for example, you have given a chapter the title *The introduction of the single permit*, you may want to make it clear in your introduction that this chapter discusses a national scheme for permits for buildings, monuments, space, nature, and environment. In itself that is fine, but in that introduction you must also use the term 'single permit'.

8.1.7 Final section

To turn your text or part of your text into a finished whole, you have to add a final section. As with the introduction, the length of such a 'closing' section depends, on the length of the text. If possible, the text should be wrapped up with a clear message to the reader.

Like an introduction, a final section can also contain various elements: a review, conclusions and recommendations, and a final word (the presentation of some remarkable example, result, or story; see also section 9.2.3, where the ending of an oral presentation is discussed). If all these elements are present, the final part of a text is often considered a separate chapter with titles such as 'Discussion', 'Conclusion', 'A Final Word', and so on. In the case of a short final part, the title 'Conclusion' is best used.

Review
'First tell what you're going to tell; then tell it; and finally, tell what you've told.' This rule of thumb, which is applied daily in news and current affairs programs on television, is the basis for the strategy of presenting an overview in the introduction and a review (or *recap*) at the end. Of course, there is a risk that readers will get annoyed when they receive the same information for the third time. The review must therefore be clearly different from what was said in the introduction.

- In the review, the emphasis is not on the questions that have been discussed, but on the answers that have been given.
- The review does not summarize all the answers but only those that are of direct relevance to the conclusion.

Furthermore, you can reduce the reader's sense of déjà-vu by choosing different formulations in the review and perhaps even a different order than in the main text. A good review shows the readers the mental journey they have made while reading: What did they first know, what do they know now, and how has this difference in knowledge come about?

> There is no need for the monthly tone function in the calendar, and how the confer-
> ence function and the mailbox function work is unclear to the vast majority of the users
> surveyed with the new software. The other functions are also not clear to significant
> percentages of users (12%-34%). The results of the research in Chapter 4 contrast sharply
> with the conclusions from the interviews with the technicians responsible (Chapter 3).
> After all, they were convinced that the information provided to users was sufficiently
> clear and that the new app was working optimally.

Looking back at research results in a research report. Only the most important results are mentioned, and they are in a different order than in the report. In this way, the necessary variation is guaranteed.

Conclusions and recommendations

The final section is also the place to formulate your conclusions concisely. It goes without saying that these must not be allowed to come out of the blue: the arguments in favor of them must have been made clear in the preceding chapters or sections. The conclusions are often complemented by recommendations, which show the reader what to do next on the basis of those conclusions. In some types of text, such as advisory reports or progress reports, the conclusions are in fact also the recommendations. These are often already included in the summary (see section 8.1.2). But there are also recommendations in other parts of the document.

- By default, research reports end with recommendations for further research.
- Evaluating texts conclude with recommendations for measures to be taken to strengthen the positive aspects of a particular case and to reduce the negative ones.

Particularly in texts with persuasive goals (see section 1.2.1), a well-formulated conclusion is crucial. This offers the author the chance to bring the core of the message clearly and convincingly to the fore.

8.1.8 Notes

Notes (*footnotes* or *endnotes*) are used to explain or justify passages in the text. Sometimes they also contain an 'aside', a remark that does not fit in the actual text but that the writer nevertheless wants to make, and sometimes they are also used to thank people who have contributed to the creation of the text. Use notes sparingly, unless the style conventions prescribe an extensive set of notes. It is important to keep the following in mind.

– Notes quickly distract the reader's attention.[14]
– If the information in a note is important, it belongs in the actual text.
– If the information is not pertinent, the note may also be deleted.

When using notes, it is best to include them at the bottom of the pages (footnotes) rather than after each chapter or at the very end of the text (endnotes). With footnotes, you can prevent the effect that your reader becomes confused or irritated by constantly having to page forward to see the endnote and then leave the text. If you still want to use endnotes, it is best to number them consecutively and not separately for each chapter.

8.1.9 Bibliography

Your bibliography (also called *References, List of references*, or *Literature*) provides an overview of the sources you refer to in your text, nothing more and nothing less. In section 8.2.3 and in section 8.2.4, you will find instructions plus an example of the content and design of a bibliography.

8.1.10 Appendices

An appendix (also referred to as an *annexure*) contains supporting and additional information that, if incorporated into the text itself, would lead to a confusing structure. The following are examples of what might be included in an appendix:

– tables with research data that are not directly relevant for the processing of the main text (often raw data);
– examples of forms or questionnaires used;
– supporting documents, printouts of computer programs and copies of letters; technical drawings.

---

14   See this example.

Number the appendices and give each one a good title. The order of the appendices is determined by the order in which they are first mentioned in the text.

Make sure that each appendix is mentioned at least once in the text and that it is clear what it is for. At the beginning of each appendix, you should spell out what kind of material is included and also refer to the page or section where the appendix is discussed. The latter is helpful for readers who do not read the report from beginning to end.

8.2   References

No matter what type of report you are writing, you should always clearly identify the sources of your information. Four important considerations apply.

- Good references show that you have studied the subject, thereby increasing the credibility of your text.
- With a proper indication of the reference, you help critical readers to properly assess the credibility of the information in your text.
- With a proper indication of the reference, you do justice to the authors of the sources consulted; you give them the honor they deserve.
- If you do not, or do not correctly, reference the sources from which you obtained the information that you present in your text, you are suggesting that what you wrote down is 'your own work'—and that is *plagiarism*.

Below, we first discuss the phenomenon of plagiarism (section 8.2.1) and demonstrate how to prevent this pitfall. In section 8.2.2 we will discuss the rules for referencing, which you must follow if you reference your sources in the text. In section 8.2.3 we will discuss the requirements that apply to the individual entries that make up the bibliography at the end of the report, and finally, in section 8.2.4 we will discuss the structure of the bibliography itself. This also includes an example of such a bibliography.

The rules presented here for source mentions, bibliographical entries, and bibliographies are based on the widely used *Publication Manual of the American Psychological Association* (2009). In this *APA Manual*, as it is often referred to, you can find more details for special cases if you wish. For more information, see the last part of this book, entitled *Suggested readings*. Obviously, there are other referencing systems too (like the *MLA*, *Harvard*, or *Oxford* systems, as any internet search will show). Should you choose to follow another system, the most important rule is to apply it consistently.

8.2.1 Plagiarism and how to prevent it

When presenting your own work, if you do not acknowledge the work of others that you have used (maybe even unintentionally), you are guilty of plagiarism. This applies to art, to fashion, and also to texts. Plagiarism is seen as a form of fraud both within and outside educational establishments, and those who plagiarize should expect the legal consequences facing any other fraudsters. Especially for beginning writers, it is sometimes difficult to recognize the phenomenon of plagiarism and to avoid the risk. That is why we give an overview of common forms of plagiarism in texts.

–   A text from another person is presented as if it were the writer's own work.
–   A text has been written in collaboration with others without explicitly mentioning this.
–   Parts of a text have been copied from another text (on paper or on the internet) without mentioning the source.
–   It is suggested that a text is one's own work, when in fact only a few amendments have been made to someone else's text.
–   Words, ideas, results, or conclusions have been taken from other sources without a complete and correct mention of the source.
–   No quotation marks have been used for literal quotations, or the quotation marks have been placed in such a way that the impression is created that part of the passages quoted is your own work.
–   Reference is made to sources but not to all places where information from those sources has been used, with the result that some of the information taken over is wrongly presented as your own work.
–   References to sources are incomplete or incorrect, so that the sources used are not available to others.

Preventing plagiarism is actually very simple: You never commit plagiarism if you do justice to the work of others by treating paraphrases, quotations, references, and source references with care.

8.2.2 References in the text

When making a reference in the main body of your text, provide a brief description of the source of your information. The rules that apply are set out below. In the entry as it appears in the bibliography, readers of your text should be able to find the complete information they need in order to trace the source mentioned.

> Personalized information is increasingly offered via the web: information adapted to the user. Think, for example, of the personal recommendations that Amazon.com sends its customers through e-mail, or of the electronic tax form that has already been partially completed by the Tax and Customs Administration. Personalization seems handy for customers or citizens; the question is whether they always appreciate it (La Strada, 2017).

A brief indication of a source is given.

A reference may also specify the type of source. This makes it easier for the reader to estimate the value of the source (assuming that they are not going to check the source themselves).

> Personalized information is increasingly offered via the web: information adapted to the user. Think, for example, of the personal recommendations that Amazon.com sends its customers by e-mail, or of the electronic tax form that has already been partially completed by the Tax and Customs Administration. Personalization may seem handy for clients or the citizens, but an experiment described in La Strada's dissertation (2017) shows that personalization is often far from being appreciated.

The information that this is an experiment presented in a dissertation can strengthen the credibility of the source.

> Does an increase in the price of admission to amusement parks put a brake on the number of visitors? Literature is not uniform on this point. Vanderbilt (2008) indicates that it is, but Daniel (2009) and Palin (2014), for example, argue against it.

> Does an increase in the price of admission to amusement parks put a brake on the number of visitors? Literature is not uniform on this point. Vanderbilt (2008) is of the opinion that it is, but without clear arguments. However, the studies by Daniel (2009) and Palin (2014) show no effect.

In the first version, it is not clear what type of sources are involved; in the second case, it is. A reader who values research will appreciate the second version, and find the results of Daniel's and Palin's studies more important than Vanderbilt's opinion.

No matter how you include your references in the main body of the text, you need to clarify exactly what your sources are, so that readers can look them up in your bibliography (see sections 8.2.3 and 8.2.4). Next, the readers can use the information provided there to find the relevant publications in the library or on the internet if they wish. Specific rules apply to the literature references in the text.

- A reference in the text must mention at least the surname of the author or authors, followed by the year of the publication.
- Do not include the initials of the author (or authors).
- For publications with two or more authors, the order in which the authors are mentioned is the same as the order of the authors' names in the publication itself.
- For publications with two authors, both authors are always named. Between their names 'and' is inserted.
- For publications with three, four, or five authors, the first time you make a reference you should mention all the authors. Before the last name, 'and' is inserted, preceded by a comma. All further references only mention the first author, followed by 'et al.' (*et alii*, Latin for *and others*).
- For publications with more than five authors, all references—including the first one—should only mention the first author, followed by 'et al.'.
- If the publication is issued by an organization, the name of the organization serves as the author's name.
- If the publication does not mention an individual author or an organization, the title of the publication serves as the author's name. If the publication is an article or a web page, use double quotation marks around its title. If the publication is a book or a report, the title is *italicized*.
- If the year of publication is not mentioned, it is replaced by 'n.d.' (= no date).
- For direct quotations, the reference should always also include the page number (preceded by 'p.') or page numbers (preceded by 'pp.') in the source where the information was found.
- When paraphrasing, it is also advised to provide page numbers, especially when it would help readers in finding the relevant passage in a long text.
- If an author's surname contains a prefix such as 'Van', 'De', or 'La', the reference to that author's name begins with the prefix.
- If you cite more than one publication by the same author published in the same year, these publications are referred to by the year, followed by a, b, and so on, with no intervening space (e.g. 2000a, 2000b, etcetera). The same rule holds for references in the bibliography.
- References that cannot be worked into the sentence should be placed between brackets. The reference should be placed in such a way that the reader's train of thought is not disrupted.
- Refrain from putting a reference in brackets immediately after the author's name in the possessive, for example: 'Bush's (2011) thesis argues that [...]', as this is likely to be experienced by the reader as disruptive. A good alternative in this example would be: 'Bush (2011) argues in her thesis that [...]'.
- If the reference is in brackets, 'and' before the last author's name is replaced by the symbol '&'; if there are three to five authors, a comma is placed before '&'.

- If the reference is not to a publication on paper but to a website, there are two possibilities.
    - If the document referred to resembles a paper document (with an author, a title, and a year), exactly the same method is used as for paper sources.
    - If the reference is to a website without an author, the title of the appropriate page on this website (between double quotation marks) is referred to, followed by the year of publication or 'n.d.'.
- The most important rule of all: the various kinds of publications should be referred to in a consistent way.

Justin (2006) and Moeninx and Bolowski (2007) briefly discuss the so-called MBI (*Model for Behavioral Intentions*). According to Maisbowns (2008), "personal characteristics can only influence a person's intention to behave if they also have an effect on his assumptions about the results of the behavior, about the ideas that others have about that behavior and about his own possibilities to actually execute that behavior" (p. 51).

Knaus (1971) already mentioned the risks of a large gap between government and people. Other authors have characterized the relationship between the government and the citizens as a bureaucratic paradox (Milner & Van der Stoor, 2004; Wagner, n.d.; "This is why", 2017). As one author states, "The more systematic and neutral the government is, the greater the gap between the government and the citizens" (Brown, 2009, pp. 265-266).

A number of recent publications have strongly criticized the *Occupational Health and Safety Directives* as they currently apply. Williams (2011a) refers to the directives as incomplete and to their legally uncertain status. According to her, it is also clear that medical examiners have major problems with their unclear status: They must serve the interests of both the employer and the employee (Williams, 2011b). Recent internet publications, such as ATC-SPD (2016), RKTVV (n.d.), and "How does it feel?" (2017) provide support for this vision.

Van Owen and Drake (2005) and Williams, De Kock, and Van Owen (2009) consider the existing rules to be bureaucratic and warn against the administrative burden they entail. Williams et al. (2009) add that the trend towards standardization of the guidelines can easily result in the specific safety and health problems of all kinds of organizations escaping attention. The vision as formulated by Williams et al. (2009) is shared by Srobanowski (2010). Other authors also take this stand (Heerkens & Jacobs, 2009; Smith, Vale, & Blanchard, 2009; Mlapuntu et al., 2011).

Examples of references in a text.

8.2.3 Bibliographical entries

The references in the text do not by any means contain all the available information. They only provide sufficient information to find the full reference in the bibliography at the end of the publication. The bibliography contains the complete bibliographical entries of all publications mentioned in the text. A complete bibliographical entry contains all the information about a publication that is needed to find it in paper and digital reference works, data files, and libraries.

There is software available in which you can enter the data of publications, after which a correctly formatted bibliography can be generated. By linking the software to your word processor, you can also have the references in the text created automatically. An additional advantage of the software is that it may also serve as an archive for all your publications, in which you can also save notes.

Different official reference systems, also called Styles or Standards, exist for bibliographical entries. In the field of science and technology, the *APA Manual* (of the *American Psychological Association*), the *Harvard System of Referencing*, the *IEEE-NORM* (of the *Institute of Electrical and Electronic Engineers*), and the rules from the *Chicago Manual of Style* are among the most authoritative ones. Whichever system you choose, it is important that you apply your choice consistently. As mentioned above, the rules presented here are based on the APA Manual: the *Publication Manual of the American Psychological Association* (2009). There you can find more detailed information on how to refer to the sources you have used.

Below, we present five models for bibliographical entries based on the *APA Manual*. The information you must include in your bibliography can be found on the publication's title page (not the cover) and, if necessary, on its colophon. A colophon is a brief section on the first pages of a book that provides detailed book production information. The following rules for bibliographical entries apply to all five models presented below.

– In a bibliographical entry, the surnames of the authors of the publication are first mentioned, followed by a comma and a space. Then their initials are given, each followed by a dot and a space.
– For publications with two or more authors, the order in which the authors are mentioned is the same as the order in which the authors' names are given in the publication itself.
– For publications with two to seven authors, the name of the last author is preceded by a comma, a space and an ampersand: ', &'.
– For publications with more than seven authors, the sixth name is followed by '…'. After this comes the name of the last author mentioned in the publication.
– If an author's surname contains a prefix such as 'Van', 'De', or 'La', all references to that author's name begin with the prefix.

- If the publication is issued by an organization, the name of the organization serves as the author's name.
- If the publication does not mention an individual author or an organization, the title (in *italics*) serves as the author's name.
- If the publication has a title and also a subtitle, both the title and the subtitle are mentioned, and both start with a capital letter. Unless the title ends with a question mark or an exclamation mark, a colon is placed between the title and the subtitle.
- If the year or the place is missing from the publication, n.d. (*no date*) or n.p. (*no place*) is used.
- If a 'DOI' (*digital object identifier*) for the publication is available, this is the last part of the bibliographical entry. Immediately after 'doi' (in lower case) comes a colon, which is immediately followed by the actual number of the DOI. After this number, there is no period.
- If you cite more than one publication by the same author published in the same year, these are referred to by the year, followed by a, b, and so on, with no intervening space (e.g. 2000a, 2000b, etcetera).
- The most important rule of all: the various kinds of publications should be referred to in a consistent way.

When using the models below, pay close attention to the weight of the font used for the various elements (upright roman or *italic*) and to spaces and punctuation marks between the elements. Examples of bibliographical entries are provided in sections 8.2.4 and 8.3.7.

[Author's surname], [Author's Initial]. [(year)]. [Title: Subtitle]. [*Journal*], [*volume*], [number of first page-number of last page]. [doi:number]

Model for the bibliographical entry of a journal article. The name of the journal is in *italics*, and all words—except articles and prepositions—start with a capital letter. After the year and a space comes the volume (in *italics*). In the rare case that each issue of the journal begins on page 1, the volume number is immediately followed (that is: without a space) by the issue number within that volume (in upright roman).

[Author's surname], [Author's initial]. [(year)]. [*Title: Subtitle*] [(number of edition ed.)]. [Location]: [Publisher]. [doi:number]

Model for the bibliographical entry of a book (not an anthology). The first edition of a book is never indicated. Other editions are indicated by a space and an opening bracket immediately after the last letter of the title, and then the appropriate abbreviation ('2nd', '3rd', 4th, and so on) followed by 'ed.' (edition), or 'Rev. ed.' (revised edition), followed by a closing bracket. The title of the book is in *italics*, and only the first word of the title and the subtitle start with a capital letter. The name of the publisher is preceded by the location that the title page mentions first, followed by a colon. If the location is in the US, its name is followed by a comma and the abbreviation of the state (in capitals). If the location is outside the US, its name is followed by a comma and the name of the country.

> [Editor's surname], [Editor's initial]. [(Ed.)]. [(year)]. [*Title: Subtitle*]. [(number of edition)]. [Location]: [Publisher]. [doi:number]

Model for the bibliographical entry of an anthology that includes contributions from different authors. After the initial of the editor or editors comes '(Ed.)' or '(Eds.)', followed by a comma.

> [Author's surname], [Author's initial]. [(year)]. [Contribution title]. In [Editor's initials and surname] [(Ed.)], [*Title: Subtitle*] [(pp. number of first page-number of last page)]. [Location]: [Publisher]. [doi:number]

Model for the bibliographical entry of a contribution in an anthology . The initials of the editor come before the surname.

> [Author's surname], [Author's initial]. [(year, plus month and day if available)]. [Title: Subtitle] [*Title of the website*]. [Retrieved from URL]

Model for the bibliographical entry of an internet source. If the author is unknown, the entry starts with the title of the publication (in upright roman). Then follows the title of the website (in *italics*). If in this case the title of the website does not add any relevant information, it may be left out. If there is neither an author nor a specific title of the publication available, the title of the website (in *italics*) takes precedence. At the end of the entry, the exact web address (URL) where the publication was found is given, preceded by 'Retrieved from' and not followed by a period.

8.2.4   Setting up the bibliography

At the end of a report, there is a bibliography that contains the complete entries of all the publications referred to in the text. In this list of literature no entries of other publications are included. Other variants are also available, however.

- A list of the literature consulted. This list may also include literature not mentioned in the text.
- A list of recommended literature. This list includes publications recommended by the author for further information or study on the subject.
- An annotated list of literature. In this list, the publications are provided with a brief indication of the content and, if necessary, an opinion on this content.

In the bibliography, the entries are arranged alphabetically. The following rules apply.

– The starting point is the surname of the first author. This is followed by the names of possible other authors.

– If there are several publications by the same author or authors, they are put in chronological order by year.

– If the same author uses both single and multiple first names (or initials), publications with a single first name (or initial) take precedence.

– If there are several publications by the same author or authors in the same year, the year is immediately followed (with no intervening space) by a, b, and so on, depending on their order in the references in the text.

– If the first author has publications alone and together with other authors that you refer to, then first the publications of the author alone are mentioned. After these come the publications in which other authors have collaborated.

– If no individual author or organization is known, the title of the publication is used as the starting point for alphabetization. In doing so, articles (the, a, an, der, die, le, le, la, un, une, and so on) are disregarded.

The most important rule of all: the publications should be listed in a consistent way.

Below is an example of an alphabetically ordered bibliography, with entries in which the rules mentioned above (in sections 8.2.3 and 8.2.4) have been followed. It is customary to format each entry as a hanging indent so that the reader can easily find an author's name.

Ariale, S. T., La Strada, W., Clayderman, H., & Sol, F. M. (2006). The layout of digital forms. *Journal of Text Production*, 12, 238-249. doi:10.1408/T15326985EV3802_2

Benzema, M. H. (1997). Determinants of interest: Which ads are processed and why? In H. Jörgensen & R. van Persie (Eds.), *Effective ads unraveled* (pp. 439-448). Cape Town, South Africa: Floris.

Content Matters Inc. (2011). *Algorithms in Learning and Instruction* (2nd ed.). Windhoek, Namibia: Namibian Press.

Henrike, P. (Ed.). (2013). *Text analysis: Between theory and praxis* (Rev. ed.). Assen, The Netherlands: Van Gorinchem.

Joelle, O., & Lennie, D. (2013). *Conversation analysis: Between theory and praxis* (4th, rev. ed.). Pittsburgh, PA: VanderBoult.

Noticeably less and better! Progress report on tax reduction for citizens (2006). Glasgow, Scotland: Bagpipe Printers. doi:12.1307/T15326985EQ3801_9

O'Grady, M. (2015, June 5). Frontal cortex deserves more research funding. *New Aduard Times*. Retrieved from http://www.nat.com

Social scientists' comments on APA guidelines. (n.d.). Retrieved from http://more_about_
        publication_guidelines.org/

Tom, K. (1993). Tips for easy to use templates revisited. *Journal of Information and Commu-
        nication Studies, 11*(1), 1-19.

Tom, K., & Mike, H. (1991). Tips for easy to use templates. *Journal of Information and Com-
        munication Studies, 9*(4), 13-26.

Why the last two Beatles are still going strong. (2018, September 20). Retrieved from
        https://music_yesterday_and_today.com

Zwegmans, F., Gardens, J., Smits, H., Gaillard, J., LeBlanche, K., Wallmach, L., … Wolfs, J.
        (1998). Cognitive load measurement and cognitive load theory. *Cognition and Emo-
        tion, 38*, 63-67. doi:10.1207/S15326985EP3802_4

Example of a bibliography (all publications are made up).

8.3   The research report

Not to report research is tantamount to not having done the research at all. A good research report will not save a bad investigation, but a bad report will prevent the quality of good research to shine. Furthermore, the research report remains the most common form for theses and dissertations in higher education.

In general, the recommendations for report components as presented in section 8.1 also apply to the research report. This section, however, provides more detail about the specific approach to this type of report. The last part of this section (8.3.8) focuses on a type of text that must be written before the research takes place: the research plan or proposal.

Goals and target groups

The main goal of a research report is to ensure that research activities and their results are recorded in a sufficiently precise and verifiable manner. What you have researched should generate new insights on your topic and should be presented so concisely that your research is replicable by others in such a way that it generates results comparable to yours. Furthermore, the report is regarded as an assessment instrument in the field of education, testing the writer's capability as a researcher.

In addition to the description of the study that was performed, the justification of the chosen approach is also necessary in a research report. Based on arguments and sources, you should show why your approach is appropriate and why other approaches would be less appropriate in this case.

Although the target groups of your report may vary, you may still expect readers to have a certain amount of expertise in terms of content (but in general they will not be as specialized as you have become through this research) and to be familiar with the conventions of a research report. It is therefore of great importance that you stick to these conventions as far as possible. If you have an overwhelming desire to stand out or to unleash your creativity, you should do so via an original research question (but always within the context in which you operate), a refined research design, or a smart approach to unexpected problems.

8.3.1   Components of a research report

A standard research report, at least in the social sciences, contains the following sections: Introduction (with problem statement and research question); Method (of research); Results; and Discussion. Each of these parts has its own specific content (see also the set research schema in section 2.2.8).

Component	Content	Details
Introduction	Problem statement	Explain what problem was investigated / what observation or knowledge gap underlies this research.
	Theoretical framework	Using relevant research literature, sketch out the broader context of this study. Do this in the form of an argument from which it is clear why, given the current state of affairs, your question was worth investigating in this field of research. When discussing this current state of affairs, explicitly refer to what earlier studies have revealed. In this section you should also present definitions of the key terms you use in the current text.
	Research questions and hypotheses	Formulate as precisely as possible—and in a logical connection to the above—the questions (or question) to which your research intended to provide an answer. If you have to use terms that readers may interpret differently than you want them to do, describe as precisely as possible the meaning in which they are used (operationalization). If you performed a quantitative study, here you might also mention the hypotheses (your explicit expectations) that you tested (also see section 8.3.2).
Method	Experimental design	In the case of an experimental study, show, preferably with the aid of a table, what the various groups of participants were asked to do and at what times, and make it clear how you divided the research participants among the different groups.

Component	Content	Details
	Participants	Accurately describe the relevant characteristics of the people who participated in the survey. For example, the minimum, maximum, and average age per group, but also the numbers per gender, origin, education, social status, and the like. Indicate the population for which this group may be considered a representative sample. Also discuss the way in which the participants were recruited.
	Instruments	Describe and justify the materials you used, the extent to which you adapted existing instruments, and how you determined the scores. Furthermore, provide information on the reliability and validity of the instruments. If necessary, present a sample item or refer the readers to a source where they can find the items.
	Procedure	Explain exactly what happened during the investigation. How was the measuring instrument used among the participants? What instructions did the participants receive and how was any aftercare arranged?
Results	Presentation of the outcomes	Present the results, where possible also in tabular form, keeping in mind the order of the research questions.
Discussion	Conclusions	Repeat your research question (or questions) and answer them based on the results you have found. Discuss what the testing of possible hypotheses has yielded. Also indicate the scope of your conclusions: what population can you say something about, and with how much certainty?
	Implications, limitations, and suggestions for research and practice	Discuss the significance of your conclusions for the theoretical or practical problem that led to the research. Also show how your findings bear upon what you found in the literature: How do the outcomes of your study relate to findings of the earlier studies that you referred to in the introduction section? Furthermore, evaluate the method you have chosen and the materials you have used. Finally, you may indicate the limitations of your study, suggest follow-up research that would be worthwhile in the light of your findings, and formulate recommendations for dealing with the problem.

The usual format of a research report.

8.3.2   Introduction

In the introduction section of your research report, you outline the problem you have addressed in your investigation. You work from a general problem to a specific question.

First, you provide a problem statement: You describe the problem or issue that your study was about in general terms, possibly illustrated by an example. After this general opening, you place the problem in a scientific context by defining the key concepts in theoretical terms. Although this theoretical framework clarifies the relevance of your problem statement, it is important that you also show that there is no satisfactory answer yet to the problem in the research literature. In this part of the report, you therefore also process an important part of the literature that you have studied about your subject (see chapter 6). In the case of an extensive research report where you deal with a lot of literature to justify the investigation into your problem, you may consider including an exhaustive literature review as a separate section or chapter. In that case, the introduction will evidently be shorter.

The introduction ends with the precise research question or questions. This is hardly ever exactly the same as the problem that gave rise to the investigation. Often you have to decide to limit yourself to a certain part of the original subject, either because it is too complex to examine in the time available, or because the literature studied gives you reason to do so. Because the type of question determines the approach to the research, it is appropriate to present the research question(s) at this early stage. This will make it clear to the reader at the outset what steps you followed to find answers to your problem and will pave the way for a discussion of your research methods.

If you performed a quantitative study and you had strong arguments for expecting certain outcomes, you may also formulate your hypotheses here: the precise predictions of the outcomes of your study. Usually, there will be both so-called *null hypotheses*, predicting the absence of any relationships between your variables (what you controlled, changed, or measured in your study), and so-called *alternative hypotheses*, predicting that such relationships did exist. For more information on research concepts such as experiments, variables, and hypotheses, see the last part of this book, entitled *Suggested readings*.

8.3.3   Method

In the method section, you describe and justify what materials you used, whom you selected as participants, what instruments you used (such as questionnaires or observation scales), and how exactly you conducted your study. In the case of an experiment, you start by presenting the experimental design you used.

What you should and should not deal with here strongly depends on the field of your research. For each discipline there are manuals for setting up and performing research that indicate what is customary in your field. It is important to realize that you not only have to describe but also justify the research method. The latter is, of course, only necessary if you made choices that are not really self-evident. You will then use arguments—derived where possible from literature—to explain why you have opted for a particular research design, and you will make it plausible that your study is methodologically sound.

8.3.4   Results

Depending on the type of study you have conducted, the results section may have a different format. If you have performed a quantitative study, the reader will expect to find tables with results, information on whether or not there are significant outcomes and relationships, and possibly graphs in which trends become clear. You can explain these data in the main text.

If you have performed qualitative research, the results section is usually a lot longer, and it often has a more narrative character. Unlike the quantitative variant, where no interpretations of the outcomes should be given in the results section, in qualitative studies, the representation and interpretation of the findings are usually integrated.

From raw data to reporting

In quantitative research, the step from raw data to report is indirect. An experiment or a survey produces a large amount of raw data that must be analyzed for relationships between the variables. You may be performing complex statistical operations to find such relationships or to test certain models. It is therefore important to continue to see the link between the research questions, the hypotheses, and the data you have collected. We therefore recommend that you first create a framework for your results section.

– Set up your own research questions or hypotheses.
– For each question or hypothesis, design a simple table containing the figures needed to answer the question or to test the hypothesis. Do not enter any digits in that table yet, but limit yourself to the title of the table and the headings of the rows and columns.
– If necessary, discuss the framework with your supervisor(s) or with others.
– Finally, fill in the numbers you get from the output of your statistical software.
– Then add the text explaining the data from the tables.

Readers of research reports often look at the tables first to draw their own conclusions before reading the explanatory text. Try to take advantage of that tendency when writing the results section.

– Formulate your text in the form of an explanation of the tables. Use sentences such as 'Table 1 shows [...]', 'Table 2 reveals [...]', or 'Table 3 suggests [...]'.

– Make a connection with the research questions and your hypotheses in your explanation. Use phrases such as 'The data from Table 5 support the hypothesis that [...]', 'Contrary to the expectation that [...], Table 6 shows no significant difference between [...]'.

8.3.5   Discussion

In the discussion section, you draw conclusions from your results in terms of the research questions and hypotheses with which you have finished the introduction section. What is the answer to those questions? And what did the tests of the hypotheses reveal? What nuances are needed in your conclusions? What do the outcomes of this study imply? In the discussion section, you also consider the limitations of your research, and you make suggestions for further research. Finally, you may mention possible recommendations for dealing with the problem.

– The discussion starts with your conclusions. Here you repeat your research questions and possibly your hypotheses, and you briefly formulate the answers and outcomes as they emerge from the results. Readers who want to know quickly what the research has yielded will want to read this information right away.

– Next comes a brief description of your conclusions in the light of the theoretical framework you outlined in the introduction. What do the results of the research mean for the development of theories and other developments in the field? Differentiate here between expected and unexpected results, and try to provide alternative explanations (explanations not based on the tested theory) for the results found.

– After mentioning the possible alternative explanations and referring to the consequences of the choices you had to make in the method of your research, you offer a critical analysis of the possible shortcomings of your study. What limitations should be mentioned, and what does this imply for the generalizability of your findings? Sometimes this is even put into a separate section with a title such as 'Limitations of this study'.

– Both the limitations of your research and the new knowledge you have acquired may give rise to new research questions. You can include these as suggestions for further research in the final part of the discussion.

- It is important to make a clear distinction between your conclusions and the recommendations you may put forward. Recommendations are based on the conclusions, but you go one step further: you give practical advice on whether to do or not do something.
- If the discussion section runs the risk of becoming too long, you can divide the discussion part into 'Conclusion', in which you return briefly to the research questions and key answers, and 'Discussion', in which you critically reflect on the research, look forward, and give practical advice.

The discussion section should be well coordinated with the results section. It is useful to take into account some rules of thumb.
- At least in quantitative studies, the results section is limited to the presentation of your observations. Your interpretations of the results do not belong here but rather in the conclusion section, where the reader expects to find the answer to the research questions.
- Always be precise in the discussion section about the results on which you are basing your conclusions.
- Do not present new results in the discussion section. However, you may indicate which assumptions that were not part of the theory you tested have become more plausible or, conversely, more implausible in the light of your results. Such tentative conclusions, which actually fall outside your research questions, are mainly intended as suggestions for further research.

8.3.6 Language used in research reports

There are some aspects of style in research reports that deserve special attention. The first of these are the verb tenses. These tenses should correspond to the stage of the research activities you are writing about. In a research report, the past tense is used ('The questionnaires were completed by 84 men and 122 women [...]'), while in a research plan (section 8.3.8) the present tense is used ('The subjects are approached as follows [...]') or the future tense ('Use will be made of [...]').

The use of the first-person personal pronouns *I*, *me*, and *my* also needs some consideration. Those opposing the use of these pronouns argue that this would affect the desired objectivity and neutrality. Those in favor contend that by not referring to the researchers, the report (or plan) has the appearance of objectivity but that, in fact, the personal preferences of the researcher are actually part of the research and the approach to the research. Therefore, if you want to use a personal style, you can opt for a more 'distanced' style by choosing to use *we*, *us*, and *our* instead of *I*, *me*, and *my*. What is important is that you are always consistent in your choice.

Although the passive voice is often used in research publications, it is good to use the active voice where possible (see section 4.2.2). This will improve the clarity and readability of the text. In passages where the participants or the instruments are discussed, the passive voice is warranted, however: It is not necessary to mention who did what; what is important is what happened to someone or something.

This theory explains the existence of false memories.
With this theory, the researchers explain the existence of false memories.
With this theory, we explain the existence of false memories.
With this theory, I explain the existence of false memories.

Some variations on the presentation of who is responsible for what is claimed. In the first sentence, the choice of the subject places the responsibility with 'this theory', as if it were above human interference. By first humanizing and then personalizing the subject in the second, the third and the fourth sentence ('the researchers'; 'we'; 'I'), the focus shifts to the argumentation of the people who work with the theory. As a result, the theory is increasingly presented as open to discussion.

A t test was used to find a possible significant difference between these groups.
By asking open-ended questions and tolerating silences in the interview, we managed to make the most painful episodes accessible for research.

Who or what is presented as responsible for what is claimed, is often associated with the type of research reported. In quantitative research, an analytical instrument is placed in the foreground. In qualitative research, the emphasis often is more on the choices of the researchers, who also more clearly take responsibility for them.

8.3.7   Example of a research report

On the following pages, we provide an example of a research report that follows the standard format. Note that this is only an example and that organizations often have their own requirements. You should therefore use this example for inspiration, not imitation. The comments in the example are limited to a few typical passages in the core text of the report. For a discussion of all report components, see the information in the sub-sections above.

1 Introduction

Berfelland's elderly of 2018 are mature, age in better health, and are expected to live independently for much longer than in the past. They often do not want to be tucked away in a care center or nursing home either. Yet there is a great deal of criticism of the government's policy that older people should live independently for as long as possible. Informal caregivers, such as spouses and children, are increasingly objecting to this.

Opening.

Care professionals experience that elderly people often have no insight into the many types of facilities and also find that potential informal caregivers prefer to outsource their task. This is mostly due to a lack of information, and improving the provision of information would therefore be useful in many cases (Edström, 2018)

[…]

Presentation of the reason for the report.

In view of the current assignment, Sol (2018) has already formulated a number of points for attention: (1) improving cooperation between the various agencies, (2) extending the scope of the information, and (3) tailoring the information to the wishes and needs of older people and informal caregivers, both in terms of content and method and organization.

[…]

Relevant literature is referred to by the name of the investigator followed by the year of publication.

In the scientific literature on the provision of information, it is often suggested that there may be considerable differences between stakeholders in terms of their information needs. This applies not only to this group of older people (Vance, 2009) but perhaps even more so to various other groups of older people, informal caregivers, and care professionals (Van Gilze, 2004). In addition to a breakdown according to the differences in information needs, a breakdown according to types of needs can also be made. For example, there are normative, experienced, pronounced, and comparative needs (Barclay, 2009; Vandersteen, 2008).

[…]

Theoretical framework based on literature.

For the current assignment it was not necessary to include all types of information needs in the research; we limited ourselves to the needs experienced and expressed by the elderly and the informal caregivers.

[…]

Based on the various theories about types of information needs, the following research question was formulated.

What are the information needs regarding care and service provision of independent elderly people and their informal caregivers in Berfelland?

The introduction concludes with the final formulation of the main research question and the sub-questions.

The sub-
questions are
particularities
or elaborations
of the main
question.

This main question is elaborated in three sub-questions.

1 To what extent do independent elderly people and informal caregivers in Berfelland need information about assistance and services?
2 On what topics relating to assistance and services would independent elderly people and informal caregivers in Berfelland need information?
3 From which persons or institutions would self-employed elderly people and informal caregivers in Berfelland like to receive information?

In order to answer these questions, a telephone survey was conducted to investigate the wishes and needs of elderly people and informal caregivers in Berfelland with regard to information about health and facilities. This research report presents the outcomes to this study.

Overview of
the rest of the
report.

The structure of this research report is as follows. Chapter 2 discusses the method by which the information needs of older people and informal caregivers have been assessed. The results are presented in chapter 3, after which conclusions are drawn and recommendations are offered in chapter 4.

The information
in the method
section should
be detailed and
clear enough
that a fellow
researcher
could repeat
the study.

2 Method

This chapter sets out the method of investigation. [...]

2.1 Participants

A total of 350 elderly people and their informal caregivers were sent a letter requesting them to take part in the survey.

[...]

Some
demographic
character-
istics of the
participants
are usually
mentioned.

The survey was successfully conducted for 212 elderly people. The remaining 138 elderly people did not respond to our request. Of the elderly people whose answers we could analyze, 144 were women and 68 men. The average age was 79.4 years, with a standard deviation of 5.2 years. Most of the elderly people had Swedish nationality; only 3 Turkish and 2 Polish elderly people participated in the study. The 212 informal caregivers who completed the survey were mostly female.

[...]

2.2 Measuring instrument(s)

RESP and the SOC-IV questionnaires were used. The subscale for measuring normative needs was removed from the first questionnaire.

[...]

2.3 Procedure

Elderly people were visited at home by the researchers, and the questionnaires were filled in in the presence of the informal carer.

[...]

3 Results

This chapter discusses the results of the survey conducted among independent elderly people in Berfelland. First of all, we give an overview of the outcomes (section 3.1). Sections 3.2 to 3.4 then discuss the results of the three research questions.

[...]

> The results should directly relate to the research questions or hypotheses formulated earlier in the report.

3.2 Older people's need for information

The first sub-question concerned the need for information. Seven subjects that have traditionally been distinguished in this type of research were asked (Van Gilze, 2004). The need for information is thereby operationalized as a reported lack of knowledge.

[...]

The second sub-question concerned the themes on which independent elderly people and informal caregivers would like to have information. The survey first examined how much knowledge older people have about the six subjects that are traditionally distinguished in the provision of information to older people (Van Gilze, 2004). The results are shown in Table 6.

[...]

Table 6. Reported knowledge by subject and category (A lot, Enough, Not much, Very little) in percentages

> A table always has a number and a title placed at the top of the table.

	A lot	Enough	Not much	Very little
Healthy behavior	42	47	4	7
Ageing phenomena	25	45	18	12
Diseases	19	43	24	14
Housing	11	26	23	40
Alternative medicine	12	24	19	45
Financial provisions	13	20	21	47
Health care facilities	28	12	19	41

> Tables consist of rows (horizontal) and colums (vertical). The reader can quickly review and compare the data.

Table 6 gives an overview of the knowledge that the group of elderly people claim to have about the different subjects. The majority of older people say they know a lot or enough about the subjects of healthy behavior (89%), old age (70%), and illness (62%). Very little or nothing is said to be known about the subjects of housing (63%), alternative medicine (64%), financial provisions (68%), and healthcare facilities (60%).

[...]

The discussion chapter opens with a repetition of the main question.

4   Discussion

Central to this study was the question of the perceived and pronounced need of independent elderly people and their informal caregivers in Berfelland for information about care and service provision. This question was answered in three steps.

[...]

Below we successively discuss the need of the elderly and informal caregivers for information about health and services, the themes on which they would like to receive information, and their preferences for the persons or bodies that should provide this information. We then discuss the limitations of the research and make suggestions for follow-up research.

The conclusions are arranged following the research questions: A concise answer is given to each question.

4.1   To what extent do older people and informal caregivers in Berfelland need information about assistance and services?

One-third of the participants do not have sufficient knowledge about assistance and services. Older people with higher incomes in particular report this. It also appears that more than half would like to have more information about at least one of the subjects mentioned in this study—illnesses, healthy behavior, symptoms of old age, alternative medicine, financial facilities, housing, and care facilities. Elderly people and informal caregivers therefore quite often experience a need for information. Among the elderly, this need is present particularly among 'younger elderly people' (55-64 years of age).

4.2   On which topics relating to assistance and services would elderly people and informal caregivers in Berfelland need information?

The elderly and informal caregivers consider it particularly important to provide information about care services, financial provisions, age-related symptoms, and healthy behavior. These topics partly correspond to those on which older people would like more information. A quarter of older people want more information about care services, especially family care, old people's alerts, home nursing, and social work. It also appears that a number of care facilities are relatively unknown, especially among the elderly between the ages of 75 and 84. This concerns social work and voluntary work. Nearly a quarter of the participants say they want more information about financial facilities and housing. Many older people in particular say they know little about this. There is less need for more information on subjects directly related to health, such as diseases, ageing, health behavior, and alternative medicine. Diseases score the lowest. It is striking that 'younger elderly people' (aged 55-64) have a greater need for information about the themes studied than the other age groups.

[...]

4.4 Restrictions of the current study

In the current study, the elderly and their informal caregivers have been approached together. The advantage of this was that the data could be collected more efficiently. The disadvantage, however, was that differences between the elderly and their informal caregivers sometimes remained unclear. In follow-up research, it may be possible to approach these groups separately.

[...]

4.5 Recommendations

Based on the conclusions, the following recommendations can be made with regard to the organization of information for the elderly and informal caregivers in Berfelland.

1 *Increase the available budget for information for older people.*
At the moment, an annual budget of 500,000 euros is available for the provision of information in Berfelland. This budget was determined in 2008, and its level has not changed since then. At the time, it was assumed that there would be a particular need for specific information for older people, particularly for people aged 65 and over. The study now shows that there is also a great need for specific information for older people among 'younger elderly people' (aged 55-64) and informal caregivers. In order to be able to serve this group adequately, an increase in the budget of 150,000 euros seems necessary.

2 *Pay more attention to the evaluation of the available set of brochures.*
The study clearly showed what subjects elderly people and informal caregivers want to be informed about. At the moment, there are several brochures about these subjects. Perhaps in the near future it will be possible to determine to what extent all relevant subjects are actually covered in these brochures and to what extent the information provided in these brochures corresponds with the prior knowledge of both groups.

3 *Develop an in-service training course for doctors.*
The research shows that elderly people prefer to turn to their general practitioner. However, many general practitioners are currently not sufficiently equipped with the specific knowledge and skills needed to provide this information. This is shown in Vance (2009), a study into the state of affairs with re-

The discussion chapter also reflects on the constraints arising from the chosen methodology and any difficulties encountered in performing this study.

Based on the conclusions of the study, recommendations can be made about actions that, according to the researcher, the organization could take.

gard to the interviewing skills of doctors. Vance (2009) found some major gaps: 'Doctors, especially general practitioners, say they have difficulty in explaining information to patients in a comprehensible manner in 78% of the conversations they characterize as information interviews' (p. 32).

Bibliography

Barclay, M. J. C. (2009). What do we really want? From survival to excess. *Psychology Journal, 45*, 415-427. doi:13.1317/Y15326985EQ3801_7

Sol, F. (2018). *Information about getting older: A study about informing the elderly on health and facilities.* Sandhamn, Sweden: Municipal Health Service.

Van Gilze, A. J. (2004). *Growing older and communicating.* Berkel-Enschot, The Netherlands: Plato.

Vance, A. G. C. (2009). *Conversations with elderly people.* Chicago, IL: ABC Publishers.

Vandersteen, I. H. (2008). Needs of the elderly. *Journal for Caregivers and Nurses, 16*(1), 32-45.

> The bibliography contains only the literature mentioned. The list is alphabetized by the last name of the authors.

Example of a research report.

8.3.8   The research plan

Before a research report can be made, the research must have been carried out, and before the research can be carried out, a research plan must have been written. The research plan or research proposal has virtually the same format as a research report (see above). Of course, the results, the conclusions, and the discussion are still lacking, and the other components are usually not yet fully elaborated either. At the moment the plan is made, you will not have read all the literature, and the details of the method will probably have to be thought through.

As an extra component, a research plan also has a planning section. This also makes the relationship with the writing plan clear (see section 7.1.2). The planning section consists of two parts.

– A plan of action that indicates what you are going to do in what time period and with which (interim) results. The deadlines that you set for obtaining these results are particularly important because they give you and your supervisor a tool to monitor the course of your research process.

– A list of conditions: what you need to be able to conduct the study properly. It can be money, materials, the cooperation of others—in short, all kinds of external factors on which success depends. Such a list is important for planning in order to prevent you from being unexpectedly stuck somewhere in the process.

Planning		
Period	**Activity**	**Deadlines**
1 May-15 June	Literature survey and development of research questions	20 June: version 2 research questions (consultation)
15 June-10 July	Draft questionnaire, justification, coding scheme	10 July: draft questionnaire with justification and coding scheme (consultation)
10-25 July	Processing comments on questionnaire; pretest	25 July: final version; comments via e-mail
1-20 August	Holiday	
21 August	Implement questionnaire on internet; invitation to participants	1 September: questionnaire ready for participants
1-15 Sept	First version chapter on method	
8 Sept	Send reminder to participants	
15-30 Sept	Data analysis	Version 1 of results chapter (consultation)

Conditions

Help from John to put the questionnaire on the internet.

1500 email addresses of potential participants via the university system.

Part of a schedule from a research plan. For more detailed planning, you can use special software for planning tasks, or special functions in your spreadsheet program. This is particularly useful if you are working with several co-researchers on one study.

8.4 Two other types of reports

In addition to the research report, there are other, often lengthy professional texts that report information. Here we discuss two main types: the short report and the portfolio.

8.4.1 The short report

Many professionals spend a lot of time meeting, consulting, gathering information, presenting, and reading. They have an interest in concise and targeted information. Within organizations, there is a lot of communication by means of so-called short reports. There are a number of document types that one can consider as short reports: policy notes, competition analyses, meeting documents, advisory reports, assessment reports, and so on. The medium can also differ: You have the option of using either paper or electronic reports.

A short report differs from a long or full report in a number of respects. Firstly, of course, there is the issue of length. A report of up to five pages is a short report and thus would not need to incorporate all the components associated with long reports. For example, the foreword can be omitted, as can the table of contents, an extensive introduction, chapter numbering, an extensive conclusion, an afterword, and the summary.

There is also a difference between short and long reports in terms of content. This is mainly due to the representation of the findings and the degree of substantiation of opinions and recommendations. While these can be worked out in detail in a lengthy report, in a short report they are only touched upon or even left out. After all, everything must be directly relevant in a short report. The reader must be provided with sufficient information to be able to base a decision on it or to become convinced of the conclusion.

Structure of a short report

Some organizations have reporting guidelines, such as rules for the size, structure, formulation, layout, and the like. Sometimes there is even a kind of standard form or template available for creating a short report. This not only saves the writer work, readers can also benefit because they recognize this standard form and thus may get a quick overview of the text.

If you want to draw up a short report yourself, you will follow the same general procedure as for drawing up the research report (see section 8.3). In general, a short report contains the following parts:
- goal of the report;
- approach and method;
- results;
- discussion (with conclusions, limitations, and recommendations).

Sometimes a comprehensive report is already available and its content needs to be made available to a broader target group. An abridged version can then be of help. Perhaps the comprehensive report already contains a good summary (see section 8.1.2). You can then use this as a basis for the short report. You will probably have to rewrite some of it. A short report, just like an investigation report, is entirely independent; therefore you will have to formulate the most important arguments and facts as explicitly as possible.

Suppose you want to make an abridged version of a more comprehensive report. You base your decision on the table of contents of the detailed report, which could be as follows:

Table of contents

Table of contents of an extensive jury report.

The set evaluation schema is a useful tool when drafting a short version of this jury report (see section 2.2.4). The structure of the short report could be as follows.
– Introduction with theme description and answer to the elaboration question. What is the Harold Miller Prize, who can participate, and who are the members of the jury? You do not have to provide background information on the history,

details, and policy information. You limit yourself to the relevant facts that are necessary to form an idea of what the contest for this prize is about.

–   In the next section, you answer the second main question: What are the relevant assessment criteria? Here you describe the criteria used by the jury, with a short explanation, and delete theoretical reflections.

–   You then briefly introduce the nominated entries, summarizing the positive and negative scores of the jury for each nomination.

–   In the final section, you will present the final judgment: the jury's conclusion. You briefly highlight the strongest points of the winning entry and link them to the criteria. If necessary, you can make a comparison with the other nominations. It is conceivable that your audience will be particularly interested in the answer to the question 'What is the final judgment?'. You could decide to reveal the name of the winner at the beginning of the report, while at the end you take the liberty to properly explain the jury's assessment of the winning entry.

Returning to a set schema such as the evaluation schema is often an effective way of working, but it does not always lead to an optimal match with the needs of the target group. Because readers are often more interested in the conclusion than in the procedure followed, they want to see results rather than research data. A more public-oriented structure fits this need. You can compare such a structure to that of a management summary, which focuses on the recommendations that usually follow at the end of the process (see section 8.1.2). You can also think of the structure of a journalistic article or news report: the headline and the intro contain the most important news facts, and the background information and elaboration follow afterwards.

What could a public-oriented structure of the short jury report look like? First of all, consider what the most relevant main question for the public could be. The key answer to that question should be the core of of the short report.

Title: Harold Miller Prize for trendsetters in innovation
–   Already with the title of the report, you respond to the curiosity of the public. Immediately following the title, in your introduction, you announce the winner of the prize.
–   The public is probably also curious about the other nominated entries and their quality. People will also want to know how many and what kind of entries there were in total. You will therefore continue with the answers to the main questions about the positive and negative aspects of the other entries.

- You can then explicitly mention the relevant assessment criteria and justify their importance.
- Finally, you will briefly explain the background of the Harold Miller Prize and, in the light of this, explain the jury's assessment of the winning entry.

Public-orientated structure for a short report. The most important information for the reader is at the beginning, and not at the end, as is the case with extensive reports. Readers who want to know more will find the background information and details later in this short report.

8.4.2 The portfolio

Although it may seem strange to consider a portfolio as a report, it is. After all, a portfolio is nothing more than a form of self-reporting. There are different types of portfolio, especially in education. We confine ourselves here to discussing the career portfolio. This portfolio is a substantiated overview of a person's education, competencies, and testimonies, along with a selection of a person's work that is used for recruitment, selection, and professionalization. Although it differs per sector, the career portfolio is becoming increasingly important for professionals as a means of distinguishing themselves from their peers.

What the career portfolio has in common with the classic curriculum vitae is that it is a document that must be continuously updated and, in that sense, is never 'finished'. Unlike a curriculum vitae, the emphasis of the portfolio is on evidence. The ability of professionals to provide evidence of qualifications such as diplomas, credentials, and own work enables them to demonstrate their suitability and expertise. The career portfolio in turn has this in common with the research report: there is evidence. Unlike the research report, the answer to the central question 'Is X a suitable candidate?' is implied and left to the reader.

Depending on your preferences, those of potential clients or employers, technical possibilities, and conventions in the sector in which you operate, you can choose to create a paper or a digital portfolio. If you create a digital portfolio, you can present it as an electronic version of what you would otherwise have created on paper. However, you can also choose to create a website for your portfolio. The latter may be more attractive, but in order for the information to be accessible to a wider public, you may have to opt for a little less detail.

Parts of the portfolio

Although the portfolio does not have a standard form, there are some parts that most career portfolios have in common.

– *Training.* Most portfolios would give an overview of the candidate's training, including school education, tertiary education, and any other specific vocational courses or programs that you might have followed. You may wish to consider adding certified copies of certificates as evidence.

– *Own work.* Originally, portfolios were used by artists and architects to show their designs, sketches, and projects. The material that is submitted is therefore the most essential part of a portfolio. You can choose to record a selection of previous work, or just extracts from it. You can base these selections on your best work or create a sample of your work to illustrate your versatility.

– *Evidence of success.* In some sectors, it is customary to show the results of your previous efforts instead of, or alongside, your own work. If so, provide information on specific tasks, projects, or designs that you have completed successfully, production achieved, quality figures, turnover, and the like. Note that if you want to create a website as a portfolio, it is not always desirable to publish strategic or sensitive information on the internet.

– *Vision document.* The content of your portfolio is held together by an explanation of all the information and evidence that you present, preferably in the form of a text in which you discuss your competencies but which also shows your own vision as a professional. This document bears some resemblance to an application letter in terms of content but not in terms of form.

– *Recommendations.* Ask colleagues, supervisors, and teachers to write a recommendation. However, it is important to ensure that the referents give specific information and that their support for you coheres with the information that you present about yourself in the portfolio.

Audience of the portfolio

Although it should be possible to use a portfolio, unlike an application letter, for several employment positions, you will only draw the necessary attention if you clearly design your portfolio keeping the specific audience you are targeting in mind. You would do well to adapt the information you present to each specific audience, adjusting your language and the form of your text where necessary. In doing so, pay attention to the following aspects.

– *Professional group.* What professional group (or groups) are you creating the portfolio for? Who are your competitors there? What backgrounds and expertise do they bring? What are your distinguishing qualities? If relevant to your job, who are your role models?

– *Inside information on the topics you deal with in your portfolio.* Does your target group consist of experts or lay people in terms of the topics in the portfolio? When you have the opportunity to present your portfolio, try to bridge the gap between your knowledge and the needs of the organization you are talking to.

– *Inside information about yourself.* Do people know you and the organizations you are describing? What kind of reputation do you have with the target group? It is important that you take the opportunity to show that you 'walk the walk and talk the talk'. In other words, the language you use can demonstrate that you are familiar with the conventions that apply in the industry in which you operate.

Key points

Reports are longer texts, usually intended for an organization.

Components of a report

The usual parts of a report are:

- cover and title page
- summary
- preface or foreword
- table of contents
- introduction
- titles and headings
- final section
- notes
- bibliography
- appendices

Source references

- If you use information from others for your own purposes by summarizing, citing, or referring, you must clearly identify the source of the information, both in the main text and in the bibliography.
- The fraudulent act of plagiarism occurs when the writing of one's own text does not do justice to the work of others. Plagiarism can be prevented with correct and complete literature references and a complete bibliography.

The research report

A research project should provide insight into the phenomenon that was studied and should be replicable on the basis of the research report. The research report must therefore contain all the information required for this purpose. In addition, you must justify the choices made in the report by discussing possible alternatives and by mentioning relevant sources.

A standard research report contains the following components:

- introduction (including the problem statement, the theoretical framework, the research questions, and, if applicable, the hypotheses);
- method (including information about the materials, the participants, the instruments, and the procedure, all of this preceded by the experimental design if applicable);

- results;
- discussion (with conclusions, limitations, and recommendations); in an applied study, the recommendations are often presented in a separate chapter.

The short report

In short reports, the following parts can be omitted: the foreword, the table of contents, an extensive introduction, chapter numbering, an extensive discussion, and a summary. Core components of a short report are:
- goal of the report,
- approach taken;
- results;
- conclusions and recommendations.

The portfolio

The portfolio is a self-report that provides a substantiated overview of a person's education, competencies, testimonies, and a selection of a person's work. The portfolio (on paper or in digital form) is often used in recruitment and selection.

Assignments

Assignment 1: Critically assess reports

Purpose of the assignment
You will practice developing a professional sensitivity to the communicative aspects of a report.

Subject matter
Introduction to this chapter
section 8.1
Section 1.1
Section 7.1.1

Tasks
In the introduction to this chapter, you will find a list of report types. Find a report that belongs to one of these types and answer the following questions about that report.
1. What do you like, what do you like less?
2. What components do you see?
3. For whom is the report intended? Be as specific as possible.
4. Who are the 'shadow readers'? Be specific here too.
5. Where and to what extent do you see each of the four sides of a communication message?
6. What suggestions for improvement would you make?

Assignment 2: The title

Purpose of the assignment
You will practice thinking up effective titles.

Subject matter
Section 8.1.6

Tasks
Think of informative and catchy main titles and subtitles for the reports below.
1   A report on the problems associated with the existence of shooting clubs.
2   A report on the way in which the live bearing tooth carp (poecilia) looks after its offspring.

3   A report on how the FIFA is managed and controlled.
4   A report on the problems of relatives of murder victims.
5   A report on what type of entry has the greatest chance of winning the Eurovision Song Contest.

Assignment 3: The preface

Purpose of the assignment
You will practice writing a preface or foreword.

Subject matter
Section 8.1.3

Tasks
1.   Think of a writing assignment for yourself that would result in a research report. At least state what you should investigate, whom you should investigate, why you should do so, and what kind of results you can expect.
2.   Your research must lead to an internal report. Write a preface to that report. Make up the information you need.

Assignment 4: The portfolio

Purpose of the assignment
You will practice creating a career portfolio.

Subject matter
Section 8.4.2

Task
Make a career portfolio about yourself, considering a specific field in which you would like to work. Because you may not yet have relevant work experience, consider how you can adapt your portfolio in due course so that it becomes a real career portfolio.

DEN ZEDELYKE EN ZINNELYKE MENSCH.

9   Oral presentations

◀ *An orator gives a speech about Kantian philosophy to a sleeping audience*, Jacob Ernst Marcus, 1800-1805. The print is part of a series of caricatures of society from around 1800.

This chapter provides you with guidelines, often based on classical insights, on how to make your speech more engaging and effective, so as to avoid the situation in this picture.

An impressive speech on a classical basis

When Barack Obama gave his election victory speech in 2008, he ended with the following words.

This election had many firsts and many stories that will be told for generations. But one that's on my mind tonight is about a woman who cast her ballot in Atlanta. She's a lot like the millions of others who stood in line to make their voice heard in this election except for one thing: Ann Nixon Cooper is 106 years old.

She was born just a generation past slavery; a time when there were no cars on the road or planes in the sky; when someone like her couldn't vote for two reasons — because she was a woman and because of the color of her skin. And tonight, I think about all that she's seen throughout her century in America — the heartache and the hope; the struggle and the progress; the times we were told that we can't, and the people who pressed on with that American creed: Yes we can.

At a time when women's voices were silenced and their hopes dismissed, she lived to see them stand up and speak out and reach out for the ballot. Yes we can.

When there was despair in the dust bowl and depression across the land, she saw a nation conquer fear itself with a New Deal, new jobs, a new sense of common purpose. Yes we can.

When the bombs fell on our harbor and tyranny threatened the world, she was there to witness a generation rise to greatness and a democracy was saved. Yes we can.

She was there for the buses in Montgomery, the hoses in Birmingham, a bridge in Selma, and a preacher from Atlanta who told a people that we shall overcome. Yes we can.

A man touched down on the moon, a wall came down in Berlin, a world was connected by our own science and imagination. And this year, in this election, she touched her finger to a screen, and cast her vote, because after 106 years in America, through the best of times and the darkest of hours, she knows how America can change. Yes we can.

America, we have come so far. We have seen so much. But there is so much more to do. So tonight, let us ask ourselves – if our children should live to see the next century; if my daughters should be so lucky to live as long as Ann Nixon Cooper, what change will they see? What progress will we have made?

This is our chance to answer that call. This is our moment. This is our time, to put our people back to work and open doors of opportunity for our kids; to restore prosperity and promote the cause of peace; to reclaim the American dream and reaffirm that fundamental truth, that, out of many, we are one; that while we breathe, we hope. And where we are met with cynicism and doubts and those who tell us that we can't, we will respond with that timeless creed that sums up the spirit of a people: Yes, we can.

Thank you; God bless you, and may God bless the United States of America.

Source: Obama (2008).[15]

Not only political supporters of Barack Obama in the US but many others too were touched by his speech. Both the content of the speech and its presentation by Obama received wide acclaim. The touching story he told, the multiple repetitions of his presidential campaign slogan, the parallelism in the construction of his sentences with hopeful contrasts between the first and second part, and the climax that the speech builds up to—all of this goes back to classical rhetorical techniques invented and described by Greek and Roman rhetoricians.

In this chapter we will discuss a number of classical rhetorical techniques. We will not do this from the idea that anyone who uses them can become as good a speaker as Obama. But knowledge of and experience with the rules of classical rhetoric will help you to make your presentations as effective as possible.

Where appropriate, we will also use the Greek and Roman terminology. However, the aim of this chapter is not to give a full overview of classical rhetoric. Its system of rules is too extensive for our purposes, and not all aspects are relevant anymore. Still, many of the classical guidelines remain useful, and that is why they form the basis of many of the recommendations in this chapter. Famous orators such as Barack Obama, Oprah Winfrey, Winston Churchill, and Archbishop Tutu prove with their speeches that knowledge of classical rhetoric can still be effective today. Every speaker can benefit from these guidelines developed more than two thousand years ago and from the terminology belonging to these theories.

15   Obama, B. H. (2008, November 4). [Victory Speech]. Retrieved from https://abcnews.go.com/Politics/Vote2008/story?id=6181477&page=1

According to classical rhetoric, an experienced speaker should be able to adequately perform five tasks. The first is the collection of material (Latin: *inventio*) in order to determine the content of the speech. After this followed the arrangement (Latin: *dispositio*): ordering the contents in a suitable structure. The third task concerned wording (Latin: *elocutio*): choosing the most effective formulations. After that, the speaker had to learn the text by heart: *memoria*. And finally, the orator delivered the speech: *actio*. These tasks are all discussed in this chapter, albeit in a slightly different order.

Section 9.1 presents recommendations for the proper preparation of a modern oral presentation (lecture, speech, or recital). In this section, we explain possible goals of the presentation, paying particular attention to three important aspects from classical rhetoric, in Greek: *ethos, logos,* and *pathos* (which we will explain below). We also discuss a number of questions regarding the audience and the context of your presentation, and we will describe the function of a speaking schedule for a presentation. The preparatory tasks of inventio and dispositio will be discussed simultaneously, because from a modern perspective these tasks are too similar to be dealt with separately.

Section 9.2 discusses the ordering of the various parts of a presentation—dispositio—in more detail. We will pay most attention to the introduction, or *exordium*, and the conclusion, or *peroratio*, because these parts are particularly important in determining the impact your presentation will have on the audience. The midsection of the presentation will naturally also be discussed.

This chapter includes only a short section on the elocutio: section 9.3. Elocutio, or style, was already central to chapter 4, because it is important for both written and spoken communication. However, in section 9.3 we do discuss a number of style recommendations that are particularly important for a presentation.

Section 9.4 discusses actio together with memoria. This section covers body language and use of voice, as well as contact with the audience and the use of visual support. This section will also explain under what circumstances it may be useful to either read your presentation (or parts of it) from paper or to learn it by heart.

Finally, in section 9.5 we will discuss two special contemporary types of presentations: the *elevator pitch* and *pecha kucha*.

9.1   Preparation

Classical rhetoric distinguishes three kinds of speeches: the judicial speech, or a plea in a court of law (in Latin: *genus iudicale*); the political speech, or a speech by a politician (in Latin: *genus deliberativum*), and the occasional speech at a party or farewell (in Latin: *genus demonstrativum*). There were special rules for each of these, and it was important not to confuse them. Nowadays the distinction between these three types of speeches is no longer very important. Still, it remains true that presentations can be very different and may therefore require different forms of preparation. In this section we will discuss possible goals of your presentation and characteristics of the audience, and the situation in which you deliver the presentation. The better you know what you want to achieve, with whom you want to achieve it, and under what circumstances, the greater your chance of success. We end this section by showing you how to use a text schema to help you create good content and a good structure, and how to record that content and structure in a speaking schedule. You may also want to take a closer look at section 7.1 about the preparation for writing a longer text. This largely corresponds to the preparation for an oral presentation.

9.1.1 Goals

In chapter 1, we mentioned five different types of sender goals: informative, instructive, persuasive, motivating, and affective. These also apply to a presentation, but there are some limitations.

– Presentations are less suitable for conveying a lot of detailed information, because they are usually too short for that. Moreover, the receiver needs some time to think about detailed information and, if necessary, to review it. Written communication is therefore more appropriate for these purposes.

– Presentations are also less suitable for giving instructions about complex tasks, for example the use of a new and unknown product or the introduction of a new procedure within an organization. Listeners are not likely to precisely remember that kind of information. An online video or a written text that the user can keep at hand while performing the task is much better.

On the other hand, presentations can be particularly suitable for persuasive, motivating, and affective purposes. Speakers are more able to emphasize their personal qualities than writers. They can also use the speed, volume, and pitch of their speaking to influence the emotions of the audience.

As a speaker, you should have a clear idea from the outset of what you want to achieve and what obstacles you may need to overcome in order to convince your audience. The answers to these questions determine what will be the right balance between the rhetorical aspects that the Greeks referred to as *ethos*, *logos*, and *pathos*.

Ethos is the impression the audience has of you as a speaker: Do you come across as an expert, and do you seem honest and sympathetic towards your audience? Considerations of honesty and expertise are related to the self-expression side of your communication, as explained in section 1.1. Sympathy for your audience is expressed through the relationship side of your communication (section 1.4). If you give a presentation for a group of people you know quite well, you can assume that your listeners will not question your honesty or the sympathy you feel for them. But sometimes your audience has no particular reason to consider you an expert on the subject you are talking about. In that case, you must put some effort into establishing yourself as a knowledgeable speaker. If your audience does not know you at all, you should also pay attention to the other two aspects of ethos. You should demonstrate your honesty in a delicate way or give your listeners the feeling that you like them and that you share their interests or at least understand them. Ethos is particularly important for the introduction of the presentation. We will return to this in section 9.2.1.

Logos refers to the matter side of your presentation. What factual information do you want to transfer? What arguments do you put forward to convince your audience of your position (see chapter 3)? For logos, the midsection of the presentation is most relevant; see section 9.2.2.

Pathos is about the feelings you try to evoke in your audience. These feelings can be very important if you want to persuade your listeners to adopt a certain position or if you want to encourage a certain behavior. Encouraging emotions mainly serves the affective goal, which was mentioned in section 1.2 with reference to the appeal side. The ending of your presentation is the appropriate place for additional pathos (see section 9.2.3).

9.1.2   Situation and audience

A presentation is always delivered for a specific audience and in a specific situation. Speakers should adapt their presentation accordingly.

Your first consideration is the reason for your presentation; that is, why the audience will come and listen to you. Someone speaking at a scientific conference about 'Using health information on the internet' will have a different message and content from someone delivering a lecture about health information in a public library or from someone speaking at the opening event of a new health program. Sometimes you are the only speaker, but it is also possible that your presentation is part of a program that includes presentations by others. How much time do you actually have for your presentation, and how much time is there for the discussion, if there is any? And what about the room where you will deliver your speech? How large is it, how many listeners can you expect, and what facilities are available to you?

The characteristics of your audience are also important, especially their prior knowledge and their interest (or possibly lack thereof) in the subject you are talking about. You should realize that the audience's inclination to listen attentively is in most cases not great. Your listeners may sit back and let their thoughts wander, and their attention span is by definition limited. It is therefore essential that you succeed in catching and keeping the attention of your audience, that you provide a clear structure so that a listener who was distracted can easily catch up, and that you create a pleasant rhythm in your presentation: a good alternation between moments with a high information density and moments of relaxation.

Reason
- What is the reason for the event?
- Why were you asked to speak, and why was your subject chosen?

Allotted time
- When does the presentation start, and how long do you have? Will there be time for a discussion after the speech? If so, how long?

Program
- Are there any other presentations? If so, by whom, and what are they about?
- Will you be introduced to the audience, and if so, by whom?
- Who is in charge of a discussion, if there is one?

Space and facilities
- How large is the space and how is it arranged? How far away are you from your audience?
- Is all the equipment you need present (and how does it work?), or do you have to bring your own? Is there technical support?
- Can you write something on a board or flipchart during the presentation? Is there an electronic whiteboard?
- Are you behind a lectern, or can you walk around freely?
- Is there a microphone? If so, is it a fixed microphone, a dynamic microphone, or a lapel microphone? In the latter case, take this into account when you choose what to wear; make sure that the microphone can be easily attached to your clothing.

Audience
- How many attendees can you expect?
- Have the attendees been invited, or is it a public presentation?
- To what extent are the attendees interested in your subject? Why?
- What do the attendees know about your subject? Do they have lay knowledge, knowledge from books, or specialist knowledge?

Questions you can ask yourself while preparing a presentation. If you have been invited to hold a presentation, you should consider discussing these points beforehand with the person who invited you.

9.1.3   Content and structure

According to classical rhetoric, the first two tasks of the speaker are inventio and dispositio. As said before, we will discuss them together. We will show you how to construct good content and a structure with the use of a short text schema and how to record your choices in a speaking schedule.

From text schema to speaking schedule

Similar to the production of a written text (see chapter 2), a text schema is a useful starting point for an oral presentation. This does not have to be a very detailed text schema. In the first phase of your project, a short text schema is often better. Your text schema also does not have to be explicitly visible (or audible) in the final presentation. Its main function is that you use it to create an adequate internal structure. In the following phases you will build on this internal structure and convert it into an effective outer structure. The requirements for a clear outer structure are discussed in section 9.2.1 (about the introduction), section 9.2.2 (about the midsection) and section 9.2.3 (about the ending).

When you are designing the internal structure, try to limit yourself to the main lines of your presentation. This includes determining the presentation's exact theme, and formulating the main questions and key answers and, where necessary, sub-questions and their answers. Always make sure that the content you choose fits together logically to deliver a clear end product for your audience. Again, you can make use of the set schemata discussed in chapter 2.

THE MYSTIFICATION OF ANIMAL TESTING

What is the problem?
1   Every year, 600,000 animals are used for animal testing.
2   Animal testing is mainly used in the pharmaceutical and cosmetic industries.
3   There is mystification surrounding amounts, goals, and methods.

Why is it a problem?
1   Ethical objections.
2   Social unrest sometimes leads to unacceptable violence.

What are the causes of the mystification?
1   Considerations of competition.
2   Fear of having to relocate laboratories abroad.
3   Fear of social unrest.

What are possible solutions?

1 More openness from the sector.
2 (Continue) looking for alternatives.

Example of a short text schema based on the set problem schema.

The short text schema forms the basis for your speaking schedule, which you use as a support during the actual delivery of the presentation. In this schedule, you write down short sentences or keywords of what you will say and at what point. If you make use of visual support, you should also include how you will use this and when (for example, 'don't forget to point out where Troy was'). We recommend that you write out some important parts completely, such as the introduction and conclusion. At a later stage, you can decide what you want to read from paper or what you want to learn by heart (see also section 9.4.1). To illustrate this, there are some examples below of speaking schedules.

SLIDE 1	INTRODUCTION
Photo of a beautiful holiday destination	Ladies and gentlemen,
	Travelling abroad has become second nature to many people. Every year, millions of our countrymen travel to all corners of the world. Statistically speaking, there is a good chance that you, too, will soon leave on a faraway journey. Of course, you're hoping that you will have a pleasant time and will have happy memories to think back on. Yet every year, many travelers return with less pleasant experiences. They were faced with theft, sickness, or underinsurance.
	You can't prevent all potential problems on your trip abroad. But you can prepare for many things. To help you with your preparation, *Continental Tours* has organized this evening for you. As tonight's chairman has already told you, I am an employee of *Continental Tours*. For the next 45 minutes, I hope to give you some tips, ideas, and advice to make your next journey a success.

The introduction is written out in full. The first digital slide should appear right at the start of the presentation.

The first part of a speaking scheme: fully written text of the introduction.

The first question from the text schema is answered. The beginning of the answer is written out in full.

Follow-up to the answer to the first main question in key-words. As soon as the deviating traffic signs are mentioned, the second slide should be shown.

How to prepare for a far journey?
What can you do beforehand to make your holiday a success? First of all: Browse through folders or books about the country you are going to visit, buy tickets, and so on.
The more you know, the more you understand about the country and the more you will enjoy it.

SLIDE 2
Collage of photographs of foreign road signs; point out an example for each of the four kinds mentioned on the slide.

Important information:
– different road signs and traffic rules
– medical risks
– customs regulations for photo and video equipment
– regulations for camping in the wild

Another part of a speaking scheme: a main question with elaboration.

The ending is written out in full. The last slide should appear on the screen immediately at the start of the last paragraph.

SLIDE 4
Photo of another beautiful holiday destination

Ladies and gentlemen,
I hope I have made it clear that you can make an effort to avoid problems, both before and during your holiday. However, it is not possible to anticipate everything. That is why I have also given you some specific advice in case you run into difficulties. In any case, you can always count on Continental Tours to try to help you in such cases.

Still, we assume that this will not be necessary. There is a reason that travelling has become our second nature. After all, there are many foreign countries to explore. Let us continue to enjoy the many beautiful holiday opportunities that are available to us.

The last part of a speaking scheme: fully written text of the ending.

You can simply write the speaking schedule on one or multiple sheets of paper. Do not use paper too sparingly. The font size should be large enough to be legibly, and you should include enough white lines to keep the schedule clear. It must be easy for you to read from some distance, especially if you put it down on a lectern but also if you are holding it in your hands. You can also choose to copy the schedule on a series of cards numbered in the correct order on A5 format, for example. If you use index cards, your presentation will look a little more polished. You also reduce the risk of losing contact with your audience because you are concentrating too much on your notes.

Practice
Crucial for a successful presentation is that you practice enough—if possible for a small and preferably somewhat critical audience that can give useful feedback (see section 1.5), or else in front of the mirror, or using the camera on your computer, tablet, or smartphone. If you practice your speech very well, you will know exactly how much time you need. You will also identify any problematic passages that you need to devote more attention to in your speaking schedule.

9.2 Parts of the presentation

According to classical rhetoric, a good speech consisted of at least five parts, each with different requirements: the introduction (Latin: *exordium*), the description of the relevant facts (*narratio*), the position taken by the speaker (Latin: *propositio*), the argumentation supporting that position (Latin: *argumentatio*), and the ending (Latin: *peroratio*). Contemporary presentations too, have different requirements for the introduction than for the midsection and the ending. These three parts of a presentation are therefore discussed separately in this section. Specific types of modern presentations still maintain a clear distinction between narratio, propositio, and argumentatio, such as a plea in a court case. For most other presentations, however, this distinction is no longer very meaningful. For this reason, we have combined these three classical parts in our discussion of the midsection of a presentation.

9.2.1 Introduction

During the introduction, you try to ease your audience into the right 'listening position'. To achieve this in your exordium, you need to do three things: Catch the attention of your audience (Latin: *attentum parare*), establish your *ethos* (Latin:

benevolum parare), and provide a preview of what you will say so that your listeners know what to expect and will be able to follow you more easily (Latin: *docilem parare*). Here we will discuss these three functions of the introduction in the context of an oral presentation. Section 8.1.5 explains how to use these functions in a written report.

Attention

At the start of a presentation, your audience is often still noisy. Attendees are talking to each other, reading and writing their last tweets or Facebook messages, or browsing the program booklet. It is up to you to ensure they stop doing this: All eyes must be on you, the speaker. A good opening is therefore essential, even if you have already been introduced as a speaker by someone else. An opening sentence such as 'Hi everyone, so, I'm George and I'm going to talk about animal testing now', is not a good way to get the undivided attention of your listeners. There are better possibilities, a number of which we list here. You can find further examples in section 8.5.1.

–   You start with a *short story*. You can tell an anecdote (preferably one that you were involved in), quote a news report, or recall a recently aired television program. Stories usually attract more attention than factual information. Still, the story you choose to tell must be worthwhile; there should be some tension in it, and it should fit well with the rest of your presentation.

–   You ask a *question* about your subject, encouraging people to raise their hands if they agree with something. 'Who among you thinks that [...]' Such an opening works particularly well if you can continue with something along the lines of, 'So the majority of you thinks that [...], but is this really the case? That's what the first part of my presentation is about.'

–   You explain the *importance* of your subject. You open with a current social problem (refugees coming to Europe, new budget cuts, climate change, quality of education, health care costs, and so on) and show that your subject is relevant in that context.

–   You go back in *history*. You start with information from the past that is probably interesting for your audience. 'Did you know that in the seventeenth century, Dutch cities such as Amsterdam, Haarlem, and Leiden did everything in their power to bring as many immigrants who were fleeing the oppression of Catholics as possible to the north? For example, immigrants from Antwerp were offered free citizenship and living space in Haarlem, and they could work there in workshops. The government sometimes even supported them in financing their businesses. If all this had not happened, the seventeenth century would never have become the famous Dutch Golden Age, characterized not only by its great freedom of religion but also by its much-acclaimed trade and economy, and perhaps most of all by its impressive art—specifically painting. Partly in this light, I would like to reflect with you today on the possible benefits that the current influx of refugees—if well managed—can bring, both for the economy and for culture.'

– You start with an attention-grabbing *one-liner*: a concise statement that touches upon the core of your speech—or goes against it. Quotations are often a good choice. Make sure that your one-liner will surprise the audience. For example, you can begin a lecture for policymakers on the subject of 'Healthy ageing' with this statement by the British health professor Karen Middleton: 'Let's add life to years, not just years to life!' And in a presentation for managers on taking proactive action, you may want to use a quote from the famous Dutch soccer player Johan Cruijff, such as: 'You have got to shoot, otherwise you can't score' or 'Every disadvantage has its own advantage'. Try to avoid over-used quotations that have developed into clichés with little or no meaning, like 'Everything happens for a reason' or 'The journey matters more than the destination'. You can find many usable (and not so usable) one-liners online or in books, for instance in aphorism collections.

– You use special *visual or sound effects*. A surprising image, sound, or video clip at the start of your presentation will certainly attract attention. A disadvantage of this approach can be that the audience's attention stays with the screen and less with you as a speaker. This is often a matter of trial and error.

– *Humor* is certainly a useful tool to attract attention. To give an example from arguably the most famous British politician and speaker, Winston Churchill: 'A good speech should be like a woman's skirt; long enough to cover the subject and short enough to create interest.' But be aware that humor is also risky. As the example from Churchill perhaps may illustrate, a small joke that appeals to part of your audience can be annoying or even offensive to other attendees. Self-deprecation often works best, though it should also not be overdone. A nice example comes from Abraham Lincoln. When he was accused of being two-faced, he replied: 'If I were two-faced, would I be wearing this one?' The best advice when it comes to using humor is to try out your ideas, preferably on a mixed audience.

Ethos

The introduction is also the appropriate moment to establish your ethos. Here you can try to create or enhance a positive impression of yourself among the audience. You show your competence and suitability as a speaker on this subject, preferably implicitly, and, if necessary, you prove that you are honest, objective, and that you have your listeners' interests in mind.

Sometimes you can explicitly mention certain ethos elements: 'I have obtained a cum laude degree in animal science and pharmacy, and I have completed a PhD on the ethical aspects of animal testing.' However, a more indirect indication of your ethos will sometimes be more appreciated by the audience, and many speakers feel better about indirect claims. Here are a number of possibilities.

–   You can express a short *word of thanks*. Thank the audience for coming, the organization for inviting you, and the moderator for her kind introduction of you. In this way, you not only encourage the audience to feel sympathy for you, but you also point out your own expertise. If the organization did not think you were an expert in the field, you would not have been invited. Similarly, if the moderator did not have a high opinion of you, he or she would not have introduced you with such kind words.

–   You can emphasize the *relationship* between yourself and the audience. You are one of them, you have the same opinion on a matter, or the same taste and interest.

–   You can *flatter* the audience. For example, you can say how honored you are that you are allowed to speak to this learned company, or you can express how important and generous the organization is. Such words of praise also indirectly apply to yourself.

Preview

The audience should be able to follow the main lines of your presentation. That is why it is important to include a brief preview in the introduction to a presentation. An explicit indication of the goal of your presentation helps your audience to understand where you are heading. Make sure that you do not take yourself and your goals as the norm but focus on what you hope your audience will take from your presentation. You should also mention how much time your presentation will take, if this is not yet clear from the program that the audience members have received.

The simplest form of preview is something along the lines of a table of contents for your presentation, which you briefly explain. You can base this on the questions from the short text schema that was the starting point during your preparation phase. Speakers often show the table of contents on a separate slide, but that is not always necessary, and you risk boring your listeners from the start. If you do put the contents on a slide, make sure that your own explanation adds something to what the listeners can already see on the slide.

> I will first explain the research question and then describe the theoretical framework. Then I will discuss the research method and after that I will show you the most important results. I will conclude with a conclusion and recommendations, after which you can ask questions.

This preview does not give any insight into the concrete research that the presentation will be about. Especially if the speaker only reads aloud what is on a slide, this is guaranteed to be a boring introduction.

You may never have noticed it, but when language users give an estimation of, for example, an amount or a distance using two numbers, they can only use certain combinations. For example, 'some ten or twelve dollars' and 'some fifteen or twenty miles' are fine. But what do you think of, for example, 'some twelve or ten dollars', or 'some fourteen or nineteen miles'? That sounds very odd, doesn't it?

Our research focuses on these fixed patterns that apparently exist when we use combinations of numbers for estimations. You may wonder how on earth we thought of this topic. I will tell you more about that in a moment, and after that I will briefly discuss the international background literature so you may better understand the subject. I will also discuss some puzzles that we had to solve in order to obtain useful data for our research. But you'll be mostly wondering what the results of our research were. Of course, these will also be discussed. At the end of my talk, I will try to answer the key question: What has this research taught us about the rules we apparently follow when we use these estimation pairs, as we call them?

I hope that my story about the estimation pairs will lead you to share in my amazement about the sometimes quite complex language rules that we all know and follow without even being aware of it. What is the reason for this, and what does it say about what may be the most essential difference between humans and other animals? After I have explained this and have thus reached the end of my presentation, you will probably have all kinds of questions and perhaps also some criticism, which I would very much like to discuss with you.

This speaker opts for a livelier approach, even including some self-deprecating humor ('You may wonder how on earth we thought of this topic'). The speaker addresses the audience with 'you' eight times as a way to involve them more. He also mentions the goal he wants to achieve with his talk and outlines a perspective that reaches far beyond the seemingly rather peculiar topic of his lecture. In this preview, you can also recognize the fixed questions from the set research schema. Particularly in the case of such a conventional structure, it is not necessary to display all points you are going to discuss on a slide.

A few more examples of introductions

For inspiration, here are a few more examples of opening parts of famous speeches by experienced speakers.

I am proud to come to this city as the guest of your distinguished Mayor, who has symbolized throughout the world the fighting spirit of West Berlin. And I am proud to visit the Federal Republic with your distinguished Chancellor who for so many years has committed Germany to democracy and freedom and progress, and to come here in the company of my fellow American, General Clay, who has been in this city during its great moments of crisis and will come again if ever needed. Two thousand years ago the proudest boast was 'civis Romanus sum'. Today, in the world of freedom, the proudest boast is 'Ich bin ein Berliner'.

Opening of the 'Ich bin ein Berliner' speech by John F. Kennedy (1963).[16]

Ladies and gentlemen,

Now and again in the course of my remarks, I will pull out a white handkerchief and wipe my eyes. Don't be worried. There is nothing wrong. It is my own unique way of attracting your attention.

I stand before you aware of the momentous times that we are traversing. These times also demand of us that we regularly account to this important assembly about the work and process to us by the electorate. [...]

At the end of the day, a yardstick that we shall all be judged by is one and only one. And that is, are we through our endeavours here creating the basis to better the lives of South Africans? This is not because the people have some subjective expectations fanned during an election campaign. Neither is it because there is a magic wand that they see in the new government. Millions have suffered deprivation for decades, and they have the right to seek redress. They fought and voted for change, and change the people of South Africa must have. Honourable members, you have been warned.

Opening of the '100 days speech' by Nelson Mandela (1994).[17]

So I would like to start by telling you about one of my greatest friends, Okoloma Ma-duewesi. Okoloma lived on my street and looked after me like a big brother. If I liked a boy, I would ask Okoloma's opinion. Okoloma died in the notorious Sosoliso plane crash in Nigeria in December of 2005. Almost exactly seven years ago. Okoloma was a person I could argue with, laugh with, and truly talk to. He was also the first person to call me a feminist.

I was about fourteen, we were at his house, arguing. Both of us bristling with half-bit knowledge from books that we had read. I don't remember what this particular argument was about, but I remember that as I argued and argued, Okoloma looked at me and said, 'You know, you're a feminist.' It was not a compliment. I could tell from his tone, the same tone that you would use to say something like, 'You're a supporter of terrorism.' I did not know exactly what this word 'feminist' meant, and I did not want Okoloma to know that I

16   Kennedy, J. F. (1963, June 26). *Remarks at the Rudolph Wilde Platz, Berlin*. Retrieved from https://www.jfklibrary.org/archives/other-resources/john-f-kennedy-speeches/berlin-w-germany-rudolph-wilde-platz-19630626

17   Mandela, N. R. (1994, Augustus 18). [100 Days Speech to Parliament]. Retrieved from http://www.africa.upenn.edu/Govern_Political/Mandel_100.html

did not know. So I brushed it aside, and I continued to argue. And the first thing I planned to do when I got home was to look up the word 'feminist' in the dictionary.

Now fast forward to some years later, I wrote a novel about a man who among other things beats his wife and whose story doesn't end very well. While I was promoting the novel in Nigeria, a journalist, a nice, well-meaning man, told me he wanted to advise me. And for the Nigerians here, I'm sure we're all familiar with how quick our people are to give unsolicited advice. He told me that people were saying that my novel was feminist and his advice to me—and he was shaking his head sadly as he spoke—was that I should never call myself a feminist because feminists are women who are unhappy because they cannot find husbands.

Opening of the 'We should all be feminists' speech by Chimamanda Ngozi Adichie (2012).[18]

9.2.2 Midsection

After the introduction with the opening and preview, it is time for you come to the point. You present your actual argument in the midsection of your presentation. Whereas in the introduction the emphasis is on ethos, and the ending is often the best place for pathos, the midsection of the presentation is usually dedicated to logos: the matter side of the information you present. In order to keep your audience's attention, it is important that you clearly convey the internal structure and thus the actual content of your presentation (see section 9.1.3). It can often be helpful to make your transitions from one point to the next explicit. Good and effective phrasing is paramount. Your wording should not only be clear but also appealing (see section 9.3).

Keeping to the structure: transitions
In the preview you gave in the introduction, you explained that your presentation will consist of a number of stages or parts. Now it is important that the audience can keep track of where you are in the presentation. Not only does this help them to better understand your main argument, but they will also know what is coming next and how close you are to the end of the presentation. After all, this is not always clear in the case of a presentation, unlike a report or other written texts.

A good rule of thumb is to make sure that each part of your presentation has a clear start and a clear ending. You can achieve this by using transition moments.

18   Adichie, C. N. (2012, December). *We Should All Be Feminists* (TED Talk). Retrieved from https://www.ted.com/talks/chimamanda_ngozi_adichie_we_should_all_be_feminists/transcript

Such a transition moment consists of two parts: a summary of what you have just said and a preview of what you will do next.

– The summary covers the main points you made in the preceding section of the lecture. For example: 'I have now identified the three causes of the perceived insecurity in our green area: the damaged street furniture and plants, the waste scattered everywhere on the street, and the dangers caused by traffic and crowds'.

– In the preview you announce the content of the next part of the presentation. For example: 'But what can we do about it?'

– Formulate the transition moments in a surprising way. Try not to use standard phrases such as 'After discussing the main causes of the perceived insecurity, I will now explain a few possible solutions.' Think of wording that sounds better and that will engage the audience more, such as 'In short, the feeling of insecurity is caused by three D's: Damage, Debris, and Density of traffic. We are going to replace this with ABC: Alternative transport, Bins, and Cops. I will now explain how we can do this.'

9.2.3   Ending

'This was what I wanted to tell you today and I will leave it at that'. This ending betrays a lack of preparation: The speaker has not put enough thought into the ending. That is a shame, because an engaging peroratio of a presentation is often what your listeners remember the most, especially if you manage to include some pathos to evoke certain feelings in the listeners. Make use of that classical insight to prevent your presentation from tapering off. You should carefully prepare your conclusion instead of relying on your ability to improvise. The ending is too important and difficult to make up on the spot. A good ending to a presentation generally contains the same elements as that of a written text: a summary, a conclusion, and a final remark (see also section 8.1.7). If you want, you can also pose a question to the listeners.

– In the *summary*, you can repeat the key answers to the questions from your short text schema that was the basis for your presentation, which you also mentioned during the introduction.

– If your speech leads to a clear *conclusion*, you should emphasize it again and, if necessary, provide some recommendations. A presentation does not always have to end with a conclusion. For example, if your goal was to provide an overview of the different applications of Blackboard in higher education, you can suffice with a summary of the points you discussed and some memorable final words. If you do draw a conclusion, for instance that Blackboard could be used more efficiently in higher education, then you can minimize your summary and instead reiterate the facts that support your conclusion.

- For the *final remark*, try to think of a remarkable example, a beautiful image or a story, where appropriate with some pathos, that the audience will remember. If you manage to link this to what you said at the opening of the presentation, the audience will feel that your speech is nicely rounded off.

- One element that specifically belongs to the ending of a presentation is the *request for reactions*. If you want the audience to ask questions or engage in a discussion, you should finish your presentation with an invitation to a follow-up. A very simple strategy is to end your presentation with 'Are there any questions?', but that is a quite worn-out ending and usually not very stimulating to the audience. A good alternative is to invite your listeners to think about a question or proposition that you saved for the ending.

Ladies and gentlemen.

At the start of this presentation, I told you the story of Josie Richards, the eldest daughter of a working-class family from Liverpool, who in the 1960s had the opportunity to be the first of her family to go to secondary school, and from there go on to university. I am sure Josie owed part of her success to her own dedication and talent. But perhaps even more important was that her head teacher felt that children from the working class should also be able to continue learning. Josie was also lucky to have parents who dared to follow the head teacher's advice, and who dared to have their daughter prepared for a way of life they did not know themselves. Last but not least, there was the government's emancipation policy, which was aimed at giving ambitious young people the chance to realize their ambitions, no matter what social class they came from.

You may wonder what happened with Josie Richards. Well, I can tell you that. But first I have to admit something. The story was completely true, except for one thing. That girl was not called Josie Richards. That girl was me. After my graduation, I immediately got a job as a university lecturer; later on I obtained my PhD and a while later I became a professor. Perhaps it would be good to remind yourself of stories like this—of which there are many—next time you hear our Minister of Education say that it 'bothers her that it seems that nowadays everyone only wants to get further in life, and claims the right to the best education possible'. Her predecessors had a very different view on this. They tried to create the conditions for every child to develop its talents to the max, no matter where they came from. And that was fortunate, I dare say on behalf of all children who indeed were given the opportunity to make full use of their talents. Let's hope that this statement of our present minister turns out to have been a slip of the tongue, and that in the coming years the emancipation of disadvantaged groups will once more receive the full attention of both herself and her successors.

This speaker goes to great lengths to make her point. She finishes the story she started her presentation with, and surprises her audience by telling them that it was her own story. In doing so, she makes the story very personal, and thus engages the feelings of the listeners. They will probably sympathize with her and may know similar stories. If the speaker succeeds in touching the emotions of the audience (which requires honesty and a certain degree of restraint), this will likely increase her chances of convincing the audience that the Minister's policy should be changed.

As is the case with every research project, in hindsight I should also mention some limitations. For example, the assignment that the participants were given may have had more influence on their behavior than we would have liked. Moreover, the analysis of the results showed that the reliability of some measurements was quite low. I may also have overlooked alternative explanations for the results. But I'm getting ahead of myself. I'm curious to hear what you have to say about it and therefore I'd now like to change my role from speaker to that of a discussion partner.

In this conclusion, the speaker already provides input for the discussion.

In the last 20 minutes, I have shown you why I think it is important for our company to start offering public and private workshops. In my opinion, the most important advantages are the financial benefits and that we will have more contact with those surrounding us. However, the investment should not be too high. This means that we should initially only offer courses on subjects we have enough knowledge on and we already have some experience with. I would now like to invite you to join me in identifying and discussing specific options. What kind of workshops can we think of? If you could come up with ideas, I will write them down; afterwards we can examine them together to determine how attractive and feasible they are.

Here too, the speaker takes the lead in the discussion, this time by proposing a brainstorm.

9.3   Style

It is not easy to formulate complex information in a clear and compelling way, especially if you have not written out the whole text of your presentation. But it certainly is important. It is not for nothing that in classical rhetoric clarity (Latin: *perspicuitas*) was considered one of the four style virtues (Latin: *virtutes dicendi*). The other style virtues were attractiveness (Latin: *ornatus*), appropriateness

(Latin: *aptum*), and correctness (among the speakers of Latin: *Latinitas*). Some two thousand years later, these are still characteristics of good and effective language use in an oral presentation. What you say should be clear, it should sound attractive and fascinating, and it should fit the occasion. When you speak at a party, you must express yourself differently than when you speak on a sad occasion, such as a funeral. And finally: Even in an oral presentation, you should avoid language errors. They can distract attention and contribute to a less positive image of you as a speaker than you would wish. Chapter 4 already includes much information about the effects of a wide range of formulation choices. Below we will briefly review some extra possibilities for a clear and attractive style in an oral presentation.

9.3.1 Clarity

For clarity, the following specific requirements apply to a presentation.
- *Use short sentences.* Long, composite sentences are often difficult to follow, not to mention the problem of breath pauses when you are pronouncing them. Especially in large rooms, you will be less intelligible if you speak in long sentences.
- *Don't be too precise with numbers.* If you talk about election results, you can of course say that 17.1% of the German voters voted for party X, but an expression such as 'party X attracted more than one-sixth of the German voters' or 'one in six of the German voters voted for party X' is more likely to stick.
- *Provide the information step by step.* Do not put all information in one sentence; first outline the context before coming to your point.

> The E26 motorway is the main thoroughfare in this part of the country. In recent years, the E26 has also been number one in the national top ten of long traffic jams. Early last year, work was started on widening the section of the road between Robinstown and New Aduard from three to six lanes. Everyone was very surprised when the work was halted at the end of last year. Why did that happen? The new minister's judgment was that at a number of places along the motorway the air would be polluted too much.

Information provided step by step with short sentences. The speaker first sketches the context (the importance of the E26, the widening of the highway) and then presents the core information (the halting of the project). Before presenting that core information, she builds up extra attention ('Everyone was very surprised [...]'). And finally, she uses a question ('Why did that happen?') to announce the explanation she wants to give for what happened.

9.3.2   Attractiveness

Your presentation should not only be clear but also attractive. We mention a number of rhetorical figures that can work well not only in political speeches and in speeches for special occasions but also in business presentations.

- *Repetition* and *parallelism* can evoke emotions and be more convincing. Especially *bicolons* and *tricolons* can render your words more compelling and easier to remember (also see section 4.4.4). You list two elements, preferably alliterative ('part and parcel', 'brains and beauty'), or three elements, also preferably alliterative, and with a climax at the end: 'Veni Vidi Vici'—'I came, saw, and conquered (Julius Caesar)'; 'Tell me and I forget, teach me and I remember, involve me and I learn' (Benjamin Franklin).
- *Metaphors and imagery* can take your lecture to a higher level: 'The world is a book and those who don't travel have only read one page' (Saint Augustine of Hippo); 'A hospital bed is a parked taxi with the meter running' (Groucho Marx).
- *Contrasts and paradoxes* (seeming contradictions) can give your audience food for thought and make your presentation more exciting: 'I can resist anything but temptation' (Oscar Wilde); 'All animals are equal, but some are more equal than others' (George Orwell).
- *Questions for the audience* can raise extra attention. The listeners are, as it were, forced to think about the issue before the speaker provides the answer.

When we allow freedom to ring, when we let it ring from every village and every hamlet, from every state and every city, we will be able to speed up that day when all of God's children, black men and white men, Jews and Gentiles, Protestants and Catholics, will be able to join hands and sing in the words of the old Negro spiritual, 'Free at last! Free at last! Thank God almighty, we are free at last!'

In his famous *I have a dream* speech[19], Martin Luther King made abundant and very effective use of the classical repetition technique, in the form of both bicolons (*'every village and every hamlet'*, *'every state and every city'*) and tricolons ('black and white, Jews and Gentiles, Protestants and Catholics'), ending in the literal repetition of the words 'Free at last!'.

We need to be prudent in our spending and remain practical and realistic in our approach, and if I may, Honorable Speaker, I borrow from the words of Antonio Gramsci, one of the Marxist scholars of Italy, who once said: 'The point of modernity is to live without illusions while not becoming disillusioned.'

19   King, M. L. (1963, August 28). *'I Have a Dream …'* Retrieved from https://www.archives.gov/files/press/exhibits/dream-speech.pdf

Indeed, we are not illusionary about the global economic situation nor disillusioned about the prospects of a brighter future. All that we need is to find new ways to contend with the constraints of the global economy and the effects it has on developing economies. In the process we must master the technique of knowing how to sail on the side of the winds to weather the storm as we navigate to our destiny, otherwise our vessel too will sink like the Titanic.

In this part of his 2013-2014 budget speech,[20] South African Paul Mosethla Sebegoe, member of the Executive Council of North West Province, used various rhetorical means to present his argument: a paradox ('living without illusions while not becoming disillusioned') and a metaphor ('weathering the storm and not sinking like the Titanic').

In the past, textbooks were light and teachers were heavy—now it's the other way around.

With this double contrast ('in the past – now' and 'light – heavy'), used in his 2007 Kohnstamm Lecture, Dutch Professor Frits van Oostrom accentuated a structural problem in modern education. In line with the problem's image that he created in this way, further in his speech he advocated 'leaner and cheaper' textbooks and 'heavier loaded, better educated' teachers.

After his wife's death, a spouse receives everything and the children's claim is only paid after his death. However, this does not mean that he has to spend everything before he can apply for social welfare, because he can also pay the children their shares earlier. If he does so and then calls on social welfare, the municipality probably cannot refuse his request.

This speaker uses only declarative sentences, creating a monotonous text.

After his wife's death, a spouse receives everything and the children's claim is only paid after his death. Does that mean that he has to spend everything before he can apply for social welfare? No, because he can also pay the children their shares earlier. If he does so and then calls on social welfare, can the municipality refuse his request? No, probably not.

Now the speaker asks two questions ('Does that mean that […]?'; 'If he does so and then calls on social welfare, can the municipality refuse his request?'), making the speech livelier and more engaging.

20   Sebego, P. M. (2013, March 12). *2013-2014 Provincial Budget Speech*. Retrieved from http://www.treasury. gov.za/documents/provincial%20budget/2013/1.%20Provincial%20Budget%20Speeches/North%20 West%20-%20Budget%20Speech%20-%2012%20March%202013.pdf

9.4   Delivery

Good preparation is essential for a good performance of the presentation, but it is no guarantee. In this section, we will discuss the most important aspects of the execution of your presentation. The same requirements from classical rhetoric that we described in section 9.3 (the *virtutes dicendi*) still apply. Your words should be clear, your presentation attractive, your performance appropriate for the occasion, and your language and pronunciation correct. In this section, we give some recommendations for meeting these classical requirements in a modern presentation.

9.4.1   Reading and improvizing

Almost every speaker makes use of a written text to some extent. Sometimes a speaker has fully written out the text, as is often the case with speeches from official dignitaries. They read aloud from the written text, although they may occasionally deviate from it and improvise. The best speakers can do this without the audience being really aware of the fact that they are reading from a written text. This is easier with the help of an autocue, which enables a speaker to read the text without losing eye contact with the public.

Speakers rarely learn their entire presentation by heart. We would not recommend this either, and not only because the preparation will then take a lot of time. An even more important reason is that if you attempt to deliver a seemingly spontaneous speech, which you in fact completely memorized, you will often sound very artificial. Still, in some cases it can be useful to practice your speaking schedule so thoroughly that you are fully familiar with the written version of certain parts of your presentation, particularly the introduction, the transition moments, and the ending. If you know those parts more or less by heart, it will be easier to stick to the text you prepared without losing contact with the public.

The most common way of delivering a speech is with the use of notes from your speaking schedule. You can find an example in section 9.1.3. Now you have to find a good way to use this schedule for your delivery. The most important thing is that you maintain a good balance between reading and improvizing and that you are sufficiently detached from your written text to make eye contact with your audience.

– Make sure that the font size is large enough for you to read it from some distance. This also applies to system cards, which are easier to hold in your hands.
– Make sure that the sheets of your speaking schedule or your system cards are in the correct order. Do not forget to number them in case you accidentally drop them.

9.4.2   Use of voice

Many speakers would prefer to have the sonorous voice of a famous actor or presenter, but sadly most people are not so lucky. Still, even if your voice is not remarkable, there is a lot you can do to make sure the audience finds it pleasant to listen to you. The most important strategy is variety.

Volume
–   Try to talk loud enough to be heard in the room, but do not put a strain on yourself. You should still be able to raise your voice somewhat at important moments. In fact, talking loudly is not the only or even the best way to catch the audience's attention. At some key moments, for example when you introduce an important problem, a central proposition, or a conclusion, you can even make your speech more intense by speaking softly, articulating the words more clearly, and including pauses.
–   When you are using a microphone, always test them carefully. Do not talk more softly if the sound is too loud, because that takes away the nuance from your voice. Instead, lower the microphone or keep it a little further away.
–   If there is noise in the room, do not try to override it by talking louder, but ask for silence, speak softly, use pauses, and keep eye contact with the audience.

Speaking style
–   Try speaking slower than you are used to do. Also try adapting your speaking speed to the length, difficulty, and importance of a passage. The best speed also depends on your articulation: If you articulate clearly, it is less of a problem if you speak faster.
–   Do not worry too much about your accent if you have one. As long as you make sure the audience can understand you, most listeners will not mind that they can hear where you are from.
–   Occasionally include a pause, especially when you are moving on to a new main question or a new key answer. Three to five seconds of silence indicate to the audience that you are going to introduce a new point. Silence also attracts attention: Experienced teachers know that you can silence a classroom by being silent yourself, so that pupils wait in suspense for what will happen.
–   If you find it difficult to remain silent in front of a room full of listeners, try to find something to do during the moment of silence: Take a sip of water or re-arrange your papers.

9.4.3 Appearance, posture, and body language

What impression do you make on your listeners? Do you appear insecure, or do you come across as serious and confident? You can make a video recording (without sound) when you are speaking to hold up a mirror to yourself, so to speak. There are several guidelines when it comes to appearance.

Clothing and accessories
–   Wear clothing that is appropriate for the situation. Make sure you feel at ease with the clothes you choose. If you normally never wear a tie, skirt, or dress, do not wear it now, unless the situation absolutely requires it. It is generally better not to dress too ostentatiously. In terms of style, you would rather be overdressed than underdressed.
–   Also pay attention to your accessories. It is usually better to avoid distracting jewelry. You should also try to avoid 'unintentional' accessories such as a jacket with stuffed pockets. They make a disorderly impression and may distract the public.
–   Make sure you have turned off your phone before starting the presentation.

Feet and posture
–   Make sure you are not swaying. Place your feet firmly on the ground, spreading your weight so that you do not slant or lose balance. Keep your back straight.
–   Do not be too static. If the setup allows, take an occasional step to the left or right, or in the direction of the audience and back. A step aside can help to draw attention to the screen, if you are using one. A step forward is appropriate when you are addressing the audience directly. You can take a step back when you summarize and finish a section. However, do not overdo it: If you walk back and forth too much, you will make a restless impression.

Hands
–   Keep your hands in the right place. We recommend the so-called applause position, the posture just before you start applauding. With this posture you make a lively, active impression, it is easy to make gestures, and you avoid some common mistakes: hand in pocket (slouching, disinterested), hands on the hips (challenging, aggressive), crossed arms (detached, authoritative), or hands clasped in front of you (shy).
–   Although a lectern may make you feel more secure, it may also create a barrier between speaker and audience. You can avoid this by occasionally taking steps sideways or backwards (see above), although this may not be possible if you

use a fixed microphone. In any case, it is better not to clasp the lectern in your hands, as this makes a static and rigid impression.

Eyes
– Be aware of the direction of your gaze. If you use digital slides, do not look at the projection screen, but use the computer's or notebook's screen to keep track of your slides. Only look at the screen if you want to draw particular attention to what it shows, or for example when you are showing a video—by watching it together with your audience, you show how interesting the video is.
– Facial expressions can also support your message. You can show (or pretend) that you are surprised, worried, happy, or disappointed. This will make your presentation livelier.
– Looking at your papers does not have to be a problem, as long as you do not do it all the time. Of course you should know the main points of your presentation, but everyone will understand if you occasionally look at the notes in your speaking schedule. If you refer to numbers or quote someone, you are more credible if you do so from the paper, because you show that you want to be precise and do not want to make mistakes.
– If you do not look at your papers, look into the room and seek eye contact with your listeners. Be careful that you do not stare and that you change who you are looking at often enough. Listeners usually appreciate it if you make eye contact, and it allows you to respond to any signals that show the audience does not understand you or is starting to get bored.

9.4.4 Visual aids

Well-chosen illustrations can clarify your message and make your presentation livelier and more attractive. But use them sparingly. Few things are more annoying than a series of digital slides with endless lists of bullet points, especially when the speaker reads them aloud almost literally. This will give listeners the impression— and sometimes not unjustly—that the slides are intended more as a reminder for the speaker than a service to the audience. Instead, you could even decide not to use slides at all. Because they are used so widely, you will stand out positively by not using them. There are also situations when slides are never recommended:
– occasional speeches at parties or sad occasions;
– recruiting or motivating presentations, for instance political speeches at meetings or demonstrations;
– presentations in situation where digital slides are not available, for example during a lunch meeting in a canteen or in the open air.

If you do use digital slides, limit them to those parts where they are really functional, for instance to show examples or trends. Recommendations for the layout and graphic design can be found in chapter 5. You can also use objects to support your speech.

If you do use illustrations, make sure that your presentation does not become a media spectacle. Images, objects, and multimedia applications can be useful to attract attention, add some variation, or clarify certain points, but they should remain *supportive*.

9.5   Two special types of presentations

However relevant the advice from classical rhetoric may still be, the world has not stood still since antiquity. Below we briefly discuss two useful presentation types from the last decades. What they have in common is an emphasis on conciseness. Many examples of these models can be found on the internet.

9.5.1   Elevator pitch

The *elevator pitch* is named after the ability of a seller who can informally sell a product or idea in the very short time that it takes an elevator to go from the lowest to the highest floor (up to two minutes). The elevator pitch is often connected with the AIDA formula from the field of marketing and advertising. You should first attract *Attention* with a surprising opening, then *Interest* by posing a question to your audience, then *Desire* by mentioning the advantages of your product or idea, and lastly facilitate an *Action* by explaining as clearly as possible what they should do to quickly benefit from your product or idea. Good preparation is essential for a successful elevator pitch. Only then will you be able to achieve maximum effect within the measured time.

The elevator pitch approach is also recommended for job interviews. When you are asked 'to tell something about yourself', you can address the questions of who you are, what you have to offer, what you can add to the organization, and what you are looking for in the right order.

9.5.2 Pecha kucha

The concept of the *pecha kucha* (pronounced peh-cha-koo-cha, with equal emphasis on each syllable) was developed in Japan by two architects, in response to the many boring and lengthy presentations they had to endure from fellow architects and other speakers. A pecha kucha—the Japanese term for the sound of conversation—adheres to a very strict template. The speaker has exactly 6 minutes and 40 seconds to present 20 slides, which contain very little or no text at all. You can use short audio or video clips. The slides appear and disappear automatically and remain on screen for exactly 20 seconds. This forces the speaker to be creative and concise and to prepare very well.

It is useful to have a system card for each slide with a text that you have written out completely, so you know it will last exactly 20 seconds. Depending on the speed of your speech, this amounts to 40 or 50 words per slide. All around the world, people organize special pecha kucha evenings, with presentations on all kinds of topics. Even in this short amount of time—6 minutes and 40 seconds—you can give an interesting, informative, and convincing presentation about research.

Key points

Preparation

- For a successful oral presentation, thorough preparation is essential. It is important that you realize what your main goal is and what barriers you may have to overcome with your audience. This determines the right balance you should aim to strike between the classical aspects of ethos, logos, and pathos.
- Pay close attention to the characteristics of the situation in which you will be speaking (reason, time, program, space, and facilities) and of the audience you are addressing (size, prior knowledge, interest).
- Taking into account the information provided by this orientation, draw up a short text schema. The theme, the main questions, and the key answers will form the basis of the content and structure of your presentation. Elaborate your short text schema, together with the introduction and the conclusion, in your speaking schedule. This will allow you to practice, preferably for a few critical listeners who will provide you with feedback.

Parts of the presentation

- In the introduction, immediately draw the attention of your audience. Work on your ethos and provide a clear preview. It is advisable to write out the introduction.
- In the midsection, discuss the questions from the text schema on which your speaking schedule is based. Preferably write out the transition moments in which you move from answering one main question to the next.
- Begin the ending of the presentation with a summary in which you mention the key answers to the main questions you discussed in the middle section. Then comes the conclusion, which is brought to a close with a final remark, preferably one that reminds the audience of the opening of your presentation. It is also best to write out the ending part of your presentation.

Style

- For an oral presentation, pay extra attention to clarity (short sentences, global indications of quantities, information presented step-by-step) and attractiveness (repetition and parallelism, metaphors and imagery, contrasts and paradoxes, questions for the audience).

Delivery

- You can read from paper the parts you have written out (introduction, transition moments, and ending), but it is better if you have practiced your speaking schedule intensively beforehand, so that you are so familiar with the written formulations of those parts that you can more or less present them by heart.
- You can formulate the parts you have not written out in an improvizing manner, based on the keywords you have written down in the speaking schedule.
- Make sure that the use of your voice is varied, that you speak loud enough without forcing yourself, that you speak more slowly than you are used to, and that you occasionally include a pause. Do not worry too much about your accent.
- Try to make a serious, confident impression by choosing appropriate clothing and by adopting a firm but non-static posture by holding your hands in the right place and by looking at your audience.
- Be sparing with visual support, especially with digital slides that contain only point-by-point enumerations. Limit the use of illustrations to those parts of the presentation where they are truly functional.

Two special types of presentations

- With an elevator pitch, you try to convince your audience in a very short time. A suitable starting point is often the AIDA formula: Attention, Interest, Desire, Action.
- For a pecha kucha, you have exactly 6 minutes and 40 seconds available. In this time frame, you present exactly 20 slides that are shown for exactly 20 seconds each, preferably with little or no text.

Assignment

Job application tips

Purpose of the assignment

You will practice making an introduction for a presentation.

Subject matter
Section 9.2.1
Section 8.1.5
Section 1.5.2

Tasks
1   Think of an introduction for the presentation in the situation below and write it out completely.
2   Explain what elements you have incorporated in the introduction with regard to attention, ethos, and preview.
3   Also practice the execution of this introduction. Ask listeners for feedback, and make a note of their most important remarks and suggestions.

Situation sketch
The *Facility Management* course from which you recently graduated is organizing a business day for the fifth time. The aim of this annual activity is to bring students into contact with the professional working environment. Several large companies such as Shell and AkzoNobel and a number of smaller companies have set up a promotion stand where students can go for information and questions. There will also be various lectures.

The organization has found five interesting speakers, including a top manager of Shell and an employee of Akzo. But the organizers are still not completely satisfied. They would prefer to also have a speaker who can talk about applying for a job, but the business day will take place very soon, and where will they find a speaker on such short notice? Ruth Baker, one of the organizers, suddenly has an idea. Six months ago, she met a former student who didn't have to look long for a nice job and who is often involved in application procedures in his organization. Maybe he would like to tell the students something about applying, given that he is a successful expert himself.

You are that former student. A few months ago you started working as an employee at Bond & Partners, a large consultancy firm. When Ruth calls you, you are not very enthusiastic, but you are flattered by her request and you say yes. Ruth is very happy with your decision. A few days later she calls you with more information. She says the business day is expected to be especially well-attended by senior students who will soon graduate. Because the course already pays some attention to writing cover letters, it would be nice if you could mainly discuss the actual job interviews. You have half an hour for your presentation. There will probably be around 120 students attending your lecture. The lecture will be held in a spacious room, and you can use digital slides or videos if you want.

    The day of the lecture is approaching and you are well on your way with the preparation. The core of your lecture is almost finished: You know what you want to say and in what order.

Text schema
For this presentation, use the following text schema.

> THE JOB INTERVIEW
> What is the goal of the organization?
> What is the goal of the applicant?
> What are the characteristics of a good applicant?
> How do you become a good applicant?
> What happens during a job interview?
> How do you make a good impression?
> How does the organization make the final decision?

10 Professional conversations

◀ *Weaver's workshop*, Cornelis Gerritsz Decker, 1659. Two weavers are bent over a loom, engaged in a conversation. On the left a spinning wheel, on the right a cradle and household goods.

For your professional career, it is not only important that you engage in informal conversations with your colleagues like these weavers seem to do, but you also need to be able to participate in professional conversations to reach specific organizational goals.

A good conversation

If you've ever gone on a date with someone you really liked and wondered if it was a success, the answer is pretty simple. Just think back on the conversations you had. As a newly released survey conducted by *Plenty of Fish* found, nine out of 10 singles say great conversation is the number one sign of a successful date.

I know it seems pretty obvious. I mean, you can't just go out with someone, stare at each other the entire night, and know you're meant to be. You have to talk to someone in order to know whether or not you really click. But according to the survey of 2,000 singles, it may not be as easy as it seems to connect on a date.

In fact, 65 percent of people believe that 'conversation is a lost art', and another 61 percent blame technology for messing with our ability to have meaningful face-to-face conversations. If fear of rejection stops you from even just talking to someone you like, you're not alone—48 percent of people say that's the number one reason why they're hesitant to make the first move. Not knowing what to say comes in at second.

Having good banter over text seems great initially. But knowing how to have a great conversation in person is much more important. According to nearly 90 percent of singles, they say they found someone more attractive after having a conversation with them. In fact, good conversations can give you the opportunity to showcase your intelligence, your 'sexy voice', or your sense of humor. According to singles, those are the top three things that made a date appear more attractive.

Source: Fellizar (2017).[21]

Despite all the modern communication tools we have at our disposal, a good person-to-person conversation is still very important when it comes to having real contact. It may even be the start of a life-changing romance. Being able to have a good conversation is not only paramount in the context of dating; for professional purposes too, it is important that you master the art of holding pleasant but effective conversations.

This chapter discusses person-to-person interaction with a focus on professional conversations, such as job interviews, performance interviews, appraisal interviews, consultation sessions, motivational interviews, journalistic interviews, and research interviews. Professional conversations differ from everyday, informal conversations in a number of ways.

– Professional conversations are institutionalized: They are always held in, with, or for an organization.
– Professional conversations are always meant to achieve an organizational goal, such as information transfer, problem-solving, consultation, or evaluation.
– Unlike most everyday conversations, professional conversations generally take place by appointment. Participants can prepare for the interaction.
– In professional conversations, the roles of the participants are generally fixed. For example, in a counseling interview there is a consultant and a client, and in a research interview there is an interviewer and an interviewee.

Characteristics of a professional conversation

The previous chapters treated communication mainly as one-way traffic: A sender sends a message to a receiver. In conversations, on the other hand, interaction is central. It is two-way traffic, with a series of messages from both sides. The participants are simultaneously senders and receivers of this series of messages: While a participant is saying something, he or she is at the same time also paying attention to the other and interpreting their attitude and behavior.

An important characteristic of such interaction is that neither the way of speaking nor what is said is determined by only one of the participants. The conversational partners together determine what they will discuss and how their conversation will develop. Because you can only partially influence the interaction and because you

21   Fellizar, K. (2017, July 19). *Singles say 'great conversation' is the mark of a successful date, so here's how to make it happen.* Retrieved from https://www.bustle.com/p/singles-say-great-conversation-is-the-mark-of-a-successful-date-so-heres-how-to-make-it-happen-71090

have to constantly respond to what your conversational partner says or does, it is not always easy to plan and hold a conversation in a systematic way. There is a risk that you will be carried away by what is discussed and have little control over the interaction. But for a well-trained professional, it is important to be able to oversee the progress of a conversation and to control it to some extent. The purpose of this chapter is to increase your knowledge and skills so that you are better able to do so.

Section 10.1 will focus on the preparation of a professional conversation. This is followed by a section on the introduction and conclusion of a professional conversation (section 10.2). Next, we will discuss the middle part (section 10.3). Finally, in section 10.4 we will discuss a number of basic techniques that you can use during a professional conversation.

10.1   Preparation

Just like an oral presentation or a written report, a conversation consists of different parts. There is an introduction, followed by the core or middle part, and finally there is a conclusion. But the planning of a conversation is much more difficult than that of one-way communication tasks. You can never fully foresee what is going to happen during the interaction, because that partly depends on your conversational partner. If during the course of the conversation you are surprised by unexpected turns, you cannot take your time to think about what strategy you should choose. You need to be able to respond quickly and adequately to your partner. This unpredictability is the reason why you have to prepare well. What tasks (or sub-tasks) will you have to deal with, what structure appeals to you, what basic techniques could you use, and what can you expect from your conversational partner in these respects?

10.1.1   Orientation

What do you want to achieve with the conversation, what does your conversational partner want to achieve, and what preconditions do you have to consider? Your goals, the goals of your partner, and the preconditions for the conversation determine to a large extent the content and the structure of the conversation and the tasks for which you need to prepare.

Your goals
As is the case when you want to write a text or give a lecture, during the preparation phase of a professional conversation you must have a clear idea of what you hope to achieve. During a conversation, you are sender and receiver at the same time. You

should therefore keep both roles in mind when you are preparing. The following table might help (see also section 1.2).

Type of goal	Orientation question as sender	Orientation question as receiver
Informative	What information do I want to transfer?	What questions do I want answered by my partner?
Instructive	What task do I want to instruct my partner to perform?	For what task do I need instructions?
Persuasive	What do I want to convince my partner of?	What do I want to form an opinion on?
Motivational	What action or behavior do I want to persuade my partner to undertake?	To what kind of action or behavior would I consent?
Affective	What emotions do I want to evoke in my partner?	What kind of behavior evokes emotions in me?

Preparation questions for familiarizing yourself with the goals of the conversation.

During the conversation, it is of great importance that you not only pay attention to the matter side and the appeal side but also to the self-expression side and the relationship side of the communication. Again, you should ask yourself beforehand what you want to achieve.

- With regard to the self-expression side: What impression do you want the other to have of you?
- With regard to the relationship side: How do you view your mutual relationship, and how do you think your partner views this? How do you want your relationship to be after the conversation, either in your view or your conversational partner's?

Your conversational partner's goals

If you have known your conversational partner for some time, it is usually not difficult to form an impression of him or her and of the goals that he or she wants to achieve beforehand. With someone you do not know, however, you will have to wait and see. Still, there are some ways you can try to form an idea of the other's goals before the conversation.

- Try to put yourself in the other's shoes and think about what their goals might be. You can do this using the questions in the right-hand column of the table above.
- See yourself through the eyes of your conversational partner. How does she view you? Is she curious about what you have to say or not? Does she see you

as a superior, a colleague, a competitor, a subordinate? What does she think you want to achieve with this conversation? Are there reasons why she might feel threatened by you?

– Are the goals of you and your partner identical, complementary, divergent, or opposite?

- *Identical*: You and your partner's goals are the same. For example, you want to solve a shared problem together.
- *Complementary*: Your goals are not the same, but they do complement each other. For instance, one of you wants to give information about an imminent policy change, while the other wants to know what this change will mean for his or her tasks.
- *Divergent*: You and your partner's goals do not correspond. A sales manager of a software company, for example, wants to sell the customer an advanced but expensive software product, while the customer is most interested in a cheap and simple package.
- *Opposite*: Your goals are not only different, but they are opposites. Achieving one goal is by definition unfavorable to the other. An example is a manager who asks the management for an expansion of her team, while the management wants to downsize due to an imminent merger.

Symmetry between conversational partners' goals.

Preconditions for the conversation

During the preparation, it is useful to consider some preconditions for a successful conversation.

– *Duration*. How long is the conversation likely to last?
– *Location*. This can be particularly important for difficult conversations. Does the conversation take place on your own familiar ground or at the other's—'in the lion's den'? The latter has the advantage that you can decide when you want to leave and thus end the conversation.
– *Report*. Will parts of the conversation be written down? If so, in what way, by whom, and who will receive the report? Do you want the minutes to remain confidential?
– *Mandate*. What subjects are you or your conversational partner allowed take decisions on, and when is it necessary to first ask your manager or client for permission?

Structure of the conversation

Although it is difficult to predict the exact course of the interaction beforehand, orienting yourself on a suitable structure is always useful. With proper preparation, you will be able to exert more influence on the structure of the conversation. Even if you do not have such influence, orientation is still important. You will be less surprised by the run of events because you can anticipate what will happen next. The set schemata discussed in section 2.2 can help you with this. For example, do you want the conversation to focus on a problem that needs to be solved, a measure that needs to be taken, a task that needs to be carried out, or a research project that you need to reach an agreement about? You can use these set schemata when you are preparing for a professional conversation in the same way as when you are thinking about the structure of a text or an oral presentation. We will discuss this in more detail in section 10.2.

Content of the conversation

If you have carefully thought about the structure of the conversation, you will have an idea of the content that may be discussed. You can then prepare for that content. If necessary, look up the information you think you need, for example by listing questions and arguments, and considering what questions and arguments your partner may bring up. Try to formulate your reaction to these as well.

It is always a good idea to make notes and take them with you. If you think that certain documents will be discussed, bring them with you too. Examples include a copy of your final thesis for a job interview or the report of your previous performance review for a new performance interview.

Make sure you not only prepare for the core of the conversation but also for the introduction and conclusion. What would be a good topic for social talk during the introduction (section 10.2.1)? What agreements should certainly be reached at the end?

Professional conversations are often seen as impersonal. However, there is no reason to assume that a good atmosphere and personal attention are not part of a professional conversation. It is sometimes said that a good professional conversation is hard on the job and soft on the person. This means that both parties should critically examine the subject of the conversation, resulting in lively discussions. At the same time, the conversational partners should both ensure that any disagreements do not affect their mutual relations.

With good preparation, you ensure that you always have a substantive response to the contributions of your partner. You are less likely to be surprised and thus less likely to react in a personal or emotional way.

Basic techniques for you and your conversational partner

As we will explain in more detail in section 10.4, various basic techniques are used in every professional conversation: informing, arguing, and enthusing; listening and observing; asking questions and follow-up questions; structuring; repeating, summarizing, and reflecting. The basic techniques you have to apply in a particular conversation are closely related to the nature of the conversation and your role. If it is a job interview and you are a member of the selection committee, there will be more emphasis on listening, observing, and asking questions (or follow-up questions). On the other hand, if you are conducting a counseling interview and you are the one giving advice, the emphasis for you will be more on providing information. Even if the conversation you are preparing for is not one of the standard conversations, it is still useful to ask yourself what basic techniques you could mainly use—and what you can expect the other to do in that respect.

10.2 Course of the conversation: introduction and conclusion

Each professional conversation unfolds in phases. These phases are partly determined by the content and the type of conversation. There are also phases that are almost always part of professional conversations, regardless of the content or the type of conversation: the introduction and the conclusion. These two phases are discussed below. In section 10.3 we will discuss the middle part, the core of the conversation.

10.2.1 Introduction

The introduction greatly determines the further course and atmosphere of the conversation. An introduction may contain the following elements, usually (but not necessarily) in this order:
– an opening during which the participants greet each other and start up the actual conversation;
– an indication of the conversation's goals during which the participants explain what they expect from the conversation and coordinate their goals with each other;
– a preview during which the participants try to agree upon an overall structure for the conversation;
– a discussion of preconditions during which the participants agree on practical matters such as the duration, reporting, and confidentiality of the conversation.

Opening
A professional conversation almost never directly starts with the actual subject. The participants first greet each other and engage in some social talk. The opening

largely determines the further tone of the conversation and thus the conversational and working atmosphere.

The greeting can be a hasty nod or simply a handshake, but it is often more extensive: 'Good afternoon, my name is Bradshaw. Take your seat.' The more formal the conversation and the less familiar the partners are with each other, the more important such a greeting becomes. The greeting phase is particularly important if there is an inequality in power or authority between the two participants. Such a difference can already be accentuated or reduced in the greeting phase.

> A manager having a conversation with a new, young employee can reduce the distance by introducing herself informally ('Hello, I'm Chareldine Swanepoel') and by not remaining at the desk in an authorative way, but standing up and walking towards the incoming assistant. The same manager can increase the distance by not introducing herself (implicit message: I am so important that you should know who I am) and by staying behind her desk.

Power differences can be accentuated or obscured in the opening phase of a conversation.

The greeting is often followed by a phase in which the participants talk about things that are not directly related to the subject of the professional conversation: social talk. For professional conversations, the goal of this social talk is often to create a conversational atmosphere in which both parties feel at ease and can talk easily. Then it is a matter of sensing and understanding when and how to start the actual conversation.

During the opening, it usually becomes clear who takes the initiative during the conversation. This is an important issue. After all, the person who has the initiative determines to a large extent the themes that are discussed, when they are discussed and for how long, and how formal the tone of the conversation is.

The division of roles during the conversation often determines who has the initiative (for example during a performance review or a job interview), but sometimes it is determined during the start-up phase. For conversations where there is no clear division of roles or power differences, participants often make proposals about the way in which the conversation is to take place.

A1:   Please continue, Mr. Putinaki. How was your trip here?
B1:   It was fine, thank you.
A2:   I'm glad you found the address so quickly. With all the diversions, our guests sometimes get lost in the neighborhood.
B2:   It took some searching indeed, but fortunately I left home early.
A3:   Great, please sit down. Can I offer you something? Coffee, tea?
B3:   Coffee please, black.

A4:   Okay, how are we going to set up this meeting? You may have some questions,
      I also have some. Shall I first give a short summary of the project so far?
B4:   That sounds good to me.

A welcomes B and starts the conversation with some social talk. In her fourth conversational turn (A4), A proposes to switch to the actual interview by addressing the content and the structure of the conversation.

Indication of the conversation's goals

To ensure an efficient and effective flow of the interaction, it is important that the participants gain insight into each other's goals at the beginning of the conversation. After all, that is what determines the course of the further conversation. Insight into those goals may prevent that one of the participants feels disappointed or annoyed after the conversation is concluded. There are various ways in which you can discuss goals during the introduction to the conversation. The participants can, for example, pay attention to:

– the reason for the conversation (why are we having this conversation?);
– the desired outcome of the conversation (what is asked of us?);
– the nature of the conversation (what kind of conversation are we going to have; do we want to familiarize ourselves with a certain issue or do we want to solve a problem?).

Sometimes there is a *hidden agenda*, for example if the participants have opposing goals, or if the mutual relationship is not very good. The exact goal of the conversation is then less clearly delineated. In such cases, too much clarity about goals may accentuate the contradictions, which will reduce the chance of success.

Okay, Linda, we agreed to talk about Karen Hayes' suggestion to draw up a memorandum on the training plan for apprentice salespeople. Well, I think she just wants some more information before the plan can be approved. So I suggest that we start reworking the parts of the plan now […].

The reason for the conversation makes it clear what goal should be achieved.

Well now, John, about that purchase of a new printer. I was actually hoping that we can come up with a clear proposal today, which I can then put on paper for dr. Flower. Does that make sense to you?

By indicating the desired outcome of the conversation, the speaker makes his goal clear.

> Hi Harry. Here we are for the appraisal interview. We're going to talk about your performance in our department […].

The type of professional conversation makes it clear what the subject will be.

> Well, Sally, let's get to the point. You'll have noticed that there have been quite a few complaints about your functioning lately. We thought it might be better to give you a different position within the company […].

> Well, I'd like to have a chat with you about your work, how things are going, how you and I feel about that, and so on. Perhaps we can start by listing the ideas that you and I have about your functioning […].

The goal of the speaker is to get Sally to accept another position. In the first fragment, the reason and the goal are formulated so directly that there is a great chance that Sally will quickly become defensive and dig her heels in. In this situation it may be better to be less explicit about the goals at the start of the conversation, as in the second fragment.

> Hello Mike. Lately, I've been hearing from some of your colleagues that you're not entirely satisfied with the way we organize our production process. That's why I thought it might be a good idea to take a closer look at your role in this company and the tasks you have.

In this example, at least one goal of the conversation is to investigate Mike's role and his tasks. What will be done with the outcome is left unresolved, however. Mike may think he is going to be reprimanded by his superior.

> Hello Mike. Lately I've been hearing from some of your colleagues that you're not entirely satisfied with the way we organize our production process. That's why I thought that it might be a good idea to take a closer look at your role in our company and the tasks you have.
>
> Although I would appreciate it if you could share your opinions about our production process with me in the first instance, I do agree with the general idea. I am pleased to have someone in our company who continues to look critically at the way in which we organize our processes, and who always sets a good example in the performance of his duties. That's why I'm thinking about proposing to the other members of our board that you will lead this department after Peter's retirement six months from now. How would you feel about that?

Only during the course of the conversation does it become clear that the ultimate goal of the manager is to offer Mike a promotion.

In daily practice, the goals of the conversational partners are often not, or only partly, made explicit. They sometimes only find out as they go along what the other wants to achieve and whether these goals are complementary or opposed to their own.

In a situation with great inequalities in status or power between the participants, it is sometimes difficult to directly ask for the other's goals. The more equal the conversational partners feel, the easier this becomes.

Preview of content and structure

Once the goal of the conversation is clear to everyone, it is useful to define the general content and structure of the conversation. This increases the chance that the conversation will be formal and systematic. If you have a list of points that you think need to be addressed, you can share them with your partner. You can also indicate which points you think have priority. If you and your partner do not have a clear structure in mind at the start of the conversation, you can look at each other's points and together determine the order in which you should deal with them.

In this respect too, good preparation can help you, but in practice this is sometimes less straightforward. You may think of some points only after you have already discussed that subject. Matters such as the goal of the conversation, the amount of effort you must put into actually conducting the conversation, but also your impression of your partner are likely to determine whether you will introduce new points during the conversation.

Agreements on preconditions

The introduction is also the moment to make agreements on a number of preconditions, if you have not done so yet when you made the appointment: How much time do you have, will you make a report, and if so, who will receive a copy, and so on. If you determine the duration of the conversation, you will know how much time you can spend on each point, which makes it more likely that you will actually address all of the points you would like to make.

10.2.2 Conclusion

During the conclusion phase of the conversation, it is customary to summarize what has been said and make a follow-up appointment. There is also often some time for social talk at the end of the actual conversation, after which the participants say goodbye.

Summary

At the end of the conversation, you should check with your conversational partner whether you have addressed all the important points and whether you have achieved your goal. You can do this by summarizing the results of the conversation for each sub-topic. By doing so, you reduce the chance that you and your partner will each go your way with different ideas about the outcome of the conversation.

A summary is always a certain selection from the content of the conversation. For this reason, there is a risk that the participants do not agree on the summary. When you summarize, you should therefore give the other party ample opportunity to put forward any corrections or additions. You can do this by asking their consent at the end ('Have I summarized our conversation correctly?'), but it is often sufficient to give the other person the opportunity to react, for example by being silent and looking at the other questioningly.

Follow-up appointments

Many professional conversations lead to specific agreements about tasks that need to be performed. Even though you have already made these agreements during the course of the conversation, it is good to list them again at the end. You repeat who is going to do what, when, and how. In the case of important tasks, it is wise to put these agreements down in writing.

Social talk and goodbye

An informal conversation often occurs 'automatically' after the actual conversation has ended. The interaction then seems to be moving on to a different subject, often also in a different tone, without any problems. However, there are always contributions to the interaction that indicate a transition from the formal, substantive part of the conversation to the informal part.

A1: If my summary is correct, we have reduced the options for solving our space problem to two: a new building on the site behind our head office, or an extension of the leasing of some of our branches.

B1: Exactly.

A2: Your advice now is to go for the first option, given the structural nature of our lack of space.

B2: That's right.

A3: Okay, I'll present both options with your advice to our board and the facility manager, and next week we'll meet again to draw up a plan that we can present at the staff meeting.

B3: That's fine. I'll give you a call about that tomorrow.

A4: Well then, we did a lot in only half an hour!

B4: Absolutely.

A5: It's nice to prepare these things in a short talk, isn't it?

B5:   Sure, if we would discuss a topic like this for the first time in an official meeting, then there is a good chance that the result would be no more than a couple of half-made plans.

A6:   By the way, will we see you at Peter's farewell party, or are you already on vacation then?

At the beginning of this fragment, A summarizes what was discussed. After confirmation of this summary by B, A closes the subject of this conversation in his fourth turn. In his last turns, he evaluates the usefulness of this conversation and finishes with some social talk.

Try to reserve some time for social talk after the actual conversation. A few moments of social talk are important to avoid an abrupt ending to the interaction, to emphasize the good relations, and to express hope for good further contact. Finally, you can encourage a good atmosphere by the manner in which you say goodbye, for example by thanking someone for the conversation or guiding them towards the exit.

10.3   Course of the conversation: middle part

To shape the content and structure of the middle part—the core of the conversation—you can start from one of the set schemata, as with a text or presentation. We will discuss the use of set schemata below.

10.3.1   Set schemata

Set schemata (see section 2.2) are often useful to ensure that the middle part of the conversation runs smoothly. If, for example, the theme concerns an undesirable situation that warrants improvement, then you could use the questions from the set problem schema to solve the problem together. And if you want to explain to someone how best to carry out a certain task, the set action schema can be a good starting point.

Edith Bécaud is the manager of a new branch of *Croscus Collations* in Le Lamentin, located in the Outre-Mer department of Martinique, in the French West Indies. Edith has a problem. Over the next few weeks, her branch has to carry out a large order. All hands on deck. But in ten days' time, the Martinique carnival will begin, which Edith, as a true Canadian, did not think of when she closed the deal. A large number of staff members have announced that they will take five days off. What to do now? Edith raises the problem with her superior, managing director Gilbert Delpech.

In their conversation, Edith and Gilbert adhere to the set problem schema. Edith explains exactly what the problem is by answering a number of *elaboration questions*: What kind of order are we talking about, what is in the contract, how many employees have taken time off, how many will be present, and so on. Together, Edith and Gilbert discuss the *consequences* of returning the order, if they choose to do so: What will it cost, and how will it influence the relationship with the client? And what would happen in the company if Edith forces the employees to keep working?

As unpleasant as it may be for Edith, Gilbert also raises the issue of the *causes* of the problem. He points out that Edith herself is responsible. She could and should have informed herself about the typical by-products of the local culture in this part of the world, as Gilbert puts it.

Edith and Gilbert spend most of their conversation discussing possible *solutions*. Canceling the order, outsourcing the work, hiring temporary staff (but where do you find them?)—every option is scrutinized. Eventually Edith and Gilbert decide to propose to the partygoers that they commit themselves to work three overtime hours daily before and after the carnival; they will be paid in money or extra days off in another period of the year. Finally, Gilbert makes it clear to Edith that he expects situations such as this one not to happen again. Edith cannot afford to make any more mistakes like this.

The set problem schema is used as a template for a professional conversation.

The main questions from a set schema often lead to a certain division of tasks during the conversation. One participant has the initiative for one question, while the other participant takes the initiative for another question. Other questions may demand equal input from both participants.

Particularly in the case of conversations that involve negotiation, that is to say when participants are pursuing different or contradictory goals, it is important to examine which schema may be most suitable for you. One subject often allows for different schemata.

Company CEO Helga Schröder is preparing an important conversation with Fritz Zondermann, chairman of the works council of her company. Helga decides to try and base the structure of the conversation on the set measure schema, with DISMISSALS IN OUR COMPANY as the theme of the conversation. But Mr. Zondermann would benefit more from a structure based on the set problem schema, with THE PROBLEMS OF THE COMPANY as the theme of the conversation. After all, following the set problem schema, dismissal of personnel would not be more or less accepted as a given, which would be in Mrs. Schröder's interest. The set problem schema also creates the opportunity to address other issues, which is more in Mr. Zondermann's interest. Moreover, the set problem schema more clearly highlights the causes of the problem, which gives Mr. Zondermann the opportunity to address the failing management policy, which is not in Mrs. Schröder's interest.

Sometimes the parties differ in terms of the conversation structure that would serve their interest best.

As explained in the introduction to this chapter, a conversation is characterized by interaction. In practice, this means that a conversation cannot be strictly controlled according to set schemata. The set schemata do, however, offer a good basis for exploring complex conversation topics.

10.4   Basic techniques

During a professional conversation, the participants should exchange information in a clear and objective way and develop positions and solutions to problems in order to ensure that the goals of the conversation are achieved. In addition to good planning, this requires certain basic techniques that you can use during a conversation: informing, arguing, and enthusing; listening and observing; asking questions and follow-up questions; structuring; repeating, summarizing, and reflecting. You should consider not only how to use these techniques, but also under what circumstances, for what purpose, and from what capacity. Here we will discuss a number of these basic techniques.

10.4.1 Informing, arguing, and enthusing

During conversations, you often put forward information and ideas that you think your conversational partner should know about. For example, you want to explain what you think should be done to successfully finish a project on which you are both working, or you want your partner to agree that the company should not purchase a new operating system. In such cases it is important that you are clear and that you are able to convincingly argue and enthuse.

If you want to convince your partner of your position, you need solid argumentation: You first provide factual information and then put forward arguments that hold up against criticism (see chapter 3). This way, you emphasize a rational approach.

Lubinga proposes a new discount system for people with the lowest incomes in our municipality. However, I do not think that we should agree with her proposal. I hope you will feel the same. First of all, the system as proposed by Lubinga would be far too expensive. A simple sum shows that the annual cost would amount to a quarter of a million euros. Our budget does not allow for this. Above all, however, I object to a side effect that would undoubtedly occur: It would stigmatize the citizens with the lowest incomes in an unacceptable way. They have to make themselves known as paupers at every cultural facility or sports association they want to be part of.

The speaker provides two arguments why she does not believe there should be a new discount system for the lowest income groups. Firstly, it would be too expensive. This argument is supported with specific information on its costs. Secondly, according to the speaker, the discount system would stigmatize citizens with low incomes.

Highlighting factual information and arguments is a great way to convince each other of positions and ideas. This ensures that you talk as professionals, that the results can be easily summarized, and that you can effectively defend decisions you took together against third parties. A good preparation can help you make a clear argument during a conversation and thus increase your chances of success.

– Make sure that you know beforehand what information and arguments you want to put forward and which ones you do not. It is better to have three strong arguments than six weaker ones. Finish with your strongest arguments.
– During your preparation, try to think of counterarguments that your conversational partner might bring up and how you can refute them. Stay one step ahead of your partner by incorporating possible counterarguments into your own argument: 'I understand that the investment costs are very high and that this may cause problems, but according to my calculations we will have earned back a second production line within a year. Look here [...]'

Of course, it is also important to present your arguments well.

– Show that you believe in your own arguments. Look at your partner, speak clearly, and avoid unnecessary hedging words such as 'perhaps' and 'probably'.
– In most cases, you are the one who provides information and arguments that are meant to convince your conversational partner of your position. However, sometimes it is more effective if you encourage your partner to come up with arguments in support of your own position. You may start to formulate your position carefully and then suggest to your partner that you think of arguments together: 'Suppose we say that [...], how would you then [...]?' But be careful of using this method too much, because it may come across as condescending.

Persuasion is not simply a matter of rational argumentation. Your arguments are more effective if you are enthusiastic about the issue that you are arguing about. That is of course not always automatically the case. But if you manage to appear enthusiastic, you will be more convincing. It is more difficult for your partner to interrupt someone who clearly believes in a case. An enthusiastic speaker is:

– *vibrant*: The speaker makes gestures, provides quick calculations, stands up and walks around sometimes, looks closely at the conversational partner, and speaks clearly and without too much reservations;

– *focused*: The speaker gives examples, outlines possibilities, and does not waste too much time on reflection;

– *cooperative*: The speaker is focused on achieving a goal together and emphasizes how pleasant it is to achieve that goal together.

10.4.2 Listening and observing

One of the most important and at the same time most underestimated conversational skills is listening. At first this may seem like an activity and not a skill, but on closer consideration you will see that listening is a lot more than 'opening your ears'.

It may sound obvious, but by listening you collect information from your partner and may find out what they want from you, what their position is, or what problems they have. In practice, however, partners often listen with different goals and only pick up those things that fit with their own goals. The rest of the information will be lost. Sometimes conversational partners also listen only partially to each other, because they are already thinking about what they will say next. They may then even experience listening as an annoying interruption of their own contributions.

Listening carefully means that you empathize with the other person and actively try to find out what he or she means. This is also referred to as *empathic listening*. For empathic listening, it is important that you really try to understand the opinion, vision, or problem of your partner. Someone who listens empathically asks good questions and follow-up questions and reflects on what the other says. These basic techniques are discussed below. Empathic listening also means that you do not judge what the other person is saying in the middle of the conversation and that you do not come up with quick solutions to problems.

A1:   Okay, we've completed the planning for next month now. Wasn't there something else you wanted to discuss with me?

B1: Yes, I've had a bit of an unpleasant feeling about what's been going on in our department lately.

A2: Okay, since when have you had that feeling?

B2: Well, actually for quite a long time already. I've been thinking about it some three months now.

A3: And what makes you have this feeling?

B3: Well, it seems lately that the number of projects we work on is becoming more and more important. This creates an unpleasant competition. Colleagues are skimping their work, only so that they'll be able to start a new project as quickly as possible.

A4: So you think that the working atmosphere has deteriorated?

B4: Exactly. We don't help each other anymore. The new targets make it seem as if an 'every man for himself' mentality has crept in. People try to hijack projects from each other in all kinds of ways.

A5: Is it correct if I conclude that you feel the new targets are creating unhealthy competition and that they are at the expense of the quality of our work on the projects?

B5: Precisely, I've been hearing that from customers lately. Of course, that makes it all pretty painful.

A6: Yes, I can see that.

A limits herself here to asking questions and reflecting on what B says, in order to better understand his problem. With her summary in the fifth turn, A checks whether she has understood B correctly.

Listening is not simply registering what the other person is saying. One of the important aspects of listening is that you let your conversational partner know that he or she has your full attention. You can do this by looking at your conversational partner while he or she is speaking. Make sure that you don't constantly look the other in the eye while he or she is speaking, as this can make people feel uncomfortable.

You should also assume an active listening position. This means that you turn your body towards the speaker. Also consider the setup of the conversation. If you are facing each other and the table you are sitting on is narrow, do not lean too far forward. This may make you appear intimidating. If you are sitting next to each other or at the corner of a table, which is sometimes the case for consultation sessions, you cannot fully turn yourself towards the other.

It is not only your gaze and the positioning of your body that you can use to indicate your attention. You can also use body gestures, facial expressions, and short encouraging expressions ('okay'; 'hmm, hmm', 'oh?', 'really?') to show that you are actively listening. Many of these signals are at the same time confirmation or encouragement to the other to continue his or her story.

A1:   In this campaign we have chosen to focus not so much on the products them-
      selves but more on the placement of our products in the store.

B1:   Hmm, hmm.

A2:   We think that consumers do want to buy our products, but they don't notice them
      when they collect their weekend groceries because of the location in the super-
      market.

B shows A with a listening signal (hmm, hmm) that B is listening to A's explanation of the
sales strategy at hand.

A1:   In this campaign we have chosen to focus not so much on the products them-
      selves, but more on the placement of our products in the store.

B1:   Really?

A2:   We think that consumers do want to buy our products, but they don't notice them
      when they collect their weekend groceries because of the location in the super-
      market.

B2:   Okay!

Now B also gives positive signals about what A is saying.

10.4.3 Asking questions and follow-up questions

The most direct way to encourage your conversational partner to provide information is to ask questions. We distinguish between open-ended questions or open
questions, and closed-ended questions or closed questions.

–   By asking an *open question*, you give your partner a lot of freedom to choose the
    type of answer he or she wants to give, and you encourage detailed answers.
    Open questions often start with an interrogative word, such as what, why, how,
    and which. But this need not necessarily be the case. So-called yes-or-no ques-
    tions such as 'Can you tell me more about this?' or 'Have you ever experienced
    a similar situation before?' can also provoke a multitude of reactions.

–   *Closed questions* leave less room for the other. Questions such as 'Is it okay with
    you if we start now?' or 'What does a subscription to *The Guardian* cost these
    days?' limit the range of possible answers

Open questions are suitable if you want your conversational partner to tell you
as much as possible or if you want to show interest in his or her experiences or
opinions. Another reason you may want to start with an open question is that you
do not know exactly what is going on with regard to the topic of the conversation.

Closed questions are especially suitable if you want to obtain factual information ('Do you work with a word processor when you make invoices?') or if you want to avoid unnecessary elaborations and irrelevant information. A closed question can also be useful if you want to prevent the other party from talking around the topic and evading your question.

Some types of professional conversations come with a specific combination of open and closed questions. A social welfare interview, for example, often begins with the counselor asking open questions in order to obtain as much information as possible. Once a specific problem comes in sight, the counselor will start asking more closed questions.

If you want to know more about something the other puts forward, you can simply ask more questions. It is often best to ask a general question first. Suitable questions are, for example, 'Can you tell me more about this?' or 'How does that work?'. After that, you may want to ask for more specific information by asking follow-up questions related to earlier answers, for example 'Could you tell me what her arguments were?' or 'What would you advise me to do to make sure that our colleagues won't make that mistake any more?' Avoid asking a question that implies a negative evaluation of your conversational partner (a *comma-fool question*, as we call it), such as 'Okay, but didn't you know how much sugar there is in a soft drink?' or 'I see, but why did you pay so little attention to this important problem?'

If you want to encourage your conversational partner to provide more information, it may also be effective to remain silent for a while. The essence of a conversation is to talk to each other. If you do not, and remain silent, people quickly feel uncomfortable and tend to say something. By consciously introducing a pause into the conversation and looking at your conversational partner questioningly, you encourage him or her to continue talking. But beware: Silences can also have an alienating effect. Silences that last too long can make conversational partners feel uncomfortable, which does not improve the conversation.

10.4.4 Repeating, summarizing, and reflecting

By literally repeating some words that the other just spoke, preferably in a questioning tone, you can encourage your conversational partner to tell you more about the topic at hand.

A: I think we should quickly take the necessary measures to eliminate this type of abuse.

B: Measures?

A: I mean, we could be clearer about the registration procedure, for example. Now people often notice far too late that the registration period has expired. The office could well give a signal when the deadline has almost passed. And they could also be a little more flexible with the registration period that we use.

Because B repeats the word 'measures' in a questioning tone, A is encouraged to tell more about the measures she has in mind. If B had not repeated the word 'measures' but had repeated the word 'abuse' in a questioning tone, there is a good chance that A would have elaborated on that topic.

If you summarize the most important information from what your conversational partner said, you show that you are listening attentively, which has a stimulating effect. In addition, your summary may contain words that will give your partner new ideas. By formulating your summary in a questioning tone, you not only encourage the other to respond, you also give him or her the opportunity to correct you if you have not fully understood what was said.

If I understand you correctly, our mechanic has connected the wrong router, and your colleague Mrs. Carstens called us twice to say that there was still no Wi-Fi signal. We then sent someone else to solve the complaint. However, this new mechanic only succeeded in connecting part of your equipment to the router's Wi-Fi signal. The next day Mrs. Carstens called again to tell us that things still weren't working properly. Is this a correct summary of what happened?

With this summary, the speaker gives his conversational partner the opportunity to make any necessary corrections to his perception of the situation.

Reflecting is a special way of summarizing. You are holding up a mirror to the other, as it were, to stimulate him or her to think about what was said. By doing this, you may perhaps change the direction that the conversation is taking.

George Moustakis, a European politician, is suspended by his own party because of an integrity investigation into his conduct. Miriam Dohanny, a journalist, asks him: 'What exactly are you suspected of?' Mr. Moustakis gives a vague answer, after which Mrs. Dohanny asks him: 'How serious is the chance that the investigative committee will find something against you?' Mr. Moustakis replies: 'You should ask the committee.' Mrs. Do-hanny responds with this reflection: 'So your memory is so bad that you don't remember what you did right or wrong?' For a moment, Mr. Moustakis doesn't know how to reply.

A journalist uses a reflection to critically question the interviewee.

You can steer a conversation in your preferred direction by placing particular emphasis in your reflections on certain sides of your conversational partner's contributions: the matter side, the self-expression side, the relationship side, or the appeal side. There is a good chance that your partner's responses will be in line with the side that you emphasized in your reflection and that the conversation will further develop in that direction.

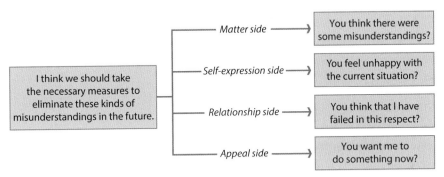

Different ways of reflecting, with emphasis on the matter side, the self-expression side, the relationship side, or the appeal side of an utterance of the conversational partner.

10.4.5 Structuring the conversation

A professional conversation should be conducted in an orderly fashion, particularly if you want to give or receive specific information about a well-defined topic in a short time. It is therefore important that you monitor the conversation structure properly and, where necessary, adjust it. Structuring is also useful to increase your own grip on the conversation: The conversational partner who succeeds in structuring the conversation most often determines to a large extent what is discussed and what is not.

Structuring the introduction
During the introduction to a professional conversation (see section 10. 2.1), the conversational partners try to agree upon the purpose, structure, and preconditions of the conversation. In some cases, these matters are pre-determined or are already known to the participants without needing to be made explicit. If this is not the case, discuss them together.

Marking transitions

You can monitor and, if necessary, adjust the structure of the conversation by indicating that you think a particular phase is finished and the next phase should begin. You can precede a transition by a summary, which helps to maintain the main line of the conversation.

> You have indicated that you have a problem in raising your youngest daughter. We have established that the cause of this problem largely lies in the lack of regularity in your daily family life. Perhaps it is a good idea to find ways to bring more regularity into your family life.

Explicit marking of a transition.

Sometimes an explicit transition such as the one in this example is necessary to indicate the next phase in the conversation. Often, however, a question or a remark that does not directly refer to a new phase is sufficient.

> You have indicated that you have a problem in raising your youngest daughter due to a lack of regularity in your daily family life. What might bring more regularity into your family life?

Implicit marking of a transition.

Correcting the structure of the conversation

Sometimes attention shifts to a side issue, a matter that is only indirectly related to the subject of the conversation. And sometimes one of the participants may anticipate the structure of the conversation by starting a new phase while the previous phase is not yet finished. In both cases, you can try to correct the structure by explicitly stating what you think you should talk about now.

> A: At the end of this conversation we must come to a decision about a possible resit for Mr. Gangla-Birir.
>
> B: But first we need to know exactly what he bases his request on. Shall we look at that first?

A request from Mr. Gangla-Birir is under discussion. A immediately starts talking about the conclusion that has to be reached. B corrects the structure of the conversation.

You can explicitly correct the structure of a conversation, but the structure of a conversation might also be more or less automatically corrected during the conversation.

A: At the end of this conversation we must come to a decision about a possible resit for Mr. Gangla-Birir.

B: Sure, he writes in his request that during the examination nothing was as it should be according to the rules. Could the exam invigilator perhaps give us information about this?

In this case, the structure of the conversation is not explicitly corrected. Now B corrects it with a substantive remark concerning the grounds on which the request for a resit was made.

Remember that it is not always necessary or even desirable to correct the structure of the conversation. Conversational partners may come up with new topics that turn out to be particularly relevant. In that case, strictly adhering to a previously devised structure does not help to achieve the goal or goals of the conversation.

Key points

A professional conversation is characterized by the fact that it:
- is institutionalized;
- serves a formal goal;
- takes place by appointment;
- has a fixed division of roles.

Preparation

Preparing a professional conversation consists of familiarizing yourself with your conversational goal, the goals of your conversational partner, and the preconditions of the conversation such as duration, location, reporting, and mandate. It is also important to anticipate the structure and content of the conversation and to look at some basic techniques that you might want to emphasize.

Structure of the conversation

- The introduction to the conversation contains four elements: the opening, the indication of the goals, the preview of the structure, and reaching agreements on the preconditions.
- In the middle part of the conversation, you discuss the content-related themes. The way in which you discuss these themes may be determined by one of the set schemata.
- In the final phase, the main points are summarized, and the conversational partners check whether they have achieved their goals. The formal part of the meeting is concluded by agreeing on any follow-up appointments. Once the formal part is finished, the conversational partners can switch to social talk to maintain or build good relationships for the next appointment.

Basic techniques

There are several basic conversation techniques that may be used in all kinds of professional conversations. Which of these techniques you should apply in a particular conversation and how emphatically you should do so, depends on the nature of the conversation and your role in it. Some basic techniques for conducting conversations are:
- informing, arguing, and enthusing;
- listening and observing;
- asking questions and follow-up questions;
- repeating, summarizing, and reflecting;
- structuring the conversation and possibly correcting it.

Assignment

Listening

Purpose of the assignment
You will practice empathic listening.

Subject matter
Section 10.4.2

Tasks
This task is carried out in a group of three: two participants (A and B) and an observer (C).
- A brings in a problem/dilemma that really exists and that is relevant to him or her: a problem that A really wants to do something about and that has not yet been solved.
- In a conversation of ten minutes, B tries to get to the heart of the problem through the technique of empathic listening, thus helping A in reflecting on possible outcomes.
- B does not express any judgments, opinions, or advice during the interview.
- C observes and notes what strikes him or her.

After about ten minutes, stop the conversation and briefly discuss what happened. A and B should first explain how they experienced the conversation. What did the conversation bring to A? To what extent does B think that he or she succeeded in listening empathically? Then the observer C should recount what he or she noticed, on the basis of the notes taken.

Repeat the assignment with the three participants taking on different roles than the first time. The assignment should be repeated twice so that in the end everyone has been an observer once.

The dilemma that A raises can be relatively superficial in nature, such as 'Should I keep attending lectures at my university, or can I limit myself to only watching them on video?' or 'What will our holiday destination be this year: Should I accept the wishes of the friends (or friend) I will travel with, or should I keep insisting that we follow my preference?'

But the dilemma can also be a problem that digs deeper, such as 'Should I keep following this educational program, or should I stop?' or 'Suppose that in the future I want to have children but my partner does not—what do I do then?'

Suggested readings

Below you will find a brief description of important background literature for each of the chapters in this book. We mention both literature that has served as a source of inspiration in writing and editing this book, and publications that we recommend for further study. The complete bibliographical entries can be found in the list of references.

For Chapter 1: Communication

The main source of inspiration for the first chapter of this book is the work of the German psychologist Schulz von Thun. He developed the concept of the *four-sides model of communication*, also known as the 'four-ears model'. His publications on this subject, including one from 1977 and from 2008, are recommended to anyone interested in the psychological aspects of communication. Schulz von Thun based his ideas on such books as *Pragmatics of Human Communication: A Study of Interactional Patterns, Pathologies and Paradoxes*, an influential publication by Watzlawick, Beavin Bavelas, and Jackson (1967).

For Chapter 2: Structure

The practical approach to understanding and generating suitable text schemata that is central to this chapter can be described as the *Theme-Questions-Answers* (TQA) approach, introduced in the Netherlands by Drop and De Vries (1977) and further elaborated in Drop (1983). The starting point of this approach is that every text has a theme. About this theme a number of questions are asked—sometimes explicitly but often implicitly—for which answers are provided. A text schema is the structure that connects the theme, the main questions, and the key answers. The idea that texts have such underlying schemata was established in classic works such as De Beaugrande and Dressler (1981): *Introduction to Text Linguistics*, and Van Dijk and Kintsch (1983): *Strategies of Discourse Comprehension*. The related

◀ *A man reading*, Anonymus, circa 1660. The young man in this painting is reading in an open book. He is depicted at half body height, with a high black hat with ribbons on his head.

In this section, we refer you to further reading materials on the topics covered by this book, so you may stay as informed as the young man in this picture—perhaps by reading from a modern tablet similar in format to the book in this picture.

concept that a text has internal coherence (established by means of a variety of cohesive ties) has been extensively discussed, including in the above references and in the seminal work by Halliday and Hassan, *Cohesion in English* (1976). Renkema's *Introduction to Discourse Studies* (2004) offers a good overview of the literature on the structure of content and on discourse connections.

For Chapter 3: Argumentation

The approach followed in this chapter is largely in line with a Dutch textbook *Argument en Tegenargument* (*Argument and Counterargument*) by Schellens and Verhoeven (1994). Like many other authors in this field, they were inspired by the work of Toulmin (1958), whose model of argumentation in its primal form can be found in *The Uses of Argument*. Another influential approach to argumentation is the so-called pragma-dialectical theory, founded by Van Eemeren and Grootendorst (1988). In this approach, argumentation is viewed as something aimed at resolving a difference of opinion by critically testing the acceptability of the positions on the issue. The theory of pragma-dialectics regards the entirety of an argumentation as a discourse activity and as ideally being part of a critical discussion. Thus, argumentation is regarded as a complex speech act that occurs as part of natural language activities and has specific communicative goals. A practical textbook based on pragma-dialectics is *Argumentation* by Van Eemeren and Snoeck Henkemans (2017). In *Strategic Maneuvering in Argumentative Discourse*, Van Eemeren (2010) discusses how the pragma-dialectical approach has been expanded to include the concept of strategic maneuvering. The *Handbook of Argumentation Theory* (Van Eemeren et al., 2014) gives an overview of the various theoretical contributions to the development of argumentation theory.

For Chapter 4: Style

One of the most famous books on style to this day is Strunk and White's *The Elements of Style*, first published in 1935. The advice presented in this seemingly 'simple' little book is valid even today. From the vast literature on style, we can recommend *The Sense of Style* by Pinker (2014), *Sin and Syntax* by Hale (2013), *Style: Lessons in Clarity and Grace* by Williams (2007), *Writing English with Style* by Shober (2010), and *On Writing Well* by Zinsser (2006). A more theoretical overview focusing on different approaches and methods of analysis and research on style is *Register, Genre and Style* by Biber (2009).

Literally thousands of books have been written on correct English usage. To present a representative selection would be impossible. We mention a few of the best-known reference works, keeping in mind that an internet search would obviously offer more references to supplement our choices. Probably one of the most famous reference guides would be *Fowler's Dictionary of Modern English Usage*. It gives practical and properly reasoned advice on issues such as grammar, style, word choice, punctuation, and spelling. This book was first published in 1926, but it has been revised to reflect English usage in the current century (Butterfield, 2015). *Garner's Modern English Usage* (Garner, 2016) started out as a reference book on American English usage; it has been reworked to reflect modern international English usage with a large number of entries on issues such as grammar, word choice, style, spelling, and punctuation. *The Cambridge Guide to English Usage* is an A-Z reference guide to a variety of issues regarding correct English usage; the distinction of this reference guide is that the advice is based on extensive corpus research (Peters, 2004). A classic but also extensive study of English grammar is offered in *A Comprehensive Grammar of the English Language* (Quirk, Greenbaum, Leech, & Svartlik, 1985). One of the truly famous publications on the history, structure, and usage of English is the *Cambridge Encyclopedia of the English Language* (Crystal, 2010).

For Chapter 5: Visualization

Schriver's much acclaimed textbook *Dynamics in Document Design* (1997) provides a great introduction to the interplay between words and pictures and the role of typography and space. *The Information Design Handbook* is a useful publication on a variety of aspects regarding visual design (O'Grady & O'Grady, 2008). The authors explore the historical, cognitive, communicative, and aesthetic aspects of the comprehensible and effective design of information and show a number of inspiring examples. *Information Design: Research and Practice* (Black, Luna, Lund, & Walker, 2017) offers a comprehensive overview of recent developments in information design and related disciplines such as document design and interaction design. *The Complete Manual of Typography* by Felici (2012) is a handy reference on typography, especially regarding font choices during the typesetting process. Instructions for the design of tables and figures in research reports can be found in the widely used *Publication Manual of the APA* (2009). Even more specific advice can be found in *Presenting Your Findings: A Practical Guide for Creating Tables* (Nicol & Pexman, 2011). *Text and Image: A Critical Introduction to the Visual/Verbal Divide* (Bateman, 2014) is a more theoretical introductory textbook dealing with different approaches to the text-image relation.

For Chapter 6: Reading and summarizing

The approach in this chapter, just like that in chapter 2, is based on the *Theme-Questions-Answers* (TQA) approach, introduced in the Netherlands by Drop and De Vries (1977) and further elaborated in Drop (1983). In *Effective Strategies for Academic Writing,* De Jong (2011) discusses reading, summarizing, and processing literature when systematically working on a thesis or another scientific text. *Summarization in Any Subject: 50 Techniques to Improve Student Learning* by Wormeli (2004) offers a wide variety of sometimes surprising techniques for teachers and students to identify and structure relevant information in a text.

For Chapter 7: Writing — the process

An important source of inspiration for this chapter was the research by Flower and Hayes conducted in the 1980s and 1990s on the writing process, the most important results of which are summarized in a didactic form by Flower (1998) in *Problem-Solving Strategies for Writing in College and Community. The Natural Creative Process in Writing* (De la Porte, 2014) is a practical guide that takes you through the different stages of the writing process. Specifically suitable for the final editing of texts is *Copyediting and Proofreading for Dummies* (Gilad, 2007). *The Now Habit* by Fiore (2007) offers a deeper knowledge and a tried-and-tested, problem-oriented approach to procrastinating behavior. The method of freewriting is discussed in detail in *Writing without Teachers* by Elbow (1998).

For Chapter 8: Writing — reporting

There is substantial literature on report writing that we cannot do justice to here. The references provided merely serve as a starting point. In *Reading and Writing Public Documents* (2001), Janssen and Neutelings provide a good overview on writing in the public sector (including report writing), dealing with the typical problems, solutions, and characteristics of writings in this sector. In their handbook *Research Writing Simplified,* Clines and Cobb (2014) provide valuable advice on writing research reports and other academic publications. In *Portfolios for Professional Development,* Smith and Tillema (2006) offer an extensive and scientifically based approach to creating a career portfolio. Precise indications for literature references in a report can be found in the *Publication Manual of the APA* (American Psychological Association, 2009) used worldwide. Other guidelines to literature references are provided in the *Chicago Manual of Style* (2017) and in *The Wadsworth Handbook*

(Kirszner & Mandell, 2014). In *Communicate as a Professional*, we follow the APA guidelines. For more special cases, it is always best to consult the most recent edition of the *APA Manual*.

For Chapter 9: Oral presentations

Thorough introductions to classical rhetoric can be found in *Classical Rhetoric and Its Christian and Secular Tradition* by Kennedy (1999) and in *Rhetoric in the European Tradition* by Conley (1990). Murphy and Wiese (2016) translated and edited three key sections of the still influential *Institutio Oratoria*, the twelve-volume textbook by the famous Roman rhetorician Quintilian on the theory and practice of rhetoric. *An Introduction to Rhetorical Communication: A Western Rhetorical Perspective* by McCroskey (2005) offers an integration of rhetorical theory and social science approaches to contemporary public communication. Anderson (2016) published *TED Talks: The official TED Guide to Public Speaking*. The book is a modern guide to effective public speaking, informed by the popular TED (Technology, Entertainment, and Design) Talks.

For Chapter 10: Professional conversations

In *Talk: The Science of Conversation*, social psychologist Stokoe (2018) offers insights about how to have better conversations. For this purpose, Stokoe collected and analyzed a great number of real conversations across various settings such as first dates, crisis negotiation, sales encounters, and medical communication. In *The 7 Habits of Highly Effective People*, Covey (2013) explains and elaborates on the importance of empathic listening, which he rightly defines as 'listening until the other person feels understood' and not as 'listening until you understand'. In *Motivational Interviewing: Helping People Change*, Miller and Rollnick (2012) provide specific and valuable guidelines on motivational interviewing—a directive, client-centered counseling style for eliciting behavior change.

References

American Psychological Association (APA). (2009). *Publication manual of the American Psychological Association* (6th ed., 2nd print). Washington, DC: American Psychological Association.

Anderson, C. (2016). *TED talks: The official TED guide to public speaking.* Boston, MA: Houghton Mifflin Harcourt.

Bateman, J. A. (2014). *Text and image: A critical introduction to the visual/verbal divide.* London, England: Routledge, Taylor & Francis.

Black, A., Luna, P., Lund, O., & Walker, S. (Eds.). (2017). *Information design: Research and practice.* London, England: Routledge.

Butterfield, J. (2015). *Fowler's dictionary of modern English* (4th ed.). Oxford, England: Oxford University Press.

Chicago Manual of Style: The essential guide for writers, editors and publishers (17th ed.). (2017). Chicago, IL: University of Chicago Press.

Clines R. H., & Cobb, E. R. (2014). *Research writing simplified: A documentation guide* (8th ed.). New York, NY: Pearson Longman.

Conley, T. M. (1990). *Rhetoric in the European tradition.* Chicago, IL: University of Chicago Press.

Covey, S. R. (2013). *The 7 habits of highly effective people* (25th ed.). New York, NY: Simon & Schuster.

Crystal, D. (2010). *The Cambridge encyclopedia of the English language* (3rd ed.). Cambridge, England: Cambridge University Press.

De Beaugrande, R., & Dressler, W. U. (1981). *Introduction to text linguistics.* London, England: Longman.

De Jong, J. (2017). *Effective strategies for academic writing.* Bussum, The Netherlands: Coutinho.

De la Porte, R. (2014). *The natural creative process in writing: A core writing and editing handbook for everyone.* Tokai, South Africa: WriteArt.

Drop, W. (1983). *Instrumentele tekstanalyse ten dienste van samenvatten, opstellen van begripsvragen en tekstverbeteren* [Instrumental text analysis for the purpose of summarizing, developing conceptual questions and improving texts]. Groningen, The Netherlands: Wolters-Noordhoff

Drop, W., & De Vries, J. (1977). *Taalbeheersing: Handboek voor taalhantering* [Language and communication: Textbook for using language]. (2nd, rev. ed.). Groningen, The Netherlands: Wolters-Noordhoff.

Elbow, P. (1998). *Writing without teachers* (2nd ed.). Oxford, England: Oxford University Press.

Felici, J. (2012). *The complete manual of typography* (2nd ed.). Berkeley, CA: Peachpit.

Fiore, N. (2007). *The now habit: A strategic program for overcoming procrastination and enjoying guilt-free play*. New York, NY: Penguin.

Flower, L. (1998). *Problem-solving strategies for writing in college and community* (Rev. ed.). Fort Worth, TX: Harcourt Brace College Publishers.

Garner, B. (2016). *Garner's modern English usage* (4th ed.). Oxford, England: Oxford University Press.

Hale, C. (2013). *Sin and syntax: How to craft wicked good prose* (Rev. ed.). New York, NY: Three Rivers Press.

Gilad, S. (2007). *Copyediting and proofreading for dummies*. Hoboken, NJ: Wiley.

Halliday, M. A. K., & Hasan, R. (1976). *Cohesion in English*. London, England: Longman.

Janssen, D., & Neutelings, R. (Eds.). (2001). *Reading and writing public documents: Problems, solutions, and characteristics*. Amsterdam, The Netherlands: John Benjamins.

Kennedy, G. A. (1999. *Classical rhetoric and its Christian and secular tradition from ancient to modern times* (2nd, rev. ed.). Chapel Hill, NC: University of North Carolina Press.

Kirszner, L. G., & Mandell, S. R. (2014). *The Wadsworth handbook* (10th ed.). Boston, MA: Wadsworth/Cengage Learning.

McCroskey, J. C. (2005). *Introduction to rhetorical communication: A Western rhetorical perspective* (9th ed.). Milton Park, PA: Routledge.

Miller, W. R., & Rollnick, S. (2012). *Motivational interviewing: Helping people change* (3rd ed.). New York, NY: Guilford Press.

Murphy, J. M., & Wiese, C. (2016). *Quintilian on the teaching of speaking and writing: Translations from books one, two, and ten of the Institutio Oratoria* (2nd ed.). Carbondale, IL: Southern Illinois University Press.

O'Grady, J. V., & O'Grady, K. V. (2008). *The information design handbook*. Cincinnati, OH: How Books.

Peters, P. (2004). *The Cambridge guide to English usage*. Cambridge, England: Cambridge University Press.

Pinker, S. (2014). *The sense of style: The thinking person's guide to writing in the 21st century*. New York, NY: Penguin.

Quirk, R., Greenbaum, S., Leech, G., & Svartvik, J. (1985). *A comprehensive grammar of the English language*. London, England: Longman.

Renkema, J. (2004). *Introduction to discourse studies*. Amsterdam. The Netherlands: John Benjamins.

Schellens, P. J., & Verhoeven, G. (1994). *Argument en tegenargument: Een inleiding in de analyse en beoordeling van betogende teksten* [Argument and counterargument: An introduction to the analysis and assessment of argumentative texts] (2nd, rev. ed.). Groningen, The Netherlands: Martinus Nijhoff.

Schriver, K. A. (1997). *Dynamics in document design: Creating texts for readers*. New York: Wiley.

Schulz von Thun, F. (1977). Psychologische Vorgänge in der zwischenmenschlichen Kommunikation [Psychological Processes in Interpersonal Communication]. In B. Fittkau, H. M. Müller-Wolf, & F. Schulz von Thun (Eds.), *Kommunizieren lernen (und umlernen)* [Learning (and re-learning) how to communicate]. Braunschweig, Germany: Westermann-Verlag.

Schulz von Thun, F. (2008). *Six tools for clear communication: The Hamburg approach in English language.* Hamburg, Germany: Schulz von Thun-Institut Für Kommunikation.

Shober, D. (2010). *Writing English with style.* Pretoria, South Afrika: Van Schaik.

Smith, K., & Tillema, H. (2006). *Portfolios for professional development: A research journey.* New York, NY: Nova Science.

Stokoe, E. (2018) *Talk: The science of conversation.* London, England: Robinson.

Strunk, W., & White, E. B. (2009). *The elements of style* (50th anniversary ed.). New York, NY: Pearson Longman.

Toulmin, S. (1958). *The uses of argument.* Cambridge, England: Cambridge University Press.

Van Dijk, T. A., & Kintsch, W. (1983). *Strategies of discourse comprehension.* New York, NY: Academic Press.

Van Eemeren, F. H. (2010). *Strategic maneuvering in argumentative discourse: Extending the pragma-dialectical theory of argumentation.* Amsterdam, The Netherlands: John Benjamins.

Van Eemeren, F. H., Garssen, B., Krabbe, E. C. W., Snoeck Henkemans, F. A., Verheij, B., & Wagemans, J. H. M. (2014). *Handbook of argumentation theory.* Dordrecht, The Netherlands: Springer.

Van Eemeren, F. H., & Grootendorst, R. (1988). Rationale for a pragma-dialectical perspective. *Argumentation, 2,* 271-291.

Van Eemeren, F. H., & Snoeck Henkemans, A. F. (2017). *Argumentation: Analysis and evaluation* (2nd ed.). New York, NY: Routledge.

Watzlawick, P., Beavin Bavelas, J. H., & Jackson, D. D. (1967). *Pragmatics of human communication: A study of interactional patterns, pathologies, and paradoxes.* New York, NY: Norton.

Williams, J. M. (2007). *Style: Lessons in clarity and grace.* New York, NY: Pearson Longman.

Wormeli, R. (2004). *Summarization in any subject: 50 techniques to improve student learning.* Alexandria, VA: ASCD.

Zinsser, W. (2006). *On writing well: The classic guide to writing nonfiction* (30th ed.). New York, NY: HarperCollins.

Index